T0301627

Radio in Africa
Publics, Cultures, Communities

Radio in Africa
Publics, Cultures, Communities

Edited by Liz Gunner, Dina Ligaga and Dumisani Moyo

JAMES CURREY

James Currey
is an imprint of Boydell & Brewer Ltd
PO Box 9, Woodbridge, Suffolk IP12 3DF (GB)
and of Boydell & Brewer Inc.
668 Mt Hope Avenue, Rochester, NY 14620-2731 (US)
www.boydellandbrewer.com
www.jamescurrey.com

First published in 2011 by Wits University Press for sale exclusively in South Africa,
Namibia, Botswana, Lesotho, Zimbabwe, Swaziland, Angola, Democratic Republic of
Congo, Madagascar, Malawi, Mozambique, Tanzania and Zambia

Wits University Press
1 Jan Smuts Avenue
Johannesburg
www.witspress.co.za

Cover photography by Nikki Rixon, African Media Online
Edited by Alex Potter
Cover design by Hothouse South Africa
Book design and layout by Sheaf Publishing
Printed and bound in Great Britain by CPI Group (UK) Ltd, Croydon, CR0 4YY

Contents

Acknowledgements

The book draws in part on a radio colloquium organised by the three co-editors in October 2007 entitled Radio, Publics and Communities in Southern Africa, which was funded by the South African National Research Foundation (NRF) and was part of a three-year research project on Radio and Community in South Africa funded by the NRF and coordinated by Liz Gunner. Their support and generous funding was invaluable for the completion of this book. An earlier colloquium, Zulu Radio Drama and Its Practitioners, was held in October 2005 at the University of KwaZulu-Natal, Pietermaritzburg. A second colloquium, Radio and the Pulse of the Times, took place at the Wits Institute for Social and Economic Research (WISER), University of the Witwatersrand in October 2006. There were many compelling speakers, such as John Perlmann, then still at the South African Broadcasting Corporation (SABC); the actor and dramatist Welcome Msomi; Anton Harber and Franz Kruger from the Journalism and Media Studies Department at the University of the Witwatersrand (Wits), Johannesburg; Thulasizwe Nkabinde, director of music at the SABC; and many others whose work we have not been able to use, but who by their very presence at these events contributed to what we now have. Without the strong support of the NRF, none of the colloquia nor this volume would have been possible, and we are deeply grateful to it.

We would also like to thank all the contributors to the October 2007 colloquium, some of whose original papers were revised and honed for publication in this book. Each presenter at the colloquium contributed to its success and the debates that emerged shaped the structure of the present book. A number of chapters were added quite some time after the initial colloquium, and we also want to thank our colleagues from distant places who contributed chapters at our request and in our view added a wider view of what radio in Africa is to the book.

Our colleagues at the University of the Witwatersrand offered us a great deal of support and encouragement as we worked on the manuscript. Among many, we would particularly like to thank Professor Tawana Kupe, Dean of Humanities, who opened the 2006 workshop and the 2007 colloquium and whose own insightful work on the media has been an inspiration to us. Isabel Hofmeyr, Dan Ojwang, Jon Soske, Jon Hyslop and Irma du Plessis all gave support and cogent criticism – our thanks to all of them. Colleagues further afield answered out-of-the-blue emails with rapidity: Wendy James answered questions about radio in Sudan, Harri Englund expanded on radio in Malawi, and Jim Brennan gave details of his work on Swahili radio rhetoric, 'poison and dope'. Our thanks too to Franz Wild for invaluable help with suggestions of who to contact on radio in central Africa. Linda Mabin provided valuable editing, research, and bibliographic skills to the final manuscript, and Lulu van Molendorff applied her excellent copy-editing and research skills to the chapters as they came in.

Our thanks for the excellent support provided by Wits Press and in particular Veronica Klipp, Julie Miller and Melanie Pequeux. Syned Mthatiwa helped with details on radio in Malawi and Euclides Gonçalves gave inspirational input on radio in Lusophone Africa.

WISER hosted the public radio events in 2006 and 2007 and provided invaluable institutional support throughout the work on this book. In this regard, we particularly thank Deborah Posel, then director of WISER, and Najibha and Adila Deshmukh for their administrative support.

Liz Gunner, Dina Ligaga and *Dumisani Moyo*
Johannesburg, March 2011

Contributors

Tanja Bosch is Senior Lecturer at the Centre for Film and Media Studies at the University of Cape Town, South Africa. She completed her MA in International Affairs while a Fulbright scholar at Ohio University, where she also graduated with a PhD in Mass Communication. Her dissertation, which was awarded the Broadcast Educational Association Outstanding Dissertation Award 2003, was an ethnographic study of community radio and identity in South Africa. She teaches radio journalism, new media, health communication, and media theory and research. Her areas of research and publication include talk radio and democracy, community radio, and youth use of mobile media, particularly cellphones and Facebook.

Monica B. Chibita is Senior Lecturer in the Department of Mass Communication, Makerere University and a senior researcher under the Makerere-Sida research collaboration. She is associate editor of the *Journal of African Media Studies*, and a member of the editorial board of *Communicatio: South African Journal for Communication Theory and Research* and of the advisory board of *Interactions: Studies in Communication and Culture*. She has presented papers at various international conferences and published on media history, media policy, law and regulation, the media and participation, and indigenous-language broadcasting. She has also been involved in various aspects of media regulation and curriculum development and review in the eastern Africa region over the last decade.

David B. Coplan began his academic career at the State University of New York in 1981 and moved to the University of Cape Town in 1993. In 1997 he became professor and chair of the Department of Anthropology at the University of the Witwatersrand, Johannesburg. Among his areas of expertise are the performing arts and media, including South African and the global music and media industries. He is the author of *In Township Tonight! Three Centuries of Black South African Music and Theatre* (Longman, 1985; Jacana & Chicago, 2007). In recent years he has extended this interest to include projects in cultural industries, heritage and tourism, and he is a frequent commentator on cultural issues on South African radio and television.

Stephen R. Davis received his PhD from the University of Florida in 2010. His dissertation is a multi-sited history of Umkhonto we Sizwe, the armed wing of the African National Congress of South Africa. He is Assistant Professor of History, University of Kentucky.

Maria Frahm-Arp is Senior Lecturer in the School of Theology at St Augustine College, Johannesburg, South Africa. Her particular research interests focus on the ways in which religion is expressed and experienced in the social context of contemporary South Africa. She was a Mellon Post-doctoral Fellow at the Wits Institute for Social and Economic Research (WISER), University of the Witwatersrand from 2006 to 2008 and completed her PhD at the University of Warwick in 2006. Her recent publications include *Professional Women in South African Pentecostal Charismatic Churches* (Brill, 2010) and *Development and Politics from Below: Exploring Religious Spaces in the African State* which she edited with Barbara Bompani (Palgrave, 2010).

Liz Gunner is Visiting Professor at WISER, University of the Witwatersrand. She has written extensively on language, media and performance in South Africa. Recent articles by her include 'Jacob Zuma, the social body and the unruly power of song' (*African Affairs*, 2009) and 'Reconfiguring diaspora: Africa on the rise and the radio voices of Lewis Nkosi and Bloke Modisane' (*Social Dynamics*, 2010). She has contributed a chapter on song, violence and masculinities in KwaZulu-Natal to the 2011 Brill/Wits University Press book *Mediations of Violence in Africa: Fashioning New Futures from Contested Pasts* edited by Lidwien Kapteijns and Annemiek Richter. She is currently one of the editors of the Wits-based journal *African Studies* and is a senior researcher on the Volkswagen Foundation-funded project on Passages of Culture: Media and Mediations of Culture in Africa.

Sekibakiba Peter Lekgoathi is Senior Lecturer in History in the School of Social Sciences, University of the Witwatersrand, Johannesburg. His research interests include ethnicity and the making of the 'Transvaal Ndebele'; the history of the South African Broadcasting Corporation's (SABC's) African-language radio, especially Northern Sotho- and isiNdebele-language services; the history of the African National Congress's (ANC's) Radio Freedom; European anthropologists, African research assistants and fieldwork in southern Africa; history teaching and teacher development; and heritage.

Dina Ligaga is Lecturer in the Department of Media Studies, University of the Witwatersrand. Her research interests include popular culture and representation, broadcasting and new media cultures and postcolonial literature. She is co-editor of an upcoming book on Eastern African intellectual landscapes which revisits theoretical and cultural nuances in Eastern African literatures and cultures. Apart from her publications in the area of radio drama, she has recently begun work on Kenyan internet cultures and has so far published two articles: '"Virtual expressions": Alternative performance spaces and the staging of Kenyan cultures online' (forthcoming) and 'Ethnic stereotypes and the ideological manifestations of ethnicity in Kenyan cyber communities' (2009).

Winston Mano is member of the Communication and Media Research Institute, director of the Africa Media Centre, and a senior lecturer in Media and Communication at the University of Westminster, London. He is also principal editor of the *Journal of African Media Studies*. He has published widely on issues related to media and communication and his current research interests include radio, audiences, new media and democracy.

Marissa J. Moorman is Associate Professor of African History at Indiana University. She is an historian of southern Africa whose research focuses on the intersection between politics and culture in colonial and independent Angola. *Intonations* (Ohio University Press, 2008) explores music as a practice in and through which Angolans living under extreme political repression imagined the nation and how the particularities of music and historical moment cast this process of imagining in gendered terms. The book argues that cultural practice is productive of politics and not just derivative of it. Her current book project, *Tuning in to Nation*, looks at the relationship between the technology of radio and the shifting politics of southern Africa as anti-colonial movements established independent states in a regional context newly charged by Cold War politics. She has written articles on Angolan cinema, dress and nation, and a contemporary Angolan music and dance genre '*kuduro*'.

Dumisani Moyo is the Media and Information and Communications Technology (ICT) manager at the Open Society Initiative for Southern Africa and is honorary research fellow in the Department of Media Studies at the University of the Witwatersrand. His research interests include alternative media, new media and society, citizen journalism, and media policy in southern Africa.

Christopher Joseph Odhiambo is Associate Professor of Post-colonial Literatures and Applied Drama in the Department of Literature, Theatre and Film Studies at Moi University, Eldoret, Kenya. His current research interests are the dynamics of FM radio stations in Kenya as well as the imagination(s) of power, politics, gender and memory in post-colonial drama. Odhiambo's book, *Theatre for Development in Kenya: In Search of an Effective Procedure and Methodology* (2008), published by Bayreuth African Studies, explores the complexities of theatre for community development, specifically in Kenya and post-colonial Africa in general.

Dorothea E. Schulz is Professor in the Department of Cultural and Social Anthropology at the University of Cologne, Germany. Her forthcoming book, *Muslims and New Media in West Africa* (Indiana University Press, 2011), deals with Islamic revivalist movements in Mali that rely on various media technologies to promote a relatively new conception of publicly enacted religiosity. She has also published widely on media practices and public culture in Sahelian West Africa, gender studies and the anthropology of the state. She is currently researching Muslim practices of coming to terms with death and mourning in a situation of continued ecological and social disaster and irruption in Uganda.

David Smith is Director of the Johannesburg-based Okapi Consulting. Okapi Consulting was the implementing agency for a United Nations-sponsored radio project, Bar-Kulan, established for the people of Somalia and the Somali diaspora. He has worked extensively with the UN on media projects in conflict and post-conflict zones from the Balkans to the Central African Republic, including the conception and implementation of the Radio Okapi network in the Democratic Republic of Congo. His background in electronic media is extensive, including producer positions at international public broadcasters of Canada and The Netherlands, and managing a commercial transformation project at South Africa's Capital Radio. His work in development began in Zimbabwe shortly after independence as part of an education programme funded by the Canadian government to help get young Zimbabweans back into classrooms after the war in that country had ended.

Scott Straus is Professor of Political Science and International Studies at the University of Wisconsin, Madison, where he also directs the Human Rights Initiative. His primary research interests include the study of genocide, violence, human rights and African politics. He is the author of *The Order of Genocide: Race, Power, and War in Rwanda* (Cornell University Press, 2006), which received the 2006 Award for Excellence in Political Science and Government from the Association of American Publishers and, with Robert Lyons, *Intimate Enemy: Images and Voices of the Rwandan Genocide* (MIT/Zone Books, 2006). He is also the co-editor, with Lars Waldorf, of *Remaking Rwanda: State Building and Human Rights after Mass Violence* (University of Wisconsin Press, 2011) and the co-author, with David Leonard, of *Africa's Stalled Development: International Causes and Cures* (Lynne Rienner, 2003). He has published articles related to genocide in *World Politics, Politics & Society, Foreign Affairs, Genocide Studies and Prevention, Journal of Genocide Research, Patterns of Prejudice* and the *Wisconsin International Law Journal,* and he has received grants from the Andrew Mellon Foundation, the Harry

Frank Guggenheim Foundation, the National Science Foundation, the Social Science Research Council and the United States Institute of Peace.

Wisdom J. Tettey is Professor and Dean of the Faculty of Creative and Critical Studies at the University of British Columbia, Canada. His research expertise and interests are in the areas of mass media and politics in Africa; ICT, civic engagement and transnational citizenship; the political economy of globalisation and ICTs; brain drain, diaspora knowledge networks and higher education capacity areas, and is author/co-author and editor/co-editor of several books, including *The Public Sphere and the Politics of Survival: Voice, Sustainability, and Public Policy in Ghana* (2010); *Challenges of Developing and Retaining the Next Generation of Academics: Deficits in Academic Staff Capacity in African Universities* (2010); *African Media and the Digital Sphere* (2009); *The African Diaspora in Canada: Negotiating Identity and Belonging* (2005); and *Critical Perspectives on Politics and Socio-Economic Development in Ghana* (2003). He has also served, and continues to serve, as a consultant to several national and international organisations in his fields of scholarly expertise.

Stephanie Wolters is a multimedia journalist, media development specialist and conflict analyst with 20 years experience working as a print and broadcast journalist and conflict analyst in Africa for organisations such as the BBC, *The Economist*, Reuters, the *Mail and Guardian*, The Economist Intelligence Unit, the World Bank and various other international institutions. She spends much of her time in Central Africa and other conflict and post-conflict countries on the continent. Wolters lived in the DRC from 1998–2004. She was Radio Okapi's first news editor.

Abbreviations and acronyms

AIS	African Information Service
a.k.a.	also known as
AMISON	African Union Mission in Somalia
ANC	African National Congress
AU	African Union
BAZ	Broadcasting Authority of Zimbabwe
BBC	British Broadcasting Corporation
CABS	Central African Broadcasting Station
CAR	Central African Republic
DIP	Department of Information and Publicity
DPKO	Department of Peacekeeping Operations
DRC	Democratic Republic of Congo
EOA	Emissora Oficial de Angola
FM	frequency modulation
FNLA	Frente Nacional para a Libertação de Angola
FRELIMO	Frente de Libertação de Moçambique
ICASA	Independent Communications Authority of South Africa
ICT	Information and Communications Technology
ICTR	International Criminal Tribunal for Rwanda
KANU	Kenya African National Union
KBC	Kenya Broadcasting Corporation
KBS	Kenya Broadcasting Service
MDC	Movement for Democratic Change
MK	Umkhonto we Sizwe
MLC	Movement for the Liberation of the Congo
MONUC	UN Organisation Mission in the DRC
MONUSCO	UN Organisation Support Mission in the DRC
MPLA	Movimento Popular da Libertação de Angola
NDC	National Democratic Congress
NEC	National Executive Committee
NGO	non-governmental organisation
NPP	New Patriotic Party
NRF	National Research Foundation
NRM	National Resistance Movement
ORTZ	Office zairois de radio-diffusion et de television
PAC	Pan Africanist Congress
PIDE	International Police for the Defence of the State

RNA	Angolan National Radio
RPF	Rwandan Patriotic Front
RTLM	Radio-Télévision Libre des Milles Collines
RTNC	Radio Television National Congolaise
SABC	South African Broadcasting Corporation
SACP	South African Communist Party
SWRA	Short Wave Radio Africa
TFG	Transitional Federal Government
TPA	Angolan Popular Television
UBC	Uganda Broadcasting Corporation
UN	United Nations
UNITA	União Naçional para a Independêçia Total de Angola
US	United States
VOK	Voice of Kenya
VOA	Voice of America
VOP	Voice of the People
ZANU-PF	Zimbabwe African National Union-Patriotic Front
ZBC	Zimbabwe Broadcasting Corporation

Introduction
The Soundscapes of Radio in Africa

Liz Gunner, Dina Ligaga and Dumisani Moyo

Africa's 'soundscapes', captured in the continent's long and extensive use of orality, may not seem to have any obvious connection with radio. Yet one reason for the continuing, possibly growing, importance of the medium of radio in Africa is its link to the oral and the aural in the history and cultural practices of the continent (Hofmeyr, 1993:85). In our use of the term 'soundscapes', we draw on Anderson's (1991) well-known formulation of 'socioscapes' and its link with print capitalism, and Appadurai's (1990) work on global cultural flows captured in the term 'mediascapes'. Our focus in this collection on radio draws attention to the aural 'eye' of radio. How, we ask in the chapters below, does radio, as a device of sound, provide landscapes that both divide and unite, or simply link publics, cultures and communities? A tension raised by a number of contributors is between the ways in which radio forms local communities and at the same time allows for the formation of national and transnational communities that may interact with the local. Thus the chapters below, working from a variety of approaches and sites, ask us to consider again how radio's soundscapes lend themselves to the mediation of people's imaginings of themselves as subjects at the multiple levels of local, national and transnational communities (Ginsberg, Abu-Lughod & Larkin, 2002:5).

Sound is a thread throughout the collection, linking the sections of the book on publics, cultures and voices of change. The role of language in forming radio communities and creating publics is also an important focus of a number of chapters in the book. The present collection, in its reach across sub-Saharan Africa down to the tip of the continent, aims to point to new directions for future research, to build on the work that has been done, and to alert readers to new research that is currently under way in terms of the publics, cultures and communities of radio from within Africa.

The sheer fluidity of radio, its pervasive presence and its links with the new media extend its range and potential. It allows African radio to be simultaneously present in metropolitan centres and in seemingly remote rural areas. Its affordability and its ability to serve rural and urban communities, including those who move between Africa's cities and towns and its dense rural spaces, make radio highly suited to African social usage. Like smoke, it sneaks round corners in the most unexpected of places and assails the senses. It travels, too, with the continent's new diasporas. One of the editors of this collection (Gunner) was surprised to have a conversation in a London cab in September 2010 that began because the Ghanaian taxi driver was listening to BBC Radio 4 – 'It's very informative!' he remarked. The topic quickly moved to the online Ghanaian station Joy FM, which operated in English and Twi, and to which the speaker often contributed and listened avidly. The usefulness of having a station where Twi (or Fante) could be used for phone-in conversations, the state of the media in Ghana and current politics were all briefly touched on before the ride came to an end, somewhere in central London. The place of the African diaspora as interactive publics for African radio and the visibility of African languages in this arena were both demonstrated within the space of the London cab.

The ways in which radio provides new linkages of the local and transnational, and its facility to provide important networks of communication and thus new kinds of imagining the self as an individual and a citizen, are among the topics explored by contributors to this volume. In relation to the former, Wisdom Tettey's chapter on talk radio in Ghana shows precisely the kind of local and transnational dialogues brought to light in the London cab in September 2010. Dumisani Moyo's chapter on resistant alternative radio in Zimbabwe shows how oppositional groups both within and outside a deeply divided state can work through radio to challenge the state radio and provide new imaginings of a nation still to be realised. Chapters in this volume by Stephanie Wolters on the crucial linkages made across the Democratic Republic of Congo (DRC) by Radio Okapi and David Smith on the role of a new radio station, Bar-Kulan, in Somalia provide powerful evidence of radio's essential role as a media technology that creates publics and makes possible the *imaginings* by radio audiences of *possible* states that struggle to exist in any meaningful way. Thus, the book locates itself within debates that identify the continued significance of radio on the continent as a product of political, historical, and social practices and processes (Bourgault, 1995; Mytton, 2000). Far from claims that radio is a dying or a forgotten medium – that the newer visual media such as television and the Internet spell its death – the book illustrates that radio has refused to die by continuing to adapt to changing circumstances and technologies. As it continues to converge with new technologies such as the Internet and the mobile phone, its uses and user gratifications continue to evolve. New socio-political dynamics also emerge with innovations such as live online streaming and podcasting, which necessitate a new theorisation of radio as a more dialogical and participatory medium. Chapters by Tanja Bosch on a Cape Town talk radio station and Maria Frahm-Arp on religious radio in Johannesburg, emphasise the ways in which the ethical significance of media engagements is brought about through standard and new uses of radio technology. Smith, Moyo and Tettey make similar points in this volume.

How does 'the imagination', to use the concept so key to Appadurai's (1990; 1991) work on mediascapes (Ginsberg, Abu-Lughod & Larkin, 2002:5), intertwine with the more accessibly measured instrumental role of radio? It is the complexity of radio's 'soundscapes', its sensuous and material 'auralities', and the relations of those to individual and social identities that remain its most elusive and under-researched components (but see Spitulnik, 1998; 2000; Moorman, 2008). Several essays in this volume address the question of radio 'sound', listener subjectivity and broader social identities. Thus, David Coplan assesses the post-colonial nationalist uses of state radio in Africa and its 'central role in post-independence political and cultural life', before outlining the 'Voices of Change' in the post-1990 restructured South African Broadcasting Corporation (SABC). He marks out a very different kind of public culture emerging from the vibrant African language stations with celebrity presenters and broadcast communities that 'bring into continual contact and creative interaction rural and urban speakers of major regional languages'. Dorothea Schulz, writing on the puzzling contradictions in the reception of women preachers on radio in Mali's new air spaces, traces this back not so much to gender and religious conservatism, but rather to the particular attachment to speech and the 'touching' sound of voice in the Sahel region. The very power of speech, she asserts, marks its ambiguous nature and its potential to generate delusion. Dina Ligaga, from a different perspective and focusing on radio in Kenya, shows how the imagination of the ordinary and 'the moral dramas of everyday lives' enabled the *Radio Theatre* programme to exist over decades with immunity within the coercive state broadcasting service of the Voice of Kenya and later the KBC (Kenyan Broadcasting Corporation). Liz Gunner's chapter on isiZulu radio drama in the 1970s, well before liberalising shifts in the SABC, shows the possibilities for multiple interpretations and imaginings of serial radio dramas that seem to fit the apartheid script, but also allow a construction of the self and community through the in-depth use of language rather than easy acceptance of the ideology of apartheid.

One of the more urgent tasks for radio research is therefore to show its complex societal value, a focus of many chapters in this volume. Valuable early scholarship often focused on the institutional structures of radio rather than what Marissa Moorman (this volume) calls the ways in which it 'structured the daily soundscape' of life (Katz & Wedell, 1977; Heath, 1986). For instance, contemporary radio can combine the sounds of the everyday with its important role in peacekeeping and post-conflict operations. Organisations such as Radio for Peacebuilding Africa, which operate in fragile post-conflict situations in states such as Sierra Leone and Rwanda, work with briefs far different from the old top-down approach of colonial or most state radios. Radio Dabanga, the Darfur station set up by the United Nations (UN), and the South Sudan station Radio Bakhita, run by the Catholic Church,[1] are further examples of stations operating as links between local communities and a wider global ecumene in tense or fragile regional situations where global media interests and commercially run stations would not venture. The chapters by Wolters on Radio Okapi and its presence in the DRC and Smith on Somalia's Radio Bar-Kulan speak to this ongoing role of radio on an unstable continent where communication is uneven and frequently under-resourced. Stations such as the Somali one of which David Smith writes often exist in the new wider context of operative modes and expanded technologies. Thus Smith (this volume) observes of Bar-Kulan: 'The Bar-Kulan website is not separate from the radio service; they are integrated as one media access operation.' And he continues: 'The days of websites being simply an add-on to radio, newspaper and television operations are long over.'

An 'ordinary' medium

It is perhaps the combination of 'ordinariness', the focus on the everyday, with the ability to engage with moments of high national and cultural drama that makes radio such a complex 'soundscape' and shapes it as both a powerful and – at times – a dangerous medium. Thus Scannell, writing on British public broadcasting, has pointed to the ways in which radio could reproduce the everyday and also weave in items of national significance through its focus on great, unifying moments (Scannell, 1989, 1992; 1995, cited in Power, 2000:613; see also Hendy, 2007). Radio can thus 'stage' the minutiae of cultural life and yet, when occasion demands, enact social memory and bind together a nation or region through such performed recall (see Connerton, 1989). Many of the chapters in the volume through rich case studies assert precisely this ordinariness and the power of the local that sits alongside the capacity for enacted cultural memory with a wider reach. This is one of the great strengths of radio in Africa.

Yet Adorno (1973:159), writing with the experience of Hitler's speeches in mind, could damn radio's capacity to unleash destructive charisma:

> The radio becomes the universal mouthpiece of the Führer; his voice rises from street loudspeakers to resemble the howling of sirens announcing panic ... The National Socialists knew that the wireless gave shape to their cause just as the printing press did to the Reformation ... The inherent tendency of radio is to make the speaker's word, the false commandment, absolute.

Certainly, this idea of radio as an all-powerful influence needs careful interrogation, as demonstrated in Straus's chapter, which revisits the case of the notorious semi-private FM station RTLM in Rwanda, owned and controlled by Hutu hardliners within the regime, which began broadcasting in 1993. His conclusion, based on meticulous fieldwork and data analysis, questions the evidence of any direct causality between RTLM's radio statements and the genocide of April/May 1994. Instead, he asks us to look carefully at the wider context of the violence and radio's role within it. We should drop, Straus urges, too easy assumptions of the lack of agency of 'simple' Rwandan listeners and the clichéd image of programmed men with a radio in one hand and a machete in the other.

Both views of the complex power of radio cited above may have echoes in its practice in the production of social meaning in Africa. Yet what is striking from available studies is the multiplicity of local practices operating within the dynamics of communication made possible through radio. As Diawara (1997) points out, writing in the mid-1990s on musical change and shifts in performance styles in Mali and the Mande region since the post-colonial era, radio and the cultural tastes it shapes interact constantly, as social categories themselves re-form. The role of *griot* (*jeli*, praise singer), once predominantly male, has become open to women:

> Radio continues to expand the influence of the famous female vocalists on numerous composers across the country and throughout the whole Mande area ... In the long term one notices a clear feminization of the artist's profession among the griots. For the average radio listener it is the voice that counts ... Radio provokes slowly, but surely, an upheaval both within the category of the addressees, the patrons, and within that of the custodian of the oral texts (Diawara, 1997:42–44).

Thus radio, along with other forms of mass media, can produce new social meaning, shift subjectivities and have huge affective power. Yet the precise way such meanings are configured varies within African societies. De Certeau's (1984) idea of 'the practice of everyday life' forms a starting point for engaging with radio's cultural practices. The anthropological 'eye' on radio and its social workings (see, for instance, Spitulnik, 2000) refocuses the agency on those who 'consume' such media. The manner in which culture is produced and consumed, and how meaning is embedded in the cultural texts become equally important in providing avenues for understanding the way that society is structured, a process that Stuart Hall (1997:1) has termed 'the circuit of culture'. Radio must therefore be seen as a process of culture involving an exchange of meanings among members of society rather than a mere instrument of power. Indeed, one of the major themes of this volume is to present the linkages between the 'enactments' of radio and 'the process of culture', through radio's interactive spoken genres, its documentary-style genres, its music programmes and its 'emergent genres' (Gunner, 2000a) such as radio dramas, talk shows hosting newscasting, and local discussion and news programmes. As Katrien Pype (2009:541) has commented in her work on television dramas, celebrity and charisma in Kinshasa: 'The mass media is [sic] dialectically connected to the social and political dynamics of any given society, remixing and reassembling signs, symbols and icons.' The emergent and unstable nature of present radio culture in Africa – its capacity to 'remix' and 'reassemble', as Pype terms it – is captured not least in this volume by the chapters on talk radio by Wisdom Tettey, Christopher Odhiambo and Tanja Bosch, writing on Ghana, Kenya and South Africa, respectively.

Language, contestation and the creation of new publics

The presence of radio in Africa has always involved the creation of new publics through the shifting and often contested use of language – both metropolitan languages and the languages of the continent. Catherine Cole's (2010:106) account of the radio transmission of testimonies from the Truth and Reconciliation Commission at a moment in South Africa's transition from apartheid to post-apartheid state captures well radio's ability to create new publics, as it carried similar news items in multiple languages into streets, laundries, taxis and bars. At such a moment, new publics, along with a re-formed nation, were brought into being, yet this making of new listening communities has historically been part of radio's communicative nature.

The process of shaping audiences and publics has been one central to radio in Africa from its inception during colonial rule. The power, popularity and affordability of the medium of radio in Africa were evident from its early inception and its widespread use during the colonial period, particularly from the 1950s onwards. New publics were brought into being and in some cases the foundations laid for listening patterns that would continue into the next millennium. Broadcasts in a number of the continent's indigenous languages were introduced alongside programmes in English, French and Portuguese.

The complexities of radio as a medium of communication in the colonial period have been pointed to in a number of commentaries (see, for instance, Mytton, 1983; 2000; Larkin, 2008). Designed primarily as a means of propaganda to serve the colonial empires, radio was always far more multifaceted and slippery than was intended by the colonial powers. Language, and the ability of radio to work from within the thick medium of cultural knowledge, was always a key element in its polysemic effectiveness and its ability to create new and sometimes unruly publics.

Fraenkel's (1959) account of what became the Central African Broadcasting Station (CABS) points to the use of a number of languages, with English set alongside Bemba, Nyanja and Lozi. This, he claims, had a dramatic effect on listenership. In the troubled 1950s, as the CABS in Lusaka ran against the ferocity of the settler press and the politicians of Federation, a programme in Bemba that revived African listeners' trust in the medium was called *Imikalile Yesu* (The Way We Live). Fraenkel (1959:211) notes that the listeners realised that '[t]hey were hearing views on the air that most emphatically did not sound like the Government handouts'. In retrospect, the Bemba programme can be seen as a new radio genre, enabling listeners to be part of the production and reproduction of the everyday, taking 'colonial' radio into a new era and setting out genres such as radio drama and talk radio that mark the power of radio on the continent half a century later.

In other contexts, in colonial Mozambique, for example, the influence of programmes in indigenous languages and the sometimes iconic status of the presenters caught colonial authorities and broadcasters by surprise (Power, 2000). Thus 'the monthly journal *Radio Mozambique* regularly commented with bewilderment and astonishment on the widespread popularity of broadcasting in African languages across the continent' (Power, 2000:617). Looking across the border to apartheid South Africa, a writer noted that 'the popularity of the programme presenters [on the SABC-controlled Radio Bantu] is quite astounding' (*Radio Mocambique*, 1962:316, 319 cited in Power, 2000:617). Power also comments incisively on the role of colonial radio in constructing a nostalgic site of belonging for Portuguese settlers, while being excessively cautious in its introduction of radio to Africans in the colony.

In other colonial areas, such as British Tanganyika, radio was instrumental in creating new, unsettled listening publics and subjects. In the 1950s, besides the broadcasts of British colonial radio, fierce anti-colonial invective in Swahili reached the east coast of Africa primarily through the broadcasts from Cairo (Brennan, 2010). Brennan notes that the radio station Sauti-al-Arab (Voice of the Arabs) allowed Egypt to 'create a public opinion where none had existed before among the illiterate and semi-literate masses of the Arab world', including East Africa (Brennan, 2010:176). Two new stations followed, Sauti ya Cairo (Voice of Cairo) in 1954 and the English-language Voice of Free Africa in April 1957. Most striking was

> ... the vivid language of invective directed against British colonial interests ... [with terms such as] 'dogs' and 'pigs' resuscitating a tradition in Swahili poetry of the competitive insult ... [and] assimilat[ing] contemporary world events into a consistent and powerful anti-colonial message (Brennan, 2010:181).

By the early 1960s the influence of both these stations waned and after the Six Day War of 1967 they closed. But the anti-colonial invective had a particular influence on the later formation of nationalist radio stations in African independent states, in Brennan's view. It produced, he argues, 'the defensive intellectual armaments of Africa's post-colonial states, whose very fragility fueled the aggressive assertion of nation-state sovereignty at the expense of transregional political movements' (Brennan, 2010:190).

The chapters by Stephen Davis and Peter Lekgoathi in the present volume speak in different ways to the themes of radio in this period of colonial and early nationalist identity in Africa and the construction of publics. Davis's chapter looks both critically and sympathetically at Radio Freedom, the voice of the African National Congress in exile from the early 1960s, and its struggle to find an audience in the face of its powerful adversary, the South African state and the SABC. Referring at one point to the station as 'a kind of political theatre', he comments that 'radio emerged as both the point and counterpoint of the construction of apartheid and of the anti-apartheid struggle'.

Peter Lekgoathi, writing on Northern Sotho radio during the apartheid era in South Africa, focuses on a contestation within the station for the loyalty of listeners. Faced with stringent mechanisms by the SABC management to pre-empt and handle possible subversion, announcers resorted to deep and subtle uses of Northern Sotho to elude their handlers, but not their listeners. Lekgoathi emphasises the role of language in the creation of publics 'drawn from different social classes and regions, literate and illiterate, townspeople and rural dwellers, all actively drawn to the new medium in their language'.

Radio and the emergence of multiple voices

Radio in Africa's high profile as a many-faceted site of communication at the end of the first decade of the new millennium signals its growing role as a 'tool of resistance' to any residual state monopoly of radio so common until the democratic waves of the early 1990s in many African countries. If radio is indeed 'Africa's medium' (Hyden, Leslie & Ogundimu, 2002), what does this mean in the present era of technological change coupled with widespread media deregulation and democratisation? These are factors that have often helped bring about a far more interactive, popular use of the electronic media on the continent, a situation with which a number of the chapters that follow engage through case studies of talk radio on stations in Ghana, Kenya and South Africa. Radio has come to be regarded as an emerging public sphere through which multiple voices have come to replace the previously omnipresent voice of despotic leaders. Often, the state used radio for its own ends through an oppressive top-down format of passing on information to the masses. For this reason, one of the earliest excitements about alternative radio spaces (see Stephen Ellis's (1989) article on popular comment through 'pavement radio') revolved around the emergence of multiple voices. An emerging body of work on talk radio turns on the democratic potential that radio now has. Bosch's chapter on South African talk radio points to the interactive nature of talk programmes and the meaning of that for remaking public space. Tettey and Odhiambo, writing on talk radio in Ghana and Kenya, respectively, also see it as a crucial remaking of the national public sphere. Tettey draws attention as well to issues of manipulation and promotion of party or commercial interest. These exist alongside the avenues of communication and genuine debate that talk radio has opened up to the Ghanaian public. Other radio shows, such as the Kenyan FM stations about which Odhiambo writes, have 'vox pop' sessions in the street. These, he argues, are open to wider cross sections of the community and can engage directly with the vibrant life of the streets and with the voices of the marginalised. Thus, as Odhiambo shows, a programme styling itself 'the people's parliament' can transform the locus of political debate in Kenya. Talk shows often heighten public awareness of specific issues concerning minority and marginalised social groups and issues such as gay and lesbian rights (Tettey, 2010). Moreover, talk radio can move debate beyond the tight linkage of current news and passing public interest. As Tettey puts it in this volume: 'Talk radio ensures that issues do not die with the news cycle, but can be kept in the public realm and in the public consciousness for some time.'

Chibita's chapter on unresolved radio policy and the power balances within language use, which she sees as one of the dilemmas facing radio practice in Uganda, prefers the idea of multiple public spheres or 'sphericules', where she sees a number of interlocking public conversations taking place. This concept of multivocality or dialogism, to quote generally from Mikhail Bakhtin (1981), allows for a more nuanced reading of radio as a media form that must be read within its context of production. Chibita argues that multivocality in the Ugandan case means working across a number of languages rather than choosing simply Swahili or simply English.

The dilemma of the new publics

More broadly, we question the roles and the differing profiles of radio in Africa where the electronic media have uneven levels of freedom and unequal capacity, depending on both the state and region in which they are situated. The relatively recent multiplicity of radio presence on the continent, a fact noted with cautious optimism by Fardon and Furniss (2000:3) in the introduction to their publication

African Broadcast Cultures, still points, we believe, to an expanding popular engagement with its genres and a steadily energised public sphere. As a part of the new publics and new listening communities that have sprung up throughout the continent since the early 1990s, new voices are on, and in, the air and the possibilities for the making of a particular kind of popular democracy 'informed by African notions of personhood and agency' are real (Nyamnjoh, 2005:20). The deregulation of radio that followed the wave of democratisation in the early 1990s in a number of countries, including South Africa, Ghana, Mali, Benin, Guinea, Burkina Faso, Mauretania and Senegal (Myers, 2000:92; Nombre, 2000:83), has indeed allowed multiple publics to come into existence, and in some instances there is a massive reshaping of publics and the public sphere.

Even in a climate of media deregulation, though, the question of how the media, including radio, are regulated remains central. Who owns the means of communication and whether a station is private, commercial, community run, state owned or a public broadcaster are all key questions. Powerful commercial and political interests, both national and global, operate in the field of radio as they do elsewhere on the media terrain. Even the site of talk radio, a forum for people's voices and 'pavement talk' on air, can become a site open to abuse (Mwesige, 2009; Tettey, this volume). The medium itself becomes a site of struggle. Alternative or resistant voices within a state or region or community often find the means of providing their own media sites for battles for power. Thus, a multitude of TV and radio stations may not mean true diversity, but a proliferation of self-serving 'voices' among which the judicious listener/viewer has to pick his/her way, a point both Wolters (this volume) and Frere (2008) make about the media in the DRC and in particular in the capital, Kinshasa.

Certainly, there is still evidence of vicious and partisan positions used by semi-private FM stations. This was the case in Rwanda's RTLM, as discussed by Straus (see above). Yet in broad terms, the move away from a single national broadcasting centre has changed the way in which ordinary citizens view local and national politics. Now listeners can imagine themselves as both global and local citizens. Marie-Soleil Frere (2007), writing on the media changes in francophone countries, sketches out both the huge gains and the pitfalls that are part of this transformation. She remarks that the new private commercial, denominational, association or community radio stations soon act as intermediaries for civil society, often all the more dynamic as the state fails to fulfil its duties. Unions, professional associations, churches and NGOs – all those entities acting as a (more or less active) counterbalance to political power – acquire greater visibility and efficiency thanks to the liberalisation of the media sector. She notes the vibrancy of the FM scene both in large centres and in small towns, and the different kinds of stations – commercial, community and international:

> Today, on the FM frequency in capitals, provincial towns and small localities, and operating side by side, are commercial private stations (often mainly musical, but launching more and more into newscasts), denominational radio stations (Catholic, Protestant and to a lesser extent Muslim), community and association radio stations (intended to promote development, these are especially frequent in rural areas) and international radio stations (RFI, Africa N1 and the BBC having been established on FM frequency in all major African cities) (Frere, 2007:39).

Proliferation does not, however, automatically ensure pluralism. This is a point well made by Tettey (2004:227–28) in his summary of broadcasting reform in Ghana. Tettey suggests that what has happened in the Ghanaian case is a 'hierarchisation of voices' with its own implications for participatory discourse. English is privileged over the Ghanaian languages in many cases and rural areas are excluded from the FM stations (Tettey, 2001:25). Often powerful means of transmission 'threaten to crowd out actual or potential channels for weaker voices, particularly of the rural poor' (Tettey, 2001:31). The same point regarding exclusion and the danger of radio in Africa becoming an elite medium with a focus on the urban and on the kind of listener whom advertisers want to cater for is made by Kruger (2007). Hendy (2000) too warns of the dangers of sameness that go together with global radio formatting and replication across stations that share a common branding. He asks – and the question is equally applicable to Africa: 'Does radio in the global age give us a wider window in the world, or expose us dreadfully to the homogenized and banal output of a few multinational media chains and record companies?' (Hendy, 2000:7).

Subjectivities, cultures, communities

The capacity of radio to engage in the 'thick' cultural expressions that mark the linguistic life of African speakers and users of the medium across the continent is the topic of a number of essays in this volume and forms the central theme of the second section, 'The Cultures of Radio: Languages of the Everyday'. How does radio engage listeners as both citizens – or would-be citizens – and self-fashioning subjects in the debates of the era? We work from the assumption that radio both shapes its listenership and is shaped by it. The complex dialogics and cultural reach of the 'voicings' of radio mean that it is not possible to block stations into such simple categories as 'repressive' and 'free' (see Gunner, Ligaga, Mano and Lekgoathi in this volume).

Winston Mano (this volume) points out this contradiction in relation to radio use in Zimbabwe. The texts carried by the different programmes of state radio, which deal with the notices of the everyday (death and funeral notices, for instance), may still function as the voices of people able to carry on conversations that, through language and cultural knowledge, knit families and group interests together and provide deep satisfaction even in the midst of poor or despotic governance. His chapter on death notices in the programme *Zviziviso Zverufu/Izaziso Zemfa* on Radio Zimbabwe argues that it is one of the key programmes on the station that continues to attract listeners. Through it, the station presents material of 'national origin' (Mytton, 1983:135). Mano draws on work by Curran and Park (2000:11–12) who, in their call for a shift towards 'de-Westernizing media studies', remark that 'perhaps the key point to emphasise is that media systems are shaped not merely by national regulatory regimes and national audience preferences, but by a complex ensemble of social relations that have taken shape in national contexts'.

Thus, Mano (citing Barnard, 2000:17) reminds us of one of radio's most important gifts, namely its ability 'to "tap" into the cultural fabric of the society to which it broadcasts'. Harri Englund's (2011) recent work on radio in Malawi has among its subjects an alternative news bulletin broadcast by the Malawi Broadcasting Corporation. Called *Nkhani za m'maboma* (News from the Districts) and broadcast in the evenings on both Radio 1 and Radio 2 FM, it uses richly idiomatic language to publicise stories about injustice and the failures of the authorities. Englund's study reveals the extent of reflection and deliberation enabled by Malawi's public radio, which is often reviled by human rights activists for maintaining a political bias in its official news bulletins. What both Mano and Englund point us to are the resonances of the local with which radio operates. Such programmes, which may run for many years through different broadcasting and political regimes, exemplify the 'complex ensemble of social relations' (to use Curran and Park's (2000) useful phrase) that radio enables people to enact. Thus, radio's capacity to assemble and reassemble items from a range of repertoires may be part of its power to voice the local and selectively incorporate the global.

Coplan (this volume) ascribes to it a unique capacity to draw people together. Using the SABC Sotho station Letshedi FM as his model, he claims that radio has the capacity to evoke 'the societal' and pull together the intersecting lines of contemporary African urban and rural culture. The point about radio and its 'spacescape' – a slightly different idea from Appadurai's (1991) 'mediascape' – is crucial. Spitulnik's (2000; 2002) seminal work on radio in Zambia has drawn our attention to the way radio remakes the listener's apprehension of the spatial; and the ways in which the radio as material object and radio sound floats through social spaces, demarcates them, and creates new networks through such tracks of sound and sociabilities.

Radio may be an apt medium for the playing out of social memory and 'the practice of everyday life' (De Certeau, 1984), even in the midst of rapid change. But the 'liberalisation of the media and the opening up of public space to the concerns and views of ordinary people' in Ghana, Kenya and South Africa, for instance (Meyer, 2004:92; see also Odhiambo, this volume; Tettey, this volume), highlight the importance of studying 'the social impact and cultural meaning of media in the everyday lives' of people (Ginsberg, Abu-Lughod & Larkin, 2002:6). The creation of a different sense of subjecthood linked to gender, public and private roles or to how one lives as a religious subject can also often come through new possibilities that radio sets out through a new configuration of public and private. Thus Schulz (this volume) comments on the proliferation of radio stations since the democratisation of the Mali media. This, she argues, can itself highlight other social tensions, as the use of the media in general reflects shifts in gender roles and understandings of religious authority.

Schulz, like Diawara's (1997) earlier work on radio in Mali cited above, draws us into a trail of deep cultural causalities that has to be followed in order to fully understand *why* women's voices as religious preachers have such a complicated reception in Mali today and why they are so enjoyed. In other words, the change in subjectivities that radio brings, as it shapes 'the production of individual and collective identities' (Ginsberg, Abu-Lughod & Larkin, 2002:3), may well be difficult and contested. In another instance, drawn from Frahm-Arp's chapter on a community station in Johannesburg, an individual's relation to his/her faith and the understanding of the believing subject can be dramatically shifted through a religious radio programme's broadcasting of the Catholic Mass. A person's subjecthood and the understanding of being a citizen may change too. Thus, a community station devoted to the Islamic faith demonstrates how individual belief may encourage a religious identity that is communal, national and part of the global *'ummah'*.

There are ways too in which a change in radioscape brings about the production of what Brigit Meyer (2004) in her discussion of the new 'pentecostalite style', particularly in visual public culture in Ghana, has termed 'alternative imaginations'. New gendered subjectivities can shape themselves through innovative ways of living one's faith (Frahm-Arp and Schulz, both in this volume). Gendered behaviour and behaviour as citizens, and modern subjects can shift dramatically due to radio (Bosch, Gunner and Ligaga in this volume).

Radio and the nation

Marissa Moorman's chapter on radio in Angola covers a broad sweep of time from colonial radio through to the post-civil war present. Not only does she demonstrate the role of music as part of the way Angolans imagined the becoming of a nation in the 1960s and 1970s, but she also shows the integral role of radio (and vinyl) in this process of imagining the nation. Thus, imagination, resistance and musical taste intertwine at a crucial period in Angola's history. Like Davis's chapter on Radio Freedom, Moorman too shows the place of *Angola Combatente* – the MPLA[2] radio programme during the war against Portugal – in creating alternative spaces of imagination. Quoting from Spitulnik (1998:68), she remarks that 'places that were minimally connected before became strongly linked ... while the horizons of people's worlds expanded ... distances overall became shorter and even more tangible'. There is no guarantee, however, that a new 'free' state will allow radio freedom. Moorman's chapter begins and ends bleakly, with an account of two killings in late 2010 – both of popular and respected journalists from Radio Despertar, the radio of the opposition party UNITA.[3]

While the politics of culture and community are themes present in essays in this volume, so too is the link between radio and the project of a state politics of identity. Moorman's chapter gives us a brief glimpse of the struggles over radio voice and its control in Angola now. Almost all the chapters in this book engage at some level with this question of the politics of state identity, radio sound, and the idea of nation and practice of the state. As Ginsberg, Abu-Lughod and Larkin (2002:11) put it:

> Even if nations are always in relations with other nations and transnational identities or ideas (Hannerz, 1992; Appadurai, 1993) ... the nation is still a potent frame of reference, especially in the many countries where the state has been the prime actor in the creation and regulation of media networks.

Can radio, carefully deployed and regulated, enable the coexistence of more multiple identities within the nation state? Chibita's chapter on the difficult question of broadcasting language in Uganda raises precisely such a problem. How, she asks, can a policy of multiple-language broadcasting that privileges African languages spoken in Uganda alongside the use of English be a way of achieving a greater sense of national unity?

Similarly, both Smith's chapter on the setting up of the new UN-funded Somalia station Bar-Kulan and Davis's historical chapter on Radio Freedom and its internal dissensions have as an underlying discourse the question of a national project.

Ligaga's chapter on radio theatre that kept afloat in the face of a repressive central broadcaster, the KBC, shows the state operating a repressive view of 'the nation' and one of the plays that survived censorship as presenting a much more complicated meditation on the nation and what has gone wrong with it. The language may be hidden, the genres different, but the fascination with the idea and project of state identity seems, on the basis of these essays, to be firmly rooted in the African imaginary at the present time. Moorman's insightful view of radio, music and the nation in Angola perhaps sums it up best. Radio, she states, 'is a cultural technology with a specific mode of communication that gives it a particular relation to the production of nation'.

The sections into which we have divided the book are in a sense as porous as radio itself: the chapters 'talk' to each other in multiple ways and cross-cut with the themes and major questions we have attempted to outline above. The sections into which the book falls are: (1) Radio, Popular Democracy and New Publics; (2) The Cultures of Radio: Languages of the Everyday; and (3) Radio and Community: Voices of Change.

Endnotes

1   Our thanks to Wendy James for providing the information on the two Sudanese stations (personal communication, 12 October 2010).
2   Movimento Popular da Libertação de Angola.
3   União Naçional para a Independênçia Total de Angola.

1

Radio, Popular Democracy and New Publics

1

Talk Radio and Politics in Ghana
Exploring Civic and (Un)Civil Discourse in the Public Sphere

Wisdom J. Tettey

Introduction

The importance of free expression in fostering and consolidating democratic governance is an indubitable fact that has been stated for centuries, from the early practitioners and theorists of democracy to contemporary advocates of democratic reform in various countries around the world (Mill, [1859] 2001; Norris, 2009). This relationship has significant resonance in post-third-wave democratic struggles on the African continent as various actors pursue, and seek to protect, a civic culture where the rights of individuals and groups to voice their points of view are affirmed and anchored in practice. It is only when citizens are able to share their thoughts and hold one another and public officials accountable, without intimidation or fear, that an informed body politic can be engendered to ensure that the affairs of state are conducted in the best interest of society.

The media are one of the means by which citizens exercise voice and attempt to engage in the deliberative processes that characterise democratic participation (Lee, 2007). While all media venues offer this possibility, their usefulness as a democratic space in Africa was constrained for a very long time by autocratic and dictatorial regimes until the early 1990s, when the continent was hit by agitations for democratic reform. Since then, the media space for democratic expression has expanded, although the vestiges of constrained engagement remain strong in certain countries (see Tettey, 2009a). Notwithstanding the fact that the preponderance of newspapers is the most observable demonstration of this opening in many countries, there is no denying the fact that radio has seen significant growth as well, providing the most geographically and linguistically transcendent, accessible and extensive medium on the continent. As the BBC World Service Trust (2006:13) notes:

> Radio dominates the mass media spectrum with state-controlled radio services still commanding the biggest audiences in most countries but regional (within country) commercial stations demonstrating the largest consistent increases in numbers, followed by community radio, where growth, although significant in certain countries, has been inconsistent.

The consistent growth in the number of non-state-controlled radio stations in several countries has led to a vibrant, pluralistic and competitive radio landscape, with the attendant potential for expansion in the media spaces available for the expression of citizens' preferences and perspectives. The extent to which that potential is harnessed very much depends on the kind of control exercised by those in charge of these channels of information flow and exchange. As Tettey (2009a:278–79; original emphasis) notes:

> ... gatekeeping is a vital process that determines the silencing or expression of various voices. Those who control the conduits for expression have the power to filter what kind of information, or whose, gets into the public realm and hence gets attention or shapes the public discourse. The media have a significant influence on the public sphere, through the exercise of this control. Depending on how they exercise this control, the media can help shape civic competence among citizens. *Civic competence* is the citizens' ability to understand, engage with, and make appropriate demands on the state while meeting their responsibilities and obligations as citizens.

Ghanaian media, in general, have grown exponentially over the course of the last two decades of democratic rule, not just in numbers, but also in their influence on the public sphere. Like a number of its counterparts in Africa, the country has seen a tremendous increase in the number of radio stations, from a monopoly of 11 state-owned, centrally controlled networks in the mid-1990s to 122 on air out of a total of 166 licences issued by 2007 (Tettey, 2004; IREX, 2008:152). A key feature of this new broadcasting landscape is talk radio. In fact, the vibrant, usually unrestrained and passionate discussions over the airwaves are one of the vivid pieces of evidence that observers of Ghana's political landscape point to in touting the country as an exemplar of democratic culture and consolidation on the African continent. According to Freedom House's 2009 report on press freedom, the country shares the top spot with Mali and Mauritius as the freest countries in sub-Saharan Africa.

The report states that 'Ghana's reputation as a country with unfettered freedom of expression was reinforced in 2008 ... and Radio remains the most popular medium' (Freedom House, 2009).

It is in the context of the foregoing developments that this chapter explores the nature of political talk radio in Ghana, with a critical interrogation of the extent to which it engages the public in issues of national and local concern; shapes the public discourse on those issues; contributes to an enriched, deliberative public sphere; facilitates democratic accountability by various actors; and creates room for a pluralistic civic culture. The chapter also examines challenges confronting this media genre vis-à-vis efforts to create a conducive environment for democratic expression, responsible citizenship and accountable journalism within a multivocal, inclusive public sphere. The chapter will explore these issues in the specific context of political discourse, because it is by far the major focus of media coverage, in general, and talk radio, in particular. A 2007 report by the National Media Commission showed that politics has the greatest share of media coverage, accounting for 22 per cent of the total (Ghanaweb, 2007a).

Talk radio and democratic citizenship

Talk radio is part of the genre of participatory media that is increasingly gaining attention from academics, as they explore the dialectics of interaction between audience and medium in shaping public discourse in the context of democratic politics (Lee, 2007). O'Sullivan (2005:719) argues that 'these fora allow the audience a presence and so create at least an illusion of access to the mass media', which is not an insignificant starting point for citizens' understanding of politics and their engagement with the public sphere. Participation in talk radio reflects active agency, which is a critical requirement for the growth, consolidation and sustenance of democracy. According to Ross (2004:787; original emphasis),

> ... listeners to and participants in public access programmes ... *do* perceive the genre as a genuine public sphere that allows the articulation of alternative (i.e. *real* people's) voices, and the explosion of talk radio shows in the US has led some commentators to suggest that this genre now constitutes a mechanism for a new electronic populism.[1]

Part of the reason for the attraction of talk radio in Ghana

> ... resides in what Michael Warner calls the 'appeal of mass subjectivity', whereby ... audience members can experience the fantastic contradiction

of being embodied and self-abstracted simultaneously ... But talk shows are also popular ... because they offer audiences a chance to speak and be heard at a time when there continues to be much to say about politics, economy, and everyday struggles (Matza, 2009:489).

Beyond the chance to directly participate, the majority of Ghanaian audiences just want to engage the public sphere vicariously as their compatriots give voice to personal circumstances and opinions that they share, and seek appropriate insights and responses. In sum, they are drawn to talk radio programmes by what O'Sullivan (2005) calls 'emotional reciprocity'.

The variegated talk radio landscape in Ghana and the opportunity that it provides for ordinary citizens to inject their voices into the public sphere through phone-in contributions or text messaging, for example, has led to a fundamental shift in the demography of contributors to political discourse. Prior to these developments, only those who were considered to have an authoritative voice on national or local issues were heard. The definition of 'authoritative voice' in these contexts was very restrictive and tended to include only those who exercised some formally recognised expertise or occupied the top echelons of the socio-economic and political ladder. The consequence was a restrictive, exclusionary public discourse environment that granted visibility and pride of place to a coterie of elite voices. Under the current dispensation, authoritative voice is being appropriated by ordinary citizens who feel empowered to comment on the realities of their lives as they see them, challenge official renditions of their reality, and call public officials to account in the open and largely unfettered spaces made possible by the instantaneity of live talk radio (see Hutchby, 2001:483).

Phone-ins are the main vehicle through which citizens participate in these talk programmes, and the opportunity for inclusive discourse is facilitated by the fact that many of these programmes allow callers to speak in local languages even when the programmes are officially in English. As Kafewo (2006:16) observes, 'a trend noticed by this researcher is that English call-in programmes, which take advantage of widespread mobile telephony access among listeners, often end up being conducted for more than three-quarters of their duration in [the] vernacular'.

A corollary to this exercise of democratic freedom is the fact that radio talk shows have given citizens the ability to set the agenda on certain issues of public concern and to serve as watchdogs not only over state institutions and public officials, but over other categories of actors as well – from private individuals, through corporate bodies and other states, to international agencies (see Owen, 2000; Nassanga, 2008). Civil society groups are also availing themselves of the opportunities provided by talk radio to pursue and champion their causes, as have international institutions, such as the World Bank. In fact, as will be demonstrated later, World Bank officials in Ghana have not only used these platforms to explain policies to the public and to share other kinds of information, but have gone as far as collaborating on a *Development Dialogue* series with some radio stations every month or two.

The challenges of getting minority and marginalised voices into the public sphere cannot be said to have been addressed simply by the mere expansion of the number of radio outlets. It is fair, however, to say that these outlets, particularly talk programmes, have enabled otherwise silent perspectives in struggles over political power and control to be shared on air, even if strained and battered by dominant voices – what Squires (2000:74) refers to as 'discursive political participation'. This is exemplified by the hitherto inconceivable opportunities that gays, lesbians and their supporters have on radio 'to challenge the inevitable erosion of citizenship rights for those whose sexual orientation does not fit the mould carved out by heteronormative and homophobic institutions, processes, and systems' (Tettey, 2010:45).

Unlike the straightforward news reporting that characterised radio broadcasts in times past and the ephemeral nature of the newscast, talk radio ensures that issues do not die with the news cycle, but can be kept in the public realm and in the public consciousness for some time. This is because the issue in question could be the subject of a panel discussion after the initial news report or could be resurrected by a member of the public in the context of the flexible interactive structure and sometimes-unpredictable flow of a live call-in programme. Consequently, it is difficult for public officials and/or those who are the subject of a particular news story to ride out an issue with the hope that it will die with the news cycle – they are compelled to address the issue in some way, even if not to the satisfaction of all.

Because talk radio is live, it allows for instantaneous responses from those who are the subject of any discussion. This gives them the advantage of addressing any misconceptions, misrepresentations or inaccuracies in discussions or to have their points of view heard in close juxtaposition to the other perspectives that are being presented. This immediacy of response has been made possible by increased access to telephones, particularly cellphones. It is not unusual to have someone call in to a talk programme while driving, because he/she feels compelled to respond to an issue in which he/she is implicated or about which he/she has an opinion. In other instances, talk radio hosts have called government officials to respond to issues raised by audience members or panellists. Cellphones allow them to respond immediately and to get involved in the discussion in ways that allow the public to get official reaction to concerns, observations, accusations, citizens' reports, etc. This live exchange provides a unique opportunity for ordinary citizens to directly confront or engage with public officials in ways that the normal ordering of power relations would otherwise not allow. Being in this open, transparent forum also compels officials to be sensitive to, attentive to and respectful of citizens' views, even if they disagree with them, because of the political repercussions that could attend untoward attitudes. This is not to suggest that all officials are reined in by this transparency, as will be discussed below. However, the likelihood of decorous response by public officials is higher in these circumstances.

Another dimension to the phenomenon of radio is, thus, the convergence that has emerged between the traditional radio platform and the new information and communication technologies, such as the Internet and cellphones. The major radio stations, mainly those in the national capital, have an Internet presence as they stream their programmes live or make on-demand access to some of their programmes available on the Internet. In fact, this convergence has allowed the stations and their programmes to extend their reach beyond the territorial confines of the country, thereby allowing anyone to be in touch with national developments and discourses. The popularity of the online services is borne out by the following disclosure by Joy FM, a leading Ghanaian radio station:

> Multimedia Broadcasting Company, owners of myjoyonline.com, has apologised to its loyal international listeners for going offline. The Online Editor … told Joy News on Friday the live streaming had to be taken off to transfer it to a larger server to accommodate the growing number of listeners. 'We have overgrown our facilities because more people are coming to our website' (Myjoyonline, 2007).

Overwhelming numbers of the online audience are Ghanaians in the diaspora, who are not only able to access news and discussions, but also have the option to join in these discussions in a variety of ways. There is, for example, a social-networking site on Facebook for listeners of Radio Gold's weekend talk programme *Alhaji Alhaji*. The site enables listeners to comment on issues being discussed on the programme (see Facebook, 2010). Radio in cyberspace has thus become a venue for multivocality and deterritorialised political discourse that defies state control. What we see now is a new mediascape characterised by a convergence of platforms that lends itself to multiple sources of information production and viewpoints, as well as the endless expanse of recipients. Tettey (2009b:149) notes:

> There are several instances where issues that have been raised within chat rooms or on websites, principally by self-identified members of the Diaspora, have found their way into mainstream national politics in terms

of influencing policy, eliciting a response from state officials, or providing fodder for domestic political actors of one stripe or another.

The following Internet exchanges on Radio Gold's online site during the 2008 elections show the extent to which online radio has become a very important means for the Ghanaian diaspora to connect with home:

written by kojo, 3 January 2009
you guys are a 'fuck' radio gold for inciting irate NDC [National Democratic Congress] supporters to come out and protect the station when danger was looming on you for the false information you kept spreading … Mind you that we the NPP [New Patriotic Party] hasn't given up the fight yet and will make sure we save Ghanaians from the dark … I love Atta Mills but not his so-called incoming government compatriots

written by NII, LONDON, 3 January 2009
RADIO GOLD PLEASE RECTIFY THE TECHNICAL ERROR. WE CANT ACCESS YOU ONLINE. I WANT TO LISTEN TO FORENSICS. CAN YOU TELL US SOMETHING OR ARE YOU UNDER ATTACK? WE ARE CONCERNED IN LONDON

written by KK, 3 January 2009
Is Radio GOLD still on-air? I can't find you on the internet anymore!!!! Njoyonline.com seems to have deleted your audio link!!!!
   Please check … I want to continue hearing your loud voices here in the Amsterdam (Radio Gold, 2009).

Text messaging has become a closely related part of the talk radio genre as listeners express their views on topical issues being covered on particular programmes. The following transcript from CITI FM's *Citi Breakfast Show* of 14 April 2010 provides some insight into how multiple media platforms are integrated into the show to allow maximum participation by listeners, enhance interactivity and promote critical discourse. On this particular occasion, the World Bank country director for Ghana, Ishac Diwan, was the guest.

Host: I want to say that if you want to contribute to this programme
            urgently, you can give us a call on 224922, 230075 and
            224959. This is strictly World Bank discussion …

Caller:	I think the alternative to weaning ourselves from the World Bank is by consolidating the building up of infrastructure in the country. When we are able to do that, then the country has appropriate legs to stand on.
Host:	Let me take a few comments [from text messages].
	Now Kuuku Ofofi-Attah says: Why is that immediately there is a government in power, they shower praises. Immediately the power leaves, it's rather the opposite. If you can come clear on this one, I will be glad.
	I think you should answer Kuuku's question: ... that when you were assessing the NPP government, 2007 World Bank Report was like, the government was doing very very well. And then you say that in their last year, they spent recklessly. They think that your comments are a bit inconsistent.
Ishac:	But I don't think that they are inconsistent. I mean that's my first answer. As I said, you can be doing very well in your Balance Sheet and be doing badly in your Income Statement for a particular year. I spoke earlier about the NPP's eight years in government as being extremely successful and the last year being delicate, difficult (Avleh, 2010).

Assessing political discourse: Tenor, tone and trends

While the value of political talk radio has been asserted, as reflected in the analysis above, there are also concerns about this genre. Some observers believe that it offers only a facade of a deliberative public sphere (see Lee, 2002). These critics share Gerstl-Pepin's (2007:4) argument that the media 'essentially operate as a "thin" public sphere ... in the sense that genuine dialogue about governance issues does not take place ... Instead, the media operate more as a billboard of opposing viewpoints rather than a forum for debates and analysis of issues'. Other critics criticise the genre for the negative streak in the tone and tenor that tends to characterise political discourse presented via these programmes, contending that it is inimical to civil, deliberative, democratic politics. Yanovitzky and Cappella (2001:379), for example, point out with regard to the United States that 'some have also been concerned that the tone of the discourse on PTR [political talk radio] is out of bounds, tending towards the uncivil and rude at least, and the racist, homophobic and chauvinistic at worst'. This section, therefore, explores the extent to which talk radio in Ghana bears out these concerns and the implications, if any, that they portend for the fledgling democratic dispensation that the country is trying to sustain.

As is the case in other countries where talk radio has been studied, some talk radio hosts in Ghana are perceived to represent particular political interests (McMillan, 2005). This reality was brought to the fore in the most vivid terms during the 2008 elections in the country when talk programmes on some radio stations, such as Radio Gold and Oman FM, which are perceived to be aligned to the NDC and NPP, respectively, put out very negative stories and allegations that heightened political tension in the country. Radio Gold's *Election Forensics* programme repeatedly played and had hosts and panellists run commentary on tape recordings allegedly showing supporters and senior members of the NPP administration plotting strategies to rig the elections and/or cause mayhem in the event that they lost (for an example, see Myjoyonline, 2008). As one analyst of Ghana's media scene laments,

> ... if issues were not put right in the media front and the public looses [sic] confidence in their work, the nation will suffer. He observed that many of the radio stations were stocked with unprofessional personnel, some of whom were 'polluting' the air with divisive messages that turn to disunite the country, especially in the area of politics and ethnicity (Myjoyonline, 2010k).

The foregoing perceptions and examples notwithstanding, hosts endeavour in most cases to come across as disinterested parties in discussions and debates about political issues, representing themselves as facilitators in efforts to help the public understand issues and diverse viewpoints. The height of partisanship in the realm of talk radio in Ghana is seen mostly among callers who tend to couch most issues in partisan political terms in order to denigrate the other side of the political divide and accentuate the advantages of their political party (see Pfau, Cho & Cho, 2001; Lee, 2002). Indeed, in Ghana's de facto two-party political environment, most contributions to debates on talk radio are usually binary, diametrically opposed viewpoints representing the two major political parties – the NDC and NPP. This approach to talk radio reflects a recognition by various political groups that these forums attract large audiences and that they constitute a very easy and cheap way to get their political messages across, from the most mundane issues to the most burning policy debates. The struggle to make political capital through these programmes is acknowledged by various political parties that regularly send their representatives to articulate their positions on panel discussions.

Indeed, the passion of partisan politics in the realm of talk radio and its use as a propaganda tool have spawned what has become known in Ghana as serial callers. These are individuals who call in to various programmes on a regular basis. In view of the fact that many Ghanaians cannot afford to call in to these programmes so regularly and across various stations, there is strong suspicion that these individuals are paid fronts for particular political parties. While parties have dismissed these suspicions and argued that these people are just ordinary citizens who happen to support the agenda of the parties, recent revelations erode the credibility of these assertions. A draft 2007/08 audit report for the Ministry of Information during the NPP administration of President Kufuor shows that funds were funnelled to various people, including 'serial callers and journalists to prosecute the party's propaganda towards the 2008 elections "under the guise of a Government Communication Strategy Programme"'. It is also worth noting that the current NDC government admits that it has a communications team that is farmed out to tell its story in various media settings, including talk radio discussion programmes (Myjoyonline, 2010d).

The talk radio scene has been further complicated by politicised journalism, as media practitioners exhibit their political leanings when serving as pundits and commentators on programmes. The regular participation of journalists in these talk programmes as partisan panellists, combined with the passion and adversarial nature of these discussions, has created some damaging fissures within the journalist fraternity, which have further compromised the public's faith in the independence of the fourth estate. A retired manager of the Ghana News Agency expressed a concern shared by many observers of the media scene in Ghana when he 'deplored the recent practice where some senior journalists had turned themselves into "politician-journalists" and move from either one television or radio station to another defending one political party or the other' (Ghanaweb, 2007b).

Some of these fissures have become very personal, degenerating into name calling and mutual accusations of malfeasance and impropriety among journalists (see, for example, Myjoyonline, 2010g). The public's loss of confidence in the objectivity and independence of media personnel was reinforced by revelations in the draft audit report, referred to earlier, which

> ... states that the money wrongfully released by the Ministry of Finance and Economic Planning was paid to some individuals who formed part of an 'Editors Forum' and media executives to defend government programmes during radio discussions .... Meanwhile, the former Minister of State at the Finance Ministry, Dr Anthony Akoto Osei, has vehemently defended the withdrawal of the GH¢6 million from the TOR Dept Recovery Fund and other government revenue sources to pay journalists to propagate government policies (Myjoyonline, 2010a).

Politicians have exploited these perceptions of partisan sympathy and attendant fissures to undermine the credibility of journalists even when they are making rational, critical arguments on these programmes in respect of the issues under discussion. By tainting these journalists as untrustworthy observers of the public realm, these political actors seek to erode the ability of media practitioners to inform and educate the public and to hold officials to account through their watchdog role. Exchanges in May 2010 between Ben Ephson, editor of the *Daily Dispatch*, and Kwaku Kwarteng, communications director of the NPP, provide an illustration to buttress the argument being made here. These followed the *Daily Dispatch*'s publication of a report by the Economist Intelligence Unit of *The Economist* predicting a win for President Mills in the 2012 elections. Kwarteng branded the *Daily Dispatch* an NDC paper on Asempa FM's *Ekosii Sen* talk programme, 'adding that Ben Ephson's one-sided politics of harping on the negatives in the NPP, including fanning (Akeym/Asante) tribal sentiments, is not helping his own reputation as a journalist' (Myjoyonline, 2010b).

Talk shows and their radio stations thrive on the controversy generated by the adversarial political intercourse that fills the airwaves. In an economically competitive climate where these stations are battling for the limited and precarious advertising revenue on which their survival depends, there is an incentive to savour controversy and rancorous, vituperative exchanges on talk programmes. As Kafewo (2006:15) points out, 'all stations, both state-owned and private, are heavily focused on generating advertising and sponsorship income'. This is not very different from what obtains in other countries, 'partly because a talk show needs to be "entertaining" as well as notionally informative' (Ross, 2004:788; see also Owen, 2000; Bennett, 2001:82).

The paradox of unrestricted voicing, made possible by call-in talk show programmes, lies in the fact that at the same time as they give space for the free expression of views and opinions, they harbour possibilities for the abuse of that freedom, without much control on the part of hosts. One of the troubling developments that have come with live call-in talk radio in Ghana is the extent to which individuals are able to make unsubstantiated assertions and impugn the reputation of others without any form of accountability. A very volatile illustration of this trend occurred on Accra-based Top Radio in February 2010 when a commentator, who was a declared supporter of the opposition NPP, was alleged to have 'made a categorical statement that the former president [Rawlings] burned his [own] house and dared ... his spokesperson to come and challenge him, and that he is aware that the former president burnt his house' (Myjoyonline, 2010h). It subsequently became evident that the commentator had no substantive evidence to back the claim, which was made in the context of an ongoing investigation by the National Fire Service into the cause of the blaze that consumed the entire home and belongings of the former president.

Talk radio has also suffered the ignominy of being hijacked by some individuals who prefer to trade personal insults rather than take advantage of its potential as a forum for deliberative political debate by informed citizens. Such exchanges almost invariably stem from political disagreements of one sort or the other – either at the level of political parties or individuals with political interests at stake. A recent high-profile case in May 2010 on Kumasi-based Fox FM involved two supporters of the two main political parties, with the NPP supporter denigrating President Mills by likening his looks to a chimpanzee's, ostensibly because the NDC supporter had likened Nana Akuffo Addo, an NPP presidential hopeful, to a frog or a corpse.

What is noticeable about reactions to these kinds of incidents by the leadership of political parties is that any criticism of the behaviour of these party surrogates is very muted in comparison to a vehement defence of their right to free expression. As a result, these individuals feel emboldened by the notoriety and support that they get for their actions, thereby encouraging similar behaviour on the part of others and perpetuating a cycle of incivility in the country's political discourse. The parliamentary caucus of the NPP decided to indefinitely boycott proceedings in parliament until the man who accused Rawlings of arson was unconditionally released from custody when the case was going through a court of competent jurisdiction. They did so in the absence of any sign that the judicial process had failed or been exhausted, thereby encouraging a spectacle in which the individual was hailed as a party hero. The importance of upholding freedom with responsibility was, therefore, sacrificed on the altar of partisan expediency, while a culture of indecorous discourse, exhibited in a number of cases by leading political figures, is allowed to fester.

Among politicians with a penchant for this kind of discourse is former President Rawlings himself and a member of parliament for the opposition NPP, Kennedy Agyapong. Agyapong, who, interestingly, owns a number of electronic media outlets in the country, is infamous for his hot-headed outbursts on the airwaves, as exemplified by the following report:

> The Member of Parliament (MP) for Assin North Constituency, Kennedy Agyapong, has threatened to kill the Municipal Chief Executive of the area following death threats he has received from the latter. 'He has threatened to kill me but I will kill him first,' he stated … 'I will beat the hell out of this guy …,' he screamed (Myjoyonline, 2010e).

In an April 2010 discussion on Hot FM about internal wrangling within the NPP regarding the nomination of a presidential candidate for the 2012 elections, Agyapong had a violent confrontation with another member of his own party who was supporting a candidate different from his. In the altercation, Agyapong 'repeatedly called Nana Asabre a "very useless man", a "useless chief" and a "villager" ... Caller after caller after the tirade, bemoaned the sense of despondency gaining grounds in the party' (Myjoyonline, 2010f).

This example shows that uncivil discourse is not limited to interactions across political parties, but is applied within parties as well when the struggle for power and the dynamics of control that come with it are at stake. Talk radio provides a venue for these struggles to be played out in the open and disseminated widely, with the calculated purpose of facilitating the self-aggrandising display of relative power and influence for political gain.

The ubiquity of irresponsible and inflammatory remarks by studio guests or callers has left the Ghanaian public and state officials with a dilemma. Should the constitutionally enshrined freedom of expression be restricted to avoid causing public disorder? The debate for and against this question is still raging and is unlikely to be resolved any time soon. There is, however, no doubt that unguarded talk is threatening the country's democratic consolidation in at least two ways. It is inflaming passions and provoking reactions that imperil public peace and order, and exposes the fact that Ghanaian society's tolerance for free speech is tenuous. In the example above involving accusation of arson against President Rawlings, an irate group of his supporters thronged the court premises where the commentator was standing trial for engaging in an act likely to cause panic and public disorder, with the obvious purpose of intimidating or causing him bodily harm. On subsequent court appearances, supporters of the NPP also showed up at the court, ready to engage the Rawlings supporters in physical exchanges.

A disquieting trend has developed whereby supporters of aggrieved parties storm radio stations while talk programmes are still on air, in order to 'discipline' a guest who, in their estimation, had said something untoward about their political party, leader(s), or some other cause to which they are affiliated. In the incident above in which President Mills was compared to an ape, the radio station was besieged by an angry mob of NDC supporters intent on attacking the individual who made the comparison (see also Citifmonline, 2010).

It is obvious that those who arrogate to themselves the power to sanction their critics – or those whose opinions they do not agree with – through physical violence and intimidation are undermining a foundational precept of democratic governance, i.e. the rule of law. The response to irresponsible and incendiary expression is not vigilante justice, but the cultivation of and civic mobilisation around a culture of civil collective revulsion towards that kind of speech and the use of appropriate institutional mechanisms for seeking redress, including the National Media Commission and the judicial system.

Threats against or attacks on radio commentators are not always carried out in the full glare of the larger public or on the premises of radio stations. The sentiments that their comments create outlive the particular programme that they were made on, with threats articulated in other settings or attacks on their person carried out later on. These situations are most terrifying when rational discourse gets drowned out by primordial attachments to institutions or ethnicity, as was the case recently when some commentators on radio talk programmes criticised the Asantehene (the head of the Asante Kingdom) for threatening the paramount chief of another town with arrest following a dispute between that chief and another who owes allegiance to the Asante Kingdom. Following talk radio discussions,

> [t]he Chief of Nsima in the Ashanti Region, Nana Nkansah Boadum Ayeboafo, has replied Kwesi Pratt Jnr. on some unsavoury remarks he made against the Asantehene, Otumfuo Osei Tutu last week on a number of radio stations in Accra .... [He] noted that 'if that Pratt does not respect his chiefs, we respect our king and will not sit unconcerned for people like him to show disrespect to our King ... We will deal with the Pratt man, and this is a promise' (Peacefmonline, 2010).

A related development is both interesting and unfortunate, because it involved one journalist using his access to the airwaves to threaten another journalist and a media organisation, and to incite a whole community against members of his profession just because they had dared to exercise their democratic right to free expression that was not to his liking:

> A Fox FM presenter in Kumasi, Captain Smart, has vowed to organise a mob attack on Joy FM's sister station in the Garden City, Luv FM, unless Ato Kwamena Dadzie apologises for writing what he described as a disparaging article about the Asantehene Otumfuo Osei Tutu II ... Those views, Captain Smart believes, were sacrilegious and Ato must atone for his 'sins' by publicly apologizing and the Multimedia Group sacking him. Anything short of that will have dire consequences for both Ato and the parent company of Luv FM, he threatened ... local radio in Kumasi Monday morning were inundated with angry callers who poured invectives on Ato Kwamena Dadzie (Myjoyonline, 2010i).

Intolerance for critique, particularly when it is construed as antipathetic to particular interests or individuals, and the unruly reaction that it engenders give an excuse for those uncomfortable with constitutionally protected free speech to justify restrictions, ostensibly in the public interest. A couple of examples will help put these concerns into perspective. In the two examples above about Presidents Rawlings and Mills, police officers were quickly dispatched to the radio stations, supposedly to prevent any disturbance of the peace and to protect commentators from attack. Invariably, in both cases, no member of the crowd that had gathered with the explicit purpose of attacking the commentators was arrested. Ironically, the commentators ended up being the ones arrested and charged with various offences, including making an offensive comment under section 207(27) of the Criminal Code Act. According to this section of the Act, '"a person who in public place or at a public meeting uses threatening, abusive or insulting words or behaviour with intent to provoke a breach of the peace or by which a breach of the peace is likely to be occasioned" commits a crime' (Myjoyonline, 2010c).

Lack of circumspection in utterances on talk radio thus leaves the country's democratic freedoms vulnerable to subjective interpretations of the Criminal Code Act by security agencies and a consequent clampdown on the right of free speech. As one legal expert notes, 'if Section 208 of the Criminal Code were to be activated, many a radio host would have problems with the law because they allow all kinds of scandalous and inflammatory statements to be made by callers and panellists on their networks' (Myjoyonline, 2010j). Incidentally, President Mills, in a commendable act of support for free speech, asked the police to discontinue prosecution of the person who likened him to a chimpanzee.

Conclusion

Political radio talk shows in Ghana are undeniably a repository of vibrant political discourse, providing an avenue for citizens to critically engage with key political issues, articulate diverse perspectives and mobilise support for different viewpoints and actions. This context is a far cry from what obtained previously:

Under the media configurations of the past, characterized by centralized control of mass-mediated information production and dissemination ... the ability of citizens to produce content and share their views was constrained by the gatekeeping role of state agents. The transformations in media ownership, control, and information dissemination ... means that counter-discourses that challenge the hegemonic viewpoint of the state are being vigorously articulated within the ... architecture of this reconfigured public sphere (Tettey, 2009a:288).

While the Ghanaian situation reflects Matza's (2009:521) and others' observation that political talk shows are, largely, 'turning political arguments into mere spectacle', it does not corroborate his argument that 'their relevance to questions of governance has become diluted'. Talk radio discourses inform and are informed by discussions in other contexts. Indeed, the Ghana talk radio scene provides a manifestation of Ross's (2004:798) position that the media allow an outlet for citizen participation in democratic practice even if we are unable to quantitatively ascertain the direct impact of the discursive interactions that characterise the mediascape (see also Hutchby, 2001:481; Yanovitzky & Cappella, 2001).

There is no denying that participants in these talk programmes reflect the expressive, exhibitionist and confessional types identified by Kivikuru (2006:26; see also Schulz, 1999a). The sole purpose of the expressive type is to create a reputation for challenging authority, the exhibitionist just wants to capture the public limelight and the confessional type wants to shine the spotlight on issues that he/she wants addressed publicly because of their relationship to public policy. Collectively, however, they all help to enrich the public discourse.

It must be acknowledged that because of the significant subjectivity that characterises the political discourse of Ghanaian talk radio and the extreme partisanship underlining the claims and counter-claims that are made, audiences are left with information that mostly serves a parochial political interest rather than enlightens. A corollary to this situation is that discussions on these programmes tend to reinforce already held views and existing beliefs, thereby mainly mobilising support for partisan causes, even if they are based largely on misinformation. The danger with this reality is that

> ... the misinformed hold their incorrect beliefs with *confidence* .... While an uninformed citizenry might not pose a threat to democracy, the presence of a largely *misinformed citizenry* may misdirect electoral outcomes and the general direction of public policy (Hofstetter et al., 1999:354; emphasis added).

Furthermore, with the diversity in and partisan politicisation of talk radio, there is concern about deepening political party cleavages and the inimical accentuation of other markers of difference such as language, region and ethnicity. This is because of the extent to which various groups are using the talk show platform to propagate their own versions of the truth, the recrimination that this engenders and the intensification of mutually orchestrated political destruction as the ultimate goal. Evidence from other countries, such as Canada (Mendelsohn & Nadeau, 1996) and the United States (Hall & Cappella, 2002; Jones, 2002), shows similar trends where targeted broadcasting or narrowcasting, aimed at particular socio-demographic groups, has sharpened polarisation among particular markers of difference. In the Ghanaian context, where FM radio stations are being established at the regional and community levels, it is important that the benefits of media expansion and diversity are not eroded by appeals to difference that undermine political stability and democratic consolidation.

While some of the comments on talk radio and the reactions to them are clearly reprehensible, the very fact that they are monitored by and generate passionate responses from various people for diverse purposes is instructive. These developments not only buttress the fact that many Ghanaians listen to these programmes, but also indicate their political impact on the body politic, the need to manage the kinds of discourse that take place on them and the pressure to address them. Notwithstanding the criticisms of political talk radio shows, therefore, there seems to be no desire on the part of many Ghanaians to eliminate them. This fact is captured in the following observation:

> Bright Kwame Blewu, general secretary of the Ghana Journalists Association … recounted how some two years ago the head of the National Commission for Civic Education proposed the banning of radio phone-in. 'There was substantial condemnation of his call,' he said (IREX, 2008:154).

Ghana will certainly suffer a major blow to its efforts at democratic consolidation if political talk radio is hamstrung by state-controlled regulations that constrict spaces for free expression, particularly counter-hegemonic discourses. It is important that the citizens of the polity collectively defend the place of this medium for political communication. Talk radio programmes also have to do their part to protect the genre's contribution to a vigorous, vibrant and civil public sphere; to enhance their role in political and civic literacy; and to prevent the curtailment of the opportunities that they provide for a discursive public sphere. A critical step towards achieving these objectives is for all those who use talk radio, both as audiences and participants, to find a reasonable balance between responsible, media-literate citizenship and free, democratic expression.

Endnote

1   See also Hartley (2000).

2

From Diffusion to Dialogic Space
FM Radio Stations in Kenya[1]

Christopher Joseph Odhiambo

> *So much has changed in the radio world. Back in the day, all we had was KBC. Now people are spoilt for choice ... There has been an evolution. The media have now become bolder, louder and more focused (Mutoko, 2009).*

Introduction

FM radio broadcasting in Kenya is a phenomenon of the late 1990s. The emergence and popularity of FM radio broadcasting can be referenced to the amendment of section 2(a) of Kenya's Constitution in 1991, which catalysed the expansion of the democratic space. This amendment heralded the reintroduction of a multiparty political system in Kenya. Before this development, the Kenya African National Union (KANU) was the only political party after a law was enacted in 1982 making Kenya a one-party state, which resulted in the suppression of all oppositional voices in the country. This not only affected political parties, but to a great extent also undermined other forms of expression such as the media, public assemblies and performance-based creative arts. Thus, it was within this newly emerging democratic landscape in the late 1990s that the airwaves were also liberalised, allowing for the licensing of FM radio stations to broadcast within a limited radius, initially covering only the capital city, Nairobi, and its immediate environs. Interestingly, though, even within this new-found democratic terrain, privately owned commercial FM radio stations were allowed to air only entertainment programmes: music, talk shows and call-ins. However, an expansion of the democratic space brought about a radical change, with FM radio stations conjuring up new styles of broadcasting that enabled them to participate in the discussion on air of serious issues that were of national interest. It is in this sense, then, that it can be argued that these radio stations have undergone a fundamentally radical paradigm shift: from entertainment sites to what can now be described as 'infotainment' sites.

As a very recent phenomenon in Kenya, FM radio stations and their emerging style(s) of broadcast presentation have not received much scholarly analysis, despite their obviously significant contribution to enhancing and nurturing a democratic culture and space. This emergent role and function seems to resonate with Ilboudo's (2000:43) observation on the advent of community radio, when he aptly reminds us:

> Recent years have seen an increasing number of initiatives to dismantle, or at least lower, the barriers to democratization which characterize the present situation of socio-political transitions. As part of the process of democratization in Africa, the advent of community radio has enabled greater popular access to information systems, enhancing people's rights to respond and criticize those who wield power. Diverse forms of feedback promote regular contacts between broadcasters and public.

The aim of this chapter, therefore, is twofold: to highlight the emerging issues regarding FM radio stations in Kenya and to lay bare some highly innovative trends discernible in their presentation and styles that in some ways closely correspond to Brecht's optimistic vision (cited in Ilboudo, 2000:42) of radio transformation when he categorically proclaims that:

> Radio must transform from being a means of diffusion to become a means of communication. Radio could become the most marvellous means of communication imaginable in public life, an immense conduit and it would be this if it were capable not only of broadcasting but also of receiving, of permitting listeners not just to listen, but also to speak; and not isolating them, but putting them in contact.

To illustrate these creative and innovative trends, examples will be drawn from Kiss 100 FM, Easy FM and Citizen Radio FM.

In Kenya, as previously noted, prior to the repeal of the infamous section 2(a) of the Constitution, the state-controlled Kenya Broadcasting Corporation (KBC) – formerly Voice of Kenya (VOK) – had for many years exemplified this 'means of diffusion', enjoying an unlimited monopoly in news dissemination and the entertainment of Kenyans. But its role as a diffusion set was more evident when it acted as the mouthpiece of the then-authoritarian, monolithic political party

KANU. As O'Doul (n.d.) reiterates: 'the government also remains acutely aware that in Kenya, as elsewhere in Africa, the radio remains the most effective means of disseminating information, ideas as well as propaganda.' However, the emergence of FM radio stations in the broadcast landscape radically shifted this character of radio as a 'means of diffusion' to a 'means of communication'.

The context of FM radio in Kenya

For a long time, KBC dominated Kenya's electronic media landscape. The station, which was founded in 1927, ran a nationwide television service and two radio channels broadcasting throughout the country in English and Kiswahili and a number of vernacular languages. At present, competing with private FM stations, KBC has started its own FM stations targeting ethnic communities in different parts of the country. The first FM radio station in Kenya was Metro FM (established in 1996), which was commercially run by KBC. It is noteworthy that this FM radio station was specifically licensed to offer entertainment, as its advertisement below explicitly announces:

> Metro FM 101.9 (KBC) is the pioneering FM station in Kenya. Set up in April 1996, Metro FM pledged to bring the listener what's in and out in International Music; what's cool and what's doomed in multimedia entertainment; what's in marking Kenya's music and what's in breaking in DRC's Lingala; what's bending in sentimental R&B and who is bending the rules in contemporary Hip-hop – in short the NEXT LEVEL in musical entertainment.[2]

Since the launch of Metro FM, more than 20 radio stations have entered the FM radio market. However, these privately owned commercial FM radio stations that came after Metro FM, although still 'pretending' to privilege entertainment, have become more dynamic, introducing creative and innovative broadcasting styles that conflate entertainment and information in their broadcast repertoire to attract listening publics.

These privately owned commercial FM radio stations have definitely made the style of broadcasting in Kenya more dynamic. Where the state-controlled KBC had fervently emphasised the 'correctness' of language and the strict observance of social morals in all its programmes, these FM radio stations seem to be intent on inverting and subverting the very fundamental ethos and principles of broadcasting. For example, regarding content, they broadcast all sorts of topics, even those that are considered taboo for public consumption. Additionally, in terms of language use, they switch and mix codes quite liberally. This free play of languages is not restricted to the utilisation of the more acceptable urban youth lingo popularly known as '*sheng*',[3] but unapologetically includes the use of either Kiswahili or English deliberately varnished with various vernacular language accents. This contrasts sharply with KBC's language policy that stresses received pronunciation in its presentations.

Whereas KBC radio services have distinctly aligned programmes with their objectives, such as 'health care', 'new agricultural methods', 'youth and drug abuse' and 'the education of the girl child', the FM radio programmes are explicitly framed around entertainment. These music-oriented entertainment programmes are interspersed with talk shows and advertisements. As such, in FM radio programming, there is apparently a very thin line between entertainment and the serious delivery of information. This is perhaps the most distinctive feature of these FM radio stations in comparison to the state-controlled KBC.

FM radio stations in Kenya can be categorised in a number of ways. This could be in terms of ownership as either private commercial and/or community owned; or in terms of language use, i.e. English/Kiswahili or the vernacular;[4] and perhaps as secular or religious. But a broad categorisation would typically be one conceived in terms of the station being either mainstream or non-mainstream. Arguably, mainstream would mostly refer to those FM radio stations that use the two official languages (Kiswahili and English) and have near-national coverage in terms of broadcasting, whereas non-mainstream would point to those whose coverage are limited to specific target listenership or communities.

Evolving dialogic and democratic cultures: FM radio talk shows in Kenya

With the proliferation of cellphone technology,[5] FM radio stations in Kenya, as elsewhere, have transformed themselves into dialogic sites where discussions and conversations on various subjects are encouraged, flavoured with variegated entertainment recipes. With the rapid communicative possibilities offered by mobile telephony, FM radio stations have become more innovative and creative in their broadcasting and presentation styles, opening up the radio stations to the public and making it relatively easy for listeners to participate in the ongoing debates as they are relayed live. This has largely contributed to the conscientisation of Kenya's citizens.

The FM stations deploy these innovative presentation strategies to deconstruct the notion of radio as a diffusion box, in the process breaking down boundaries that had traditionally separated broadcasters from listeners; more so in the Kenyan context of a unidirectional model of communication that had characterised the state-controlled broadcaster, KBC. This new dialogic model of communication indeed enhances conscientisation exponentially, thus expanding democratic space and culture. FM radio stations have become popular because they speak directly to listeners, as opposed to state-owned and state-controlled radio that was framed in ways that imposed ideologies originating from the post-independent African authoritarian leaders. (Although Dina Ligaga, in her chapter in this book, argues that there is a sense in which radio theatre provided alternative readings that went a long way in undermining the state ideology, my contention is that the overt objectives of these plays were obviously to privilege and circulate the dominant ideology of the state.) The way in which the state radio as a tool of oppression has been used by despotic leaders is brilliantly explored by Soyinka (1967) in his satirical play *Kongi's Harvest*. In this play, the Oba Danlola character ridicules the use of radio in ways that are very similar to the way that the ruling party KANU in Kenya manipulated radio to create a culture of silence and in turn created for President Moi a much-larger-than-life image. Oba Danlola ridicules the role of radio as a 'means of diffusion' in the post-colony thus (Soyinka, 1967:1–2; emphasis added):

> They say oh how
> They say it all on silent skull
> But who cares? Who but a lunatic
> Will bandy words with boxes
> With government rediffusion sets
> Which talk and talk and never
> Take a lone word in reply.
> I cannot counter words, oh
> I cannot bandy words of
> A rediffusion set
> My years are sore
> But my mouth is agbayon
> For I do not bandy words
> No I do not bandy words
> With a government
> Loudspeaker

Oba Danlola aptly refers to radio broadcast in an autocratic state as a 'loudspeaker' for the government. As such, whatever is pronounced by the radio remains incontestable, as there is no avenue for dialogue, leading to a culture of silence among members of the public. Indeed, Oba Danlola's view of the radio as that which 'say[s] it all on silent skull' immediately draws attention to Paulo Freire's (1972) ideas about traditional methods of pedagogy, which he describes as the 'banking concept of education' where learners' minds are seen as *tabula rasa* waiting to be filled with knowledge from the all-knowing teacher. This mode of pedagogy resonates with the way that radio was deployed in Kenya before the emergence of both community-owned and privately owned commercial FM radio stations. In Kenya, I see FM radio stations as participating in the process of debunking the myth of radio as the 'government loudspeaker'. But more important is the question of how these FM radio stations frame their broadcasting styles to promote dialogue and democratic practices.

Unlike the diffusion set that only speaks and speaks, as Oba Danlola points out, Kenyan FM radio stations appear to deliberately and persistently strive to break out of the strictures of traditional radio communication and metaphorically move out to invite their listeners into the studio or literally go out of the studio to connect with their publics. It is in this sense that one can argue that these new radio broadcast presenters have reinvented the style of radio communication. In a way, they seem to be deliberately aiming at debunking the myth of the radio presenter as an all-knowing figure, that 'god in the box' – invisible and mysterious – whose voice was such an authority that no one could afford to doubt his truth.

Through the use of variegated strategies, presenters have managed to break out of this notion of the 'box' and have transformed radio into a dialogic space where there are numerous possibilities for listeners to engage more actively with information as it flows out of the radio into the public sphere. Through call-ins, members of the listening public are encouraged to participate in the analysis, interrogation and interpretation of news relayed by the radio as if they were in the studio. These creative and innovative strategies that FM radio stations have conjured up effect a bidirectional channel of communication with their listening publics and in turn help evolve a culture of participatory democracy in Kenya. In fact, it is these strategies, sometimes unorthodox, that set these FM radio stations apart from the state-controlled broadcaster, KBC. A few examples from selected FM radio stations' programmes will illustrate this point.

Kiss FM breakfast show: The big issue of the day
Kiss FM has a breakfast show programme that runs from 06:00 to 10:00 every weekday. It used to be co-presented by Caroline Mutoko and Walter Mongare, also known as (a.k.a.) Nyambane, a.k.a. Baby J. Nyambs,[6] but it is now presented by Mutoko, Larry Asego and Felix Odiwuor, a.k.a. Jalang'o. The breakfast show has a very loose structure in terms of programming. It comprises music, advertisements,

information on road traffic, general conversations on all sorts of issues and topics among the presenters, and sometimes a detailed conversation with an invited guest to discuss a specific issue in order to illuminate aspects that might not be clear to the listening public. This is usually an issue that is deemed to be of significance to the general public and as such requires detailed analysis and clarification. But the more innovative and interesting dimension to the show is its performance-oriented framing. It emerges as a dramatic performance with the presenters appearing as if they are involved in a well-scripted and rehearsed drama, with each one of them playing a well-defined role. For instance, it is worth noting that on the days when Mutoko and Baby J. Nyambs presented the programme, Mutoko took on the persona of a serious, well-educated and informed radio presenter, though occasionally getting carried away by the antics of the joker (Baby J. Nyambs) into the world of the 'play'. Thus Mutoko never dissolved her personality into a fictional persona during the show. Baby J. Nyambs, on the other hand, right from the outset indicated that he was playing the role of a fictitious persona, a joker/clown. Throughout the show, he never revealed his real identity: Walter Mongare. Baby J. Nyambs and Mutoko presented an interactive talk show known as the *The Big Issue of the Day*, which followed immediately after the 07:00 prime hour news. The big issue was framed as a debate emerging from a major news item from the lead story of one of the leading daily newspapers. The debate was structured in a way that allowed the two presenters to take antagonistic views of the issue. More often, Baby J. Nyambs, the character representing the ordinary Kenyan, would take what can be construed as a rather ridiculous, sometimes simplistic position on the issue, whereas Mutoko would take a more apparently complex, sophisticated, serious and rational stance in relation. The debate would normally begin with the two presenters immersing themselves in an animated argument about the issue. Predictably, they would fail to reach consensus or a compromise because of their 'persuasions' regarding the issue. It is at this point that they would ask listeners to call in and contribute their views and perspectives on the issue. As members of the public became more passionately involved in the debate, the two presenters would then change their roles into those of moderators, ensuring that the debate did not lose its focus. Baby J. Nyambs would still remain in his role as a joker, however, every now and again cutting into the debate and breaking the tension with his jokes.

This show in some very profound ways followed the model of Boal's (1979) forum theatre where actors are transformed into 'spec-actors'. In this particular talk show, the listeners became active in the sense that they acted by calling in and making contributions to the debate, thus ceasing to be passive recipients of information and messages. During the debate, the listening public through call-ins were actively involved in the interactive show, analysing and interrogating the issues at hand, reflecting on the issues, and most probably gaining new insights about them. At the end of the debate, the presenters conducted an opinion poll to show which side of the issue had carried the day. Usually the debates and the subsequent opinion polls acted as very valid instruments for testing the mood of the nation about certain sensitive issues facing it. In many instances, the government changed its position on certain issues as a result of these debates.

Since Baby J. Nyambs left the station in 2009 for Kiu (Q) FM, a Kiswahili FM radio station run by Nation Media, the structure of the show has slightly changed. As mentioned earlier, there are now three presenters, Mutoko and the two jokers, Larry Asego and Felix Odiwuor, a.k.a. Jalang'o. The programme currently takes a more conversational tone with the three engaging in a conversation, although occasionally they invite guests who provide expert insight on the burning issues of the day. But the show has maintained the joker's persona in Jalang'o, who plays the role previously played by Baby J. Nyambs.

Easy FM: Breakfast Show

Easy FM also used to run a slightly differently structured talk show that also intended to intervene using the Boalian concept of the joker. Here again one found two presenters: Bernard Otieno,[7] who was the official host of the programme and remained in his official role as a serious radio presenter, taking a similar posture as that of Mutoko, whereas the joker/clown Maurice Ochieng', a.k.a. 'Mudomo Baggy',[8] played more or less a similar role to that of Baby J. Nyambs of Kiss FM. Their show was called the *Breakfast Show* and ran from around 2005 to 2007. Otieno stayed within the conventional rules of broadcasting, whereas Mudomo Baggy undermined all those rules of 'correctness'. Unlike the Kiss FM show, where both presenters were usually in the studio (except for the occasional moments when Baby J. Nyambs went out in the street to talk to members of the public), in the case of Easy FM, only Otieno, the chief host, was ever in the studio. Mudomo Baggy, the joker, was always an 'outsider' and was often in the street. Like Baby J. Nyambs, he relied heavily on a vernacular-accent-coated English. Although of the Luo-speaking nation, Mudomo Baggy exploited the Gikuyu accent and its various stereotypes in his performance. Because Mudomo Baggy was always outside the studio, his role could be interpreted as being chiefly to act as a kind of mediator between Otieno and his listening public. Just like Baby J. Nyambs, Mudomo Baggy was an accomplished stage actor, as well as a stand-up comedian and a member of the Reddykulus group of stand-up comedians. Because Baggy came out in the street as a 'double villager', he resonated with the common man and woman in the street, pretending, like the oral narrative trickster, to be unsophisticated and naive. This endeared him to the members of the public, who were always ready to participate in his discussions out in the street, which were transmitted live on Easy FM.

In this programme, Otieno and Mudomo Baggy (un)consciously employed one of Boal's forms of intervention theatre known as invisible or ambush theatre, which implies the presentation of a scene in an environment other than theatre to people who are not spectators. The place can be a restaurant, a sidewalk, a marketplace, a train, a bus queue, etc. The people who witness the scene are there by chance. During the spectacle, these people are not supposed to have the slightest idea that it is a 'spectacle', for this would make them spectators. They are supposed to be made to believe that the spectacle is real. In the Easy FM case, the host presenter in the studio, Otieno, raised an issue that he thought was of great significance to the public. Akin to Kiss FM's talk show, this was usually one of the main news items in the local dailies. After raising the issue, Otieno would call Mudomo Baggy, who was already out in the street, to ascertain his opinion on the issue. In a characteristically predictable way, Mudomo Baggy would take a stance diametrically opposed to that of Otieno. This then led to a conflict that needed resolution. To resolve the conflict, Otieno would ask Mudomo Baggy to find out from the people in the street what their opinion was on the issue in a conversation that was carried live on air.[9] More significantly, these people, because they were out in the street or involved in their daily routines, were usually not aware of the fact that the conversation was being broadcast live on air. As such, their comments and opinions tended to be spontaneous and relatively objective. In a way, they provided an alternative view and interpretation of the news item. This helped to take the pulse of the nation about certain matters, especially those that government wished to implement without consulting the general public.

Citizen FM: Jambo Kenya

Citizen FM, broadcasting in the Kiswahili language, also has a similar talk show, *Jambo Kenya*, presented alternately by two different presenters, Vincent Ateya or Lincoln Njogu, running daily on weekdays from 08:00 to 10:00. This show is also interactive and, in a style characteristic of other major FM radio stations in Kenya, deploys clowns tasked to provide the perspective of the common citizen on the issue under discussion. This show exploits drama techniques in the form of short skits enacted by three popular comedians, Mwala (Davis Mwambili), Oloibon (Allan Namisi) and Mama Boi (Celestine Buluti), interspersed with the presenters' analysis of the issue. Closely following the style of other FM radio stations, these comedians also exploit the popular ethnic-coated accents in their Kiswahili speech. This is supposed not only to arouse humour, but also to signify the status of the characters as ordinary, unsophisticated citizens. In this talk show, the presenters also invite specialists or experts in the field of the topic of the day to provide a more illuminating perspective.

The people's parliament: No more culture of silence

In the run-up to the 2002 general elections in Kenya, Kiss FM started a call-in programme that popularly came to be known as the 'people's parliament'. The host of the programme, Jimmy Gathu,[10] doubled up as the 'speaker' of this imaginary parliament. In the programme, the participants took up roles and referred to themselves as honourable members of parliament of real and imagined constituencies. As both the host and 'speaker', Gathu guided and moderated the debate. The participants, through call-in services offered by the various cellphone providers, passionately debated the night's motion. The programme became a site for those marginalised from the mainstream political arena to voice and articulate their political views and perspectives. Participants analysed politics, gender issues, culture, development, citizenship, etc. Thus, for the first time, the programme provided the ordinary Kenyan citizen with a forum to discuss political issues that for a long time had been deemed taboo. Although referring to intervention in applied theatre, Nicholson's (2005:163) comment that 'practitioners should recognise that their role is not to give participants a voice … but to create spaces and places that enable the participants' voices to be heard' succinctly captures the role played by the 'people's parliament', as participants not only analysed, but were vocal enough to lampoon even the then-outgoing dictator, President Daniel Arap Moi, and his clique of sycophants. An interesting feature of this forum was that in a very profound way it deconstructed the hierarchies of power that had been created by the country's political class. In this programme, those from mainstream politics had to jostle with the ordinary people to get to the 'platform' to air their views. More importantly, ordinary people could respond to their views almost immediately. Ordinary Kenyans thus moved from the periphery to the mainstream of political discourse, creating, analysing and interpreting issues using the rhetoric of politicians and, to echo Boal (1979), becoming active participants or 'spec-actors' in the performance of national politics.

This was definitely the beginning of the death of the culture of silence that had engulfed Kenya for many years. Although it has not been empirically evaluated, the programme must have contributed a great deal towards the civic education of Kenyan voters and the new consciousness that led to the demise of the independence party, KANU. This programme has been replicated in other FM radio stations with varying degrees of success. For instance, Citizen FM's Kiswahili service runs its version of the people's parliament *Jambo Kenya* (Good Morning Kenya) every weekday morning. These creative and innovative dialogic sites created by FM radio stations are usually more common and frequent when a crisis is facing the nation. The talk shows do not only intervene in the crisis, but provide ordinary Kenyans with a platform to give their perspective on the issue at hand. This interactive approach obviously transcends the traditional role of radio, especially where it had previously been controlled and manipulated by autocratic states and ruling political parties, as was the case in Kenya during KANU rule.

These kinds of strategies that consciously involve the listeners are what define the process of intervention. Mda's (1993) idea of intervention in applied theatre is invaluable in this analysis when transposed to the realm of radio broadcasting. Thus, in radio communication, intervention occurs when the broadcaster invites listeners to participate in deeper analysis, interpretation and consequent reflection on issues emerging from news items and other burning questions that affect them. These intervention strategies of FM radio presenters seem to have some resonance with Freire's (1972) ideas of a problem-posing and conscientising pedagogy in his seminal work *Pedagogy of the Oppressed*. In terms of Freirean pedagogy, in their intervention programmes, FM radio presenters in Kenya appear to gesture explicitly towards a more democratic, dialogic and, in fact, interactive analysis of issues. If we stretch this analogy between this problem-posing pedagogy and FM stations' strategies of intervention a little further, a number of similarities can be discerned. In problem-posing pedagogy, for instance, a cod(e)ification in the form of a narrative, play, newspaper or radio news item is used as a catalyst to initiate a dialogue that leads community participants to identify, analyse, and interpret the conditions and situations that limit their path to progress and development. Here, teachers and 'learners' become collaborators in the research and learning processes and none of them occupies a superior position in the search for this knowledge. The same seems to be reflected in the dialogic strategies that FM radio presenters employ in some of their programmes when they involve listeners through the call-in sessions to air their views publicly, thus in a way contributing to the unpacking, analysis, and interpretation of certain news items and burning issues of the day, which can be described as cod(e)ification. It is assumed that in these talk shows the presenters act only as catalysts/moderators and not as originators of ideas, but this is not always the case. At times, one can easily detect that the presenters subtly engage in manipulation to direct the ensuing debate towards a particular outcome. Furthermore, these presenters often fail to observe the cardinal principle of objectivity and impartiality, and end up expressing their own personal, ideological, political or gender commitments.

Conclusion

FM radio stations in Kenya have played a fundamental and significant role in confronting the country's previous culture of silence and in the process have nurtured a democratic culture by providing dialogic space, i.e. the liminal space between education and entertainment. Although these FM radio stations have been criticised for subverting the finer principles of broadcasting, their employment of concepts such as those of the 'joker' and dialogic forum sites should be appreciated within the larger context of wittingly, like the trickster in African oral narratives, using enticing strategies to intervene in diverse aspects of the nation's life. Other than these creative and innovative ventures witnessed in the FM radio broadcasting landscape in Kenya, an emerging and interesting phenomenon, which is not discussed in this chapter, is that of community FM radio stations, of which the most striking feature is their locations. They are mostly a phenomenon of the slums in the capital city, Nairobi, and are popularly referred to as ghetto FM radio.

Endnotes

1   Some parts of this chapter have been published in articles under the titles 'Accentuating FM radio' in *Jahazi*, vol. 1, 2006 and 'Reading FM radio stations in Kenya: Opening a Pandora's Box' in *Cultural Production and Social Change in Kenya: Art, Culture & Society*, vol. 1, 2007.

2   < http://www.kenyatravelideas.com/kenyaradiostation.html > .

3   '*Sheng*' is an elision of 'Swahili' and 'English'. It refers to a kind of Creole language developed by the youth in the urban spaces in Kenya. It draws its vocabulary and syntax from Kiswahili, English and many local Kenyan languages.

4   In Kenya especially, with reference to radio stations, the term 'vernacular' is used in a positive sense, in opposition to English or Kiswahili.

5   A number of research studies on cellphone distribution indicate that there are more than eight million users with slightly more than 20 per cent use in rural areas. However, this might have changed considerably with the new service known as M-Pesa offered by Safaricom, one of the four cellphone service providers in Kenya, where money can now be transferred using cellphones. It is important to note that many Kenyans in urban areas financially support their relatives in rural areas. Thus, many people have bought cellphones for their relatives in rural areas to benefit from this service. But this does not mean that such people will use their phones to participate in radio talk shows. Arguably, there is obviously an unequal participation in favour of urban dwellers in these radio talk shows. There is, however, no concrete research to show the regional or socio-economic class patterns of callers. This is because callers are required to give only their names and

locations. For details on the distribution of mobile telephony in Kenya, the work of Mary Omosa and Dorothy McCormick (2004) would be useful.

6   Mongare has since left Kiss 100 FM for Kiu (Q) FM.

7   Bernard Otieno is also an accomplished stage and TV actor.

8   Mudomo Baggy has since left Easy FM after standing in the 2007 legislative elections in the Kamukunji seat in Nairobi.

9   It is interesting to note that because this programme is live, it is sometimes very difficult to monitor what comes from members of the public. However, I have noticed that when participants make an outrageous statement or comment, the presenters intervene almost immediately by cutting off such participants and subsequently putting the record straight.

10 Jimmy Gathu has since left Kiss FM, initially for KBC, but he is now with Citizen TV and Radio. Gathu, like Bay J. Nyambs and Mudomo Baggy, is a reputed actor and musician who acted with the Mbalamwezi Theatre Company and sang with Impulse Band in the capital city, Nairobi.

3

Contesting Mainstream Media Power
Mediating the Zimbabwe Crisis through Clandestine Radio

Dumisani Moyo

> *A society's lack of openness is the surest predictor that clandestine stations will appear, whether the nondemocratic government is a military junta, communist or capitalist (Soley, 1995:139–40).*

Introduction

Throughout what has come to be known as the Zimbabwe crisis and in the negotiations aimed at pulling the country out of this crisis, the question of media policy reform has always been central. This is because the democratic and communicative space in that country shrank considerably in the period between 2000 and 2009, as the government of President Robert Mugabe tightened and consolidated its grip on the media landscape through the passing of restrictive media laws and the banning of 'hostile' publications. Article XIX of the agreement signed on 15 September 2008 between Mugabe's Zimbabwe African National Union-Patriotic Front (ZANU-PF) and rival Morgan Tsvangirai's Movement for Democratic Change (MDC) on 'resolving the challenges facing Zimbabwe' broadly focused on freedom of expression, but paid particular attention to the broadcast media.[1] While it articulated the old concerns of the opposition about opening up broadcasting to non-state players, it also carried the ruling ZANU-PF's demand for the immediate disbandment or demobilisation of 'foreign-based' and 'foreign government funded external' radio stations beaming into Zimbabwe since the beginning of the crisis in 2000.[2]

One could read Article XIX as a trade-off between the two political parties over the contested terrain of broadcasting. The ZANU-PF government promised the immediate processing of all applications for broadcasting licences, while the opposition in turn pledged to call upon the governments hosting and/or funding external radio stations broadcasting into Zimbabwe to cease such hosting and funding and encourage all Zimbabweans running or working for these radio stations to return home and seek licences to operate legally.[3] The close attention given to radio broadcasting by both parties here is illustrative of the perceived power and importance attached to this medium in the country's political discourse. While in May 2010 the Zimbabwe Media Commission licensed four private daily newspapers, including the previously banned *The Daily News*, the long-awaited opening up of the broadcasting sector is yet to happen.

Radio has been aptly described as 'Africa's medium' and it remains by far the most powerful tool of communication on the continent, as African governments and opposition political parties alike have understood all too well. Thus, despite the growing global discourse on the liberalisation and deregulation of broadcasting, many governments on the continent have not shown any keenness to open up this sector to competition. The majority of those that have done so have not displayed a great degree of enthusiasm and sincerity either, as licences are generally doled out to trusted cronies or to 'communities' that are not allowed to use the stations to discuss 'politics'. For example, in Zambia, one of the first countries to open up broadcasting in the region following political transition in 1991, a good number of community radio licences have been given to supposedly 'harmless' Christian groups, while the general rule is that community broadcasters should not delve into politics (see Banda, 2003; Moyo, 2006).

In Zimbabwe, not much change has taken place in the broadcasting landscape since independence in 1980. Mugabe is on record as having stood against private broadcasting on the grounds that 'you don't know what propaganda a non-state radio might broadcast' (quoted in Maja-Pearce, 1995:123). It is therefore no wonder that the old broadcasting law (the Broadcasting Act of 1957), which gave monopoly status to the Zimbabwe Broadcasting Corporation (ZBC), remained in force for two decades after independence, even though it clearly presented a stark contradiction to the democratic values that had informed the struggle for that independence.

It took a court challenge in 2000, spearheaded by aspirant broadcaster Capital Radio, to bring an end to state monopoly broadcasting.[4] Capital Radio immediately exploited the policy vacuum created by the nullification of monopoly broadcasting and went on air on 28 September 2000, six days after the ruling. The government immediately declared Capital Radio a pirate station and shut it down on 4 October 2000, confiscating its equipment from its hidden location on the roof of a Harare hotel. To plug the policy vacuum, the government hurriedly put together new regulations that provided for the establishment of a regulatory authority – the Broadcasting Authority of Zimbabwe (BAZ) – whose mandate was to license operators and oversee the broadcasting sector. However, the autonomy of the BAZ has remained questionable, as real licensing powers still reside with the minister of information. It is therefore not surprising that by the end of 2011 the BAZ had not licensed a single broadcaster, some ten years after coming into existence.[5]

The rebirth of clandestine radio

The closure of Capital Radio should not be viewed in isolation from other media-related acts of repression taking place in those early years of the Zimbabwe crisis. In July 2001 the government withdrew accreditation for British Broadcasting Corporation (BBC) journalists because of their negative reports on Zimbabwe. On 12 September 2003 it closed down the country's only private daily newspaper, *The Daily News*. This was followed by the closure of three other private newspapers. These developments led to a mass exodus of journalists from Zimbabwe, mainly to countries such as South Africa, the United Kingdom, the United States, Australia, New Zealand and Canada, where they joined the increasing number of Zimbabweans pushed into the diaspora by the worsening political and economic crises.[6] Keen to keep up their profession and to continue to tell the Zimbabwe story as they understood it, some of these journalists set up news websites, radio stations and even newspapers that served as alternative voices on Zimbabwe from abroad. Capital Radio staffers went on to start a clandestine radio station, Short Wave Radio Africa (SWRA), in London, broadcasting into Zimbabwe. This station is the focus of this chapter.

The chapter explores and analyses the strategies used by SWRA to connect with listeners back home in the context of a repressive system that has unleashed a set of counter-strategies that attempt to maintain a dominant voice in the country's media landscape. At the same time, it analyses the different ways in which clandestine radio serves as a counterpoint to mainstream media representations of the crises unfolding in the country. The study specifically addresses the following questions: firstly, how does SWRA strive to create its publics in Zimbabwe's restricted communicative environment? Secondly, how has the government responded to the rise of clandestine radio in post-independence Zimbabwe? And, thirdly, in what ways does clandestine radio contest mainstream media representations of the ongoing crisis in Zimbabwe?

The chapter is based on document analysis, Internet research and qualitative interviews with individuals working for SWRA in London. It argues that the repressive environment in Zimbabwe has created conditions that are conducive to the rise of clandestine radio, which has used a variety of strategies to provide alternative viewpoints and thereby contest mainstream media hegemony. A brief comparative discourse analysis of related content from the state-owned daily newspaper, *The Herald*, and SWRA is provided to illustrate the role of clandestine radio in resisting state propaganda.

Three foreign-funded stations operated by Zimbabweans in exile and beaming into the country, namely SWRA, Voice of the People (VOP) and Studio 7 of the Voice of America (VOA), have emerged since 2000.[7] These stations, operating outside the purview of the repressive media laws, provide alternative discourse to the propaganda churned out by the long-discredited state-owned media.[8] This development in the post-independence era somewhat reproduces the anti-establishment strategies used by liberation movements during the colonial era, together with their opposites – the counter-strategies that were used by the regime of Ian Smith to silence the nationalist broadcasts. As such, clandestine radio has become part of the site for contestation of the definition of the problems facing Zimbabwe.

The clandestine broadcasters, on the one hand, see themselves as rightfully challenging the government's desire to monopolise the communicative space and remain the primary definer of the crisis, while the government, on the other hand, considers it its legitimate right at this time of crisis to muster all the media at its disposal and silence all dissenting voices in the fight against its detractors. In other words, the Zimbabwe government's reaction to these radio stations can be taken as a form of resistance to what it perceives as Western-sponsored definitions of the crisis communicated through the clandestine radio stations. This has created an interesting dynamic where both sides lay claim to the 'revolutionary' concepts of 'alternative' and 'resistance' – with the government-controlled media seeing themselves as providing 'alternative' views to what is described as 'Western-sponsored propaganda' churned out by the clandestine radio stations.

The re-emergence of clandestine radio at this stage can also be seen as a case of history repeating itself – only in a different context of post-independence. As such, the morphing of ZANU-PF from being the operator of clandestine radio during the liberation struggle into becoming both its target and the persecutor that criminalises opposing viewpoints is an ironic twist of history. This chapter thus makes passing comment on how the new breed of clandestine radio stations is similar to, and also different from, the old clandestine radio stations of the liberation era. Using some examples, the chapter will illustrate that clandestine radio operates as an alternative medium in the sense that it contests some of the mainstream media representations of the crisis at home.

The rest of the chapter introduces the clandestine radio stations beaming into Zimbabwe and focuses specifically on SWRA. The chapter concludes with some general comments about the challenges facing clandestine radio in Zimbabwe.

Short Wave Radio Africa: Connecting to publics in a restricted environment

As already pointed out, the origins of SWRA can be traced back to the closure of the short-lived Capital Radio in 2000. Upon closure of the station, one of its co-founders, Gerry Jackson, went on to set up a short-wave radio station in London as a way of getting 'independent' radio broadcasts into Zimbabwe.[9] SWRA, which calls itself 'the independent voice of Zimbabwe', began its broadcasts via short wave and the Internet on 19 December 2001. SWRA broadcasts live two hours per day between 17:00 and 19:00, covering a wide range of programmes, including news and current affairs.[10] However, its programmes are also archived and available for streaming from the station's website.[11] The goal of the station is to expose corruption and human rights abuses in Zimbabwe. It claims to provide 'balanced and in-depth coverage; a comprehensive look at current affairs and social issues, especially HIV, health and voter education; interactive discussions and debates; entertainment, music, arts and culture' (cited in Biener, 2008).

Although the location of the station and its transmitters has remained a closely guarded secret, former information minister Jonathan Moyo once alleged that the BBC was hosting the station – a claim the British authorities have dismissed. South Africa and Lesotho have also been named as possible sources of its transmissions, given the strength of the signal in South Africa and the southern parts of Zimbabwe (Biener, 2008).

Owing to the hostility of the Zimbabwe government to its operations, SWRA uses a variety of strategies to cultivate audiences both inside and outside the country. This includes a creative convergence of new and old media to ensure that the station reaches as many Zimbabweans located in various parts of the world as possible. SWRA conducts interviews with representatives from civil society organisations, members of the opposition, and Zimbabwean academics located both inside and outside the country. To ensure a wider reach, these interviews and news bulletins are posted on the station's website[12] and can be streamed live. Full transcriptions, including comments from listeners in Zimbabwe, are also archived on the website, which is linked to other news websites on Zimbabwe. The station also has a call-back facility where listeners inside Zimbabwe who cannot afford exorbitant international calls can call a given cellphone number in Harare and leave their details for the station operators to call them back. Presented every night for an hour by John Matinde and Mandisa Mundawarara, the programme *Callback* allows Zimbabweans to speak (using pseudonyms) about their experiences of life in Zimbabwe. Unlike mainstream media, which tend to focus on elite sources, SWRA allows ordinary people to give eyewitness accounts of the torture, killings and harassment perpetrated by ZANU-PF youth militias and Mugabe's security agents. Protest music banned on the state-controlled ZBC is also played as interludes on SWRA, including self-exiled Thomas Mapfumo's Chimurenga music, to galvanise listeners against the Mugabe regime.

SWRA has also introduced a free short message service[13] news headline service as a way of circumventing the jamming of its signal (see Mobile Industry Review, 2007). The station boasts some 30 000 subscribers to this free service and it has been forced to cap the number of subscribers because of the cost implications.[14] News headlines are 'texted' to registered cellphone users in Zimbabwe on a daily basis. This service is advertised via both the radio broadcasts and the station's website, and all that you have to do to access the service is to email your cellphone number to the station. The station's ability to operate on multiple media platforms – via short wave, the Internet and cellphones – ensures that its messages are as widely distributed as possible. The station also benefits from efforts made by other clandestine stations and non-governmental organisations (NGOs) to promote short-wave radio listenership by providing free radio sets to rural communities. VOP, for example, ran competitions in which short-wave radio sets were given as prizes.[15]

Another important strategy employed by the station to attract more listeners is to bring back old favourite Zimbabwean DJs who are now residing in the United Kingdom, including Peter Johns, Gerry Jackson and John Matinde. The idea of re-creating the old popular ZBC station Radio Three through these DJs has attracted nostalgic Zimbabweans both in the diaspora and at home.[16]

Breaking down gates and contesting mainstream media power

There is no doubt that the clandestine radio stations beaming their programmes into Zimbabwe have made a tremendous contribution to public debate on the constantly shifting Zimbabwe crisis. Their ability to propagate uncensored messages clandestinely sourced from Zimbabwe, but processed and distributed from outside the purview of the repressive system, has enabled these stations to provide counter-discourses to the propaganda in the state-controlled media. Until the arrival of clandestine radio and other new forms of alternative media, the Zimbabwe government had enjoyed a monopoly of the power to define the political and economic crises facing the nation. As Ranger (2004) argues, a form of 'patriotic history' has emerged in Zimbabwe that divides the nation into revolutionaries and sell-outs, and this is particularly promoted in the mainstream, state-controlled media. Almost invariably, the state-owned media have blamed 'Western imperialists', 'illegal economic sanctions', the 'pirate' or foreign-funded radio stations and an unpatriotic, intransigent, puppet opposition that does everything to please its foreign handlers at the expense of the national interest for the economic malaise facing the country.[17] This is pitted, the argument goes, against a revolutionary, progressive and patriotic ruling party whose strong liberation credentials are used to legitimise all its policies and actions, while at the same time delegitimising members of the opposition, who are generally referred to as 'traitors', 'political dissidents' and *mafikizolos* (late arrivals).[18] Since 2000 the ZBC has mounted a sustained propaganda drive to remind the nation of the pains and sacrifices endured by ZANU-PF in the war of liberation. Programmes such as *Nhaka Yedu* and *National Ethos*, and sustained 'nationalist' columns penned by ZANU-PF ideologues became the mainstay of government-controlled media.

If the mainstream media have been playing a gatekeeping role where they filtered and selected what to circulate in the Zimbabwean public domain, it is clear today that this role has been undermined by clandestine radio and a multitude of other alternative forms of communication that emerged in recent years. Clandestine radio stations, for example, have enabled Zimbabwean citizens abroad and at home to bypass the gatekeepers and debate issues that the mainstream media often present in one-dimensional form or choose to push under the carpet altogether: from the larger economic crisis, the water crisis in the cities, the closure of schools and hospitals and the stalled negotiations to the more recent cholera outbreak. In contrast to the shorthand response from the mainstream media and government officials of blaming the West for all the problems facing the nation, SWRA, for example, enables citizens to question the credibility and ability of the Zimbabwean leadership. As Gonda and Jackson point out:

> Zimbabwe is in a major crisis because of misgovernance and corruption by a handful of the ruling elite, and not because of foreign-based radio stations. It is sad that instead of addressing the needs of the suffering masses the authorities spend crucial time on imaginary enemies.[19]

Following the outbreak of cholera in August 2008, for example, government reaction was slow and the official figures initially given were conservative – until SWRA and other alternative and foreign media made an issue of it, forcing the government on 3 December to declare a national emergency and appeal for help.[20] The state-controlled daily newspaper, *The Herald*, unexpectedly acknowledged the scale of the crisis, reporting that

> ... the Harare City Council yesterday remained mum as cholera continued to take its toll. Yesterday afternoon *The Herald* witnessed two trucks ferrying bodies of cholera victims from Budiriro Polyclinic to Beatrice Road Infectious Diseases Hospital mortuary (*The Herald*, 2008).

In this way, clandestine radio and other forms of alternative media create information warfare by breaking news on crises that mainstream media would otherwise have remained silent about, thereby forcing the latter to acknowledge these crises.

Another telling example of how clandestine radio is playing a critical role in uncovering the truth where government-controlled media would rather hide it is the reporting on the killing of illegal diamond miners in the Chiadzwa diamond fields in Marange. While *The Herald* story on 12 December 2008 entitled 'Call to relocate Chiadzwa families' concentrated on the need to relocate villagers occupying the diamond fields and pave the way for an unnamed 'investor' to start proper mining and create much needed revenue for the state, and hailed 'the successful joint blitz codenamed "Operation Hakudzokwi" (Operation No Return) … that has flushed out over 35 000 illegal panners and diamond dealers' (Matambanadzo, 2008), it was totally silent about casualties in that operation. The SWRA story on the same day, however, was entitled 'Government looking for land for mass burial, after killing 78 miners' (Gonda, 2008). The story illustrates how the government was trying to conceal the killing of 78 people by burying them in a mass grave.

It is notable that the government-controlled media use sanitised language (e.g. 'successful blitz' and 'flushed out') to give the impression of a casualty-free, surgical operation. The 'noble' idea of 'relocating' some 500 Chiadzwa families and bringing in an 'investor' to start 'proper mining' is projected as potentially serving the national good, including the generation of revenue of up to US$1.2 billion per month. In other words, the government is projected as executing a noble task of restoring order after 'rapes, robberies, thefts, assaults and murders' had become the order of the day in the diamond fields. The SWRA story, on the other hand, is replete with negative terms that serve to condemn the government's high-handedness. Phrases such as 'murdered', 'mass burial', 'killed in the volatile diamond minefield', 'bodies piling up in mortuaries', 'murderous actions', 'slaughtered in the mining fields', 'mass grave', 'campaign of terror', 'warlords battle for control', 'resembling a war' and 'a pile of 50 bodies' are used in the story to demonstrate the gratuitous killing of defenceless villagers who are simply struggling to find ways to cope with a severe economic situation by exploiting what nature had provided them with.

Government strategies to silence clandestine broadcasters

As already mentioned, the government of Zimbabwe has not been sitting idle as the clandestine radio stations devised other ways of reaching listeners with their alternative viewpoints. Its clear agenda, as indicated earlier, is to create a coherent, uncontested narrative of the Zimbabwe situation through a centralised media system. The increasing number of clandestine radio stations and an array of other forms of alternative media pose a serious challenge to this ideal. Different strategies have therefore been employed to try to silence 'offensive' broadcasts from the clandestine radio stations.

Jamming and countermeasures from below

Since March 2005 SWRA has been experiencing interference on its frequency, which has been linked to jamming from the Zimbabwe government. This has forced the station to operate on multiple frequencies to evade 'Bob's Fire Dragon', as Biener (2008) refers to the Chinese-sourced jamming technology used by the Zimbabwe government.[21] However, the station managed to evade the jamming only for a few weeks, as the cost became unsustainable.[22] In fact, the station had to suspend its short-wave signal for a while and operate on medium wave, which allowed it to have a strong signal in South Africa (home to an estimated three million Zimbabweans) and some parts of Zimbabwe (Jackson, quoted in Biener, 2008). As Gonda and Jackson revealed:

> For about a year listeners were unable to hear us at all. At that time we were broadcasting for three hours but were forced financially to scale down to two hours. It was also difficult to get information back from people on the ground as to the extent of the jamming.[23]

On 18 April 2007 SWRA reportedly 'launched a massive use of short-wave frequencies to strain Zimbabwe's jamming resources' and also to 'eclipse' the much publicised News 24 external short-wave service that the Mugabe regime was planning to launch (Biener, 2008). As a way of further countering 'anti-government propaganda' from clandestine radio and influencing international public opinion, News 24 was meant to be a 24-hour external news service whose primary mission was 'to tell our own story', as Information Minister Sikhanyiso Ndlovu reportedly put it. Recently, the government admitted that it was behind the jamming of clandestine radio frequencies. Deputy Information Minister Bright Matongo told parliament: 'We cannot allow foreigners to invade our airwaves without our authority.'[24] What is clear from this effort is the government's fear of the power of alternative radio. As Gonda and Jackson emphasise:

> We should point out that it is VERY expensive to jam radio signals – so it shows that the regime fully understands the importance of independent radio, and what financial lengths they are prepared to go, to ensure that people have no access to independent information.[25]

There is nothing wholly new about both the SWRA strategies and government counter-strategies. As pointed out earlier, the Smith regime had used the same approach to silence liberation broadcasts using equipment based at Thornhill Airbase in Gweru.

Condemning, criminalising and delegitimising clandestine radio

Although SWRA claimed that it received its funding from human rights and media freedom groups, a report by Chris McGreal in *The Guardian* in 2002 suggesting that the US government, through the Office of Transition Initiatives, was giving large sums of money to the station has served to confirm the accusations made by the Zimbabwe government. The former information minister, Jonathan Moyo, accused Western nations of creating the stations and described the tone of the stations as inflammatory and 'fanning tribal divisions and ethnic hatred among Zimbabweans' in order to make the country ungovernable. The clandestine radio broadcasts were likened to the Rwandan station RTML, whose broadcasts have been accused of promoting tribal hatred that led to the 1994 genocide. By so doing, the government has criminalised the clandestine radio station, whose staff have been banned from returning to Zimbabwe.

Another approach used by the government has been to put pressure on regional governments to condemn the foreign broadcasts. Invoking regional solidarity, the Zimbabwe government called upon the Southern African Development Community to make a stand against these 'offensive' broadcasts. It accused the Botswana government, for example, of allowing the erection of transmitters that were relaying VOA's Studio 7 signal into Zimbabwe. The government of Botswana has, however, consistently denied hosting such transmitters and has even invited Zimbabwean authorities to come and verify the claim.[26]

Threats to both clandestine broadcasters and listeners

Different forms of overt and covert threats are directed at both people working for these stations and their listeners inside Zimbabwe. Warnings have also been issued against NGOs distributing radio sets in rural areas, and security agents have reportedly harassed SWRA stringers (or 'informal journalists'[27]), and civil society and political activists (see *The Herald*, 2007). Government officials accused the British and Americans of sponsoring a 'radio for free project', which was seen as a way of encouraging rural people to listen to anti-government messages. These threats have often been transformed into action: security agents have allegedly been confiscating radio sets distributed by NGOs from teachers and other individuals in rural areas. VOP reported on 22 January 2007 that at least 42 radio sets were allegedly confiscated by state security agents from rural areas. Teachers are generally considered key opinion leaders in rural areas and form the core of intelligentsia in these areas. The government has been uneasy about rural teachers and the power they wield in shaping public opinion, and they have been targets of attacks in elections during the past few years.

Although no clear evidence has been found linking the government to the bombing of one of the clandestine radio stations' offices (VOP) in Harare in August 2002, the government's slow pace of investigation has led many to point fingers at security agents seeking to silence clandestine radio. The dismissive response from then-Minister of Information Jonathan Moyo stating that 'something went wrong and they bombed themselves so they could blame the government' while in the same breath describing the station as a pirate radio sponsored by Western imperialists to cause disharmony in the country partly justifies these interpretations (see Masuku, 2006:69).

Conclusion

The chapter has argued that the Zimbabwe crisis led to the re-emergence of clandestine radio, which has become a critical player in the mediation of the crises facing the country. These radio stations provide alternative spaces to groups that are generally excluded from the restricted Zimbabwean public sphere. In the process, they are contesting mainstream media power by often setting the agenda in terms of bringing into the public domain stories that government-controlled media choose to ignore. The growing importance of these alternative media suggests that the power of gatekeepers in the dissemination of information is rapidly receding. SWRA in particular has come up with innovative ways of creating and sustaining publics in a restrictive political environment that criminalises listening to its broadcasts. The government of Zimbabwe has responded by introducing countermeasures to silence these stations, which it perceives as foreign-sponsored and hence seeking to cultivate anti-government sentiments among the citizens. These measures are in many ways a replay of the handling of nationalist broadcasts by the Smith regime in the 1960s and 1970s. Ironically, government reaction to these stations has inadvertently given them much-needed publicity and therefore created curiosity among people who perhaps never tuned in to the stations in the first place.

Although it operates as a clandestine radio station, which, as suggested earlier, locates it within the domain of alternative media, it is important to point out that there are ways in which SWRA is run more like the ordinary stations that it attempts to challenge. The institutionalisation of the station – with a salaried staff in London and a number of dedicated stringers on the ground inside Zimbabwe – and the nature of news and programme production and distribution are all features of mass radio. In fact, SWRA operators do not see their station as clandestine (see Wachanga, 2007), but as an independent radio station like any other that has been forced to operate from outside Zimbabwe. Unlike clandestine stations of the liberation war era, which signed off after the dawning of freedom, SWRA sees itself as having a future in the 'new Zimbabwe': 'Our role in future, back home, would be that of any normal independent radio station and – what we try to do now – it would have the additional task of trying to "heal" an extremely traumatised and brutalised nation.'[28]

Another clear distinction between today's clandestine radio stations in Zimbabwe and the clandestine radio stations of the liberation era is that whereas the latter were officially mouthpieces of the liberation movements, the former are not directly linked to or operated by the opposition, although they generally champion opposition politics. This to some degree gives them the critical distance their predecessors did not enjoy. Furthermore, today's clandestine radio enjoys the possibility of the amplification of its messages from a variety of other platforms, thanks to the rapid technological developments of the past two decades.

Endnotes

1   The full text of the agreement can be downloaded from < http://www.kubatana.net/html/ archive/demgg/080915agreement.asp?sector = DEMGG > , accessed 27 October 2008.

2   For almost a decade, Zimbabwe has been experiencing what amounts to a war of the airwaves between the mainstream state broadcaster (the Zimbabwe Broadcasting Corporation), which has long been suffering a credibility crisis, and clandestine radio stations beaming into the country from outside its borders.

3   Although the opposition MDC did not have an official external radio station, it was believed that the party was supported by the hosting and funding governments.

4   On 22 September 2000 the court invalidated the ZBC monopoly status on the basis that it was inconsistent with section 20 of the Constitution of Zimbabwe, which guarantees freedom of expression.

5   The announcement in May 2011 by the BAZ of two national commercial radio licences available for application has been widely seen as a ploy to placate growing criticism from the Southern African Development Community (SADC) leaders over lack of media reform since the formation of the Government of National Unity.

6   About four million Zimbabweans are estimated to have emigrated since the beginning of the crisis. An estimated three million are believed to be living in South Africa alone, while about a million are spread across the United Kingdom, United States, Canada and Australia. However, there is no authentic figure for their numbers, as these are estimates coming from the press.

7   These are the most prominent clandestine radio stations beaming into Zimbabwe. There are, however, several other initiatives whose visibility and impact are rather limited – particularly the Internet-based radio stations, which are mostly entertainment oriented. The impact of a newly introduced 'community' radio station beaming on short wave from the Middle East, for example, is yet to be established.

8   While government-controlled radio stations serve as government mouthpieces and give support to the ruling party in the run-up to national elections, it must be pointed out that they are not propaganda mouthpieces through and through, as Mano's chapter in this volume testifies.

9   Gerry Jackson is a former DJ on the ZBC. She was fired from the station after allowing on air callers who were critical of government.

10 See weekly schedule of programmes at < http://www.swradioafrica.com/pages/schedule. php > , accessed 3 December 2008.

11 See archives at < http://www.swradioafrica.com/pages/archives.php > , accessed 3 December 2008.

12 < http://www.swrafrica.com > .

13 Better known by its abbreviation SMS.

14 Email interview with V. Gonda and G. Jackson, 27 November 2008. This is not a small figure, given the tendency among recipients of these messages to forward them to their networks of friends and relatives, thereby amplifying the distribution of the message.

15 This is also a strategy borrowed from the Smith regime, which, after stopping production of short-wave radios to prevent people from listening to foreign broadcasts in the 1970s, went on a drive to promote listening to government stations by distributing free FM sets to the chiefs.

16 See SWRA website at < http://www.swradioafrica.com/ > , accessed 4 December 2008.

17 It is clear that a combination of economic sanctions, and government ineptitude and corruption has contributed to the worsening crisis in Zimbabwe. However, both government and its opponents have tended to take polar positions to defend themselves.

18 For a detailed discussion on patriotic history and perceptions of nationalism and nationhood, see Ranger (2004), Chiumbu (2004) and Bull-Christiansen (2004).

19 Email interview with Gonda and Jackson.

20 With most hospitals closed down, the country's disease surveillance system has collapsed, meaning that many cholera-related deaths go unreported across the country.

21 See < http://www.evrel.ewf.uni-erlangen.de/pesc/peaceradio-ZBW.html > , accessed 3 December 2008.

22 Email interview with Gonda and Jackson.

23 Ibid.

24 See < http://www.zimbabwesituation.com/mar1a_2007.html > , accessed 1 December 2008.

25 Email interview with Gonda and Jackson.

25 See Wachanga (2007:52).

26 A recent leak from the whistleblower website, Wikileaks suggests that Botswana sought American deployment of troops in 2008 to guard the transmitters, fearing possible Zimbabwean military invasion. See http://cima.ned.org/botswana-invited-us-troops-over-zimbabwe-attack-fears. Accessed 11 September 2011.

28 Email interview with Gonda and Jackson.

4

Equivocal Resonances
Islamic Revival and Female Radio 'Preachers' in Urban Mali

Dorothea E. Schulz

Introduction

In September 1999, a few months into my research on Islamic revival in urban Mali, I listened to a sermon by an elderly woman broadcast on a private radio station in Mali's capital, Bamako, together with Khadidja, a close friend and neighbour. I had known Khadidja from my earlier research in the early 1990s and, upon my return to Mali in 1998, learned that she had become a stout supporter of Islamic moral renewal, which prompted her to revise not only her dress habits and choice of peers, but also her daily schedule of chores and activities. Three times a week she attended the learning sessions of one of the numerous 'Muslim women's groups' (singular, *silame musow ton*) that have been mushrooming in urban areas since the 1990s. Even outside these formal meetings, Khadidja socialised with fellow 'Muslim women', who visited one another and together listened to sermon audio recordings or religious radio programmes. As I had learned over the weeks I spent together with Khadidja and her fellow Muslim women, they particularly cherished the radio lectures delivered by women who were often also heading a Muslim women's group. Knowing well that Khadidja and her friends respected these women as their 'teachers' and moral guides, I was surprised to overhear the following self-effacing opening remark by the female radio preacher:

Women, if I speak to you, I do this not in the role of a teacher (*karamògò*[1]) or of someone who is authorised to give a sermon (*wajuli*). As a woman, it is my vocation to lecture to fellow women, to offer them moral lessons (*ladili*) and to show them the right path to God (*alasira*). I can only educate you about women's duties and rights in Islam, about how a woman should behave so that on the Day of Judgement, God will reward her for her striving and sufferings by granting her eternal life.

The speaker's explicit denial of her role as a teacher piqued my curiosity. After all, the 'moral lessons' delivered by women on local radio were just that: teachings on the 'rules of Islam' offered to female audiences. But, as I realised over the months to come, similar denials of the formal position of a 'teacher' were common among the women who appeared in religious programmes of private radio stations. As I started to compare Muslim women's radio lectures with those of their male counterparts, I came to understand these women's downplaying of their role as teachers as a pre-emptive defence against the disapprobation they encountered on the part of the numerous male preachers who upbraided women's radio appearances as an indication of an appalling want of modesty. These charges of immodesty were all the more striking in light of the internationally acclaimed, public and mass-mediated presence that women, in their role as musicians and singers, have enjoyed in Mali since the early years of post-independence (Schulz, 2001a; 2001b). At the same time, it was evident that the allegations of impropriety levelled by male preachers against women delivering religious education on private radio, as well as the attempt by women to forestall them, indicated recent transformations in the field of religious authority. As such, they illustrate the insecurities and contestations generated by the recent appearance of female 'preachers' on Malian national and local radio, which point to controversies over the validity of their 'teachings'. These controversies are in themselves a reflection of the heterogeneous field of Muslim debate that emerged along with the recent diversification of the Malian media landscape.[2] Since the early 1990s, the time when multiparty democracy was introduced, Mali's public arenas have been permeated with emblems and idioms of Muslim piety and with a mushrooming infrastructure of Islamic proselytising (da'wa). The political opening following the breakdown of President Traore's single-party rule in 1991 allowed supporters of Islamic renewal – as they themselves refer to their endeavour – to gain an unprecedented prominence in public debates and daily life. Their activities tend to be associated by many Malians with practices and interpretations of Islam that draw inspiration from Salafi–Sunni reformist trends in Egypt and Saudi Arabia. The public presence of these supporters of Islamic renewal not only brings them into collision with those who view themselves as defenders of the principle of laicité against the onslaught of Islamic 'fundamentalism', but their activism has also spawned new controversies among themselves over what it means to be a proper Muslim (Schulz, 2007).

The emergence of these Muslim actors and groups, and their marked presence in Mali's public arenas and debates, parallels developments elsewhere in Muslim Africa. In Senegal, Nigeria and Niger, for instance, recent political liberalisation, paired with long-standing processes of broadening access to religious education, has similarly resulted in significant transformations in the field of Muslim debate and activism, and in the ways in which various Muslim actors engage the actors and institutions of the state to make their claims heard in public arenas. What is particularly remarkable about the recent developments is the great number and prominence of women who, in their endeavour to invite others to join their 'search for greater closeness to God', place a special weight on the public practice of their religiosity. Although these women often assume a key role in contemporary reform-oriented Islamic movements and enjoy great (often iconic) visibility, they have received surprisingly little attention in the scholarly literature on Muslim Africa.[3]

In southern Mali, these women refer to themselves simply as 'Muslim women' (*silame musow*) and thereby distance themselves from 'other women' (*musow to*) who, in their eyes, are not 'true believers' because of their lax attitude towards the Islamic duties of worship.[4] 'Muslim women' organise themselves into neighbourhood groups to 'learn to read and write' the Qur'an, and to engage in joint religious practice. Their female leaders, referred to as 'group leaders' (singular *tontigi*) or by the honorific title *hadja*,[5] offer admonition and advice on proper female conduct in ritual and daily settings, and emphasise the key role of Muslim women in effecting the moral transformation of Malian society, a role they consider to be closely related to a woman's 'natural' role as mother and spouse. Some *hadjas* disseminate their moral advice in local radio broadcasts and in audio recordings that circulate beyond the networks of their immediate followers. As this chapter's introductory quote illustrates, they do not to frame their interventions as 'preaching' or 'sermons' (*wajuli*), but describe them as 'moral lessons' (*ladili*), a category of edifying speech associated conventionally with older women and with professional specialists of the spoken word, the *jeliw* (Schulz, 2001b). Their disciples, on the other hand, consider their *tontigi*'s moral advice to be a form of religious instruction that complements that of male preachers.

In contrast to the *hadjas* who rely on audio recordings and local radio broadcasts to disseminate their moral summons, other female leaders limit their moral instruction to unmediated settings, such as educational circles associated with certain mosques. A third, and numerically rather insignificant, category of female 'preachers' is made up by younger married women whose advanced training in the religious sciences (most often at institutions of higher learning in North Africa) makes them much-solicited speakers in the religious programmes of national radio and television. Although these different 'types' of female educators opt for different venues for public sermonising, they all share the conviction that women's vocation as mothers and wives makes them key agents of Islamic moral renewal.

Spokespeople of the Islamic renewal movement echo their view of Muslim women's role as moral guides. However, many male activists also voice a dominant, yet contested Muslim scholarly opinion that women should not be allowed to preach in public because the sensuality of their voices risks arousing male desire. In theory, this danger could be seen to emanate from the teachings of the *hadjas* who preach on private local radio as much as from those offered by the younger, foreign-trained women who are explicitly invited to speak on national radio. Yet, curiously enough, most of the apprehensions by male Muslim activists are directed towards the *hadjas*, who, they maintain, should not be mistaken for Islamic 'teachers' in the proper sense of the term. They maintain that the *hadjas'* level of religious erudition is appallingly low and conclude that their access to local radio stations should be limited to the bare minimum. Their scepticism is shared by many men who work in administrative structures geared towards implementing what the state defines as 'proper' Islam.[6] Those in charge of Muslim religious programmes on national radio, for instance, speak condescendingly of 'these "radio *hadjas*" who talk on local radio without knowing much about Islam'. Their dismissal of the validity of the teachings of the *hadjas* is echoed by the younger, highly educated women who, at the behest of the religious programmes director of the Office de Radio and Television du Mali, deliver lectures on 'women's rights and duties in Islam' on national radio.

Clearly, there is a strong tension between these critics' dismissal of the *hadjas* as women who lack both religious erudition, and a sense of modesty and moral responsibility, and the authority that these female leaders enjoy in the eyes of their 'disciples'. Whereas their male critics deny these female leaders the scholarly credentials that would invest them with the authority to interpret texts and deliver formal teachings, their female followers highlight the moral and intellectual guidance they provide. These dissonant valuations of the authority and role of the radio *hadjas* deserve closer scrutiny and are the subject of this chapter.

At first sight, the contested public presence of radio *hadjas* seems to illustrate the argument that new media technologies contribute to the diversification of forms of authority; undermine the foundations of traditional, text-based forms of authority; and foster a 'democratisation' of religious interpretation[7] – a democratisation that allows women, similar to other formerly marginalised groups, to 'carve out' new spaces in a formerly male-dominated field of religious interpretation and authority. This view of media technologies' transformative workings, i.e. of their instrumental role in enabling women's gradual 'empowerment' vis-à-vis established (male) religious authority, reiterates the – somewhat schematic – ways some scholars conceive of the reworking of conventional authority structures of Muslim religious practices under the 'effect' of new media technologies (e.g. Robinson, 1993; Mandaville, 2007; Turner, 2007; Volpi & Turner, 2007; also see Castells, 1996).

It also echoes a long-standing tendency in studies of Muslim societies to conceive of gender relations in terms of oppression and struggle. Although this perspective has recently been subject to sustained critique (Abu-Lughod, 1998; Mahmood, 2001; 2005), the preoccupation with gender struggle proves to be remarkably tenacious.[8]

As compelling as a stress on media's subversive and 'empowering' effects appears at first sight, it proves unsatisfactory in the case at hand, on several grounds. Firstly, it starts from a purely instrumentalist view of the workings of media technologies and assumes that media simply transport, rather than affect, the 'message' they carry and the media engagements to which they give rise. As recent scholarship demonstrates, one way of exploring the complex interplay between religion and media, and of religion *as* media (De Vries & Weber, 2001; Stolow, 2005) is to pay close attention to the perceptive and sensuous processes accompanying and, indeed, constituting the mediation of religious experience (Schulz, 2003; 2006b; 2010; Meyer, 2005; 2009; De Witte, 2008). Secondly, a preoccupation with mass-media technologies' subversive effects also fails to elucidate why the *hadjas*, although 'gaining a voice' in public, do not challenge the authority of male representatives of the movement, such as by articulating independent religious interpretations.[9] Thirdly, emphasising women's 'empowerment' does not explain why these women's mass-mediated interventions generate such critique among other types of female 'preachers'. The *hadjas* and their female critics owe their prominence to the use of mass media, but interpretations that focus on technological innovation as a central venue of transformations in religious practice and hierarchy cannot explain the conflicted relationship between these two types of female leaders. Clearly, to interpret these dynamics as one of gender opposition does not do justice to the heterogeneous field of female Muslim activism, or to the variety of types of female 'educators', their agenda and positions in the broader field of Muslim debate.

We therefore need to explore how new technologies of 'mediating religion' inflect the 'message' that is publicised and facilitate certain engagements with it while foreclosing or limiting others; and how these processes reset the conditions for public debate by fostering imaginations of community, yet also of moral particularity and difference (Meyer, 2005; Meyer & Moors, 2006; Schulz, 2007). Moreover, rather than focusing on the radical changes introduced by new media technologies and the disruptions in the foundations of religious authority they engender, we should also recognise important continuities in the ways in which authority is claimed and assigned (Gaffney, 1994) and the ethical significance of media engagements is generated (Hirschkind, 2006).

How, then, can we make sense of the fact that these female educators are cherished as moral guides and as religious authorities by their followers, even though they downplay their role as 'teachers' and the text-based, interpretive authority for which the teacher stands? In what source(s) of authority is the standing grounded that they enjoy among their 'disciples' and that generates such resentment among other, male and female, representatives of Islamic moral renewal? Wherein consists the challenge of the *hadjas*' mass-mediated moralising activities? And what is the specific role that audio-recording and broadcasting technologies play in bringing about these changes and attendant contestations?

The social and political locations of Islamic moral renewal

Much of the 'moralising' of the *hadjas* and of other female leaders of the moral renewal movement takes place during Muslim women's learning activities. Until, roughly, the 1970s, these activities were restricted to older women from privileged families of religious specialists and merchants. The written traditions of Islam, whether passed on in Arabic or regional vernaculars, had only scant influence on the understandings and practices of the majority of Muslim women, whose knowledge in ritual matters and in the different Islamic religious disciplines remained very limited.

In all areas with a significant Muslim presence, however, a small group of highly educated women existed who owed their considerable religious erudition to their fathers' and husbands' support. They excelled through pious conduct, verbal proficiency and oratory skills, and enjoyed considerable respect and authority among their female disciples who were offered religious and ritual instruction. To lead a life withdrawn from the pressures of public opinion and worldly matters was an ideal many women aspired to, yet one that only the economically privileged ones could realise.

The mushrooming of Muslim organisational forms since the 1980s, supported by aid money from the Arab Muslim world, evidenced a historical process since the 1930s in the course of which opportunities to learn about religious and ritual matters had been extended to new segments of society, especially to 'younger' (married) women from the urban middle and lower-middle classes.[10] These changes also affected conventional sites and appreciations of female leaders' 'moralising' activities.

In spite of the current learning efforts of Muslim women, they often acquire only very basic knowledge in Arabic and of the teachings of Islam. Levels of erudition among the *hadjas* vary greatly. Some of them display a more advanced level of interpretive knowledge; others tend to reiterate very 'basic' rules of proper ritual behaviour and female conduct they learned from their male teachers. As a consequence, their views reflect the level and kind of education their teachers received at local schools or at institutions of higher religious learning in North Africa or other Arab-speaking countries.

The 'moral advice' many *hadjas* offer on local radio stations and on audio recordings forms part of a broader culture of moralising that existed prior to these social and political changes and to recent technological innovation. In this traditional culture of moralising, women of particular social origin, the so-called *jeliw*, were expected to play a key role as articulators of gender-specific ideals of proper moral conduct. I will return to this point below. For now, suffice to say that the task the radio *hadjas* accomplish as 'educators' resonates deeply with long-standing aesthetic and social understandings of the moral guidance a woman was to provide for her social surroundings. The *hadjas'* moral lessons are thus rooted in long-standing conventions; they have become more diversified, however, with the increasing reliance on new (mostly audio) reproduction technologies. Female 'educators' understand their moral instructions as part of an endeavour to return to more authentic modes of interpreting and living God's word. Yet the topics on which they lecture actually reflect their engagement with the radically transforming economy of gender relations in urban households. They also advise their disciples on proper comportment in domestic and public settings, and on their duty to invite others 'to embark on the path to God'. True religiosity, the teachers argue, should manifest itself not only in the performance of the conventional obligations of worship, such as the five daily prayers, but in a range of acts that are religious and social in nature.[11] Women's self-disciplinary endeavour should materialise in the acquisition of specific dispositional and emotional capabilities, among them the capacity to feel 'shame' and 'modesty' (*maloya*), to display endurance and patience, and to exercise self-control and submissiveness. Women should practise these virtues in various social and ritual activities in public and semi-public settings to 'profess' their ethical quest to a broader, potentially nationwide, audience.

The emphasis on the collective relevance of individual women's propriety is in line with the moral leadership elite Muslim women were historically expected to display. Relatively novel, in contrast, is the stress on women's individual responsibility for salvation and on the necessity to become a 'public' example of moral excellence. This self-conscious adoption by women of a public persona departs from the traditional relegation of female religiosity and devotional practices to an intimate, secluded space within the domestic realm. Whereas before women's spiritual experiences were predicated upon their withdrawal from the area of worldly matters and mundane daily activities, Muslim women's public worship establishes a direct link between the practice of piety and its public profession (Schulz, 2008; 2011).

The attempts by leading figures of the renewal movement, both men and women, to be heard as representatives of 'civil society' lead to often-uneasy relationships with the current political elite. This uneasiness is reinforced by the fact that numerous initiators of 'Muslim women's groups' belong to the political elite that enjoyed power and privilege under former President Traoré (who governed in the period 1968–91). The group leaders (among them many of the *hadjas* who lecture on local radio stations) owe their respected and often influential position at the neighbourhood level to a combination of different credentials, among them a Western education, (former) employment in the state administration and an economically privileged family background. In this way, they seem to confirm the interpretation of scholars who assess the striving for public prominence by Muslim movements and their leaders primarily in terms of a struggle over state institutions and resources. But as I want to show, these elements of political and economic capital do not exhaust the sources of authority on which the radio *hadjas* draw and that allow them to be viewed and revered by their followers as moral guides and 'teachers'.

Voice, mediation and charismatic authority

Wherein lies the force of the moral and intellectual authority that the 'radio *hadjas*' enjoy? On what sources and on what processes of authority making do they draw in addition to the textual knowledge that puts them in the position of 'educators'? In other words, what is so special about the current broadcast interventions of the *hadjas* that increases their authority in the eyes of their female disciples? What significance do their followers attribute to their mass-mediated moral advice – and to the practice of listening to it – that these lectures are so strongly resented by other Muslims who participate in Muslim activism and debate?

Answering these questions requires an investigation into how the process of transmitting – and indeed mediating – the *hadja*'s 'moral lesson' affects the significance and value it holds in the eyes of listeners. This investigation presupposes an historical reconstruction of conventional forms of Muslim women's moralising activities and of the evaluatory framework within which they were appreciated and received significance. Such reconstruction would allow us to understand the extent to which the activities of many *hadjas* constitute a departure from earlier sermonising practices.[12] Yet this endeavour of historical reconstruction also confronts us with a methodological difficulty: the presence of written Islamic texts and scholarly debate in the area cannot be taken as an historical indicator of the actual practices and evaluatory frameworks on which the majority of Muslims relied – and continue to rely. Even if, starting in the 1920s, more and more people in southern Mali converted to Islam, the promulgation of these Arabic texts remained restricted to a small educational elite. Accordingly, the written traditions of Islam played a very limited role in informing people's appreciations of the moralising activities of these Muslim female educators or their disciples' understandings of the ethical relevance of their listening practices. The same observation holds true today: most believers in Mali do not have the knowledge or institutional capacities that would allow them to frame their practices of listening to sermons as an appropriation of particular disciplinary traditions of Islam, similar to the 'ethics of cassette listening' analysed so brilliantly by Hirschkind (2006). I therefore propose to understand their views of the relevance of this practice against the backdrop of broader cultural valuations of the spoken word – valuations that are articulated in an explicit taxonomy or performatively elaborated.

Throughout Sahelian West Africa, speech was – and is – considered to have a special capacity to mobilise people's affective and agentive capabilities through the 'touching' sound of voice. In Mali, it is common practice among listeners to assess the efficiency and ethical quality of speech by references to its effects; i.e. by its capacity to mobilise a person's sensual, cognitive, and ethical qualities and to move her from stillness to action and to the performance of heroic 'deeds' (kewale). The central significance of 'moving speech' is paralleled by the importance attributed to listeners' aural perceptual predisposition. A person's *capacity* to feel touched by sound is considered an essential prerequisite for moral being and action. Hearing and speaking thus go in tandem in validating an educator's 'moral lesson'; being touched or 'captivated' by the (sound of a) voice is the principal marker of 'truthful' and compelling speech (Schulz, 1999b). Yet, along with the high value attributed to speech and voice throughout Sahelian West Africa, people also feel highly ambivalent towards the spoken word. Precisely because human speech has such enormous potential to move the human senses, speech is distrusted as the act that releases the damaging forces of untruth, delusion and human betrayal (Camara, 1976; Kendall, 1982; Hoffman, 1995; Diawara, 2003).

How, then, does this cultural conception of the moving capacities of voice and speech inform listeners' appreciations of the female educators' moralising activities? Elsewhere, I show that the authority that followers assign to their leaders in their radio- and cassette-mediated interactions is predicated on their understanding of the 'touching' effects of voice, and of voice as an essential medium for facilitating and generating spiritual experience and moral subjectivity (Schulz, 2003; forthcoming).[13] The experience of audition as a tactile sensation that radio broadcasts and audio recordings enhance reinforces the sense of the shared experience of women and the emotional identification that *hadjas* evoke in their 'moral lessons'. Both technologies of mediation thus allow women leaders to establish their authority as figures of ethical guidance and as examples of moral excellence.[14] This means that female leaders claim and constantly reassert a form of leadership that is only partly – and not always primarily – based on authoritative or informed textual interpretation. Sensually mediated feelings of trust, empathy and common experience as women play an important role in the interactive creation of authority and emotional attachment. Voice, by virtue of the tactile qualities that people attribute to it and the perceptive modes it facilitates, is pivotal to the interactive generation of a form of authority that, following Max Weber, could be seen as emanating from a form of 'charismatic' attachment, yet that clearly is at variance with how scholars of Islam in Africa and beyond have tended to conceive of 'charismatic authority' and its sources. To the listeners and followers who experience this charismatic spell, the various sources and forms of authority mobilised by the radio *hadjas* (as well as by some male preachers; see Schulz, 2006a; 2006b) do not contradict or exclude one another. Rather, their sensually mediated and experienced identification with the example set by a leader adds further substance to the intellectual guidance and leadership these *hadjas* are seen to hold and that they make available to their disciples during learning and sermon sessions.

These female believers' understandings of authority, in their appropriation of local conceptions of compelling speech and of genuine, 'heartfelt' hearing experience, form an essential part of the symbolic and discursive parameters in which the practice of Islam is grounded in West Africa. I therefore suggest that they should be conceptualised, and explicitly acknowledged by scholars as a constitutive element of a locally or regionally specific discursive tradition of Islam (see Asad, 1986; Bowen, 1993).

Voice and (dis)embodied authority

So far, I have argued that the authority of the *hadjas* and their mass-mediated lectures is grounded importantly in (what their followers identify as) the compelling force of their voice. If read along these lines, the vociferous criticism that the *hadjas* encounter on the part of state officials and some representatives of the Islamic renewal movement could be seen as a reflection of the challenge these female 'preachers' pose to text-based forms of religious (interpretive) authority. Yet, as I want to suggest, this argument or perspective does not exhaust the reasons that make female educators' public interventions so debatable. Rather, the denigration of female educators' mass-mediated interventions seems to reflect on the deep ambivalence that many representatives of the movement experience about the separation of the voice from body and authorship that the introduction of audio-recording technologies generates. This ambivalence is projected onto the assessment of female preaching activities; it is not rooted exclusively in a struggle between men and women. The following quote, drawn from a sermon delivered in June 2006 by a prominent preacher of Radio Islamique, one of the two Muslim radio stations in the capital, Bamako, illustrates this ambivalence articulated by male critics about the increasingly publicised, yet simultaneously strangely disembodied, presence of women in mass-mediated realms of everyday experience.

> There have been a number of women who, in recent years, have asserted that they received a divine calling to lecture about things Islamic. In doing so, they are not ready to limit themselves to teaching groups, no, no! They go to various radio stations and offer their services, they think they now have the knowledge and the (technical) means to lecture in public, to give people moral lessons. All of this is pure presumption. Having learned some passages from the Qur'an does not make you a teacher. The radios that have been popping up everywhere, they aggravate this problem. They delude women into thinking they can do and say whatever they deem right and important. With these radios, it is no longer possible to know who speaks, who are her parents, and what is her upbringing. One no longer knows who this person is, and whether her demeanour, her bodily comportment and dress make her a valid candidate to speak to others. Radios aggravate this problem, I tell you!

Rather than engaging in a textual argument about the unacceptability of women's mass-mediated lecturing activities, the preacher frames his critique as a moralising discourse on the alleged lack of modesty and propriety of female 'preachers'.[15] His attribution of these alleged developments to the spread of radios also communicates an unease about the radio-mediated dissociation of voice, physical presence, and authorship that, in his mind, casts doubt on the authority and moral integrity of the speaker. His dismissal of Muslim women's mass-media lectures reveals the ambivalence generated by the disembodiment of voice effected through audio-recording technologies, an ambivalence that translates into deep feelings of insecurity about the dissemination of the disembodied female voice.

My interpretation of these allegations of female preachers' immodesty as manifestations of people's unease about radical technological and social change echoes recent work by authors such as Macho (2006), Schmidt (2000) and Peters (2004), who are similarly interested in the ways in which media technologies intervene in processes involving the (dis)embodiment of voice. Thomas Macho (2006), in his historical reconstruction of media practices relating to the different technologies of storing and broadcasting sound and voice since the late

19th century, argues that these media practices went hand in hand with sustained efforts to re-embody 'voice', which was perceived to have been disembodied through the reliance on particular technologies of storing and amplifying sound (also see Sterne, 2003). Macho's perspective draws attention to the tension-ridden relationship among voice, different recording and mediation technologies, and processes of disembodiment in contemporary Mali. Following his analytical lead, we need to explore how the relationship among voice, physical presence, authorship and authority has been conventionally organised in this area of Muslim West Africa; and how new technologies of mediation intervene in these constructions and conventions. This will allow me to reflect on whether the controversial reception of the mass-mediated interventions of the Muslim 'educators' can be read along these lines.

Historically, the performative construction of political authority in the Mande-speaking cultural realm of southern Mali was based on a division of labour between families of free or aristocratic descent (singular, *horon*) who held power (singular, *keletigi, mansalen*), on the one hand, and professional praise speakers and singers, the *jeliw* (singular, *jeli*), on the other. The *jeliw* belonged to a group of endogamous artisanal specialists, the *nyamakalaw*,[16] who lived next door to powerful and rich families and for whom they performed various tasks of social and political mediation (e.g. Camara, 1976; Conrad & Frank, 1995; Schulz, 2001b). Throughout the colonial period (and until today), *jeli* men and women with outstanding musical and rhetorical skills spoke for their patron families at public events and thereby played a crucial role in sustaining and enhancing the honourable reputation of these families. They also assumed important functions in political negotiations. Because loud and self-appreciative speech was (and still is) considered unworthy of a person of aristocratic rank, *jeliw* repeated and elaborated at high volume on what their patron uttered in a low voice, thereby assuming the role of 'ventriloquators' (Goffman, 1981). In their public speech interventions, they thus effected a separation of voice and authorship that was pivotal to the assertion and reaffirmation of political authority. The loud and 'shameless' speech of these professional orators could affect listeners' hearts and minds even against their will.

Patrons and audiences felt highly ambivalent about the interventions of *jeli* speakers whose public speech and knowledge of intimate details of the patron family they both feared and depended upon. *Jeli* oratory was thus iconic of the ambiguous nature of speech and of its potential for delusion and betrayal (Schulz, 1999b; Diawara, 2003). In this situation, the physical presence of the *jeli* speaker served as a precondition of – and a kind of guarantee for – the truthfulness of his assertions. The co-presence of *jeli* and patron in the same time space indexed the long-lasting patronage relationship between the two. The physical presence of the *jeli* speaker-as-ventriloquator, and his palpable and visual embodiment of the patron's voice formed a sign ('proof') of the truthfulness of both *jeli* speech and the patron's claim to political leadership. This means that, while *jeli* speech effected and implied a separation of voice and political authority, its effectiveness depended upon the inseparability of (his) voice and body and thus on his embodied – and embodiment of – voice.

Jeli clients, and the values and claims of social hierarchy for which they stood were in a relationship of competition with the moral and social universe proclaimed and represented by Muslim scholars and traders. The '*jeli* principle' of ventriloquation, of separating voice from authorship (and the ambivalences that this separation created), constituted the conceptual opposite of the practice of religious preaching: whereas the making of political authority was predicated on a subtle *separation* of voice and authorship, Muslim religious authority rested on the embodiment of voice and authorship in the person of the (male) preacher. Their respective speech interventions also followed contrasting protocols of presentation and *voicing*. While 'loud' and 'shameless' speech was considered a genuine feature of *jeli* oratory, male preachers were expected to display their capacity for self-control and restraint through controlled, low-pitched speech. Besides, as some of them seem to have claimed, they sought to convince through the force of argument, not through presentational style.[17] The lecturing activities of the (few) elite Muslim women were restricted to women-only settings; these women were expected (and are remembered) to have drawn their female audiences by their warm, 'piercing', yet restrained voice. Thus, gender-specific norms of religious 'preaching' applied less to the mode of presentation and more to the spatial organisation of the lectures, as Muslim women's teaching activities were relegated to same-sex, domestic and semi-public settings.

The adoption of radio broadcasting technologies, and the heavy reliance of the first two regimes of independent Mali on *jeli* praise as a mode of promoting governmental policy and a sense of national identity, reinforced people's ambivalences towards *jeli* speech as a medium of political power. Over the years, radio-mediated *jeli* praise came to represent the empty official rhetoric and delusions of Mali's subsequent single-party and military regimes. Disembodied praise (on behalf of patrons who had a similarly disembodied, merely alluded-to presence in radio-mediated performances) cast greater doubt on the truthfulness (and faithfulness) of *jeli* speech. Also, as most of the *jeliw* whose praise was broadcast on national radio were women, *jeli* women, rather than men, became emblems of this form of 'empty praise' (as listeners usually referred to it). Four processes were key to this development. Firstly, the radio-mediated dissociation of voice and embodiment; secondly, the disembedding of *jeli* praise from the social and political context of long-standing patronage relations, and its concomitant insertion into the institutional context and rationalities of modern state power; thirdly, the commercialisation of *jeli* praise; and, fourthly, a move towards greater prominence of female *jeli* praise, a development that was reinforced by the introduction of television (in 1983). Each of these processes merits detailed attention, yet for the purpose of my argument, I will focus on the first one.[18] The radio-mediated disembodiment of voice reasserted and reinforced listeners' ambivalent perceptions of the Janus-faced quality of speech (and of the voice and its capacities to move the heart against one's own will).

Contemporary controversies over mass-mediated religious sermonising, and over the 'preaching' activities of Muslim women in particular, should be read in the light of listeners' general ambivalences towards speech that have been invigorated by the radio-mediated dissociation of voice and body. These ambivalences and insecurities tend to translate into gender-specific evaluations of the acceptability and validity of preaching on radio. They lead to different judgements regarding the preaching activities of men as opposed to women. Sermonising by male preachers on national and local radio is a commonly accepted practice, even if some controversies around specific radio preachers suggest that in their case, too (at least in the eyes of certain representatives of the religious establishment), their disembodied, mass-mediated interventions generate new anxieties about the uncontrollable nature of voice and its repercussions (Schulz, 2003). But in the case of the male radio preachers, the anxieties are expressed mostly as a matter of interpretive authority, i.e. of the validity of their textual interpretations; the anxieties are reinforced by the preachers' claim to make the Qur'an 'accessible to everyone' by translating important passages into the national lingua franca, Bamanakan (Schulz, 2006b).

The radio-mediated interventions by female 'educators' seem to generate similar anxieties, yet they are articulated differently. These women are challenged not only on the grounds of interpretive authority, but, most significantly, through a moralising discourse on their lack of modesty and propriety. What we see here is how long-standing ambivalences about the voice and its 'uncontrollable' nature – ambivalences that have been exacerbated by the disembodiment of voice through new mass-media technologies – are translated into a gender-specific moralising discourse on the acceptability and validity of male as opposed to female preaching.

Conclusion

In this chapter I have analysed the relatively novel and embattled public presence of female radio 'preachers' in urban Mali as a way to explore the dynamics emerging at the interface of a shifting field of Muslim activism and debate, changing articulations between the Malian state and society on which these debates reflect, and the spread of decentralised audio-recording and broadcasting technologies. These dynamics, and the controversies over proper religious practice and conduct that they simultaneously reflect and inspire, cannot be understood in their complexity if examined primarily with reference to doctrinal positions and to believers' appropriation of the written sources of Islam. Nor can they be adequately understood as a struggle over the control of textual interpretation that opposes women to men. Rather, they illustrate in rather complex ways the insecurities and anxieties surrounding the integration of a new media technology into existing religious and discursive practices. Although these insecurities take on specific discursive and symbolic forms in this particular social setting, they are by no means unique to this historical and cultural situation; nor are they limited to the introduction of audio-recording and broadcasting technologies (Sterne, 2003; Gitelman, 2006).

The *hadjas* who currently appear on Mali's private radio stations, and the disagreements and controversies they generate *among* women representatives of the Islamic renewal movement suggest that more attention should be paid to the diversity of sources of authority on which these female leaders and 'preachers' draw, both in Mali and elsewhere in Muslim Africa. Of particular relevance is a closer analysis of the younger generation of female preachers whose training abroad qualifies them to sermonise on national radio. A more nuanced approach to these women, and to their sources of knowledge and the interpretations they promote, would allow us to generate a more nuanced (and realistic) portrayal of the forms of women's participation in Islamic revivalist trends and the concerns that animate their involvement.

What emerges from the preceding analysis is that the respect and admiration that the '*hadjas*' of private radio programmes garner among their female disciples, and the position of moral guidance and authority they enjoy are not exhausted by text-interpretation-based forms of religious authority. The sources of authority on which female preachers draw may vary greatly from one woman to another. Religious erudition may count as much as the touching effects of a female preacher's voice in conjuring up the image of a woman whose 'completeness' makes her an authoritative guide in moral matters. Future research on the trends of Islamic renewal and reform in Muslim Africa and beyond should therefore pay closer attention to the ways in which these different foundations and parameters of religiously relevant practice interact with and feed on one another.

Endnotes

1   Unless noted otherwise, all foreign terms are rendered in Bamanakan, which, although officially represented as the national lingua franca, is spoken mostly by the peoples of the southern triangle of Mali.

2   Since the end of single-party rule in 1991, numerous newspapers have been created along with more than 80 local radio stations. Most of these radio stations are private and broadcast from the urban areas in Mali's southern triangle. In response to the great popularity of local radio stations, national radio launched a number of reforms in broadcasting policy and format to enable greater audience response and participation (Schulz, 1999a).

3   Notable exceptions are Alidou (2005) and the (rather cursory) discussion by Kleiner-Bosaller & Loimeier (1994). Miran (1998; 2005), LeBlanc (1999) and Augis (2002) deal primarily with the disciples of these female 'teachers'. Other scholarship on female religiosity in Muslim West Africa tends to focus on Sufi-related practices and understandings of authority (e.g. Coulon, 1988; Coulon & Reveyrand, 1990; Reveyrand-Coulon, 1993; Evers Rosander, 1997; see Dunbar, 2000).

4   Some 'Muslim women' and male activists mark, if often only implicitly, their distance from the representatives of local Sufi orders and their practices, which are in local parlance referred to as 'traditional' Islam. 'Traditional' religious practices include the veneration of religious leaders and other acts that are inspired by the assumption that a believer needs the mediation of spiritually blessed leaders in order to communicate with God. The proponents of Islamic renewal also denounce as unlawful innovation (*bid'a*) the use of Islamic esoteric knowledge (for purposes of divination or protection) and spirit possession cults.

5   The honorific title *hadja* usually refers to a woman who has accomplished the pilgrimage to Mecca. In Mali, it is often extended to honour a woman for her age and pious conduct.

6   Among these structures are the national Muslim association, Association Malienne pour le Progrès et l'Unité de l'Islam; the Bureau des Ulemas, the section of the national broadcast station that supervises (Muslim) religious programming; and the Haut Conseil Islamique, a committee initiated by the Ministry of Interior Affairs.

7   For example, Eickelman and Anderson (1999); also see Eickelman (1992).

8   Numerous anthropological studies on Muslim women's educational activities still study them in terms of a struggle between men and women over 'gaining a voice' and 'carving out new spaces' in a male-dominated religious field (e.g. Weix, 1998; Nageeb, 2004; Alidou, 2005).

9   Interpretations of women's public interventions as indications of their 'empowerment' also ignore the long-standing importance of elite women's educational and organisational activities in Muslim West Africa (Trevor, 1975; Asma'u, 1997; Hutson, 1999; Boyd, 2001; Umar, 2001; also see Purpura, 1997).

10 Instrumental for this development were the activities of a younger generation of Muslims who, after prolonged stays in Saudi Arabia, Egypt, and sometimes North Africa, initiated educational and other reforms to respond to the new situation established under French colonial rule. Their reformist endeavour was inspired by intellectual trends throughout the early 20th-century Arab-speaking world. The interventions of this earlier generation of Muslim activists had far-reaching effects for segments of the population of the French Sudan, particularly for women and adolescents, who hitherto had been widely excluded from opportunities to gain sustained Arabic literacy skills and knowledge on religious interpretation. Most importantly, they contributed to the ongoing unsettling of conventional foundations of religious interpretive authority (Brenner, 1993; 2001; Soares, 2005).

11 Stress on women's individual responsibility in cultivating an ethically *superior* disposition suggests that prevalent conceptions of Muslim religiosity are currently being reassessed, partly in response to broader societal transformations and transnational influences. A Muslim identity is no longer conceptualised primarily as a marker of family or ethnic identity, but as the result of personal conviction and daily practice (see Launay, 1992, chaps. 3–5).

12 For the African context, such an historical *reconstruction* is marred with methodological difficulties resulting from the scarce (written) documentation on female Muslim leadership and on 'ordinary' female believers' practices. Oral historical material has to be treated with care because of its tendency to 'telescope' critical events, meanings and forms of practices that belong to different historical periods. Colonial reports and contemporary scholarship, on the other hand, reveal a 'scripturalist bent' in their approach to questions of religious practice and authority. They fail to do justice to forms of authority that are not, or are not exclusively, rooted in the interpretation of the written foundations of Islam, yet that are of particular relevance to an understanding of female forms of leadership.

13 Listeners (sometimes) spontaneously remark on the capacity of audio recordings and radio broadcasts to 'intensify' the 'touching' effects of a speaker's voice, a vocabulary that intimates that listeners explicitly recognise and value the synaesthetic nature of both sound and sound transmission facilitated by these sound reproduction technologies. However, most of the time listeners downplay (or dismiss) any mediating effects of these technologies and emphasise their instrumental 'utility' in 'broadcasting' a message, thus allowing disciples to listen to their *tontigi*'s advice in a broad variety of mundane settings.

14 One could argue that the hearing experiences generated by audio recordings differ in many ways from those of radio broadcasts: in the sound patterns coupled with the two technologies (such as the radio frequency interferences as opposed to the 'scratching' and other 'noises' associated with the frequent use of audio tapes); and in the temporal, spatial and social organisation of the listening event (affecting, for instance, women's and men's unequal opportunities to access and control the technological equipment

necessary for sermon tape consumption). Ideologies inscribed in the use of the two sound reproduction technologies differ slightly, too. Radio consumption tends to be associated with an ideology of transparency, personal enlightenment, civic education and informed debate. The consumption of audio tapes, in contrast, tends to be associated with notions of sharing, mutual trust and empathy. The markedly communal 'personality' of tapes is closely related to the collective form of their reception; they are more frequently consumed during group gatherings, and their circulation establishes and sustains communality, bonding and a sense of empathy (Schulz, 2007). Interestingly, however, listeners, both men and women, only occasionally acknowledge the discrepancies between sound experiences generated by radio and by audio tape, discrepancies partly related to the respective social organisation and appraisal of these media products.

15 In another intervention, the same preacher also warned his listeners of the sexual evocativeness of the female voice.

16 These groups of specialists included blacksmiths (*numun*), leathermakers (*garanke*) and people specialising in public speech (*fune*).

17 This argument is based on oral testimony I collected in the period between 1998 and 2004 in the towns of Segu, San and Kayes.

18 For a detailed analysis of these interlocking transformations and their effects on the contents, forms and political effectiveness of *jeli* praise, see Schulz (2001b).

2

The Cultures of Radio

Languages of the Everyday

5

What Is the Relationship between Hate Radio and Violence?
Rethinking Rwanda's 'Radio Machete'[1]

Scott Straus

Introduction

In 1994 government and military officials in Rwanda orchestrated one of the 20th century's most extreme human rights crimes. During a three-month period, in the midst of a civil war that they were losing, Rwandan officials led an extermination campaign against the country's minority Tutsi population that left some 500 000 civilians dead (Des Forges, 1999). At the time it occurred, despite the magnitude and character of the violence, the genocide in Rwanda received relatively little attention in the English-speaking developed world. Rwanda was a small, landlocked, coffee-and-tea-exporting, francophone and strategically insignificant country. However, more than a decade later, interest in Rwanda has surged, as evidenced by a slew of major motion pictures, documentaries and books (both scholarly and popular) about the country. Through these various media, Rwanda has emerged as one of the most recognisable contemporary cases of mass violence and as a textbook example of the international community's inaction in the face of genocide.

A prominent theme within the corpus of commentary on Rwanda is the pervasive and pernicious role that modern media, in particular 'hate radio', played in stoking the genocide (Chrétien et al., 1995; Kellow & Steeves, 1998; Schabas, 2000; Melvern, 2004; Moghalu, 2005; Thompson, 2007). In popular settings, films on the Rwandan genocide invariably feature radio as a contributing factor in the genocide.[2] In policy circles, debates on how to contain genocide often focus on jamming the radio.[3] For sceptics of rapid democratisation, Rwandan private radio is a showcase example of the dangers of media liberalisation (Snyder & Ballentine, 1996; Snyder, 2000; see also Kirschke, 2000). In addition, students of genocide (Chalk, 1999), journalism

(Internews, n.d.; Gatwa, 1995; Article 19, 1996; Temple-Raston, 2002; 2005) and international law (Metzl, 1997; Schabas, 2000) all highlight Rwandan radio. And in a major decision in 2003, the United Nations (UN) International Criminal Tribunal for Rwanda (ICTR) found two radio journalists and a print journalist guilty of inciting genocide, the first international court to do so since the Nuremberg conviction of Julius Streicher (ICTR, 2003a). In short, radio has become a symbol of the genocide in Rwanda, and Rwanda has become a paradigmatic case of hate radio sparking genocide (Metzl, 1997:629; Levene, 2005:116).

However, despite the central role regularly attributed to radio, there has been little sustained social scientific analysis of radio media effects in the Rwandan genocide. Many of the standard methods and concepts of political communications empirical research – such as exposure, timing, frequency, reception, audience selectivity and survey research – have found little application in the literature on Rwanda. This is the case despite the presence of often quite strong claims about media effects, found especially in film and popular writings. Such claims often assert or imply undifferentiated, direct and massive media effects – effects that, if true, would be at odds with decades of political communications empirical research. Scholarship on Rwanda shows greater differentiation, but many scholars suggest large-scale media effects or employ somewhat vague terms, such as radio 'fomenting' genocide (Thompson, 2007:6).

Given the importance of the Rwandan case and given the centrality of hate radio to the commentary on Rwanda, a better assessment of radio media effects in the genocide is needed. At stake is not only getting the Rwandan story right, which has implications for a series of related issue areas, including genocide studies, humanitarian intervention and democratisation, but also bringing the issue of media effects in Rwanda to the attention of the political communications field, where the bulk of research focuses on voting behaviour and electoral outcomes in Western countries. At stake is yet another broad issue: the way in which outside observers conceptualise extreme behaviour in poor, non-Western settings. The conventional wisdom on hate radio and massive media effects in Rwanda is undoubtedly an improvement on ahistorical and empirically untenable claims that 'ancient tribal hatred' drove the violence – a view common to press commentary on Rwanda and ethnic conflict in general. Nonetheless, much of the conventional wisdom on hate radio reproduces simplistic models of political behaviour that attribute little or no agency to Rwandans and that minimise the context in which extreme violence took place. Re-examining radio effects in Rwanda thus allows for a reintroduction of causal complexity to help explain a multidimensional outcome.

To gain analytical leverage on the issues at hand, the chapter focuses on two researchable questions: firstly, did radio broadcasts account for the onset of genocidal violence in Rwanda and, secondly, was radio responsible for prompting ordinary citizens to become genocide perpetrators? I examine the questions by using a series of different methodologies, and by triangulating available information and original field research, including a survey of convicted perpetrators. On the whole, I conclude that radio alone could not account for either the onset of most Rwandan genocidal violence or the participation of most perpetrators. That said, I find some evidence of conditional media effects. Radio in some instances coordinated elites, reinforced the connection between violence and authority, and catalysed a small but significant number of individuals and incidents of violence. Situated in context – i.e. seen alongside the primary dynamics of violence and mobilisation that drove the genocide – I hypothesise that the effects had a marginal but important impact on the outcome. To be clear, the overall point is not to exonerate, legally or morally, journalists found guilty of incitement; radio broadcasts were at times racist and openly inflammatory and those responsible deserve punishment. Rather, the point is to evaluate systematically and empirically, using the tools of social science, the conventional wisdom about media effects for what has become a world historical event.

Media and media effects in the Rwandan genocide

Most discussions of media effects in the Rwandan genocide focus on radio, in particular a notorious semi-private FM station called Radio-Télévision Libre des Milles Collines (RTLM), which began broadcasting in 1993. The focus on radio is appropriate, given that radio in Rwanda and throughout much of sub-Saharan Africa is the most important medium of public communication (Mytton, 2000). Transistor radios and the batteries that power them are comparatively plentiful and cheap in Rwanda, as they are throughout Africa. By contrast, print media have limited circulation outside the capital and are accessible primarily to urban and educated elites. Television has similar demographics.

RTLM was not the only radio station accessible in Rwanda on the eve of and during the 1994 genocide. Rwandans could listen to the more staid, state-owned station Radio Rwanda. In addition, the Tutsi-led rebels, who were fighting the government in a war that began in 1990, operated a station called Radio Muhabura. Several foreign stations were also accessible.[4] But for discussions of the relationship between media and genocide, RTLM garners the most attention. The station was owned and controlled by Hutu hardliners within the ruling regime who ultimately organised the genocidal violence (Chrétien et al., 1995; Article 19, 1996; Kirschke, 2000; ICTR, 2003a). Before the genocide, RTLM broadcast a steady digest of belligerent, nationalist, anti-rebel and often openly inflammatory statements.

During the genocide, RTLM announcers encouraged listeners to fight, and in some cases the announcers broadcast names of individuals and places that were subsequently attacked by citizen bands. For these reasons, RTLM is the subject of most commentary on genocidal media effects and is the focus here.

Within the literature on Rwanda, a number of claims about RTLM's effects are evident. The strongest and most common assertion – the conventional wisdom – is that RTLM broadcasts had large-scale and direct effects on behaviour. For example, Roméo Dallaire (2004:272), the celebrated former UN force commander in Rwanda, claims: 'In Rwanda the radio was akin to the voice of God, and if the radio called for violence, many Rwandans would respond, believing they were being sanctioned to commit these actions.' Another well-known author on Rwanda, Linda Melvern (2000:71), writes that RTLM radio was 'a propaganda weapon unlike any other'. She claims: 'The influence of hate radio … must never be underestimated' (2004:25). Similarly, Pulitzer-Prize-winner Samantha Power (2001:89) claims: 'Killers in Rwanda often carried a machete in one hand and a radio transistor in the other' (the implication being that radio delivered instructions and then men attacked with machetes). Such conceptualisations suggest a strong causal link between radio broadcasts and genocidal violence, as do expressions about RTLM such as 'radio genocide' (Mitchell, 2004:42), 'death by radio' (Misse & Jaumain, 1994) and the 'radio dispatcher of murder' (*New York Times*, 2003:A38), among others. The most common sobriquet – 'Radio Machete'[5] – directly equates RTLM with a violent weapon.

Some observers – a minority in the literature – hold more moderate views or are openly sceptical. For example, Rwandan analysts Jean-Marie Vianney Higiro (2007:86) and Charles Mironko (2007:134) argue that media had some effect, but cannot alone account for citizen mobilisation during the genocide. After interviewing perpetrators in Rwanda, researcher Darryl Li concluded that RTLM communicated ideology and constituted 'performances' that listeners subsequently re-enacted. Radio routinised and legitimised violence, he argues (Li, 2004); RTLM 'may have been the key thing that helped transform the genocide from a state-led campaign into a nationwide project' (Li, 2002:82). But Li distances himself from claims that radio had direct media effects capable of instantly causing violence. Richard Carver (2000), a rare sceptic, faults most commentary on hate radio in Rwanda for failing to establish a causal relationship between radio propaganda and the violence. Similarly, Alan Kuperman (2001:91) doubts that radio broadcasts were essential to the genocide outcome, because military officials had separate communication networks and moderate Rwandans were not convinced by such broadcasts. Nonetheless, the bulk of commentary asserts or suggests a significant causal link between radio broadcasts and genocidal violence.

Although not always clearly specified, the literature indicates two prominent causal mechanisms. The first is that radio broadcasts implanted ideas in listeners that subsequently caused them to hate, dehumanise and fear Tutsis. Radio thereby conditioned, facilitated, and legitimised violence and became a tool for the mobilisation of genocide. Writing in the preface to a seminal study, for example, a UN investigator claimed that Rwandan media were the vector by which 'the poison of racist propaganda is spread' (Chrétien et al., 1995:7; my translation). Similarly, Melvern (2004:25) claims: 'In order to commit genocide, it is necessary to define the victim as being outside human existence – vermin and subhuman. In Rwanda, the propaganda campaign against the minority Tutsi was relentless in its incitement to ethnic hatred and violence.' In another study, communication scholars Christine Kellow and H. Leslie Steeves (1998:124) assert that radio indoctrinated the public by 'instill[ing] a pronounced fear and hatred that previously had not been part of the everyday culture'. Such views are fairly common in the commentary on radio media in Rwanda.[6]

The second major theme is that radio was a voice of authority and that when it issued orders to kill, Rwandans obeyed. In their seminal study *Les médias du génocide*, French historian Jean-Pierre Chrétien and co-authors claim that the Rwandan genocide had two main tools: 'the radio and the machete, the first to give and receive orders, the second to execute them' (1995:191; my translation). Another observer, a journalist, asserts: 'When the radio said it was time to kill the people opposed to the government, the masses slid off a dark edge into insanity' (quoted in Kellow & Steeves, 1998:124). The UN investigator quoted above similarly concluded that the 'poison' of radio propaganda 'is all the more effective because, it is said, the Rwandan peasant has a radio culture of holding a transistor up to his ear in one hand and holding a machete in the other, waiting for orders emitted by RTLM' (Chrétien et al., 1995:7; my translation). The ICTR decision is a variation on these themes. The judges essentially make two arguments. The first, and the emphasis in the decision, is about indirect incitement. The judges find that media 'spread hatred and scorn' and equated the Tutsi ethnic group as a whole with the Tutsi-led rebels, the Rwandan Patriotic Front (RPF) (ICTR, 2003a:165). The second argument that the court makes is about direct incitement. The court recounts instances when people or places were named on the radio; that naming was followed by attacks (ICTR, 2003a:165). In short, the court finds that radio played an essential role in the genocide by indirectly and directly inciting listeners to commit genocidal violence.

Problems with the conventional wisdom

Nothing a priori discredits a causal relationship between RTLM radio broadcasts and the bulk of genocidal violence in Rwanda. However, to be persuasive, the strong claims found in the literature should be well grounded theoretically and empirically. As I show in this section, neither is the case.

Theoretically, the strong claims that radio indirectly instilled ideas that led to violence and issued orders that directly led to mobilisation have three primary weaknesses. Firstly, the claims are at odds with mainstream political communication research. The claims closely resemble a 'hypodermic needle' model of media effects, whereby media purportedly injects ideas into the body politic and thereby has a direct impact. That view – and similar elementary models of propaganda stimulus and behavioural response – have been largely discredited after more than four decades of empirical research.[7] Even if political communication scholars no longer agree, as they did for many years, that mass media have 'minimal effects' (Zaller, 1996), contemporary scholarship still focuses on effects of much smaller magnitude than what is claimed for Rwanda. The focus of most contemporary political communication scholarship is on voting behaviour and electoral outcomes.[8] The common causal mechanisms found in the literature include agenda setting, elite persuasion and reinforcing predispositions (Zaller, 1992; 1996). To be sure, the field is considerably more complex than this truncated summary indicates, but the point is to highlight the very large gap between the effects claimed in mainstream political communication research and those commonly attributed to the Rwandan case. Candidate preference, voting turnout, and agenda setting are quite different media effects than murder and genocide.

Secondly, the strong claims found in the literature on Rwanda imply a simplistic and improbable model of agency. With the exception of Li and Mironko – both of whom conducted interviews with listeners and perpetrators – most discussions of Rwandan media effects attribute little or no agency to listeners. The Rwandan public is often characterised as hearing a drumbeat of racist messages and directly internalising them or as hearing orders to kill and heeding the command. These views are consistent with stereotypes about Rwandans, namely that they obey orders blindly; that they are poorly educated and thus easily manipulated; and that they are immersed in a culture of prejudice.[9] But being based on stereotypes, the assumptions deserve close scrutiny. Thirdly, most discussions of media effects are not situated in a broader discussion of the dynamics of violence or of an assessment of rival explanations.[10] None of these latter assumptions – minimal agency; an obedient, pliant and hateful public; or uncomplicated dynamics of violence – should be dismissed out of hand. But to have validity, the claims require empirical substantiation.

However, the existing empirical case is as weak as the theoretical one. The most common method of analysis in the literature on Rwanda is non-systematic content analysis.[11] One exception is a study by Kenyan journalist Mary Kimani (2007), who conducted a detailed content analysis of RTLM transcripts. Even so, Kimani's and other studies do not systematically address questions of timing (whether content correlates with violence) or audience selectivity (whether and how media effects varied by social category, education level, region, political party affiliation, or some other potentially relevant variable). Some studies suggest RTLM appealed to young listeners because of the station's talk-show format. If true, the finding runs contrary to expectations, because the two existing published studies on the demographic profile of genocide perpetrators indicate that they were a cross-section of the adult male population (Fujii, 2006; Straus, 2006). In addition, some commonly cited broadcasts – such as the evocative command 'the graves are not yet full'[12] – may never have been aired.[13]

Perhaps the most glaring absences are questions of exposure and reception. As I discuss below, it is not clear that RTLM reached all the areas of Rwanda where violence occurred. Moreover, with the exception of Li and Mironko, the existing literature does not assess media effects through interviews or survey research. Even Li's study has empirical limits. Li primarily interviewed detainees and sentenced perpetrators in Kigali's Central Prison, thus drawing an urban (as well as a non-random) sample. Mironko (2007) had a larger and more rural sample, but he concludes that media had minimal effects and that most of the perpetrators he interviewed thought that broadcasts were destined for the urban, elite and educated. In short, despite very strong causal claims about media effects commonly found in commentary on Rwanda, the supporting evidence is weak.

Hypothesis testing

Given the attention Rwanda receives and the prominence of hate radio in the commentary on Rwanda, a better appraisal of media effects is critical. While existing data to test hypotheses is not extensive, enough evidence exists to test in various ways some of the claims found in the literature. In this section I pursue several approaches. Each method is independently inconclusive, but triangulating the approaches yields a cumulative evaluation of the conventional wisdom.

Exposure

A central issue for assessing media effects is exposure: in this case, how many Rwandans had access to RTLM broadcasts? One way to answer the question is by looking at radio ownership rates. UN statistics indicate that less than 10 per cent of the Rwandan population in 1994 owned radios, which is comparatively low for Africa.[14] But the data is weak and individuals could have listened collectively.

A better measure is broadcast range: did RTLM reach the areas where the genocide took place? The genocide itself was national. The violence occurred in all 11 prefectures and in all but one commune (an administrative unit equivalent to a town) under government control. By contrast, while the data to evaluate RTLM's range is inconclusive, most indicators suggest that the broadcast range was not national.[15] Several studies claim that RTLM had little reach in rural areas (Kellow & Steeves, 1998:118; Kirschke, 2000:241), even if Rwanda's population was 90–95 per cent rural in the early 1990s (République du Rwanda, 1994). The ICTR decision does not address the question of broadcast range, but during the trial the prosecution produced a Rwandan radio technician who testified that RTLM had two transmitters. He claimed RTLM had a 100-watt transmitter that could reach the whole of the capital Kigali and a few areas south and east of Kigali, as well as a less-powerful transmitter on Mount Muhe in western Rwanda that could reach some areas in that part of the country.[16] If true, then RTLM would not have reached large segments of the country where genocide occurred, including northern, north-eastern, southern and south-west areas.

Another way to consider broadcast range is through an analysis of topography and elevation. The assumption would be that hilly and mountainous areas have comparatively limited exposure to radio broadcasts. Here again, the evidence from Rwanda points to non-national range. Rwanda's nickname is the 'land of a thousand hills', which reflects the country's mountainous and hilly terrain and many changes in elevation. Rwanda's topography thus makes the country a poor exemplar for mass effects from FM broadcast media. In short, the available evidence suggests a significant exposure gap between broadcast range and the places where the genocide occurred.

Timing 1: Broadcast range and regional patterns of violence

Another way to test media effects is through an analysis of timing, here operationalised in terms of whether broadcast range corresponds to regional temporal patterns of violence. Even though the genocide occurred nationally, the violence started at different times in different regions. In some regions, violence started immediately after President Juvénal Habyarimana's assassination on 6 April 1994. In other regions, the violence took two weeks or longer to materialise. Moreover, in one commune (Giti) under government control, genocidal violence did not occur. The temporal variation is small, but nonetheless it represents different levels of local willingness to commit genocide and of resistance to it.

Since RTLM's exact range is unknown, I compare four hypothetical broadcast models against a data set of onset variation. The data set includes onset estimates for about two-thirds of Rwanda's 145 communes that existed in 1994.[17] The four hypothetical models of RTLM's broadcast range are as follows: (1) national coverage; (2) urban coverage (including the capital, Kigali, and its environs); (3) coverage as stipulated in the ICTR testimony (Kigali and its environs and Mount Muhe and its environs); and (4) coverage in Kigali plus flatter and lower-elevation regions. All told, the mapping analysis indicates that broadcast range does not correlate well with the onset of genocidal violence in different regions. Of four tested hypothetical models of broadcast range, only one (the third) lends minimal support to the hypothesis that violence started earliest where RTLM reached. The three other models show either no correlation between early onset and broadcast range or an inverted relationship. Moreover, the third model leaves out many areas where violence started earliest.

Timing II: Broadcasts and violence

A related timing issue is whether violence tended to take place when broadcasts tended to air. In some cases, the answer to the question is 'yes'. There are examples where RTLM broadcast specific names and places, which were followed by attacks on those individuals and locations. However, the cases comprise a tiny fraction of the total violence and appear to be limited to the capital and its environs. The ICTR Media Trial decision, for example, lists about ten instances. The ICTR may not have discovered or reported all such incidents, but even if the number was increased twenty-fold to 200, the percentage of attacks would be small compared to the total number of attacks and murders during the genocide, which left at least 500 000 dead countrywide.

With regard to general trends of broadcasts and violence, the existing data shows a limited temporal relationship at best. Most violence during the genocide occurred in April. The only comprehensive data on the timing of deaths comes from Kibuye Prefecture, where a survivor's organisation conducted a household survey documenting the date and location of deaths. The organisation's findings show that some 85 per cent of all reported deaths took place between 7 April and 20 April (Ibuka, 2001). Kibuye was a mid-onset prefecture, meaning that violence spiked earlier in Kigali, Gisenyi and Rugengeri. By contrast, violence spiked later in Gitarama and Butare between 21 April and the first week of May. By mid-May, moreover, the RPF rebels had won control over large areas of the country.

For simplicity, I categorise the genocide into two periods: a 'high-genocide' period (between 6 April and 7 May) and a 'low-genocide' period (between 8 May and early July).

When, then, did most inflammatory broadcasts take place? The ICTR decision lists relatively few specific broadcasts from the high-genocide period, and those that are listed focus on the Kigali area. The decision discusses three broadcasts in which people were named on 7 and 8 April and subsequently killed (ICTR, 2003a:151, 162). A separate broadcast took place 'days after' the president's assassination, according to the ICTR, and it encouraged listeners in three locations in and around Kigali to search for '*inyenzi*' (ICTR, 2003a :133). (The Kinyarwanda word means 'cockroach' and was a pejorative term for the rebels and sometimes all Tutsis.) A broadcast on 11 April encouraged Tutsis to return from their hiding places to their homes, which a court witness testified led to some who returned being murdered. On 12 April an RTLM announcer claimed armed '*inyenzi*' were at an Islamic centre in Kigali; a day later, attackers stormed the centre's mosque and massacred hundreds of unarmed civilians there (ICTR, 2003a:152). On 13 April the same announcer implied that Tutsis, as a minority, should be exterminated for seeking to take power (ICTR, 2003a :136–37).

The broadcasts provide evidence of direct media effects, especially where attacks followed the broadcasting of a name or location. At the same time, the broadcasts amount to a handful of examples from the high-genocide period and they focus on the capital, Kigali. The ICTR decision cites many other broadcasts in the decision, but they date from 13 May onwards. The later broadcasts are indeed consistently inflammatory, in some cases urging Hutus to quash the rebels and their Tutsi 'accomplices'. On several occasions, the broadcasts refer to 'exterminating' the rebels and the 'enemy'. Indeed, as Kimani (2007:122) concludes, RTLM broadcasts appear to become more extreme during the later stages of the genocide, as the government side lost ground to Tutsi rebels. However, by mid-May most killings of Tutsi civilians had already taken place. Thus, citing mid-May or later broadcasts is weak evidence to support the hypothesis that broadcasts drove the violence and participation in it.

Other sources show similar patterns. In the seminal book *Les médias du génocide*, Chrétien et al. (1995:393) list only three specific April 1994 RTLM broadcasts. Almost all of the most explicit and inflammatory RTLM broadcasts cited in the book are dated from mid-May onwards. Communication scholars Kellow and Steeves (1998) make generalisations about radio broadcasts after 6 April, but the earliest specific RTLM broadcast they cite is on 14 May. The report *Broadcasting Genocide* from media watchdog group Article 19 (1996:114–19) cites five specific broadcasts in the high-genocide period. According to the report, on 8 April listeners at roadblocks (where violence frequently occurred) were told to remain 'strong' and to know that the radio supported them. On 10 April listeners were told to 'remain vigilant', to 'defend themselves' and to man roadblocks. On 13 April listeners were additionally told to 'give punishment', to remain 'heroic' and to prepare for 'battle'. On 15 April listeners were told to 'stand up' and 'take action', lest they be exterminated. The report provides some evidence of a temporal link between belligerent broadcasts and the bulk of killing countrywide. Even so, the frequency of hate-filled broadcasts and their reception are not documented. Moreover, while the broadcasts were inflammatory, they were not clearly communiqués to exterminate Tutsi civilians.

Content analysis

Another way to consider media effects is to examine the content of entire RTLM transcripts systematically. The ICTR produced transcripts of 34 distinct broadcasts, which were translated from Kinyarwanda to French and English, and which were provided to me. The transcripts include nine that aired before the genocide, four that aired during the high-genocide period, ten that aired during the low-genocide period and eleven that are undated. In total, the transcripts amount to 973 pages and an estimated 2 070 minutes of airtime. My analysis proceeds in two ways, first quantitatively and second qualitatively; the latter focuses on the broadcasts from the high-genocide period.

To conduct the quantitative content analysis, I selected five indicators of inflammatory broadcasts: (1) calls to be 'vigilant'; (2) calls to 'fight' or 'kill'; (3) calls to 'defend' the nation or themselves; (4) mention of the word 'exterminate'; and (5) mention of the word *inyenzi* (or cockroach – the derogatory term for Tutsi rebels and Tutsi civilians). The results are fairly consistent with the pattern seen so far. During the high-genocide period, there are some hateful and inciting messages, but they are not overwhelmingly frequent. During the low-genocide period, the inflammatory broadcasts are more frequent and virulent, but again citing broadcasts from mid-May onwards is weak evidence to show that radio broadcasts sowed violence.

The qualitative analysis reveals the same patterns. The pre-genocide broadcasts present Rwandan history in a tendentious, nationalist and anti-rebel fashion, often accompanied by negative commentary about Tutsi behaviour. The low-genocide broadcasts include inflammatory calls to arms. Broadcasters urge listeners to fight the '*inyenzi*' and 'their accomplices' (references to Tutsi civilians). However, a close reading of the four available broadcasts from the high-genocide period reveals little evidence of direct calls for violence against Tutsis. In fact, on several occasions announcers or interviewees urge listeners *not* to attack civilians; they also advocate negotiation with the rebels. To be sure, the tone of the broadcasts is decidedly hostile towards the rebels. The announcers refute claims made on the rival rebel radio station, Radio Muhabura. Speakers urge the population to assist the armed forces and, on two occasions, broadcasters mention place names where listeners are supposed to go to find '*inkotanyi*' (another Kinyarwanda synonym for rebels). But the consistently official line is that listeners should avoid excesses and spare civilians.

Reception I: Quantitative analysis of perpetrator interviews

It is possible that RTLM aired more virulent broadcasts during key periods in the genocide, but that the broadcasts were not recorded, have since disappeared or are otherwise inaccessible. Thus, another way to triangulate evidence is through interviews: do those who took part in the genocide say that radio influenced them to commit violence? To answer the question, I draw on results from a survey of 210 sentenced and self-confessed perpetrators who were sampled randomly in 15 prisons nationwide in 2002. The results are consistent with the thread of analysis so far: radio broadcasts had an influence – it catalysed some hard-line individuals – but most respondents claim radio was not the primary reason that they joined attacks. Most commonly, individuals say they chose to participate in the genocide after face-to-face solicitation, usually from an authority, an elite figure or a group of violent men.

The general pattern of mobilisation at the local level reported by respondents is that elites and young toughs formed a core of violence. They then traversed their communities, recruiting a large number of Hutu men to participate in manhunts of Tutsis or to participate in other forms of 'self-defence', such as manning roadblocks. The recruiting most often was done house to house, at markets or rural commercial centres, at rural bars, or at meetings called by local authorities. Radio, in short, was not the principal reason why men participated in violence; rather, mobilisation was locally organised and took place face to face. Those results are consistent with other extended, interview-based studies of genocide perpetrators in Rwanda. Researchers consistently find that face-to-face mobilisation and social ties were the primary vectors through which ordinary citizens joined the killings (Fujii, 2006; Mironko, 2006).

In the survey, respondents claimed that they participated in the violence for various reasons. The stated motivations included intra-ethnic coercion and intimidation, obedience, wartime fear, a desire for revenge, anger, a desire to loot or gain land, and interpersonal rivalries, among other factors. The two most commonly cited responses were intimidation from other Hutus – respondents said they feared negative consequences for themselves and their families if they refused to take part in the violence after being solicited to do so – and wartime fear and anger – they said they feared Tutsi rebels and wanted to attack their supposed ethnic supporters first or they said they were angry at the president's assassination and sought revenge. Asked to name the most important reason why they participated, not one respondent said radio broadcasts (though many claimed that they participated because 'the authorities' instructed them to). Asked to name the most important reason why the genocide took place, not one respondent cited radio broadcasts. Most blamed the genocide on the assassination of the president, which they attributed to the rebels.

Close-ended questions in the survey reveal much the same. The most direct question about radio media effects put to respondents was: 'Did the radio lead you to take part in the attacks?' About 85 per cent of respondents said 'no'; 15 per cent said 'yes' (N = 176). About 52 per cent of respondents said they owned a radio (N = 157). A subsample of these was asked what stations they listened to during or prior to the genocide. About 60 per cent did not cite RTLM; 34 per cent named RTLM and at least one other radio station; and 6 per cent said they listened to RTLM exclusively (N = 65). Cross-tabulated with age, the results about RTLM listening conform to expectation. The majority of RTLM listeners (exclusive or not) were 20–39 years old in 1994. As for education, RTLM listeners tended to have above-average education (which in the sample meant completion of primary school or greater).

Reception II: Qualitative analysis of perpetrator interviews

To probe the issue further, I examine the interviews qualitatively. I start with a typical example of face-to-face mobilisation in the survey. The respondent describes how national government officials travelled to his commune and held meetings, and then local officials instructed the population to attack Tutsis (questions put to the respondent are in italics):

> After the death of the president, the Hutu authorities thought that they would lose power. The high authorities of Kigali went to their home areas … [and] met the local authorities, notably the burgomasters [local officials] who had never before incited people to kill others …. Afterwards, our burgomaster changed his behavior and started to look for others to join him. He called a meeting of leaders from political parties and the local administration … *How did you become involved in these events?* I left to go and loot.[18]

Radio plays little evident role here. Rather, national elites fanned out to local areas to meet with local officials; the latter in turn mobilised citizens directly.

Another excerpt mentions the radio, but only as relaying information about the president's assassination and violence elsewhere in the country. As in the excerpt above, the respondent described how violence started after high authorities (in this case President Théodore Sindikubwabo) travelled to the region:

> After the crash of the president's plane, on April 7th we heard on the radio that in other regions the massacres started immediately. On April 19th, when Théodore came ... he met the leaders of the administration. After the meeting, these leaders of the administration told us that the Tutsis had to be killed as it was in other regions ... In a meeting by the *conseiller* [a local official], he told us, 'One must look for the *inyenzi* among us and put them to one side.' When we left the meeting, people began to burn Tutsi homes. Then one looted and took cows. The next day, roadblocks were erected to look for Tutsis.

As in the first excerpt, face-to-face mobilisation and coordination among officials precipitated the anti-Tutsi killing. National elites travelled to local areas to order the killing to start. Having initially opposed the violence, local officials in turn decided to join the programme. They then held meetings and instructed Hutus under their jurisdiction to attack Tutsis. Radio did not unleash the violence; meetings and direct mobilisation did. Rather, radio conveyed information and framed the context in which political action took place.

The two excerpts are representative of the dynamics most respondents described. Below is a series of different excerpts from respondents who, in the survey, answered negatively when asked if radio led them to participate in the genocide (again, interview questions are in italics):

> Radio is where we learned that the president died. But radio is not what led me to join. I went in order to obey the authorities.
> *Did the radio lead you to take arms?* No. *Why not?* I am not a politician. I was not part of the state. *So the broadcasts were for the authorities?* Yes.
> The radio did not lead me to take part in the attacks. It was the meetings.
> *Did the radio lead you to take arms?* No. If other people did not demand this of me, I would not have gone.
> I participated because all Rwandans had to participate ... to save his own life. Those who did not participate were considered enemies and the penalty was death.
> *Did the radio encourage you?* No, but it did for others. *Why do you say that?* Because after the radio said the enemy is such and such, it was then

that the leaders said that to the population and that is when the killings began.

We were people convinced the Tutsis would kill us. I would not say that RTLM encouraged us. To the contrary, it lied saying we were winning.

In these excerpts, the principal motivations to join attacks are coercion, compliance with authorities and wartime fear. Radio mattered, but according to the respondents, broadcasts were intended for the authorities; radio also shaped and encouraged elite actions.[19] In that sense, radio broadcasts served as a coordinating device and as a tool that strengthened the hand of the elites who advocated violence. But the broadcasts were not the reason why the respondents participated.

In contrast is a series of excerpts from respondents (again a significant minority) who claimed that radio did encourage them to commit violence. But the described dynamics of mobilisation are not altogether different from the excerpts above:

Yes, the radio encouraged this. *Did you listen and go out to attack?* No. We waited for the order from the authorities. We had to wait for the order from them. We knew them and they were closer.

Did the radio have an effect? Yes, the radio confirmed what the *responsable* [a local official] directed us to do.

Yes [the radio had an effect]. When we were in the fields and we heard that the enemy was the Tutsi and that came from the high authorities, we understood it was serious.

The radio encouraged people to participate because it said 'the enemy is the Tutsi'.

If the radio had not declared things, people would not have gone into the attacks. *What declarations?* There was a communiqué that came over the radio that said Habyarimana's plane was shot down by the RPF and that there was a combat between the FAR [the Rwandan government army] and the RPF and that the Tutsis were the enemy .... Leaders' ideas were on the radio.

The station that encouraged me was RTLM .... *Was there a specific broadcast?* There were songs about how Hutus had to rise up and fight for their country.

RTLM said the Tutsi is the enemy. That is where I heard the word '*inyenzi*'. They said you could not sleep: you had to look everywhere for the enemy.

In these accounts, respondents claim several radio media effects. Firstly, radio broadcasts communicated the intent and instructions of authorities. Secondly, radio broadcasts reinforced messages that authorities communicated in person. And thirdly, radio broadcasts framed the political crisis: broadcasts categorised Tutsis as 'the enemy' or as '*inyenzi*'. In these accounts – again a minority in the survey of 210 perpetrators – radio is not the only or even the primary cause of onset or mobilisation. Rather, radio broadcasts had more marginal and conditional effects. Radio communicated who had power, what 'authorities' supposedly wanted and how to think about the crisis.

An alternative model of media effects in the Rwandan genocide

The evidence presented above consistently contradicts the conventional wisdom. There appears to be a substantial gap between RTLM's broadcast range and where genocidal violence took place; there is little positive and much negative evidence that broadcast range corresponds to where violence started earliest in different regions; the bulk of violence appears to have occurred before the most inflammatory broadcasts aired; most perpetrators in a survey say face-to-face mobilisation, not radio, led them to join attacks; and, when asked, no respondent identified radio as the primary determinant of the genocide. Each piece of evidence has its limits. RTLM's range is not conclusively known; a full transcript record of RTLM broadcasts does not exist; convicted perpetrators may not tell the truth. But together, the evidence amounts to a persuasive refutation of the commonly held beliefs that radio had widespread, direct effects and that hate radio was the primary driver of the genocide and participation in it.

That said, the evidence suggests that radio had some marginal and conditional effects. RTLM broadcasts instigated certain attacks, particularly in and around the capital. Survey research shows statistically significant correlations between RTLM listening and holding racialist and negative views of Tutsis, on the one hand, and between radio incitement and higher levels of violence among perpetrators, on the other (results not reported here). From that, it might be deduced that RTLM at a minimum reinforced violence-supportive ideas and catalysed some key agents of violence. Qualitative analysis additionally shows that some genocide perpetrators believed that radio coordinated elites, signalled that authorities wanted the population to fight the enemy and reinforced local mobilisation for violence. In sum, then, the positive evidence of radio media effects is that radio instigated a limited number of acts of violence, reinforced racialist views, catalysed some key actors, coordinated elites, signalled power and belligerence, and bolstered local messages of violence. Based on these findings, it is plausible to hypothesise that in this specific context radio empowered those advocating violence and framed political action, which had the overall effect of helping the hardliners assert dominance. Radio media effects were not direct, undifferentiated or massive; rather, they were marginal yet important in consolidating an extremist position.

If radio was not the primary catalyst, how then did the Rwandan genocide happen – and happen so quickly? Answering this question is not the focus of this chapter. Nonetheless, field research conducted in Rwanda yielded three primary factors: an intense civil war following a presidential assassination, a state with strong local mobilisational capacity and a pronounced history of ethnic categorisation. The civil war had two principal effects. The war underpinned the logic of killing and violence, and created a sense of acute uncertainty and fear, which catalysed some and led others to be convinced to join the killing. Rwanda is a low-income country, but Rwanda's state is compact and dense at the local level, with multiple layers of administration. Rwanda additionally has entrenched practices of civilian labour mobilisation that date back to the pre-colonial era. State power in Rwanda thus bequeathed to those authorities and elites who promulgated violence the means to carry out the violence quickly and with widespread participation. Finally, there is the issue of ethnic categories: the logic of genocide was basically an equation between 'enemy' and 'Tutsis' – military officials and other influential hardliners encouraged the population to eliminate the Tutsi enemy, which became an extermination campaign. A condition for the success of such an order depended on the resonance and pre-existence of the Tutsi category – and, indeed, ethnicity has a long and pronounced political history in Rwanda, dating back to the colonial period. Hutus did not, in general, hate Tutsis before the genocide, but ethnic categories were meaningful and salient, especially in wartime.

The unfolding of the genocide was not mechanical. In early April, immediately after the president's assassination and the renewed onset of civil war, hardliners within the military and ruling political party engineered control of the central state. They set out to eliminate their immediate political rivals, Hutu and Tutsi alike, and proceeded to advocate or suggest violence against the Tutsi minority. They did so through military channels, through officials and hardliners fanning out to the countryside, and on occasion through calls on the radio for vigilance and citizen participation in the war. Once the violence started, it also had momentum. At the subnational level in rural areas, the crisis triggered different responses. In areas with strong support for the deceased president and ruling party, coalitions of local hardliners quickly formed and initiated violence against Tutsi civilians. In other areas, moderates sought to prevent violence from starting. Over time, however, in all areas not yet lost to the rebels, hardliners succeeded in undermining moderates, eventually consolidating control. Once they did, these hardliners – usually local authorities and violent young men – would mobilise a large number of ordinary Hutu citizens to commit violence. Communities in turn switched from a period of heightened anxiety and confusion due to the president's assassination and the resumption of civil war to a period of participatory and exterminatory violence.[20]

What role did radio play in this process? The primary means of communication and mobilisation was face-to-face solicitation. In rural areas, interpersonal mobilisation was made effective by a strong local state apparatus, dense human settlement and community norms of compliance (which were based on Rwanda's history of state power). To the extent that hate radio mattered, media had a second-order impact. In the capital, RTLM's broadcasting of names and locations of Tutsis, as well as its generally hostile tone, inspired attacks and were a factor in the hardliners' ability to assert dominance. But radio was not the only reason that Hutu hardliners advocating genocide won the upper hand. Most importantly, the hardliners controlled the balance of power among Hutus in the country; they controlled key military units and militia. Moreover, the civil war and the advance of the rebels undermined moderates and moderate calls for peace. By broadcasting a belligerent and jingoistic tone and catalysing acts of violence, RTLM signalled that hardliners had power and reinforced their messages. Locally, mobilisation ultimately was interpersonal and face to face. Most individuals chose to enter the violence because they were afraid of the consequences of disobeying or afraid of what a rebel victory meant. But in reinforcing the hardliners' positions, signalling who had power and setting a tone of war and belligerence, radio narrowed the choices individuals believed they had.

The conceptions of media effects hypothesised here – of empowering hardliners, reinforcing beliefs and framing public choice – point to real impacts. Hate radio constituted one dimension by which hardliners achieved dominance and persuaded individuals to join attacks against Tutsi civilians. But the conceptualised effects are more nuanced and conditional than the conventional wisdom would have. They emphasise the importance of context and they are embedded alongside discussion of the broader dynamics of mobilisation and violence. Moreover, the claims avoid what the chapter has shown to be the empirically untenable notion that radio media had widespread effects and were a primary determinant of violence. The claims are also consistent with cumulative findings in the political communications field, which stress agenda setting, elite persuasion and marginal media impacts. Hate radio mattered in Rwanda, but the dynamics of genocide are considerably more complex than the popular image of 'Radio Machete' suggests.

Endnotes

1 The chapter is a condensed version of an article previously published in 2007 in *Politics and Society*, 35(4):609–37.

2 See, for example, the films *Hotel Rwanda*, *Sometimes in April* and *Sleeping Dogs*, as well as the PBS documentaries *The Triumph of Evil* and *Ghosts of Rwanda*, and the 30 November 2006 *Sixty Minutes* show 'Rwandan genocide survivor recalls horror'.

3 See Metzl (1997) and US Department of Defense memos online at the National Security Archive, < http://www.gwu.edu/ ~ nsarchiv/NSAEBB/NSAEBB53/rw050594.pdf > .

4 These included Radio France International, the Voice of America, the British Broadcasting Corporation and Deutsche Welle.

5 The term is found throughout the ICTR Media Trial decision; see also ICTR (2003b).

6 For some additional examples, see Chrétien (2007); Chalk (2007:375); Orth (2006:221).

7 On the 'hypodermic needle', see Zaller (1992:311). On stimulus and response, see Perse (2001) and Bryant and Thompson (2002).

8 This is true even in a non-US setting. For examples, see Lawson and McCann (2005) and White, Oates and McAllister (2005).

9 On the latter point, see also Carver (2000).

10 A similar point is made in Kirschke (2000:239).

11 Two of the most important studies are good examples: the ICTR Media Trial judgment and Chrétien et al. (1995).

12 The broadcast is attributed to RTLM and was the basis for the title of a popular book on Africa: *The Graves Are Not Yet Full: Race, Tribe, and Power in the Heart of Africa* (Berkeley, 2001).

13 There is no record of the broadcast (Article 19, 1996:112) and the ICTR does not cite it.

14 Rwanda in 1994 had 67 radio receivers for every 1,000 inhabitants, making it the country with the eleventh-fewest per capita radio receivers in Africa, as reported in UNESCO (1996).

15 An exception is Mironko (2007:126).

16 See the 4 July 2001 testimony in the Media Trial at < http://www.hirondelle.org/hirondelle. nsf/0/54b248bce49a1b54c1256721007ae35c?OpenDocument > .

17 For greater details on onset dates in the data set and their sources, see Straus (2006:249–55).

18 A longer excerpt from the same interview, as well as a number of other interview transcripts, can be found in Lyons and Straus (2006:39–96).

19 This is consistent with Mironko's (2007) findings.

20 For a fuller elaboration of the argument, see Straus (2006).

6

Why Radio Is Africa's Medium of Choice in the Global Age

Winston Mano

Introduction

Radio has remained the top medium in Africa in the global era because of its ready adaptability to rapidly changing living conditions on the continent. It is much more important and more widespread than any other mass medium. In her paper on gender in radio, technology and development in Africa, Mary Myers (2009:13) makes a very interesting observation about how many researchers find it 'exciting to contemplate the possibilities for interactivity, information provision and advocacy offered by the Internet, email and mobile communications' and yet forget about the continued importance of radio in Africa. The migration to digital platforms will in fact strengthen the position and penetration of radio, as it will no 'longer be limited to linear and non-interactive transmission' (Berger, 2009:7). In the digital age, radio in Africa will be received on television, cellphones and other new devices, which will help cement its place as the continent's main mass medium.

The crucial point is that in many developing contexts, it is easily 'forgotten that radio access far outstrips computer and mobile phone access throughout the population of sub-Saharan Africa' (Myers, 2009:13). Radio listenership has consistently remained high. This is confirmed by feedback from male and female respondents who listened to radio the day before various surveys were taken in several African countries. For instance, a survey of five cities in Mozambique showed 73 per cent of male and 64 per cent of female respondents had listened to the radio the previous day. In Senegal, the male:female ratio of those who listened to the radio the previous day was 95:92; in Tanzania, 78:64; and in Uganda, 73:63 (Balancing Act, 2008, cited in Myers, 2009).

In Africa, radio's main advantage is its ability to overcome the main communication barriers on the continent: poverty, illiteracy and linguistic diversity. Radio is relatively more affordable than other media, and small, portable radio sets, mainly from Japan and China, have made radio more widespread. It can be listened to in many contexts. The case study in this chapter of a popular 'death notices' programme on Radio Zimbabwe (a public service station) and how it is received by its actual listeners offers clear evidence of how radio will remain the main medium in Africa for many years to come.[1] This can be seen in terms of what Berger (2009:7) sees as 'an age of people being receivers of mass information ... expanding into one where they are participants in mass communication'. This phenomenon, it is argued here, will not start with the adoption of new digital technologies, but rather will be deepened by it. The chapter shows clearly that radio in Africa has a close relationship with its listeners. It is the high level of participation by listeners that makes radio integral to and closely implicated in the processes of modernity and globalisation on the continent.

Radio in Africa is part of broadcasting systems inherited from colonial governments. Most publicly funded radio stations still enjoy monopoly status in return for national transmission, and also 'because they are supposed to be custodians of public service broadcasting, which indeed they sometimes are, in areas such as cultural programming' (Berger, 2009:8). Not much research has been done to illustrate such cultural programming. The chapter discusses how listeners in Zimbabwe have engaged with a 'death notices' programme. The research can be seen as part of the debate and controversy around the transfer of technology and products of the mass media, at various stages, from the industrialised countries of Europe and North America to developing countries in Asia, Africa and Latin Africa. For example, the mass media in developing countries are often seen as purveying a 'homogenised brand of popular culture' that is in the main 'either copied or borrowed from broadcasting in the West' (Katz & Wedell, 1978:vii). Such views, although valid in relation to particular media and in specific societies, are to an extent technologically deterministic because they neglect the fact that the history of media technologies shows that in most cases uptake is dependent on meeting the genuine social and cultural needs of the society into which media technology is introduced. In most cases, there is what the media historian Brian Winston (1998:8) calls a 'supervening social necessity' before any media technology is diffused in a particular society. The history of media technologies shows that they mainly develop in response to specific social and economic factors that may either accelerate or block their development. The primacy of human social needs in the development of technologies such as radio is an issue largely ignored in international communication debates about 'life in the South'. The overwhelming focus is on an inevitable adoption rather than a more selective and purposeful adoption based on social and other factors.

Radio particularly challenges the idea that Western technologies are merely implanted in an African continent that has no need for them. Graham Mytton, former head of the BBC World Service Audience Research Department and a researcher of mass communication in Africa, aptly reports how the rapid diffusion of the transistor radio in Africa challenges much of the thesis on the transfer of technologies. He argues:

> Here was an example of a technological innovation developed in the West, meeting one kind of demand there, being transferred very successfully to non-industrialised countries and becoming a very significant innovation there – making, perhaps, even more social, cultural and political impact than in the West from where it came (Mytton, 2000:25).

However, Mytton's point is not the common view of the role of radio in Africa. Boafo (1991) exemplifies the widespread perspective when he generalises about how foreign content is predominant in African radio and other mass media. Such a view unfortunately characterises African media mainly in terms of political propaganda and Western-produced entertainment:

> Opportunities for reaction and feedback through the centralised systems, from the many to the few, on national development policies, programmes, and other issues with significant implications and effects on their daily lives are minimal or non-existent in many instances. Thus the content of mass communication media in black African countries abounds in propaganda, demagogy, cheap entertainment, empty promises and far-fetched ideologies of dubious significance or relevance to individual or societal development ... Electronic media in black African countries allocate only a small proportion of their content to cultural programmes of relevance and value to the local environment (Boafo, 1991:116).

The uses of technologies and communication models adopted from Western countries in contexts other than those for which they were originally meant are seen in two rather contradictory ways. On the one hand, such mass media are seen as agents of 'modernisation insofar as the national sharing of images is concerned', while, on the other hand, the mass media are seen as 'destructive of indigenous political and cultural self-expression' (Katz & Wedell, 1978:vii). While I do not dispute the abuse of the media by political regimes, I believe some of the critiques overestimate the effects involved and rarely support their descriptions of the African mass media by empirical research. The current study is aware of the problems posed by such generalisations within cultural imperialism debates and international communication scholarship.

Research on the mass media in Africa also suffers from the influence of Katz and Wedell's analytical framework, which is mainly concerned with the extent to which the mass media 'may be seen as transferring or imposing imperialistic values' and are 'derivative from or imitative of those of the dominant capitalist societies' (Reeves, 1993:63). It is true that issues are raised by the way communication technologies are mainly acquired from Western Europe, Japan and North America or from other industrialised societies and used in the Third World, while the know-how, skills and capacity to manufacture them remain in the hands of the few in developed countries (Hamelink, 1986, cited in Boafo, 1991:110). After all, broadcasting was initially extended to developing countries mainly to serve a variety of colonial interests that included 'prestige and influence' (Hills, 2002:279).

I believe that international communication scholarship needs to research national and local contexts of everyday life and focus on specific mass media such as radio. It is imperative to engage with the specific contexts of everyday life if one is to unravel the complexities of international communication. The cultural imperialism debate must also start focusing on ordinary people rather than on the structural carriers of imperialism alone. Sreberny-Mohammadi (1997:51) insightfully advocates a return to the ordinary everyday-life issues that were introduced long ago by Raymond Williams, the prominent British social commentator:

> If Raymond Williams (1961) oriented us to the essential ordinariness, everydayness, of culture, then part of the function of a global cultural analysis is to identify the many ordinary, everyday ways that life in the South has been affected by the social structures of imperialism.

I conducted a study on national radio that identifies the connection between radio and real life in Zimbabwe. My study complements rather than opposes some of the work mentioned above. The findings partly answer Golding and Harris's (1997:5) call for scholarship that focuses on the radical, resistant and creative dynamics of human agency in the face of cultural imperialism.

From the point of view of this research, cultural and media imperialism analysts have yet to recognise the processes of and extent to which some of the previously Westernised communication models and media systems have been indigenised to serve local needs. For example, in Africa and Asia in particular, the British and

French models of broadcasting, and to a lesser extent print media and journalistic practices, have generally been indigenised. Reeves (1993:69) crucially suggests that

> ... such models underwent transformation after independence when conflicts between international and national forces, and internal social structural factors such as class relations, became decisive in the determination of state media and communications policies, and in media organisational change.

In the face of such indigenous transformation, there is a need to focus on what happens to those commodities and technologies produced and consumed in the specific contexts of different national societies. There is a need to spread the focus on the 'indigenised' mass media to deepen our understanding of specific media and their contexts. I suggest that studying the reception of national radio helps unpick the character and role of such indigenised media institutions in post-colonial societies.

In Africa and other developing areas, radio has more resonance with local life than other media. This is particularly true of television, which depends largely on programmes produced in Western countries. Radio is the dominant mass medium in most contexts and, as Reeves (1993:55) insightfully puts it, it is the medium 'most open to local programming. Receivers are relatively cheap and widely distributed, and more-or-less continuous programming can be maintained at a fraction of the cost of television programming and production'. The local content of radio and its technical simplicity are behind its high reception and widespread use on the continent. In her study of technological convergence and gendered use of radio in Africa, Myers (2009:13) sums up the main reason why radio is attractive particularly to women in terms of both its production and consumption:

> The beauty of radio for the female audience is that, as an affordable, portable, oral/aural medium, it overcomes many of the barriers posed by other ICTs. The advantage of radio for female producers and managers is its relative accessibility in terms of technical specifications and its affordability in terms of initial equipment investment.

Examples of how radio has practical relevance in Africa are provided by Myers, and these include Radio Mang'elete in Kenya, which, since its establishment in 2004, has helped rural women address problems with such things as water provision: 'This came about because the radio station publicised the fact that some local politicians were closing boreholes in the area so that they could sell water to the village from their own boreholes' (Myers, 2009:10). In western Uganda, Kigadi-kibaale Community Radio has helped its listeners deal with sensitive issues around domestic and sexual violence. In this case, the station manager, Mwalimu Musheshe, reported a 60 per cent reduction in domestic and gender-based violence as a result of programmes aired on the station (Musheshe, 2007, cited in Myers, 2009:10). These examples clearly show ways in which radio is an important medium in Africa.

Radio is part of popular cultural practices in the continent. As discussed above, it helps ordinary people question and challenge circumstances that oppress them. It makes them aware of their condition and allows them to fight back against oppressive authorities that ignore the popular will. Radio reflects battles from below, often by the poor for the poor, and in Africa can be seen as a means of alternative communication (Atton, 2002) that enables those at the margins to understand their situation and try to do something about it. 'Popular' has a dual reference here: it points to how radio is consumed by many people in huge numbers. The other reference is political and has to do with how radio creates spaces and offers an ability to speak against the 'power blocs' in society (Sparks, 1992:24). Citing Stuart Hall (1980), Fiske (1992) suggests that this opposition derives from the way in which public communication (news) has traditionally been produced and dominated by a 'power bloc', whereas popularity is the product of 'the people'. Popular culture comes, therefore, from below and differs from and challenges that which those in power wish the people to have, and in many ways this applies to radio in Africa.

In the continent, popular music serves as journalism in situations where public communication is constrained. It expresses the majority will when all other avenues seem to be closed. It is effectively journalism in the way that it sets the agenda for the people and in the way music texts meet with and generate new forms of knowledge among members of the audience. This awareness not only induces 'sceptical laughter', but it opens up to 'pleasures of disbelief, the pleasures of not being taken in' (Fiske, 1992:49). Popular culture makes the oppressed more aware of their circumstances, which is precisely the reason why those in positions of power campaign to have it controlled or banned. Although music texts are polysemic, it is important to note that the meanings that listeners derive from popular music depend at least in part on what musicians have actually 'written in the first place' (Sparks, 1992:37).

Radio Zimbabwe

Radio Zimbabwe is one of the four monopoly public service radio stations run by Zimbabwe Broadcasting Holdings, a parastatal that before 2005 was known as the Zimbabwe Broadcasting Corporation (ZBC).[2] At the time of writing (May 2010), the

Zimbabwe government, in spite of ongoing economic and political reforms, was maintaining a monopoly of the country's broadcasting sector. Radio has a high penetration in Zimbabwe, as shown by a 2006 study that reports up to 85.3 per cent of the population listening to radio in the previous 12 months (see Mukundu, 2006). A number of alternative and foreign-sponsored radio stations (Studio 7, Short Wave Radio Africa and Voice of the People) broadcast to Zimbabweans online and via short wave, but their reach is limited (Mukundu, 2006). Radio Zimbabwe dominates, and registers its largest share of listeners compared to any other radio station in Zimbabwe during the early afternoon shift (12:00 to 14:30). Throughout the week, the midday shift is most popular with all types of listeners. The share of midday adult listenership dramatically increases until it spectacularly peaks at 13:00 with the lunch-hour broadcast of *Kwaziso/Ukubingelelana* (a write-in greetings and music dedication programme), *Zviziviso Zverufu/Izaziso Zemfa* (death notices), *Nhau/Izindaba* (news) and weather reports. The audience rating figures show that Radio Zimbabwe garners more listeners between 12:00 and 16:00 p.m. than at any other time during the day. The chapter discusses the reception of *Zviziviso Zverufu/Izaziso Zemfa* as an example of why radio is so popular in Africa.

Methodology

The choice among different research methods should depend on what one is trying to find out (Silverman, 2000). Rather than coming to the research with fixed preferences, it is important that the topic being examined should influence the methods that one adopts to carry out the research. The current research project was interested in the production and consumption aspects of *Zviziviso Zverufu/Izaziso Zemfa* in the context of Zimbabwean everyday life. From 2000 to 2003 I sought to find out how the programme was produced and organised for listeners of different ages, speaking different languages and from different geographic regions. I chose the following sites:

- Harare, the country's capital city and largest area of varied chiShona speakers;
- Bulawayo, the second-largest city and bastion of isiNdebele speakers;
- Entumbane, a high-density suburb in Bulawayo;
- Ntabazinduna, a village on the outskirts of Bulawayo in Matabeleland;
- Tsanzaguru Growth Point, a peri-urban settlement near Mutare in Manicaland, a province with speakers of different dialects; and
- Beitbridge, on the border with South Africa, an area with Tshivenda speakers who experience poor reception of ZBC signals.

I also went to three regional sites from which ZBC broadcasts: Pockets Hill in Highlands, Mbare Studios in Harare and Montrose Studios in Bulawayo.

Although I interviewed over 50 people in Harare, the research analyses the responses of 20 interviewees: 13 men and 7 women. The 30 interviews I left out would have given my study an urban male bias and one that predominantly reflects views from Harare. I therefore analysed 20 interviews selected on the basis of being more factual, audible and responsive to my research questions. Bulawayo, Zimbabwe's second-largest city and home to isiNdebele speakers, is the commercial capital of the southern half of the country. It has very close geographic, cultural and commercial links with South Africa. At the time of the interviews, its urban population worked largely for the government and the commercial sector. Most businesses, including the ZBC, had regional offices in Bulawayo, but in most cases they were headquartered in Harare. My face-to-face interviews in Bulawayo took place in the busy work environments following appointments. I would have liked to have interviewed more people, but some of the potential respondents kept shifting their appointments. I managed six in-depth interviews with individuals from varied backgrounds: a broadcaster, two print journalists, an entrepreneur, a cadet and an apprentice, all aged between 22 and 36 years. I saw them as representing the young mobile population of Bulawayo that listens to radio both at home and at work. Some respondents from central Bulawayo wanted to be interviewed in English, although they still dropped isiNdebele phrases into the interview. My respondents allowed me to record the interviews with a tape recorder.

In Bulawayo's Entumbane suburb, I managed to hold a focus group meeting with the help of a local resident from the area. I carefully briefed him about the objectives of my study. The group had six isiNdebele-speaking listeners who were permanent residents of Entumbane, a high-density suburb in Bulawayo. The focus group was made up of three men and three women.[3] All the women were housewives (3); while one of the men was working for a private company (1), another was retired (1) and the last was a student (1). The ages of the participants ranged from 16 to 71 years. The female respondents were all housewives and neighbours of the Gwalala family, at whose house the meeting took place.

In Entumbane, discussion was in English, chiShona and isiNdebele[4] and took place in the shade of the Gwalala's house. It was a three-bedroomed house with a kitchen, a living room and all the modern conveniences: sofas, a fridge, a colour television, a fixed telephone and a big, oldish Tempest radio (I was told that another small radio was kept in the parents' bedroom). In the neighbourhood I could hear loud ZBC broadcasts echoing from one house to another. The group discussion took place at 14:00 on a hot afternoon.

Other interviews were held in the area on the outskirts of Bulawayo in rural Matabeleland. I went to the busy Ntabazinduna shopping centre on a Sunday when most villagers were at the service centre. There were grocery shops, grinding mills and butcheries, as well as a number of pubs, where most villagers came to shop or for recreation. There was loud music from both the beer hall and the pub, intended to attract villagers to either of the two establishments. I had not made any appointments, and the intention was to establish contacts before holding interviews with the respondents the next day. There were many people – young and old, men and women – sitting and talking in groups. I contacted individuals within these natural groups, via my two isiNdebele-speaking assistants, who knew the language and local norms. One of my assistants was from the area and the other from Entumbane. Some potential interviewees shied away, probably mistaking us for government operatives.

I also interviewed people in Manicaland, where the majority of people speak chiShona in the form of a distinct Manyika dialect. The Manyika dialect is different from the more dominant Zezuru dialect spoken in the Zvimba area in central Mashonaland (which, incidentally, is home to Robert Mugabe, the president of Zimbabwe). The standard chiShona employed by Radio Zimbabwe has more in common with Zezuru than with the Manyika dialect of chiShona. The tension surrounding the usage of dialects on Radio Zimbabwe was clear in the responses from this province. My respondents from Tsanzaguru, a Maungwe dialect area, were made up of five males and five females. Once again, it was a convenient sample of people who regularly listened to Radio Zimbabwe. I interviewed most of them in their living rooms, with Radio Zimbabwe playing in the background. (Members of the Indian and white communities living in Rusape informally told me that although they did not listen to Radio Zimbabwe, they were concerned with the level of political propaganda on national radio. They read independent newspapers and listened to alternative channels from outside the country. Indian Zimbabweans in Rusape complained about their lack of representation on national public radio. One couple wanted ZBC radio to introduce at least 'an hour a day of Indian music'.) My respondents from Tsanzaguru comprised employed and unemployed youths and adults, with ages ranging from 17 to 50 years. These included students, drivers, headmasters, secretaries and teachers.

The other key site for my interviews was Beitbridge, which received next to nothing in terms of signals from all ZBC broadcasting services. The settlement is on the border with South Africa. The residents share much in common with South Africans on the other side of the border, especially in terms of language and commercial activities. Beitbridge residents listen to South African radio, which is easily accessible. They were exempted from paying listeners' licence fees to ZBC.

I interviewed two groups of respondents. The first group was a natural focus group that I approached in a café at Dulibadzimu, Beitbridge's rundown high-density suburb with mud and pole structures. The discussion was spontaneous, but focused on Radio Zimbabwe and ZBC. The second was a focus group discussion with drivers, bus loaders, ticket checkers and unemployed people. I talked to them in one of the buses at the busy international bus terminus in the town. They had consented to being interviewed and recorded. All the respondents confirmed that they lived in the border town. Cassette music was playing in the bus as we discussed various aspects of listening to the radio in Beitbridge. The respondents were predominantly males whose ages ranged from 38 to 74 years. The second group talked freely, with some members dominating the discussion.

The study is also based on findings from structured questionnaires from a total of 120 out of a possible 200 students who completed a questionnaire on ZBC radio and on Radio Zimbabwe in particular. In Harare, 70 students from four secondary schools completed a structured questionnaire. The students were from Mt Pleasant, Morgan and Highfields High Schools. Fifty students at Tsanzaguru Secondary School in Rusape, Manicaland, completed the same questionnaire. The two-page questionnaire had 18 open- and closed-ended questions. The qualitative explanations provided vital clues about attitudes to ZBC national radio stations. The questionnaire findings shed light on how and when the youths listen to radio.

It is important to realise that study sites or samples can be selected on the grounds that they are critical, 'in that they are different and their examination would not only illuminate the dynamics that inform those differences, but also heighten a sensitivity towards what is taken to be "normal" in other cases' (May, 2000:173). My samples and selections were driven by the need to answer the study research questions. On the reception side, I chose methods that helped me unpick the various types of views, perceptions, mediated experiences and interactions resulting from involvement with the death notices programme. In terms of its design, the research closely matches the qualitative case study approach, which involves different methods: individual interviews, textual analysis, focus group interviews, participant observation and content analysis. These methods were divided between those examining the production aspects and those investigating reception aspects of *Zviziviso Zverufu/Izaziso Zemfa*.

My focus on radio production aspects was meant to serve two main purposes. Firstly, I discovered that it was important for me to understand the history and structure of *Zviziviso Zverufu/Izaziso Zemfa* before conducting interviews with some of Radio Zimbabwe's broadcasters and listeners. Interviews were more meaningful after I had gathered key data about the programme. Secondly, I was concerned with projecting Radio Zimbabwe listeners as individuals with unlimited creativity in their interpretations of the station's output. As Kitzinger (1999:20) reminds us, in audience studies it is 'vital to maintain concern with media "impact", besides being attentive to the ways in which people engage with, criticise, use and resist media messages. Attention to the latter should not prevent us from acknowledging media power'. I believe Radio Zimbabwe could influence listeners, particularly on political matters. After all, advertisers would not spend money on the station were it not able to do this. I therefore sought to portray how individuals negotiated radio production strategies in their day-to-day lives. I did not want to portray individuals as dupes without the ability to question what they receive. My objective therefore was to critically evaluate the dynamic relationship between a public-service radio programme and its national listeners.

Death notices on air: *Zviziviso Zverufu/Izaziso Zemfa*

The programme *Zviziviso Zverufu/Izaziso Zemfa* (death notices) was broadcast between 12:50 and 13:00 every day, and in two other slots later in the day (see below). Timothy Makoni, who later became the manager of Radio Zimbabwe, introduced the 'death notices' programme in 1981:

> It is an idea I stole from Zambia broadcasting. The then-ZBC head of marketing resisted the idea. He, however, eventually agreed to try it. Initially the responses were low. Mr Mutsinze, a bilingual presenter, mischievously one day announced that 'there is nothing from Bulawayo. Does this mean people are not dying there?' But the programme is now one of our most successful and longest running programmes, with 25 minutes per day. It is enjoying more and more airtime.[5]

The death notices programme was offered as a free public service to all Radio Zimbabwe listeners so that they could inform friends and relatives about the deaths of members of their families. The broadcast was especially targeted at close relatives and friends of a dead person.[6] Most messages to *Zviziviso Zverufu/Izaziso Zemfa* include a general notice directed to 'all friends and relatives' of the departed, especially workmates, former schoolmates, neighbours and whoever knew the dead person. The notice specified when and where the deceased person was to be buried.

Prohibitive transport costs and the likelihood of reaching most if not all of the relatives and friends of the departed meant that *Zviziviso Zverufu/Izaziso Zemfa* was a relatively quicker, cheaper and more efficient option than others. Telephones and newspaper advertisements do not match radio's instantaneous wide reach. A Radio Zimbabwe employee responsible for compiling the death notices told me how listeners to other ZBC radio stations come to place notices on the programme: 'What is strange about such listeners is that they only come to recognise the significance of Radio Zimbabwe at the time of their bereavement.'[7]

The death notices programme was so popular that the producers could not cope with the number of notices. During his tenure as manager of Radio Zimbabwe, Makoni designed a number of strategies to cope with the rising demand for the service, as it increasingly became impossible to include all the death notices that the programme was receiving:

> We have come up with a strategy where we only accept notices of people not yet buried. If we broadcast all the notices, we would spend half a day. It is also run on [a] first-come-first-served basis. We have stretched ourselves. We started with five minutes, and then ten minutes and now we have added three more slots. However, members of staff can broadcast notices outside the stipulated hours.[8]

The afternoon death notices programme had a huge listenership, as it was sandwiched between other popular programmes at a time when Zimbabweans were taking a break. A good example is when a relative of mine learned about the death of her maternal grandmother through the programme while she was a teacher at a remote rural primary school in the Marange district of Manicaland. On the afternoon in question, she was queuing in a rural retail shop where a receiver was tuned to Radio Zimbabwe while the popular *Kwaziso/Ukubingelelana*, the afternoon greetings and music dedication programme, was being aired. At 12:50, after the end of the first segment of *Kwaziso/Ukubingelelana*, came *Zviziviso Zverufu/Izaziso Zemfa*. It so happened that the first notice came from a close relative of hers informing others and herself about the death of their maternal grandmother in Mashonaland East. She remembered breaking down in tears inside the shop. She never purchased the refreshments and before the end of that day she was on her way to the funeral in Goromonzi.

Zviziviso Zverufu/Izaziso Zemfa was described as significant in the life of most of the respondents in Harare, Bulawayo, Rusape and Ntabazinduna. One adult male respondent said: 'I once went to some commercial farms where I saw how important the programme is. Out there, there are no phones or newspapers. The farm workers take breaks to enable them to listen to *Zviziviso Zverufu*.'[9] A 20-year-old gardener living and working in Harare's posh Mount Peasant suburb said: '*Zviziviso Zverufu* provides important information. In fact, one can know if and when relatives have died through that programme.'[10] People wrote and phoned in or visited the broadcasting centre to place the death notices. Depending on the number of notices received for the programme on a given day, the notices are broadcast up to three times daily, at 12:50, 18:50 and 22:10 for ten minutes before the main news slots.

In Matabeleland, both urban and rural respondents described *Izaziso Zemfa* (the isiNdebele version of the programme) as very useful. A 30-year-old Bulawayo entrepreneur described the programme as an efficient way of 'rounding up relatives when death occurs within families', while a 33-year-old housewife thought that *Izaziso Zemfa*

> ... is a good programme because at times you may not be aware that your relative has passed away. You then hear of it on radio. I think it is a good programme. Since people live away from others, they can only hear about a death if it is announced on radio. It is more effective to use the radio, as it takes long to send (death) messages by letter.[11]

Respondents from Entumbane in Bulawayo had a very high regard for *Izaziso Zemfa*. Owing to intermarriages and work placements, most of them had relatives living outside Bulawayo or Matabeleland and hence found the programme key to their daily lives. For a 51-year-old housewife who had married into an Ndebele family, the death notices programme kept her abreast of news about the death of her Shona relatives. One respondent added:

> People are entitled to their negative views about the programme, but I insist that the programme is very useful. We should not feel uncomfortable with such programmes because life revolves around life and death. Even as we live on a daily basis we are waiting for the day we will die. So it is important for people to be informed about their dead relatives.[12]

There was widespread consensus that *Izaziso Zemfa* provided crucial information about death in modern-day Zimbabwe.

A key feature of *Izaziso Zemfa* was that it conveyed the death messages to its listeners in an impromptu manner – one that was remarkably different from the more measured traditional way. The Entumbane respondents did not mind the directness and the immediacy with which the death notices were delivered. There was a belief that bad things would happen to anyone who remained ignorant of the death of a loved one. It was therefore preferable to be informed about the death in an impromptu way rather than risk experiencing these bad things:

I don't have any problems with that. For example, people like us have got relatives in places like Harare. It might take a long time before you hear that your relative has passed away. Of course, we panic and possibly collapse, but as soon as I regain my consciousness I go to attend the funeral, unlike in a situation where I don't even know that one of my relatives has passed. In our Shona [and Ndebele] culture a lot of mysterious things might occur because you have not been informed about the death of your relative, so it is not bad to promptly hear about it on radio so that you [can] arrange to attend the funeral in time.[13]

The above extract from the Entumbane discussion group generally illustrates the usefulness of and high regard for *Izaziso Zemfa* in the life of the participants, most of whom find it useful owing to the fact that they now live separately from members of their immediate and extended families in modern Zimbabwe.

Conclusion

The research was conducted at a time of intense political and economic challenges in Zimbabwe. The authority of Robert Mugabe, the long-time ruler of Zimbabwe (since 1980), and his Zimbabwe African National Union-Patriotic Front (ZANU-PF) supporters was under fierce challenge from Morgan Tsvangirai's worker-based Movement for Democratic Change (MDC), which was formed in 1999. The resultant infrastructural problems meant that the death notices programme was much more useful for families in Zimbabwe. Even after an MDC–ZANU-PF coalition government was formed in February 2009, the economic challenges Zimbabweans face have continued to make the death notices programme relevant.

The findings clearly show that the death notices programme is one of the key programmes on Radio Zimbabwe that continues to attract listeners to the station. Through it, Radio Zimbabwe presents radio that is of 'national origin' (Mytton, 1983:135). In their call for a shift towards 'de-Westernizing media studies', Curran and Park (2000:11–12) hold

… a suspicion that perhaps nations are still centrally important, and that their continuing significance tends to be underplayed by globalisation theory …. But perhaps the key point to emphasise is that media systems are shaped not merely by national regulatory regimes and national audience preferences, but by a complex ensemble of social relations that have taken shape in national contexts.

My case study shows that the centrality of the national radio content is clearly more than a 'suspicion'. My findings show how national listeners were central to the production and consumption of *Zviziviso Zverufu/Izaziso Zemfa*. The popularity of such a radio programme derives from what Barnard (2000:17) describes as the ability of radio to tap into the cultural fabric of the society to which it broadcasts. National radio organises and is itself organised by particular habits of national life (Ellis, 2000:25). *Zviziviso Zverufu/Izaziso Zemfa* and its reception revealed important dimensions of national everyday life.

I believe my analysis of *Zviziviso Zverufu/Izaziso Zemfa* and its reception was also important in terms of what Nyamnjoh (1999:34) describes as an 'African text conceived and written in accordance with a cultural perspective in tune with the African experience'. The African text in the contemporary post-colonial framework is informed by the lived experiences of African people, and I believe that radio in indigenous languages mediates this African text in a special way, providing a public service that many in Africa appreciate on a daily basis.

Endnotes

1   The evidence on which the chapter draws is drawn from my PhD study, 'African National Radio and Everyday Life: A Study of Radio Zimbabwe and Its Listeners', University of Westminster, 2004.

2   Despite the name change to Zimbabwe Broadcasting Holdings, the station is still popularly known as the ZBC, and it is to this that the chapter will refer.

3   I found it difficult to exclude family members from the focus group because they all wanted to take part in the discussion.

4   Although we agreed to have the discussion in isiNdebele, some of the participants talked in chiShona and English, showing their versatility with Zimbabwean languages.

5   Interview with Timothy Makoni, ZBC Mbare Studios, Harare, 30 August 2001.

6   Funerals in Zimbabwe are community events freely attended by anyone who wants to. They are public events, sometimes attracting thousands of people, who make financial and logistical contributions.

7   Interview with Radio Zimbabwe employee, ZBC Mbare Studios, Harare, 30 August 2001.

8   Interview with Makoni.

9   Interview, Harare, 18 July 2001.

10 Interview, Harare, July 2001.

11 Interview, Ntabazinduna, 23 December 2001.

12 Entumbane focus group, 2001.

13 Ibid.

7

Bantustan Identity, Censorship and Subversion on Northern Sotho Radio under Apartheid, 1960s–80s

Sekibakiba Peter Lekgoathi

Broadcasting ... is used for government propaganda purposes. It is a battle for the minds of the people. Control of [the] dissemination of information was the main reason behind the formation of black radio, more especially control of political information ... There was on radio some covert ways of disseminating information, especially through news bulletins.[1]

Verwoerd's messages of apartheid were transmitted to the masses of our people through radio .... But some announcers resisted because they did not want to be parrots.[2]

Introduction

The South African Broadcasting Corporation (SABC) launched Radio Bantu as a fully fledged radio station early in 1960. Targeted specifically at African listeners, this radio service was made available in different African languages. It was intended to serve as the propaganda machinery of the National Party government, i.e. as a platform to propagate and justify its policies of separate development or apartheid. In an effort to legitimise the vernacular radio service and make it more appealing to the African public, the SABC employed black announcers, but kept them on a short leash so as to have control over their utterances. Censorship on radio and the particular relationship that developed under apartheid between the SABC management and black announcers remain grossly under-researched topics.

Only a handful of notable studies have looked at the various aspects of black radio that have an important bearing on questions of censorship (Phelan, 1987; Tomaselli, Tomaselli & Muller, 1989; Nixon, 1994; Gunner, 2000a; 2000b; 2002; 2005; 2006).

This chapter adds to this literature by exploring Northern Sotho radio and using it as a window to view some aspects of the history of Radio Bantu as a whole. Based primarily on interviews that I conducted with former radio announcers in 2006 and 2007, plus a handful of archival documents and interviews stored in the SABC's sound archives, I focus on programming – particularly the news and editorial comments – as a critical site of contestation between the SABC management and some of the black radio presenters (referred to as 'announcers' by the SABC[3]) over the shaping of black public opinion under apartheid. I explore the surveillance mechanisms employed by SABC management to pre-empt and deal with possible subversion, as well as strategies utilised by a tiny fraction of the announcers to subvert such censorship. In short, the chapter highlights the more ambiguous position of the announcers, operating in one sense as pioneers of the new medium and path breakers of new language use in a new medium, but at the same time being almost prisoners in the oppressive apartheid system.

The chapter makes a twofold argument. The first is that vernacular radio was a powerful medium used effectively by the apartheid state to disseminate and popularise the Bantustan ideology through the medium of African languages. This ideology involved fostering the major African ethnic identities (Zulu, Xhosa, North and South Sotho, Tswana, etc.) in order to form separate ethnic 'nations' demarcated within their own clearly defined territories with distinct cultural practices and even bureaucracies. Radio broadcasting in apartheid South Africa was monopolised by the state and used as the ruling party's propaganda tool, just like in many other independent African countries (e.g. Kenya, Zambia and Nigeria). However, unlike its usage in post-colonial Africa as a tool for nation building, vernacular radio was used to reinforce ethnic separatism in apartheid South Africa. The second argument is that the exclusively white, male SABC management, out of fear of subversion, tried to maintain tight control by policing the translation of news and editorial comment programmes into Northern Sotho and keeping a tight hold over black employees, especially the announcers. A tiny fraction of announcers, however, refused to lie down and proved adept at skilfully sneaking in subversive information through 'the thicket of the medium of language', to borrow from Liz Gunner (2000a; 2000b), or at using 'weapons of the weak', to adapt James C. Scott's (1985) notion of everyday forms of resistance.

Vernacular radio and Bantustan identity: Northern Sotho Radio, 1960–80s

The story of the establishment of African-language radio on a small scale in the 1940s and of full-scale separate ethnic radio stations (Radio Bantu) in the 1960s has been explored elsewhere (Rosenthal, 1974; Theunissen, Nikitin & Pillay, 1996:5, 18; Gunner, 2000a; 2000b; 2002; 2005; 2006; Lekgoathi, 2009; Mhlambi, 2009) and will thus not be rehashed here. This section will briefly discuss the reasons why African-language radio was extended in the 1960s, before exploring more fully the history of Northern Sotho radio.

Ideological imperatives were undoubtedly paramount in the creation of Radio Bantu. This was made clear by the director-general of Radio Bantu services, Carl Fuchs, who stated that

> Radio Bantu was introduced to serve the seven Bantu peoples of the country, according to the nature, needs and character of each, and, by encouraging language consciousness among each of the Bantu peoples, to strengthen national consciousness' (cited in Tomaselli, Tomaselli & Muller, 1989:95).

This statement must be seen against the background of the apartheid policy, which emphasised not only the separation of South Africans by race, but also the division of Africans by ethnicity. The former announcers of Northern Sotho radio that I interviewed spoke at length about this form of 'divide and rule'. Justice Tshungu, former principal radio announcer, station manager and one of the pioneering staff members of the Northern Sotho section of Radio Bantu, attributes the establishment of vernacular radio to the then-prime minister of the country, Hendrik F. Verwoerd, in consultation with key members of his 'brain trust', among them his right-hand man, Dr W. M. M. Eiselen. In Tshungu's own words:

> Dr Hendrik Verwoerd, the architect of apartheid, founded Radio Bantu, not because he loved Africans, but because he saw radio as an important instrument in achieving the goal of separate development ... Radio was one of the three things that Verwoerd initiated. The first was a vernacular newsletter called *Tšwelopele*. Then he came up with bioscope or film, the idea being to control the minds of black people. The third and by far the most important was radio. Radio Bantu was very important for the government because it was speaking face to face with its audiences.[4]

Radio could most effectively reach a larger audience, including listeners in remote rural villages, most of whom were illiterate, in a way that newspapers and films could not. It was also an immediate medium of communication. For a government that was facing popular opposition to its policies, radio's immediacy (its nearness, closeness and directness) was crucial. The government sought to fully utilise vernacular radio to broaden support for its political project. Virtually all of my interviewees strongly emphasised that Radio Bantu was introduced to serve the government's propaganda purposes. As Valerie Aphane, one of the first female announcers of the Northern Sotho service, so succinctly put it: 'The government decided to create black radio so that black people could access its information in their own languages … Radio Bantu was a form of divide and rule.'[5] Similarly, Solly Kgamedi, another former announcer, stressed that the government's intention was 'to conquer the minds of Africans using the medium of radio in their own languages'.[6] Maje Serudu, a retired professor of African languages at the University of South Africa and a former announcer, was more elaborate:

> Basically, Radio Bantu was established to be a sort of government's propaganda machinery in the country, to disseminate government information to the people. That was the basic thing, because it started off for specific languages, or for specific groups … It started off being a Tswana radio, Pedi or Northern Sotho radio, Zulu radio and so forth, which was in line with the government policy of separate development. I think that is how it started in order to reach all Africans in their own languages.[7]

The apartheid state had become aware that in the context of heightened political opposition against its policies, state hegemony could not be maintained by brute force alone, but that the battle also needed to be waged on the ideological front. There was a need to replace repression with expression. It was fully aware of the important role that the mass media, especially radio, could play in shaping public opinion. The most distinctive advantage of radio was its ability to reach, through the medium of African languages, even the most illiterate African adults in the remote parts of the country.

The introduction of vernacular radio where in most cases none existed before, and the availability of seemingly useful and relevant programmes in the languages that most people spoke struck a resonating chord that went beyond the sort of control envisaged by separate development. It created listening publics drawn from different social classes and regions, the literate and the illiterate, townspeople and rural dwellers, all actively drawn to the new medium in their language – what Michael Warner (2002:60–61) calls 'a public constituted through mere attention', or a public that exists 'only by virtue of address'. As the chapter will show a little later, it was at the level of address that the black announcers had some degree of agency.

Turning now to the history of Northern Sotho radio, which today goes by the name of Thobela FM, its establishment cannot be divorced from the making of the mother station, i.e. Radio Bantu. Northern Sotho radio was first established at Broadcast House on Commissioner Street in Johannesburg on 1 June 1960, five months after the inauguration of Radio Bantu on 1 January. It was added to the three other major African-language services already in existence, namely isiZulu, isiXhosa and Sesotho services (Theunissen, Nikitin & Pillay, 1996:80). In 1962 the first rediffused high frequency modulation (FM) system was introduced, extending both medium-wave broadcasts and the existing services. Consequently, Northern Sotho radio was transferred from Johannesburg to the new SABC broadcasting studios on Minnaar Street in Pretoria, where it became a fully grown station on 1 June 1962.[8] In the same year, Setswana radio was added to it (Engelbrecht, 1962:495).

In its 50 years of existence, Northern Sotho radio has changed its name three times. Initially it was called the Northern Sotho Service of Radio Bantu. With its relocation to the SABC's regional centre in Polokwane in 1976 it was given the new name of Radio Lebowa, a linguistic 'home' to the Northern Sotho-/Sepedi-speaking people in the northern parts of South Africa. On the surface, both the transfer and the naming of the station after the 'homeland' of Lebowa might seem to suggest that control was now vested in the hands of the Bantustan political elite. In reality, however, the station remained tightly controlled by the SABC headquarters in Auckland Park. The relocation stemmed from the policy of decentralisation, which was about bringing the African-language stations closer to their audiences in different regions while retaining control at the centre. After the scrapping of the apartheid laws, the station finally became Thobela FM in 1996 (Theunissen, Nikitin & Pillay, 1996:80).[9]

The name 'Thobela' derives from a Northern Sotho proverb '*Šako la hloka thobela ke mojano*', which means that a community without proper leadership ('*thobela*' means chief, the ultimate authority in traditional African society) descends into self-destruction. This is a full-spectrum radio station that, according to the latest Radio Audience Measurement Survey of June 2009, has an average of 2 989 000 (i.e. nearly three million) listeners per day.[10] Its broadcasting language is Northern Sotho and it targets listeners that look to radio for music, information, education and entertainment. However, it has become a norm for younger presenters to switch from the vernacular to English with greater frequency, a practice that, while appealing to younger listeners, tends to alienate elderly audience members. Thobela FM currently broadcasts to the provinces of Limpopo, Gauteng and Mpumalanga, but it can also be accessed in parts of North West Province.

To conclude this part of the chapter, Northern Sotho radio was among the first language services to be established during the expansion phase of the SABC's African-language radio service in the early 1960s. This expansion was a response to the upsurge of political activism in African communities in towns and the countryside in the previous decade. The mass demonstrations of the ANC-led Defiance Campaign in the urban areas against a series of apartheid laws that were rapidly passed in the early 1950s (e.g. the Bantu Authorities Act, the Separate Amenities Act and the Pass Laws) and the negative media publicity they triggered had alerted the government to its serious limitations in the sphere of communication. The apartheid state was not as yet in possession of effective tools to control the dissemination of information. The homeland system being conceptualised at the time needed an effective tool of popularisation and a medium through which to disseminate its own views among African communities. The state had become convinced that a more sustainable approach to influencing public opinion was through expression, not repression; through propaganda, not only through censorship. The answer was vernacular radio, to be used to inform listeners of national and international developments, albeit from a conservative perspective (SABC, 1961:6).

'Motheeletši, theeletša ka tsebe tše tharo': Censorship, translation and subversion on Northern Sotho radio

Radio Bantu's mandate was the promotion of the government's perspectives. Towards this end, the SABC's Bantu Programme Control Board – the body responsible, among other things, for recruiting staff – had to carefully select the right type of announcer for the new positions in the radio stations. It was discovered that during the 1950s some black announcers had used the rediffusion service (predecessor to Radio Bantu) subversively as a channel for anti-government propaganda (Tomaselli, Tomaselli & Muller, 1989:94–95). Justice Tshungu – who called himself and was addressed affectionately by his listeners as 'malome'atšona', meaning 'senior uncle' – remembers the two announcers, Stanley Mtshali and Stanley Nkosi, who were deeply involved in black politics at the time. They once played the song 'Hlanganani mawethu' on radio, a song that called on Africans to unite, thus directly turning the apartheid message of ethnic division on its head. 'This really disturbed the Boers', he recalls, 'and the two men were expelled from radio allegedly because they were "communists"' (SABC Sound Archive, 2001). They were blacklisted and this brought major hardships for them as they could not get employment in teaching, office work or the few other areas open to black professionals under apartheid.

SABC management thus made an example of them. Although Nkosi eventually got his job back, he was barred from the broadcasting studio (SABC Sound Archive, 2001). Thus, to avoid similar forms of sedition from the 1960s, the Control Board made it its business to try to weed out politically minded people and to employ only those who seemed compliant and willing to parrot instructions from above.

Serudu, who was a Northern Sotho radio announcer from 1966 to 1973 (and for three months in 1975), has vivid memories of the SABC's selection process. Once suitable candidates had passed through the rigorous interview process involving a practical broadcasting component, they still had to go to the office of State Intelligence for screening and to check

> ... whether you are not politically active and if you are also ready to sell out ... Then after they have appointed you they would send another detective to you. He would come there and say: 'Do you think you could work for us?' And then if you were a weakling then you would say 'okay'. But we were so politicised that if a person said that, it was an insult to me, to say that I must become a pimp. I couldn't allow that. I was too politicised to fall for that.[11]

The method of involving the Special Branch detectives and State Intelligence in vetting prospective employees was in place well into the 1970s.[12] Hlajwe Mahlase, former radio announcer, remembers being followed around by an unmarked Special Branch police vehicle just prior to his appointment in 1975: 'When you were applying for a job on radio and got shortlisted, you had to be investigated for possible involvement in politics.'[13] This method of screening prospective employees seems to have been gradually phased out, so that by the 1980s none of the former or present announcers that I interviewed had to undergo this intrusive procedure.

For most of the apartheid era, it was not a prerequisite that vernacular radio announcers be in possession of media qualifications. The basic requirements were a Standard 8 certificate plus a three-year teacher's diploma (Bantu, 1961:151). This perhaps explains the dominance of former teachers in radio broadcasting. But the board's preferences may also have been influenced by teachers' strong attachment to petite bourgeois notions of politically neutral professionalism, which manifested in their overwhelming affiliation to moderate teachers' associations that pledged to work collaboratively with the authorities.[14] In any case, it was a primary consideration that the prospective employees should belong to or identify with the ethnic group for which the radio station had been established.

The vast proportion of announcers who joined Northern Sotho radio in the 1960s had previously been associated with Botšhabelo, the educational institution run by the Berlin (Lutheran) Missionary Society school and training institute in Middelburg (in today's Mpumalanga Province). A small proportion of broadcasters were members of the Dutch Reformed Church, which was the church of the state. The Berlin Missionary Society was renowned firstly for its emphasis on the use of local languages in converting Africans to Christianity and for turning the spoken Northern Sotho into a written language. Secondly, like the Dutch Reformed Church, it was very conservative and authoritarian, and radical student politics – a phenomenon largely associated with Anglican or Methodist mission schools in the country – had a minimal impact on Lutheran schools. If anything, Lutheran missionaries were known to be quite sympathetic to the National Party's separatist policies.[15] It was not by accident, therefore, that the Broederbond-dominated[16] SABC would select and employ mostly individuals who professed to be Lutherans or Dutch Reformed Church-goers, as it was assumed that they would be less likely to challenge the authority of the state. With respect to individuals from Botšhabelo specifically, the SABC Board possibly assumed that they would also share a common interest with government in seeking to develop the Northern Sotho language.

One of the products of Botšhabelo was Justice Tshungu. Like K. E. Masinga of Radio Zulu (Gunner, 2000b:224), Tshungu was clearly a very complex figure, considered by some as a pioneer and by others as a sell-out. He had been the principal of a local school in Heidelberg, east of Johannesburg, before Radio Bantu was established. His move to radio followed the broad trajectory taken by many black radio personalities from teaching, through radio and finally to television.[17] He was an avid advocate of more public recognition of Northern Sotho and his letters were regularly published in Afrikaans newspapers 'asking if the Northern Sotho people could also have their own mouthpiece' (SABC Sound Archive, 1980). This made it easy for the SABC to identify him as an ideal, safe and pliable leader in the formation of the Northern Sotho service of Radio Bantu. Teens van Heerden, then-director of Black Services of SABC radio and former Botšhabelo teacher, handpicked Tshungu seemingly because he knew him well. Tshungu attributes his selection to his impeccable Afrikaans language skills, his work ethic and a cooperative demeanour (SABC Sound Archive, 2001). He recalls receiving a call from Douglas Fuchs, director of radio programmes at the SABC in Johannesburg, and being told:

> You are now going back to your people. We have selected you to build a Northern Sotho nation, which will be proud of its nationality and in this way build one culture. We want you to be totally committed to this endeavour .... If you are uncertain about this step, don't come back here and without you we would rather not have Northern Sotho radio (SABC Sound Archive, 1980).

Always willing to go beyond the call of duty and publicly declaring his commitment to the cause of the Northern Sotho 'nation', Tshungu was amply rewarded for his loyalty and service by being appointed principal radio announcer and representative of black radio. Until his retirement, he was one of the most highly esteemed and popular black announcers.[18]

If we return to the 1960s, the establishment of Northern Sotho radio triggered a flurry of applications from mostly teachers in their quest for greener pastures, as well as for the glamour and novelty of radio. Radio had a reputation for paying better salaries than the teaching profession, with the average announcer earning a monthly income twice or three times the normal teacher's salary (Tshungu, 2006; Nokaneng, 2007; Serudu, 2007).[19] Radio offered members of the new educated black elite a rare opportunity to climb up the socio-economic ladder outside of teaching, nursing or the priesthood (SABC Sound Archive, 1980). Many remember a substantial improvement in their quality of life the moment they started working on radio because of better remuneration by the SABC. Perhaps this was incentive enough to keep many presenters acquiescent to apartheid, even though they may have felt seriously at odds with their occupation. Tshungu notes that 'radio improved the lives of the presenters', putting them securely into the middle class.[20]

All through the 1960s and 1970s, the SABC's Bantu Programme Control Board saw programming as critical for shaping public opinion and thus asserted maximum control in that arena. The news and editorial comment broadcasts were heavily censored in an effort to exercise the utmost control. As another informant reiterated, 'news was used to brainwash or channel black people'.[21] News bulletins were compiled and screened centrally at the SABC headquarters in Johannesburg before being sent to the regional stations via fax or telegraph (SABC Sound Archive, 2001).[22] The original transcript of the news was in either English or Afrikaans (albeit mostly in the latter), and the announcers had to translate and type the bulletin into Northern Sotho. According to Rudolph Letsoalo, at present a sports commentator on Thobela FM, a carbon paper was used to produce a copy for the white controller and sometimes the news had to be read to him about ten minutes before going on air.[23]

Controllers were whites employed to police the black announcers in the translation particularly of news bulletins. Only those with some knowledge of local African languages were employed. My informants are adamant that formal training in those languages was not a prerequisite for white controllers. Similar to Khaya Gqibitole's (2002:34) findings on Xhosa radio, these were mainly Afrikaner men who grew up around Africans on rural farms and so could understand local languages. Many supported apartheid and 'were there to perform a surveillance function'.[24] Their responsibilities included comparing the translations with the original scripts, scrutinising them for any form of subversion and deleting inconsistencies before the news could go on air.[25] A controller would sit in the control box adjoining the studio monitoring the announcer's utterances, noting any slippages in his report book (*Bantu*, 1961:151).[26]

Even in the most authoritarian regimes, however, individuals did not completely lose their agency and resourcefulness. On Northern Sotho radio, creative responses to authoritarianism manifested themselves in various forms. The first form involved the use of idioms and metaphors by African announcers as a way of challenging the white officials' control over the programme content. For example, several of my interviewees recall Alfred Jack Rasebotsa, one of the pioneering newscasters and a former interpreter in the Department of Native Affairs, who often disregarded the injunction not to use proverbs. He once translated an Afrikaans news bulletin about the outbreak of conflict in Nkrumah's Ghana as follows: '*Kua Ghana, go fula tlou le tšhukudu.*' The direct translation of this is: 'In Ghana, an elephant and a rhinoceros are grazing.' This was an idiomatic way of saying that violent conflict had erupted. But the white controller could not grasp the nuances of this expression and insisted that the announcer provide a literal, word-by-word translation of the original script (SABC Sound Archive, 2001).[27] The attempt to control all aspects of a language by outlawing the use of idioms and proverbs proved rather unsuccessful because of the dynamic ability to communicate multiple messages to speakers with a deeper knowledge of the language. And by insisting on using idioms, Rasebotsa was trying to emphasise that listeners had a kind of ownership of the language that always gave them a freedom of interpretation and usage that censors could never completely control.

Struggles over the meaning of idioms and proverbs played themselves out on other vernacular radio stations, which suggest that it was not peculiar to Northern Sotho radio. Gqibitole (2002) gives the example of Given Ntlebi, the widely celebrated veteran isiXhosa radio newsreader who, on the occasion of the assassination of Prime Minister H. F. Verwoerd on 6 September 1966, read the breaking news and used the following words: '*UVerwoerd uhlatjwe nguTsafendas itshoba lalala umbethe*' (Verwoerd was stabbed to death by Tsafendas). For this commendable use of the Xhosa language, Ntlebi was hauled before the management and given the third degree. His offence was the use of the phrase '*itshoba lalala umbethe*', a popular Xhosa idiom, which is a polite way of saying someone died. The managers, however, had a narrow understanding of *itshoba* as the tail of an animal. A literal translation of the phrase would be 'the tail has collected some dew', which is derived from the belief that when an animal dies its tail collects dew in the morning. The managers thought that by using this particular phrase, Ntlebi associated Verwoerd with an animal, and this was an affront to the master race (Gqibitole, 2002:37–38).

On Northern Sotho radio, announcers like Rasebotsa used idioms not only for aesthetic reasons, but also for purposes of trying to create their own space, using 'the thicket of the medium of language' to outmanoeuvre the system. Besides his usage of metaphors and idioms, Rasebotsa is remembered by his contemporaries for his courage in employing inventive phrases such as *'Mongwadi o re ...'* (The author says ...) or *'Go realo mongwadi'* (So says the author) to distance himself from the news that he was broadcasting and to alert the listeners that he was not the source of the news or editorial comments, but merely the messenger. Liz Gunner (2002) shows that Thokozani Nene, the veteran newscaster on Radio Zulu, used a similar strategy. He often prefaced his reading of the carefully prepared and censored news 'with the disclaimer that he was reading not what he believed but what had been prepared', the style that other Zulu newscasters soon adopted in those years (Gunner, 2002:269). As for Rasebotsa, the Northern Sotho puppet masters in the control room grilled him for his subversive antics and in the end he despaired and left broadcasting for other economic ventures.[28]

The subversive activities of Rasebotsa and Nene point to individuals being able to take their own subject position even in a severely repressive climate. In a critique of structuralist Marxism, Ian Craib contends, following Althusser, that people are not simply created by underlying social structures. In his own words:

> The experience of subjectivity, of being the author of one's actions, comes from recognising an image in oneself – in a mirror, to use Lacan's metaphor, or in a 'material practice' – and then identifying with that image. Now this presupposes that the individual already possesses certain characteristics of subjectivity; she must be able to recognise an image and identify with it, and if she is the author of these actions, there is no a priori reason why she should not be the author of others. If Althusser's theory is intended to explain why – as he puts it – people 'work by themselves', it seems to presuppose what it is trying to demonstrate. The explanation holds only if individuals already possess that quality. The subject refuses to lie down (Craib, 1992:179–80).

There is certainly sufficient evidence of other individuals who worked by themselves and refused to lie down despite the costs of such actions. Maje Serudu was one such individual. He was a very forthright and courageous announcer who questioned authority without flinching. He openly refused to present certain programmes, particularly the ones about current affairs and editorial comments, which he found insulting to his principles and political beliefs. Despite the injunction 'to translate news literally and to work within the law', Serudu was consistently defiant.

A regular newsreader, he insisted on using the word '*makgowa*' (the whites) instead of the new terminology '*batho-bašweu*' (literally meaning people who had a lighter or white complexion). For this he was constantly taken to task, but eventually he won a momentary victory when he vigorously argued that '*batho-bašweu*' was not an appropriate translation for the term 'whites', as the coloureds and other light-skinned Africans can also be referred to as '*batho-bašweu*'.[29]

Fearing that their power was being questioned, the white managers were determined to frustrate Serudu. He eventually resigned in order to pursue his studies in television in England between 1973 and 1974. After the completion of his studies, the SABC refused to give him his old job back, and when it eventually did re-employ him, it refused to recognise his television qualifications. This led him to take up a position as a language expert at the University of South Africa, where he advanced his career up to a professorship (SABC Sound Archive, 2001).[30] Coming at a time when state repression had severely crippled the organised black resistance movement in the country, timidity became the hallmark of most people's relations with state institutions, but few showed boldness and engaged in subversive activities.

The announcers employed subtle forms of resistance not only in the news and editorial comments, but also in other programmes that sought to promote the apartheid state's views of developments in the cultural and social spheres. Mogobo Boy Nokaneng, as presenter charged with broadcasting programmes about Northern Sotho culture and language, often resorted to his favourite punch line '*Motheeletši, theeletša ka tsebe tše tharo. Ka ya boraro o nyakišiše*', meaning 'Listener, listen with three ears. With the third one you should analyse'. This was a subtle warning to the audiences to be more vigilant and to be critical of how culture was being used on radio to propagate an apartheid political agenda.[31]

The level of surveillance and control was so extreme as to verge on the absurd. This farce is evident in the case of Justice Tshungu, who, as we saw earlier, was considered a model presenter by the station's management. He had a tendency to use the phrase '*bana ba tšiye kgalaka*' on his programmes, a phrase that is a common Northern Sotho expression of affection for black people. The statement directly translates as 'children of the bitter grasshopper', a type of grasshopper that is tough, exudes a dreadful stench when touched, and is considered unsuitable for human consumption. The announcer was clearly using the phrase as a metaphor of affection for his listeners. But it was hard for the white puppet masters in the control room even with some smattering of the Northern Sotho language to grasp such nuanced expressions. Constantly suspicious of subversion, they left no room for uncertainty and thus called in a white Northern Sotho linguist to analyse what appeared to be a coded political message. He concluded that blacks were analogous to the 'tšiye kgalaka' in terms of their robustness and the bitter taste implied that whites would never break them down; that blacks would eventually overthrow whites. So the aphorism was seen as incitement, Tshungu was taken to task over this, and he and other announcers were warned to desist from using metaphors (SABC Sound Archive, 2001). Such high-handed and ill-informed decisions were a major cause of disenchantment among the announcers, who felt that the richness of their language was being compromised, which was tantamount to asphyxiating or killing the language.

David Coplan (1979:148), in his study of African musicians and the development of the entertainment industry in Johannesburg, similarly explores the relationship between strict censorship and the SABC's employment of a staff of linguistic experts in a bid to search out even the most oblique and idiomatic references to political issues. This resulted in the censoring of songs that carried covertly political messages and in many instances a systematic self-censoring on the part of recording studios or record producers unwilling to lose broadcasting facilities for their products. Censorship was even more severe for the announcers, as they were not allowed to air their views. When I interviewed him, Justice Tshungu more appropriately stated that 'everything that we said came from white men's hands or mouths ... We were reminded that we were not employed to do the thinking part but simply to read the news'.[32] Letswalela Mothiba, former radio announcer who moved to black television when it was introduced in the early 1980s, also recalls his employer's words (more emphatically in Afrikaans): '*Jy is gehuur om te werk en nie om te dink nie*' (You have been employed to work and not to think).[33] In staff meetings, black employees were expected to wait for orders rather than make suggestions.[34] They had to 'carefully choose the words' that they used in translation.[35] Staupitz Makopo, who left radio broadcasting for academia and television, explains why there was such tight control of information:

Broadcasting everywhere, but more especially in developing countries, is controlled by governments. It is used for government propaganda purposes. It is a battle for the minds of the people. Control of the dissemination of information was the main reason behind the formation of black radio, more especially control of political information. Entertainment was a side issue. There was on radio some covert ways of disseminating information, especially through news bulletins. The government's perspective always got the upper hand. Other points of view were commonly dismissed as 'the views of the agitators' (*baferehli*) and these were not given coverage.[36]

Mothiba makes a similar point about the editorial commentary (called '*Tabakgolo*' in Northern Sotho), which was simply a translation of a column by Van Schoor, the SABC's political editor. Relishing the moment to reminisce about the experiences and frustrations of working on radio in the 1970s, Mothiba recalls that the announcers had to make a verbatim reproduction of the original scripts of this programme. Van Schoor always vilified the then-banned African National Congress's freedom fighters as 'terrorists' and 'communist-inspired', and he promoted apartheid as the only solution to the country's political quagmire. Van Schoor, Mothiba continues, 'sought to conscientise the people listening to radio that the Bantustans were their real homes'. Reporting on the rest of Africa was always negative, stressing stories about mayhem and strife, all this in order to channel local African listeners into thinking that the homeland system was a better deal for them.[37]

Nevertheless, despite being monitored, some announcers managed to slip some cunningly 'seditious' material through the cracks of white bureaucratic surveillance. Staff meetings were often used to generate new words for concepts that were not easily translatable into African languages. Many former announcers argue that they used translation subversively 'to water down the worst effects of propaganda'.[38] Announcers were involved in the SABC's language services alongside academics in contriving new words for some English or Afrikaans terms, aimed at creating 'linguistic purity'.[39] Whereas in the original news bulletins or editorial comments the guerrillas of the liberation movements were called 'terrorists', the announcers manufactured the concept '*batšhošetši*', which translates as intimidators.[40] This was apparently done to disguise the announcers' sympathies and to alert listeners to the fact that the motives of the freedom fighters were not to kill, but to put pressure on the government to change its policies.[41] Some courageous announcers – certainly a tiny fraction – tried to manoeuvre within the very limited space available to them, even when their heroic deeds sometimes proved suicidal, especially in the early days of African-language radio.

Conclusion

The apartheid state considered news programming, which sought to foster a conservative worldview among listeners, as vital in promoting apartheid social engineering and the state's own views on national and global developments. For this mission to be realised, certain programmes, particularly news and news commentary, were carefully edited and closely scrutinised at the level of translation to the vernacular languages, using white controllers. Black radio announcers were closely monitored and the words they used on air closely scrutinised for possible subversive undertones.

This chapter has shown that even at the height of apartheid repression, a small fraction of black announcers assumed the mantle of subjectivity and very subtly subverted censorship. Seeing themselves as agents of change, as a conduit through which broader social transformation could be effected, they refused to lie down and be used as pawns by their SABC puppet masters. This was not a popular position to occupy and only a handful of courageous individuals were willing to make the ultimate sacrifice of losing their jobs for their political beliefs. However, for the majority of the Northern Sotho announcers, it was 'life as usual', just as it was for most people in all spheres of South African society. Out of fear of losing their positions, higher salaries and elevated social status, many opted for the more conservative route and acquiesced or worked within the framework of apartheid, even as they found this policy reprehensible.

Endnotes

1 Interview with S. A. Makopo, Atteridgeville, Pretoria, 22 February 2007.

2 Interview with H. J. Tshungu, Atteridgeville, Pretoria, 12 December 2006.

3 Black radio presenters were called 'announcers' to underline their expected role as functionaries of the apartheid state, as mere conduits and translators of government messages, with absolutely no space to do their own thing. This is certainly a very problematic term and an unsatisfactory description of the presenters, as a section of this chapter shows. Despite its limitations, however, I have used 'announcer' throughout the chapter as it aptly describes their stipulated position within the SABC.

4 Interview with Tshungu.

5 Interview with V. Aphane, Mamelodi Gardens, Pretoria, 23 February 2007.

6 Interview with S. Kgamedi, Lebowakgomo, Limpopo, 9 December 2006.

7 Interview with M. Serudu, Mamelodi Gardens, Pretoria, 16 February 2007.

8 Interview with Kgamedi.

9 As a result of the new reconfigurations that were intended to indicate a turning away from the separatist ethnic politics propounded by the apartheid regime and a realignment with the new values of a unitary South Africa, vernacular radio stations had to come up with new names and logos. Radio Zulu became Ukhozi FM; Radio Xhosa adopted the name Umhlobo Wenene; Radio Sesotho was relaunched as Lesedi FM; Radio Tswana was renamed Motsweding FM; Radio Venda changed to Phalaphala FM; Radio Tsonga identified itself as Munghana Lo'nene; Radio Ndebele was rechristened Ikwekwezi FM; and, finally, Radio Swazi was given the name LiGwalagwala FM.

10 < http://www.rab.co.za/radio-stations/african-language/ > , accessed 20 May 2010.

11 Interview with Serudu.

12 Ibid.; interview with H. A. Mahlase, Lebowakgomo, Limpopo, 27 December 2006; interview with Makopo; interview with L. A. Mothiba, Polokwane, 7 December 2006; interview with M. B. Nokaneng, Mamelodi Gardens, Pretoria, 21 February 2006.

13 Interview with Mahlase.

14 This is a subject that I discuss at length elsewhere. See, for example, Lekgoathi (1995).

15 Interview with Makopo.

16 The Broederbond was a secret Afrikaans organisation whose membership included most key decision makers in the National Party.

17 Moses M. Mphahlele was another example of men who made a shift to radio in 1963 after 12 years in the teaching profession. His specialties were the programmes called *Majasane* and *Thaka e Tshesane*, which focused on entertaining young people with music and jokes. Mabuse Mpe shifted from teaching, where he had been for five years, to working in the office of the Bantu Affairs Department in 1960 and moving to radio shortly thereafter. Finally, Mogobo Boy Nokaneng made a move to radio in 1964 after many years in the teaching profession in both town and countryside. Refer to SABC Sound Archive (n.d.).

18 Some of Tshungu's former colleagues remember him as someone who always received an above-average performance-related bonus annually, while the rest of them got below average (interview with Nokaneng). Tshungu was exalted by the SABC to be the voice of the black people. He was the only black speaker to deliver a paper at the RSA 2000 conference organised by the Human Sciences Research Council in 1980 and entitled Die Radio en Kultuurbevordering, met Besondere Verwysing na Swart Kultuur (Radio and Cultural Advancement, with Specific Reference to Black Culture), which claimed to look at South Africa up to the year 2000. In this paper, Tshungu argued: 'Every nation needs its own mouthpiece – a mouthpiece to inform, to inspire and to educate him. Our black people use these mouthpieces with pride, as a driving power in building up their community. The radio does far more: it serves as a vehicle for self-determination and encourages service towards their own community' (extract translated from Afrikaans). Tomaselli, Tomaselli and Muller (1989) argue that Tshungu's presence at the conference clearly hinged on his passive and, indeed, cooperative manner with regard to his alliance with the SABC and its associated discursive practices.

19 Interviews with Tshungu, Nokaneng and Serudu.

20 Interview with Tshungu.

21 Interview with Nokaneng.

22 Interview with S. Maswanganyi, Polokwane, 8 December 2006; interview with Serudu.

23 Interview with R. Letsoalo, Polokwane, 19 February 2007.

24 Interview with Serudu.

25 Interview with Mothiba.

26 Interview with R. Phetla, Lebowakgomo, Limpopo, 21 December 2006; interview with Serudu; interview with Makopo; interview with Mahlase.

27 Interview with Kgamedi.

28 Interviews with Kgamedi, Tshungu and Nokaneng.

29 Interview with Serudu.

30 Ibid.

31 Interview with Nokaneng.

32 Interview with Tshungu.

33 Interview with Mothiba.

34 Interviews with Mahlase and Makopo.

35 Interview with Serudu.

36 Interview with Makopo.

37 Interview with Mothiba.

38 Interview with Kgamedi.

39 The SABC claimed the over 100 000 terms contrived by the language services until 1980 as the valuable contribution to black languages made by Radio Bantu (cited in Tomaselli, Tomaselli & Muller, 1989:101).

40 Similarly, Tomaselli, Tomaselli and Muller (1989) find that in the isiZulu programme the term '*amaphekulazikhuni*' was devised to describe 'guerrilla', but here too the concept actually translates as 'troublemaker'.

41 Interview with Mahlase.

8

South African Radio in a Saucepan

David B. Coplan

Introduction

This chapter offers a reflection on the development of radio in South Africa against the comparative backdrop of the history of the medium in sub-Saharan Africa more generally. It is by now a truism to note that television has nowhere in the world replaced radio as once was feared, and this is nowhere more true than in sub-Saharan Africa, where only South Africa provides near-universal access to television. Rather, the impact of television and now the Internet, cellphones and hyper-portable video, as well as audio technology, has radically reorientated the content and direction of radio programming so as to serve communicative functions that television and other media have not done, and possibly cannot do. Hence 'community access' cable TV channels in the urban centres of the United States draw a small fraction of the audiences who regularly listen to 'community radio'. In Africa, recent trends towards privatisation and specialisation have made radio, always popular, more a part of daily life than ever. The infrastructure, expense and competition in television, by contrast, not to mention the reluctance of unstable, nervous central governments to relinquish control over content, have made such successful 'niche marketing' unfeasible for the medium. Of course, the story of radio in South Africa and its continental neighbours is not a linear narrative of 'up from slavery' towards higher quality and greater prosperity as an industry. There have been and still are ups and downs from the political and economic to the communicative, cultural and aesthetic.[1] So then, through the static, let us lend an ear.

From metropolitan relay to household saucepan

Briefly, from the late 1920s, colonial powers began broadcasting relay services from Europe to serve the communication needs of their settlers and officials in Africa.

The British and French led the way, and by the 1930s, both a British Empire Service and the French Radio Dakar, along with centralised local services, were instituted in English, French and, in the case of anglophone colonies, even some African languages (Bourgault, 1995:69). The intention was to support the local acceptance of colonial rule and policy; to tie emerging African elites into the system; and, as war clouds gathered in Europe and Asia, to prevent 'the discussions of educated Africans turning rapidly to subversive and anti-government ideas' (Tudesq, 1983:15). In the Belgian Congo and the Portuguese possessions, radio was left to the church and a few private institutions and entrepreneurs. From the 1940s, the British led with a British Broadcasting Corporation (BBC) 'indirect rule' (public service) model that served colonial peoples in their own languages as well as English. The French model, based on 'direct rule' and cultural assimilation, broadcast in French. In 1950, a techno-social revolution began with the introduction to Africa of the 'saucepan special' – a portable battery-powered radio set, so called after the large aluminium aerial attached above the back (Mytton, 2000).

Way down south

In South Africa, meanwhile, at the end of the 1920s, radio pioneer and African music enthusiast Hugh Tracey, who had been involved in the establishment of the South African Broadcasting Corporation (SABC) in Durban in 1924, began touring subequatorial Africa cutting master discs of African music live and in situ. These gramophone recordings were sold to labour migrants and rural-born workers in the large towns, not played on radio. Black people who wished to broadcast their aspirations to 'modernity' by purchasing a radio set listened to the state's municipal services for whites. By 1941, however, there was concern on the part of government that German propaganda heralding the 'liberation' of the British Empire was spreading positively among urban Africans. In that year the ironically named isiZulu teacher and cultural nationalist King Edward Masinga convinced Hugh Tracey to let him present a five-minute daily report of war news in isiZulu, broadcast over SABC from Durban. Soon, this service was extended to Johannesburg and the Eastern Cape, increased to 15 and then 35 minutes (three times a week), and made available to migrant workers through ground-line rediffusion hook-ups to their hostels.

With Tracey's support, Masinga, a talented writer, introduced African radio drama. The first play was Masinga's musical script of a Zulu folk tale, *Chief Above and Chief Below*, with original songs by the author in the rural folk idiom. The plays proved popular, especially among the migrant hostel dwellers. For more urbanised listeners, the leader of the musical variety troupe Gay Gaieties, J. P. Tutu, composed a number of musical plays in isiZulu for the Johannesburg SABC. City musical forms dominated the SABC programmes, while the rediffusion hook-ups emphasised neo-traditional and syncretic styles popular with non-literate workers. The SABC initiated a regular programme on Tuesday, Thursday and Saturday from 09:45 to 10:20. Its wide variety of musical styles did not entirely please any sector of the Johannesburg audience, but as the only African programme, it was extremely popular. Radio dramas of all kinds enjoyed general popularity and in 1953, K. E. Masinga's isiZulu translations of *King Lear* and *The Tempest* were serialised over SABC (Kruger, 1999:73). By the early 1950s the SABC was also presenting different African languages and musical styles on separate days. Once a week, jazz pianist-composer Gideon Nxumalo entertained urban Africans with his regular feature *This Is Bantu Jazz*. Meanwhile, the record companies, taking advantage of the commercial possibilities of radio, processed or mass-produced 'township jazz' in the studios, pursuing a common denominator of urban African taste. This became known as *msakazo*, a disdainful term meaning 'broadcast', intended as a criticism of musical programming for Africans. In 1952 a commercial company installed a rediffusion cable service in Orlando, Soweto to help remedy the lack of recreational amenities in the townships and it featured a lot of music. The African National Congress feared (rightly) that radio would become an instrument of government propaganda. African journalists attacked rediffusion as a 'back-to-the-kraal, apartheid and never-never-land service' that used African languages (rather than English) and migrant and *msakazo* music in a 'develop-along-your-own-lines pattern' (*Ilanga laseNatal*, 1952). However, rediffusion and the SABC programmes increased cultural communication, exposing urban Africans to traditional music and rural migrants to 'township jazz'.

Post-independence radio beyond the Limpopo

In 1960, as the 'winds of change' gained momentum towards the independence of most of Africa (South Africa, Rhodesia and the Portuguese territories excepted), another communications revolution little noted elsewhere occurred: the affordable portable transistor radio arrived in Africa. As a result, radio listenership soared coterminously with the 'independence decade' (1957–1967), reaching its highest levels by the 1970s where transistor radios have remained, unaffected by the introduction of television. The governments of the newly independent African states, their boundaries set by trade-offs and treaties negotiated among the European colonial powers, were quick to realise the potential of radio for creating national identities for the disparate groups of people they governed and entrenching their power. National broadcasting services, building on the already existing colonial ones, began spreading their mantras of 'nationhood and progress' to the population in local languages almost immediately. Thus, the historical commitment to 'national', state broadcasting monopoly and control was rooted deeply in virtually all African countries. State radio played a central role in post-independence political and cultural life, and in the overdetermination of nationalist consciousness as the ideological programme of the ruling elites. This is why among the first actions of insurgents seeking or succeeding in staging *coups d'état* in Africa is the capture of state broadcasting facilities.

Indeed, the story of African state broadcasting, like that of the governments it spoke for, has not been a happy one. The world's expectations for post-colonial Africa, like those of Africans themselves, were of progress towards peace, democracy and economic development, not the endless marauding of the Four Horsemen of the Apocalypse. Radio played a positive role in inculcating a sense of new nationality and advancing programmes for development. Radio for development proved popular with the new authorities, as 'radio permitted elites and governments to talk directly to villagers, thereby reorienting existing (pre-colonial) village hierarchies toward the central government, and ... politically sensitising the rural people' (Bourgault, 1995:74). Fearing subversion and ethnic disunity, these governments did not establish or even allow regional stations, but rather provided central stations in the capitals with relays. This situation continues today. These state services soon abandoned the 'public broadcasting' model and commercialised, enabling them to both advance 'etatization' (Dutkiewicz & Shenton, 1986) and bring in revenue to supplement operating budgets bloated with superfluous personnel (Bourgault, 1995:75–76).

Educational programming proved especially popular with listeners, but was hampered by top-down communication, ministry turf wars and the reluctance of governments to actually use donor funding for the kind of programming envisioned by the funders, a response Sydney Head (1974:364–65) labelled 'defective reciprocation'. Rural and community-based radio projects were sometimes initiated in order to please donors, but were not trusted and later often allowed to die from neglect. And everywhere on the continent, the tight grip of government produced a relentless rhetoric of administrative direction and involvement, in inverse relation to the decreasing capacity of governments to preside over anything except parasitic interference in the lives of their citizens. Some governments, including South Africa, even initiated external services meant to reinforce the voice of government and to counter the alternative voices broadcast from beyond national borders. Soon radio became the 'personal address systems of presidents' of one-party states. Radio proved the ideal medium for creating and enhancing cults of personality among a population where newspapers were almost unknown (Bourgault, 1995:76–77). So, for example, the many names that President Kwame 'Oseigyafo' ('The Saviour')

Nkrumah (1957–66) of Ghana awarded himself and had read over the radio during every newscast included 'Creator of the African Personality'.

Outside the studios and the halls of state power in the capitals, the increasingly disempowered population was becoming increasingly disillusioned by the growing chasm between the improving representations of national life offered by government over the radio and the steadily worsening reality of daily life. It was not that people could not believe anything they heard over the airwaves; it was that they knew not what to believe. And so sprang up everywhere the famous *radio trottoir* (Ellis, 1993:463), or 'sidewalk radio', on which overwise tales of intrigues and manoeuvrings behind the walls of government and high society were broadcast by word of mouth on city pavements. In this alternative service, it was rumour rather than radio, the unofficial rather than the official story, that had the ring of truth. Meanwhile, national broadcasting channels lumbered from nation building to nation boring, turning off listeners who were tired not simply of misinformation, but of programmes that the powers that be considered 'good for the people'. Directors-general of radio were most often politicians or military men, not broadcasters. If they toed the line, they were promoted, and if they showed any independence, they were removed. In either case, there was a constant shifting of men at the top, while the confused and worried civil servants who actually ran radio had to respond to a host of contradictory directives from a range of ministries and the president (Bourgault, 1995:77–80). Labouring under censorship and political interference, national news reports declined to the soporific chanting of the lead line 'the president/minister said', while broadcasting technology and training stagnated or even declined. Daily programming featured a strange marriage of government media hegemony and American popular music, while state radio, regional audiences and indigenous, rural cultural expression underwent a painful divorce.

Revolt of the ordinary

With the 1990s, the fall of the Soviet Union and the coming of democracy (however unsteadily) to the former Soviet republics and satellites, post-colonial Africa got a second wind of change. 'Civil society' and new political and social actors began demanding from inside countries progress towards democratisation and decentralisation (in broadcasting as well), formerly demanded only by outside critics. National conferences and elections (however manipulated and conflicted the results) proliferated and even the most unreconstructed tyrants had to learn at least the *discourse* of democracy. South Africa moved towards democratic majority rule. Economic liberalisation led to demands for private access to investment in radio. As part of this new 'pluralism', if you will, governments not only expanded the number of state-owned radio channels, but also allowed commercial entrepreneurs and non-governmental organisations (NGOs) to establish independent stations. The end of the 20th century was characterised by privatisation, commercialisation and globalisation in African radio, and by the turn of the century the number of non-government radio broadcasters in Africa had grown from three to three hundred. Donor-driven rural and community radio projects increased and enjoyed greater success. Foreign services such as the BBC, Voice of America, Radio France and Gabon's own racy Africa No. 1 became easier to receive. In the rush to make radio into a profitable urban business for the middle class, of course the rural masses are often forgotten. Politics still intrudes, as one-size-fits-all state broadcasters now find it difficult to compete with private 'target audience' stations, and governments routinely shut down those that are too openly or aggressively critical of their officials and policies. African radio, it seems, will always 'battle against an entrenched penchant for suppressing controversial views' (Bourgault, 1995:102).

South Africa: The post-apartheid radioscape

During the 1950s state radio's hodgepodge of vernacular voice dramas and traditional and urban, foreign-influenced and religious music intended to attract the mix of migrants, urban workers and petit bourgeoisie that made up the urban black population pleased hardly any of them. Still, the use of the full range of whatever the rapidly expanding black-orientated recording industry and the 'transcription service' of the SABC studios themselves could find to record did demonstrate an attempt to provide entertainment that the newly forming black urban audience might want to hear. Afrikaans- and English-speaking services were provided for whites. In order to remind the English speakers that the National Party did not consider them as fully fledged South Africans, English-language services were conspicuously orientated to British cultural concerns and featured announcers with self-consciously bourgeois British accents.

Building on the programming base of the rediffusion service in Johannesburg, the National Party government set about creating a stable of African-language radio stations to address the politically disenfranchised majority. This was consonant with its desire not only to programme and control the kind of information and entertainment reaching them, but also to further the aim of the apartheid policy of 'separate development' to nurture ethnic divisions among black people. For, as political comedian Pieter-Dirk Uys noted, the aim of apartheid was not simply to keep blacks away from whites, but to keep blacks away from one another. So was inaugurated 'Radio Bantu', comprising a total of seven anti-national

African-language stations broadcasting from Johannesburg and relayed through local transmitters to the regional centres where each language was dominant.

Charles Hamm (1991:160–72) has reviewed the history and ideological principles of Radio Bantu in superb detail, even though his analysis of its impact may be somewhat overbalanced in favour of the controlling power of the state. I will not review Hamm's argument here, but rather employ Radio Bantu and the subsequent history of South African radio after 1993 to support arguments of my own. On Radio Bantu, music, drama, news, and information were linguistically segregated and grammatically and lexically 'purified'. Programming was 'ruralised' as much as possible while being made consistent with commercial appeal (something of a contradiction in itself in view of black urbanisation), in an effort to promote identification with insular language communities and with ethnic 'Bantustans' in which blacks resident in urban areas were supposed to find political self-expression. Coloured people, ironically, had to make do with the white stations and Indians had limited programming in Indian languages in Natal.

Language separation aside, programming on SABC was remarkably narrow overall, with a mix of musical styles and other programming material on 'national' stations for each group, rather than the demographic/stylistic 'format' stations common in Western countries. As a result, South African radio before the mid-1980s was disliked by virtually everyone except those who hadn't imagined the alternatives, and more-liberated and -responsive services from Swaziland, Mozambique and some of the quasi-independent homelands (Venda's Radio Tohoyando and Bophuthatswana's Radio Bop) became instantly popular. Interestingly, the SABC itself participated in the liberalisation of radio. In 1986, at the height of the Struggle, Radio METRO, managed by Koos Hadebe, opened on medium wave targeting specifically long-haul lorry drivers and more generally the urban black market. The station's presenters gained wide celebrity and appeal, although the 'radical' aspect of their programmes consisted primarily of progressive and cosmopolitan music that was meant to enable the SABC to compete with the popular stations from neighbouring countries and the homelands.

Voices of change

With the 1990s and negotiations leading up to democratic elections, transformation began at the SABC. In both talk and music, radio diversification and responsiveness to audience demand were far more effective and far-reaching than in state television. SABC Radio sold a number of its stations to private sector investors after 1994. But this was not simply to balance its books. Those stations that were retained were in most cases radically reformed as an outcome of the debate between those who wished the SABC to play an expanded, 'developmental', nation-building role and those who pushed for a market-driven, diversified and more 'popular' service more in tune with audience preferences. As Robert Horwitz (2001:46) explains in his detailed review of debates within the communications sector at that fateful time:

> The SABC was conceived as a cardinal ally in the nation-building project. The SABC itself lobbied heavily for a large portfolio but envisioned the broadcast system, particularly in television, as essentially market-driven. Anticipating – correctly – that little money would come from government, the SABC planned for two of its television channels to become commercial, and would cross-subsidise the third, public service channel with their proceeds. In contrast, those who argued for a smaller SABC portfolio, including the Independent Broadcasting Authority and several of the civil society media groups, fought for a leaner SABC better able to concentrate on its public service mission, and for more opportunities for new broadcast innovators – including private commercial broadcasters – particularly at the regional or provincial level. But, they argued, public service obligations and local content requirements should be imposed on *all* broadcasters so as to establish an overall public service broadcast *system*, rather than to ghettoize public broadcasting as the sole responsibility of the SABC.

In the establishment of Radio Bantu, the apartheid government, in its beneficence and wisdom, had provided the infrastructure and productive capacity that would serve as a platform for new African-language services. All at once the old Radio Bantu stations changed their names, with Radio Sesotho becoming Lesedi, Radio Setswana becoming Motsweding, Radio Zulu becoming Ukhozi, and so forth, with an additional two stations to cover siSwati and isiNdebele. These were not changes in name only, but were characterised by a cultural dynamism energised by the newly liberated society. They also surged in popularity, with Ukhozi FM (in isiZulu) soon becoming the most popular station in the country. A parallel surge in popularity occurred among stations presenting contemporary popular music to black urban youth in English, such as Johannesburg's Yfm. Significantly, this audience was not constituted only around imported black contemporary youth styles from the United States. After years of lobbying by local musicians, a quota was introduced requiring 25 per cent local content in all music programming. While broadcasters at first feared a fall-off in listenership, the result was rather a post-apartheid renaissance in local music in all its unappreciated variety. As wider opportunities for recording opened up, local musicians rushed to create new ensembles, sounds and styles. The dominance of American 'rhythm and blues' was successfully challenged by a new local style, *kwaito*. While much of what could now be heard was not particularly polished, a lot of interesting and original music that would otherwise never have been recorded suddenly appeared over the airwaves.

Just as important, the new government allowed for the licensing of various categories of independent broadcasters. Oversight of independent broadcasting had roots in civil society, but soon developed into the arena for state regulation. So it moved from the Campaign for Open Media in the early 1990s to the Campaign for Independent Broadcasting to the Independent Broadcasting Authority to the Independent Communications Authority of South Africa, initiating a struggle for the political soul of the public broadcaster. Ideally, the new government wanted a mix of public, private, and community ownership, and public service and commercial programming. The new South African radio industry was supposed to comprise three categories of broadcasters: (1) public stations that are state funded but publicly owned, financed by Parliament, but unlike 'state' broadcasters, independent from government. As we are now witnessing, the line between public and state broadcasting is rather porous and in times of tension a cause for political dispute; (2) commercial services, privately owned and operated for profit, controlled by business interests in 'civil society'. Government's worries in this sector relate to foreign investment and ownership that may crowd out domestic broadcasters and bias programming content; and (3) community broadcasting, a non-profit service owned, controlled and produced by a particular community organisation or role players, or an NGO.

Considering the first two briefly, public interest and information stations such as the redoubtable SAfm have managed to retain an admirable degree of independence and objectivity, often featuring 'expert' commentators, spokespersons, call-in programmes and documentaries that are critical of powerful social, economic, and political role players and raise the concerns of ordinary citizens. When Thabo Mbeki was summarily 'recalled' from the presidency in 2008, however, his adversaries immediately drafted legislation to dismiss the SABC Board that he had appointed. Among the specific reasons given for this initiative was that the SABC was giving coverage in both quantity and quality that was biased towards the Congress of the People, a new political party formed of Mbeki supporters against the governing African National Congress.

Commercial radio is quite popular in the urban areas where its signals can be received, and its American-style format of music and talk is dependent on a steady supply of American popular musical genres as well. Even so, most commercial stations willingly meet the quota of 25 per cent demanded by the Independent Communications Authority of South Africa for 'South African' music, however uncertainly this might be defined. They also commonly devote the early hours of weekday evenings to talk shows and listener call-ins that have a public interest and opinion focus. More illustrative of some challenges facing South African radio, however, is 'community radio', which we will now consider in its several forms in greater detail.

As regards 'community radio', we might well start at the beginning and ask just what a community *is*. Conventionally, a community is defined as a geographically and/or socially based group or sector of the public that has common outlooks and interests. This definition is highly problematic as a description of social relations on the ground, but it informs the concept of 'community' envisioned in South African 'community radio'. The first problem is how to decide who may be allowed (i.e. given a licence) to speak for the community on the air. Ideally, according to the Department of Communications, location, access, ownership, control, participation, staffing, programming, policy, purpose and accountability must all be in the hands or within reach of 'the community'. The idea, the regulations state, is 'ownership and participation *of* the community, not just *for* the community'. But what in practice might all this mean? How might it lead to 'empowerment'? Where does the finance come from and where does revenue go to? What is the definition of 'public service'? Should advertising be allowed? Is there a role for an individual or a small group of entrepreneurs to start a station that 'serves the community?' When the community station Voice of Soweto relocated to studios in central Johannesburg, it was subsequently denied a renewal of its licence because it was no longer located 'in the community', even though its signal could be clearly heard in Soweto.

Other problems involve the criteria and processes used to recruit, train and professionalise staff members. Two examples might illustrate this. The little town of Ficksburg in the eastern Free State decided to engage the youth of its sprawling township of Meqheleng by starting a community station, Radio Setsoto, and studio space was provided in the town hall. The station was much enjoyed by young people for its 'local knowledge' when it came to talk and music, and it competed successfully for listeners with the large commercial stations and Lesedi FM. But soon the list of presenters had grown from 15 to 40, as the station became an employment subagency for staff members and their friends, and the municipality closed Radio Setsoto pending reorganisation. The deservedly famous Bush Radio out on the Cape Flats near Cape Town was a different story. Not only did it achieve wide appeal among the majority of coloured youth of the Flats, soon going from 12 to 24 hours of broadcasting time daily, but it also instituted staff training and programming development through well-directed appeals for funding to foreign donors. The station competed successfully for listeners with the commercial radio and SABC outlets in the Cape Metro. But these stations, blessed with more advertising revenue and with private and even public funding, were quick to poach popular presenters and other staff from Bush Radio, turning community radio into a nursery for commercial radio and the SABC. There was also the question whether community radio ought to offer 'something for everyone' (serving the *whole* 'community') or be allowed to target a particular profile of underserved or eager audiences ('niche market') as commercial radio does. Further issues involved the responsibility of community radio to adhere to local-content regulations and the role of advertising, given the uncertainty of non-profit sponsorship, in making community radio sustainable.

In other countries in the region, the question must still be asked whether government can tolerate alternative local voices. In Lesotho, Harvest FM, which featured robust debate and commentary on political issues, was closed down by executive order in 2008. In Namibia, in Windhoek's Katatura township, Katatura Community Radio was deliberately drowned out by the ruling party's commercial station, broadcasting on a nearby frequency. In Africa as a whole, the relationship between state and community radio everywhere is uneasy and conflicted, and community radio is closely bound up with issues of democracy and economic development. One problem for government is that community radio is in general more *trusted* than the state broadcaster, and the source of the message affects its reception. Most broadly of all, more research is needed into understanding how community radio *sounds* differently from public or commercial stations.

Back in South Africa, as the South African government has decentralised its ownership and control, pluralistic language communities have strongly reinforced radio's transformation from a national into a regional or local community voice. Overall, English-language radio listenership is down and that of African- and Afrikaans-language radio stations is up. This raises the issue of the ways in which African-language radio may function as community radio. From translating (in the profound sense) global 'information culture' into local language and knowledge concepts, to providing the ever-popular (since the 1940s) radio dramas that express a common sense of character and experience to speakers of common language, African-language radio not only expresses, but *creates* cultural identities while tying these into national and global discourses of belonging and location. Certainly, since 1991, African-language radio programming has changed radically. The development of the 'community' aspect is evidenced by a higher ratio of talk to music than on urban English-language stations, as racy, heavily interactive 'call-in' shows proliferate. Presenters become regional celebrities as public personalities and 'radio friends'. As long ago as 2004, Chomane Chomane, the famous veteran presenter on Lesedi FM, was recognised by the SABC:

SABC PBS Radio is honouring its legends and last week it celebrated Chomane Chomane's success in his role as on-air personality at LesediFM. It is also an acknowledgement of the valued contribution he has made to the growth of LesediFM and to the SABC. According to Judi Nwokedi, managing director of SABC PBS Radio:

'The event was essentially a demonstration of SABC's support of its people and talent, as well as a platform on which we can inspire and motivate other radio personalities to strive for similar achievements as Chomane Chomane.' Chomane Chomane's commitment to the growth of LesediFM, his Sesotho heritage and listener base have yielded great results with 1.6 million listeners tuned in every morning to LesediFM. Chomane Chomane currently hosts the top morning drive show on Gauteng radio. With over half a million listeners tuning into his *Ha Re Ye* breakfast show every weekday, Chomane Chomane reaches almost one in ten of Gauteng's citizens and almost half of the Free State population. Of the half million audience in Gauteng, 90% are in the LSM 4–8 category, making Chomane's breakfast show an attractive proposition to advertisers and sponsors. 'Chomane Chomane is the mark of success, a reward reserved for legends, such as those from whom he has learned and shared his story. As a leader in motion, he continues to ensure that his work grooms leaders of positive change able to apply what they learn to sustain their development and that of the communities they serve,' concludes Nwokedi.[2]

We might note here Nwokedi's naturalised use of the term 'communities' to describe Lesedi's audience. Of course, the 'footprint' of African-language radio stations covers not only members, but whole geographically based sections of more than one 'language community'. Thobela FM, nominally a Northern Sotho station, uses a niche programming model to broadcast in other languages, such as a regular Tshivenda women's programme, or public affairs in siSwati. Thobela's management further takes very seriously the revalourisation of African languages and cultures promoted by the concept of the 'African Renaissance', long out of fashion with government (Mbeki, 1998; Venter & Neuland, 2005), but not at Thobela, which plays up to 75 per cent local music in various languages. This commitment raises the much larger and imponderable issue of the future of African languages in South Africa. Are they destined for obscurity, as Kopano Matlwa (2007a), author of the recent novel *Coconut* (2007b), contends? Can African languages play any effective role in formal education beyond Grade 2? Even the well-worn argument for 'mother tongue' instruction in the early grades is far from proven. Lesotho, which follows such a policy in state schools in order to preserve its national language and introduces English as a medium of instruction only in later grades, experiences a massive annual failure rate in the Cambridge Overseas School Certificate examinations.

Publishing in African languages, apart from state-funded textbooks, is not viable either. African readers prefer to read in English. English is the de facto language of Parliament, even among Afrikaans first-language speakers.

African-language radio, however, is a different, much more encouraging story. The African stations are tied to language communities of usage and identity, and unite those who can use English with those who cannot, those who can and do read with those who cannot or do not. They are not confined to listeners who are first-language speakers of the medium of a particular station. Moving about Johannesburg, one will find many Sesotho or isiXhosa speakers listening to Ukhozi FM, the isiZulu station, because they like the lively variety of local music it plays, or to Radio Thobela for its African jazz show, even if they do not quite understand Northern Sotho. Inevitably, the stations based in the major urban areas, especially Johannesburg/Pretoria, where all local languages and quite a few foreign African languages are widely spoken, begin to mix languages on the air. Local phrases and topical expressions in a variety of tongues are blended into the rapid, emphatic, unfailingly cheerful patter of the presenters, who play to their audiences' desire to become more linguistically cosmopolitan themselves. The same may be said of their musical programming. Thus, African-language broadcasting provides a vehicle for language-based, national and even global cultural identity formation.

Another de facto unifying format not to be ignored in this process of African-language and culture-community development is Christian religious programming. On Saturdays and Sundays radio stations, but by far most commonly the African-language stations, are crowded with religious programming. Formerly the nonpareil among these preachers was the redoubtable Thuso Motaung, host of *Makhulong a Matala* ('Among Green Pastures') on Sundays and also sometimes co-host of the pop-traditional multi-ethnic weekly music show on SATV1, *Ezodumo* (meaning, aptly enough, 'It Sounded!'). Thuso was famous not only for his booming, gravelly moral exhortations to the strong-spirited but carnally weak faithful, but also for dialogic, even polylogic, impromptu 'call-in' exchanges with other, like-voiced preachers with whom he competed in stentorian righteous instruction to the unseen but always heard-from faithful. Regrettably, Thuso's own moral character may not have been as incorruptible as it should be in a servant of the Lord's electronic flock. In 2007 he and his wife Mmamontha were given six-year prison sentences for defrauding the SABC of R42 million in advertising revenue over three years. They were, however, cleared and released in March 2008, but Thuso has not been heard on the airwaves since.[3] Equally if not more popular is local gospel music, sung in African languages over radio stations throughout the weekend. Part of the appeal of this form of Christian popular music lies in its irresistible vocal harmonies and rhythmic swing. Equally important, however, is the role of religion in general and spiritualistic musical catharsis, specifically in the formation and operation of contemporary social networks in a harsh neoliberal economic environment. Thus has gospel music taken its indispensible place in the deep fellowship of believers in what Marx (1970:1) called 'the heart of a heartless world'. This role is reflected as well in the music industry as a whole, where gospel recordings are among the best sellers for local companies, and established singing stars in almost every other genre feature at least one gospel number on their releases and in live performances.

Conclusion: nation, community and market

Radio has very much held its own in Africa, including South Africa, despite the rapid growth of TV and other visual media, and not only owing to a lack of advanced communications infrastructure or limited funds. Indeed, the growth of audio-visual media has in practice 'liberated' radio from its global responsibilities to government and development and provided it with a particular set of socially prized, indispensable identities. This sociability extends as well to the involvement of professionals in the industry, very different from that felt by their counterparts in television. And while, not to coin a phrase, the medium is the message in African radio, we have seen how it could be used to both create a colonial imaginary and transform it into an African nationalist one.

In South Africa, early radio for Africans did more than simply control or direct the flow of information reaching the burgeoning African urban population. It also tied rural homes to distant industrial workplaces and unintentionally spread the emerging black popular culture of cosmopolitan consumerism, fashion, drama and music among an insatiable, unpreventably urbanising audience. Even the use of African languages and an overemphasis on rural and migrant workers' music and narratives served to promote rather than hinder the creation of a cross-ethnic, African working-class consciousness.

Elsewhere in Africa, the story of post-independence radio – state radio – was ironically ultimately less favourable even than that of South Africa's apartheid Radio Bantu. No right-thinking observer wants to hear this, but there it is. While the subordination of state radio to the goals of nation building and identity formation was perhaps inevitable in the immediate post-independence period, the continuation of this subordination half a century or so later has hampered the development of both the industry and the political maturity of the societies in which it is the case. Indeed, it is post-apartheid South Africa's relative success, parallel with the slow but steady demonstrable progress towards multiparty democracy in a significant number of African states, that has inspired a limited but vitally important decentralisation and diversification of radio on the continent. Not that this has meant the death of *radio trottoir* – far from it. 'Sidewalk radio' has rather stepped off the street and into the broadcasting studio.

Lastly, we must consider more thoughtfully the varied ways in which African-language radio, locally or even internationally based, may serve as an expanded form of community radio. Such broadcast communities help to create a public language culture and bring into continual contact and creative interaction rural and urban speakers of major regional languages. Liberalisation in government policies towards mass communication media in Africa cannot but advance their future contribution, both to democratic institutions and to the local economy. New global digital technologies have fortunately made the outmoded attempts of dictatorships such as that in Zimbabwe to control the airwaves as futile as they are malevolent. Yet in many countries, state radio is still nearly the only legal, publicly funded outlet. Radio in South Africa at least, freed from its exclusive role elsewhere in 'nation building' and as a primary source of government information, has not only transformed the soundscape of political and social perspective and debate, but also expanded rapidly into a constellation of other roles and services. In a near frenzy of self-expression, call-in shows where members of the public can question all but the presidents of the ruling party and the state themselves, proliferate. In a kind of self-generating meta-communication, statements made by journalists, public commentators, experts, officials and politicians on the air then become subjects of dialogic discourse and criticism, including, of course, the distribution of local-language music and information, and commentary about it. Some may criticise the new and increasing dependence on the market – listener numbers and advertising revenues – and consider advertising as the new censorship in African broadcasting. But there is also democracy in money, for it allows listeners to vote with their time and purchasing power for what is made available that they like, and not what government or self-appointed quota-crats or guardians of culture insist they must like or would like if only we could prevent them from hearing what we do not like. Unlike written literature in African languages, the future of African-language radio sounds irrepressibly self-promoting and multivocal.

Endnotes

1   For a longer, more detailed historical view of the development of radio in South Africa, see Coplan (1979; 2007).

2   < http://www.bizcommunity.com/Article/196/59.4224/html > .

3   < http://www.news24.com/City_Press/News/0,186-187_2042795,00.html > ; < http:// www.fraudinvestigator.co.za/news_march_2008.htm > .

9

Radio Theatre
The Moral Play in the Historical Context of State Control and Censorship of Broadcasting in Kenya

Dina Ligaga

Introduction

Until the early 1990s broadcasting in Africa was closely linked to state control, propaganda and hegemony. This meant that citizen participation in the production of programmes was minimal, and the production of such programmes was measured and controlled according to what was acceptable to the state. In such a context, it was difficult, if not impossible, to go against the state and to produce overtly controversial or openly subversive programmes. In the Kenyan context, censorship affected all kinds of cultural production, from music (Mutonya, 2005) to theatre (Bjorkman, 1989). The censorship of Ngugi wa Thiong'o's plays in the 1970s and 1980s is a case in point. Given this kind of 'tense' relationship between creative cultural products and the state, it is interesting to study one of Kenya's longest-running radio plays programme, *Radio Theatre*, which was first produced in 1982, a period in which the country's second president, Daniel Arap Moi, tightened his hold on power. This programme, consisting of one-act plays aired weekly, focused on themes drawn from everyday life and often existed as 'harmless' moral plays that were apolitical in nature. However, as the chapter will show, this programme, because of its embrace of the moral play form, contained spaces for survival and counter-reading. Also, by virtue of dealing with the everyday, it contained 'ways of reading' that went against the state's 'narrative'. The chapter is therefore interested in locating *Radio Theatre* within a historical context in which programmes of its kind 'survived' the harsh censorship either by embracing mundane, seemingly harmless themes or by providing spaces for counter-hegemonic narratives. The chapter uses examples of plays that, although aired much later after the liberalisation of the media, demonstrate the continued focus on the everyday moral narratives that *Radio Theatre* has used to 'remain on the margins' of the state's focus. As Liz Gunner (2000a) and Khaya Gqibitole (2002) have shown in their various studies, the radio drama genre has the ability to escape hawk-eyed state censors, while still managing to address itself to its perceived audience in ways that continue to be relevant to this audience.

The chapter argues that one of the ways that *Radio Theatre* has been able to remain invisible is through its embrace of the moral play. The moral play presents itself as a form that can be consumed within the confines of everyday life, where it addresses its audience by providing lessons that it encourages this perceived audience to consume as real (see Barber, 2000). It also encourages diverse interpretations of its meanings because, by its nature, the moral play can be applied to situations beyond its immediate context. Given this framework, it is possible to understand how the moral play has been applied to the reading of modern mass-media forms of soap operas and melodramas in the African context (Abu-Lughod, 2002). In fact, there are those who have argued that because of the moral lessons contained in soap operas, it is possible to use such forms to influence behaviour change in Africa, leading to better health and social conditions (Singhal & Rogers, 2003; Njogu, 2005). The moral play also lends itself to multiple interpretations. It is this quality that allows one to argue that in situations of censorship and the restricted production of cultural products, the moral play becomes an interesting form that allows meanings to hide within its language (Gunner, 2000a). This means that the moral play can contain more than one meaning, without necessarily being imbued with such meaning, a theory well explored in Stuart Hall's (1980) essay on the encoding and decoding of meaning. Characteristically, moral plays therefore encourage parallel readings and applications to situations beyond the context of their production.

In spite of the interpretation of the moral radio drama as a space of creativity for both producers and perceived listeners, the chapter acknowledges the contradictions of the moral play as a genre, especially in a context such as Kenya. Within the colonial and post-colonial contexts of production, the idea of the moral drama as a tool of control can be debated, especially in the way that it has been used for control – such plays enable the circulation of hegemonic notions of morality that aid in sustaining power over modern African subjectivities. In addition, the moral drama is often stuck in its Manichean propositions of good and evil, thereby preventing a more nuanced reading of social interactions. In spite of these glaring contradictions, this chapter suggests that one can read beyond them to engage more meaningfully with the way in which this genre contradicts the institutional policies of radio broadcasting in an environment of censorship and authoritarianism.

Radio Theatre: An historical glance

Radio Theatre is a programme produced for the Kenya Broadcasting Corporation (KBC) and features one-act plays that run for about 30 minutes each week. The plays are aired every Sunday at 21:30, with repeats on Thursdays at 10:00.[1] It produces an average of 50 plays a year, providing a large spectrum of themes that speak to various aspects of Kenyan everyday realities. According to one of its producers, Nzau Kalulu, it was first aired in 1982, although there are indications that it could have existed before this date.[2] Programme line-ups from as early as 1954 show the existence of a *Radio Theatre* programme that was aired for a white audience (Heath, 1986). There was also a Kiswahili 'version' of *Radio Theatre* called *Mchezo wa Wiki* (play of the week) in the late 1970s and early 1980s. Although there is little evidence to connect these various 'versions' of *Radio Theatre*, one can argue that *Radio Theatre* is an umbrella title for plays that deal with themes that mainly circulate around the moral dramas of everyday lives.

While it began production in 1982, *Radio Theatre* has continued to air the same format of plays embracing the moral play. As such, little change in the programme structure has been observed since its inception. It is for this reason that in this chapter I maintain that plays aired in the 2000s bear commonalities with those that were aired in the 1980s and thus use examples of plays drawn from different periods interchangeably to reinforce certain points that are made. Evidence of this similarity is presented through plays that have been re-aired in different eras. For instance, one play, *Immoral Network*, which deals with HIV/AIDS and its spread through traditional cultural practices, was aired for *Radio Theatre* in 1987 and replayed in 2003. Another play, *Not Now*, first aired in 1995, was re-aired in 2002 with only a change in characters' names. *Not Now* is a play about the practice of early and/or forced marriage among certain communities in Kenya. It is a rendition of the effect of such a practice on a young girl, Sophia, and takes on melodramatic proportions to highlight the dangers of the practice. The point of raising this aspect of repetitiveness is to emphasise the fact that the themes of *Radio Theatre* have maintained a specific moral content that producers of the programme feel are enduringly relevant to their public.[3]

Given this brief background, it is interesting to note that historically *Radio Theatre* has existed in a context of extreme state control, where it could only have survived by embracing the moral play form. Because of its production in a state-run broadcaster, Voice of Kenya (VOK) (currently the KBC), it is interesting to investigate the conditions under which it survived in the 1980s, and perhaps what makes it continue to survive to date. It is also interesting, using the example of a play, *Jamhuri Day Special*, to show how *Radio Theatre* has embraced the moral play, which has allowed it to provide spaces for multiple readings.

A culture of censorship and control in Kenya

Any study of radio drama in Kenya must begin from the understanding that the genre has always been produced for the state broadcaster.[4] Whether one considers the colonially controlled KenyaRadio, African Information Service (AIS), the Kenya Broadcasting Services (KBS)[5] (Armour, 1984; Heath, 1986) or the national state-run KBC, which was renamed VOK in July 1964 and then changed back to KBC in 1989, radio drama is a genre that cannot be read outside of the institutional confines of broadcasting in Kenya. As such, one must understand that the state always saw broadcasting as a useful tool of administration, mass education and political propaganda in Kenya (Heath, 1986). Both VOK and the KBC were moulded around colonial structures that defined and dictated the way that broadcasting could be used by the state. The colonial government had used broadcasting as a tool for propaganda, education and administration, leaving little room for opposing voices. By the time of independence in 1963, the Kenyan government, alongside other government institutions, adopted existing structures put in place by colonial officers and continued to use them as they had been used in the pre-independence era (Heath, 1986). Therefore, even before *Radio Theatre* was ever produced, policies regarding its existence had already been put in place.

Like other programmes, *Radio Theatre* would follow the official VOK objective to educate, inform and entertain the public (VOK, 1984:3). *Radio Theatre* was to be used to spread the government ideologies of development, with minimal spaces for democratic engagement with the public. However, it was its production during the rule of President Moi, Kenya's second president, that suffered from predetermined censorship. While it was produced under conditions of control of VOK by the state, it existed in an environment of intense censorship that was hostile especially to theatrical and musical productions in Kenya. While VOK suffered under the manipulative demands of the Kenyatta government, these were compounded by the high levels of censorship imposed on all cultural productions, including radio drama, during Moi's rule. Moi became the president of Kenya in 1978, sworn in just days after Kenyatta's death. Moi's rule was paradoxical in that while, on the one hand, he sought to uphold Kenyatta's rhetoric of peace, love and unity by laying the foundations of the so-called 'Nyayo' era,[6] his leadership, on the other hand, was marked by high levels of suspicion and paranoia. Moi's incessant 'paramoia'[7] about 'threats' to his leadership throughout the 1980s and 1990s, as well as how he reacted to these threats, affected the manner in which institutions such as the broadcasting corporation were operated (Ochieng & Kirimi, 1980; Heath, 1986; Schatzberg & Khadiagala, 1987; Haugerud, 1995; Kariuki, 1996).

One of the most obvious trouble spots in such a repressive regime was theatre. While *Radio Theatre* is produced for radio, the fact that it shares certain dramatic characteristics with other stage theatre productions in Kenya makes it necessary to look at how these other productions were being treated around the time of its production. Even before Moi's regime, theatre had been targeted through the arrest of Ngugi wa Thiong'o. Ngugi, who at the time of his arrest in 1978 was a leading novelist and the chairperson of the Department of Literature at the University of Nairobi, had established a community-based theatre group at Kamiriithu village in Limuru. The Kamiriithu Community Education and Cultural Centre was started in 1976/77 and attracted poor peasants, factory workers and primary school teachers, who, through theatre, learned of the various ways in which they could empower themselves and gain consciousness about their conditions (Bjorkman, 1989). The first play that Ngugi wrote in 1977, together with Ngugi wa Mirii, was called *Ngahika Ndeeda* ('I Will Marry when I Want'). It was directed by Kimani Gecau and was a direct attack on Kenyatta's government for its treatment of the working class or peasants. For Ngugi, it was important to underline the involvement of the peasants in the play, and he says 'although the script was drafted by Ngugi wa Mirii and me, the peasants and workers added to it, making the end product a far cry from the original draft' (Ngugi, 1997:133). In January 1978 Ngugi was arrested and Ngugi wa Mirii had to flee the country. Ngugi 'became the first Kenyan intellectual to be detained because of his works' (Ogot, 1995:198). Ngugi's second play, *Maitu Njugira* ('Mother, Sing for Me'), was banned even before it was ever shown publicly in 1982 during Moi's rule. The Kamiriithu Centre, where Ngugi directed his plays, was shut down and in its place a technical centre was built (Bjorkman, 1989; Ngugi, 1997).

Operating under the radar: *Radio Theatre* as a moral play

From this standpoint, *Radio Theatre*'s production in 1982 is important in understanding how cultural productions evaded censorship at the time. *Radio Theatre* was produced in the same year that Moi's regime was threatened by a coup, therefore any kind of opposition or dissident voice was completely suppressed.[8] From an interview with producer Nzau Kalulu, it seems quite clear that *Radio Theatre* deliberately occupied itself with moral themes taken from everyday life for a number of reasons.[9]

The moral play provided it with a space for survival. Because of its thematic focus, the state paid little attention to the programme, ensuring its survival through the years. Part of the strategy then was to always focus on the non-political, for as Barber observes, with such plays, there are no 'hidden transcripts' that are politically laden, 'encoding the "real", politically subversive message[s] within an apparently innocent tale' (Scott, 1985, cited in Barber, 2000:300). *Radio Theatre* plays were moral plays, where 'messages about the government, regime or political party are not uniquely privileged or even especially salient themes' (Barber, 2000:300). Within the realm of the moral play, what was of the utmost importance was the moral lesson that the plays intend to deliver. Barber (2000:300) mentions that 'what seems important is the larger and more generalized moral framework which encompasses them'. Inasmuch as *Radio Theatre* operated within stringent VOK/KBC policies, and despite the fact that it operated in a genre whose creative potential was under continuous scrutiny from the government, it was able to survive any interference from the state. As a survival strategy, *Radio Theatre*, like several other VOK programmes, affiliated itself with the government in order to 'minimize the element of uncertainty' within which it could operate (Heath, 1986:346). An example of this allegiance to the state could be seen through its plays, which embraced politically correct themes that either enhanced the government's agenda of development or supported its moral stance. A play such as *Immoral Network* (1987), for instance, demonstrated the government's need to encourage abstinence in the face of the AIDS epidemic. *Immoral Network* is a play based on a family whose members all contract HIV because of their irresponsible sexual behaviour. The play emphasises characters as a point of focus, using these characters to capture the imagination of the perceived listeners in order to influence such listeners into embracing more responsible sexual behaviour. Apart from *Immoral Network*, other plays, such as *Bottoms Up*, which was produced in 2004, continued to show this characteristic of the state broadcaster. *Bottoms Up* is a play about a young man who mistakenly receives the HIV test results of his friend. Thinking they are his, he lives through a month of trauma trying to deal with the extreme stigma attached to the disease. The play, just like *Immoral Network*, ends on a punitive note, emphasising more the consequences of immorality than embracing the need to live with the condition. In both examples, *Radio Theatre* is seen to use the moral play to demonstrate its themes.

The engagement with themes drawn from everyday life showed *Radio Theatre*'s reluctance to engage with politics. This is because, according to Carla Heath (1986:379–80), cumbersome bureaucratic procedures and constant interference by government officials

... seriously hamper[ed] VOK staff in their efforts to provide the nation with timely information about matters of public concern and to encourage artistic excellence .... Furthermore, obsessive concern with proper political messages in music and drama, as well as in news and information programmes ... made it difficult for VOK producers to explore the possibilities of using a wide range of artistic talent and modes of expression.

Working within VOK and later KBC therefore made it difficult for *Radio Theatre* producers to expand the programme beyond certain levels. As Kalulu succinctly put it: 'nobody ever tells you "do not". You just know ... politics and issues pertaining to it are a no-go area and you [producers] all know that. You do not want to be called and told you are breaking policy rules.'[10] Thus, *Radio Theatre*'s preoccupation with themes of ordinary occurrences in the domestic space worked to its advantage, because it operated away from the direct gaze of the government. Its routine engagements with everyday experiences lent it the ability to appear unproblematic, thus ensuring continued funding and support from the government.

A general sense of the radio drama programme can best be demonstrated through the range of plays that were and continue to be aired for KBC. For instance, one play, *Three Times a Lady*, is a three-part play about a young woman, Tabitha, who waits for her fiancé, James, for five years, all the while remaining faithful to him. The play highlights the many doubts and temptations she faces during this period. Another play, *Whatever It Takes*, is about a multimillionaire who falls in love with a village school teacher, but because she is married, he cannot be with her. He attempts to use his money as leverage, but ends up killing her, her husband and eventually himself. Other plays are developmental in their agendas, for example, *Immoral Network*, which is about HIV/AIDS and the consequences of irresponsible sexual behaviour, and *Bottoms Up*, which deals with the stigma surrounding those living with HIV in society. Such themes are considered harmless because of their engagement with themes drawn from everyday life.

Radio Theatre was not the only drama programme that 'survived' the system because of its genre. Other popular productions from the 1970s ought to be mentioned to draw attention to the context in which this radio programme was produced. The most popular structure used by many dramatic productions on VOK television and radio from the 1980s was comedy. Swahili programmes such as *Vitimbi* ('Happenings'), *Vioja Mahakamani* ('Dramas in the Courtroom') and *Vituko* ('Drama') were among the most popular. These are programmes that were and continue to be celebrated because they are comic renditions of everyday realities in Kenya. *Vitimbi*, for instance, is a situational comedy series that presents different crises in the everyday lives of characters such as Ojwang, Mama Kayai, Maliwaza,

Masaku, Masanduku and Othorong'ong'o, characters who became household names in Kenya during the 1970s and 1980s and who still remain popular to date. Like several contemporary comic genres in Africa today, *Vitimbi* represents society's attempt to resolve problems in everyday life through laughter. *Vioja Mahakamani* is a courtroom drama series also based on comic relief. Like *Vitimbi*, several characters from *Vioja Mahakamani* became household names in the 1980s, including Tamaa bin Tamaa, Otoyo and Ondiek Nyuka Kwota. *Vituko*, likewise, brought to life characters such as Kerekani and Mzee Mombasa. The function of these dramas as social commentaries with moral resolutions at the end is reflective of the kind of dramatic narrative style used in *Radio Theatre*. Some of these programmes are still being aired on the KBC.

Another type of drama that defined the Kenyan broadcasting scene in the 1980s was the educational soap opera. These dramas were moulded around real-life issues, such as wife inheritance, teenage pregnancies and forced marriages. Three of the most popular were *Tushauriane* ('Let Us Consult Each Other') and *Usiniharakishe* ('Do Not Rush Me'), both produced for VOK television, and *Ushikwapo Shikamana* ('If Assisted, Assist Yourself') which was being produced for the VOK Kiswahili radio service (Ligaga, 2005; Njogu, 2005). Unlike *Radio Theatre*, these plays were well funded by non-governmental organisations (NGOs) and adopted a theoretical model, the entertainment-education model, for effectively reaching communities and changing behaviour. According to Kimani Njogu (2005:25), these serial dramas are used to entertain and educate, and the producers adopt an entertainment-education strategy used for 'increasing levels of knowledge, changing attitudes, increasing dialogue in families and communities, and influencing the behaviour of individuals'. However, the presentation of these plays differs from that of *Radio Theatre*, whose narratives are not predetermined by NGOs or other kinds of sponsoring organisations. Their educational content is in line with general VOK/ KBC broadcasting policies.

The multiple meanings of the moral play: A question of interpretation

Radio Theatre's survival could also be attributed to another factor – the potential for multiple interpretations of the moral play. Radio drama is a genre that provides many spaces through which these plays can be read in alternative ways. Liz Gunner (2000a) and Khaya Gqibitole (2002) demonstrate how isiZulu and isiXhosa radio dramas were able to survive the apartheid regime in South Africa because they hid in the 'thicket of language', where room for several readings and interpretations of the plays resided. Radio drama, although under constant scrutiny by white managers and the government, survived through such messages hidden within language. In the case of *Radio Theatre* plays, these messages were hidden in the form/structure. The moral play is structured around the dichotomy of good and bad. It is about excess in its demonstration of the crises of virtue and villainy (Brooks, 1976). Yet, beneath these excesses are dramas that may allow for a counter-reading through the presentation of various issues.

A close reading of one of *Radio Theatre*'s plays, *Jamhuri Day Special*, aired on 12 December 2004, can provide more insight into this claim. The play is set against Kenya's Independence Day celebrations and is clearly one that is supposed to support state ideology. However, as is shown, the play provided several spaces for alternative reading. *Jamhuri Day Special* was aired to help circulate ideologies of Kenyan struggles for independence and its sovereignty. The play is a combination of narratives and memories of 1963, the year when Kenya was formally granted its independence by its British colonisers. Through its renditions of a Kenyan past, the play doubly served as a way of unifying the nation, encouraging a sense of reconciliation and smoothing ethnic differences. The play was produced during the first term of President Mwai Kibaki, Kenya's third president. Kibaki was elected to office in 2002, following a major victory that saw the displacement of President Moi, who had ruled Kenya with an iron fist for 24 years. As opposed to Moi's dictatorial style of leadership, Kibaki was ushered in by a majority vote that saw Kenyans temporarily suspending ethnic differences and coming together to overthrow a government that had caused much pain and suffering. Kibaki's victory generated feelings of nationalism, captured in the play.

Jamhuri Day Special follows the character of Gakuo, a young man whose intentions are to marry Njambi, the woman he loves. Gakuo, who is very patriotic, intends to have his wedding coincide with Jamhuri Day (Independence Day) celebrations, a day that embodies his love for Kenya. He visits his grandfather, Mzee Gakuo, to find out whether he can have his wedding reception under a Mukuyu tree (a traditional Gikuyu tree believed to be the source of creation) that was planted on the day that Kenya gained its independence. Mzee Gakuo is a Mau Mau war veteran who fought for Kenya's independence. When Mzee Gakuo learns, however, that Gakuo's fiancée is the granddaughter of a former colonial home guard, Tobiko, he refuses to allow the wedding to take place, arguing that Tobiko had betrayed the cause of freedom by working with the enemy. Gakuo seeks his father's advice on the matter, but although his father disagrees with Mzee Gakuo, he is not able to help. He is a hopeless drunkard who blames all his problems on Kenya, which, he argues, never presented him with any opportunities to develop economically. Gakuo is unable to imagine a life without Njambi and attempts to commit suicide by jumping from the Mukuyu tree. Njambi, on hearing that the wedding has been cancelled, goes into a coma.

The play, primarily about marriage, is an allegory of national consciousness and unity. It is a layered play that uses characters, presented as either virtuous victims of a backward tradition (Gakuo and Njambi) or villains (Mzee Gakuo) to present two competing narratives, each encouraging a parallel reading of the other. For instance, the characters of Gakuo and Njambi are meant to encourage listeners to sympathise with them because they are victims of Mzee Gakuo's villainy and as such encourage a positive reading of these two characters. For this reason, Gakuo is used to present Kenya in a positive light through a dramatic monologue. In this monologue, for instance, Kenya is presented as a desirable tourist destination, much as it has been represented in the colonial/post-colonial writings of Karen Blixen and other colonial fictional writers. Gakuo's choice of language betrays his embrace of the official lexicon in which Kenya becomes 'a beautiful country, full of beautiful animals and land'. This colonial gaze betrays the dominant discourse with which the government seeks to encourage a reading of Kenya. Njambi constantly corroborates Gakuo's words and they become the representatives of a new generation of Kenyans, the 'perfect' citizens.

The imagined listeners are set up to be sympathetic towards both characters, so that when their wedding is prevented by Mzee Gakuo, the imagined audience immediately sees the old man as the enemy. This encouragement of a double reading is deliberate in its attempt to encourage a reading of national unity and an erasure of difference. This is especially relevant in the context of Kenya's 2008 ethnically influenced post-election violence. The play thus cleverly uses a moral drama on marriage to present a government ideology mirroring that of the current government. It also acts as an introduction of Kibaki's ideology of *uhuru na kazi* (freedom and work), a philosophy that echoes that of Mzee Jomo Kenyatta several years before, captured in the monologue of Gakuo's father, a drunk who hates Kenya because he is poor. Through a dramatic monologue, he comes to the realisation that it is he, not the country, who is to blame for his poverty. Kibaki's philosophy encourages Kenyans to work hard in a country that has opportunities waiting to be discovered. It is a philosophy informed by an economic ideal that can only be sustained through a peaceful and unified front. The play pushes this official narrative forward to encourage Kenyans to forget the past and begin looking at a unified nation in which Kenyans coexist as one nation.

The character of Mzee Gakuo, on the other hand, is presented as evil and backward, signifying a refusal to change with the times. The fact that Mzee Gakuo holds a grudge against Mzee Tobiko, Njambi's grandfather, and uses this grudge to prevent a marriage from taking place is seen as ridiculous, selfish and backward. He supports past traditions and social cultures that do not fit well with the modernisation plans that are being encouraged through the radio drama. The creation of his character is, however, even more important because it embraces the grand narrative of Kenya's national struggles against colonial occupation. While the contribution of freedom fighters is appreciated in the play (this is evidenced through Mzee Gakuo's lengthy storytelling about the struggle), the larger narrative is one of forgiveness and leaving behind the bitterness felt against those who collaborated.

In spite of this clear-cut presentation of one character type against another, plays such as *Jamhuri Day Special* encourage a counter-reading by having hidden alternative narratives. While it may encourage one to read Mzee Gakuo negatively, it also brings to the fore a narrative that the Kenyan state has attempted to suppress since independence, i.e. the narrative of the Mau Mau participation in Kenya's independence struggles. Kenya's independence story has been a point of critical engagement at various levels (Furedi, 1990; Ogot & Ochieng, 1995; Ogude, 1999; Lonsdale, 2004). Central to the narrative of independence is the story of how the Mau Mau fighters (often *read* collectively as Kenyans) fought for independence. However, this narrative was often at cross purposes with the national narrative that was promoted by the Kenyan government after independence.

Briefly, the Mau Mau was a militant group that was formed in the 1940s, an offshoot of the Kikuyu squatter community that had revolted against the British settlers in the White Highlands in Kenya. It was an underground movement that was defined through a radical oath-taking campaign that 'was designed to cement the Kikuyu community behind as yet undefined radical action' (Furedi, 1990:105). The Mau Mau was eventually defeated through a number of tactics applied by the settler community. At independence, however, the government was reluctant to engage with the Mau Mau movement and the role it played towards Kenya's independence. According to Frank Furedi (1990:4), 'the Kenyatta regime, composed of politicians hostile to Mau Mau, tried to portray the revolt as a relatively minor incident ... Kenyatta himself took the lead by emphasizing the theme of "forgive and forget"'. James Ogude (1999:128) also argues that at independence, 'the majority of the Kenyan elite, chiefly represented by Kenyatta, saw the Mau Mau as a discredited organization whose role in the struggle for independence had to be repressed'. The Kenya African National Union government at independence was 'openly calling for people to forget the past, eschew violence and rally behind Kenyatta, who was increasingly beginning to replace the Mau Mau as the central force behind Kenya's independence' (Ogude, 1999:128). In fact, in his book *Suffering without Bitterness*, Kenyatta (1968:189) expressly says that 'Mau Mau was a disease which had to be eradicated, and must never be remembered again'.

To therefore embrace the Mau Mau narrative within *Jamhuri Day Special* as if it has always occupied an unproblematic space in Kenya's official narrative is a fallacy. Mzee Gakuo as a character demands to be read as a hero if the idea of national memory and history is to be taken seriously. To neatly relegate him to the category of the villain without taking into consideration his meta-role in this play would be to deny him agency in the larger context of Kenyan history. In much the same way, to read Gakuo as a positive character would involve a denial of the government's manipulation of cultural productions to embrace its ideologies. Gakuo, and Njambi too, is merely an extension of the state's mouthpiece. He almost mechanically spews words that support the official and preferred narrative of the government regarding Kenya.

To read *Radio Theatre* plays, therefore, one has to constantly pay attention to what is not being said. By mapping the plays against current social realities, the contradictions that arise from their melodramatic presentations become even clearer. Plays such as *Jamhuri Day Special*, although meant to be consumed as the correct ideology of the state and in many ways meant to uphold the state's hegemonic rule, can offer spaces for contradiction and counter-reading. *Radio Theatre*'s existence is therefore one of ambiguity.

Conclusion

The genre of radio drama can be read both as a form that embraces basic mundane themes and one that contains multiple readings. Against a state broadcaster that is controlled and therefore prone to censor information, such characteristics of radio drama allow it to survive and exist under the radar while still revealing and offering interesting moral lessons that are useful to its perceived listeners. Such lessons can also be extended beyond the confines of the everyday and can be applied to the reading of political situations. Within this context, the radio drama genre emerges as a powerful and ambiguous form that can be used in conditions of censorship and restriction.

Using the example of the programme *Radio Theatre*, the chapter has demonstrated how it survived in the context of a closely controlled cultural space that smothered the growth of theatrical and other cultural productions. Significantly, products such as *Radio Theatre* survived, and it is argued that this was because of its embrace of the moral play that tended to focus on the everyday and away from political themes. It is also within the format of radio drama that such forms continued to remain relevant to their perceived audiences. On a continent where the state still holds a fair amount of control over broadcasting (Mak'Ochieng, 1996; Mbaine, 2003), such a discussion is important. At present, countries such as Zimbabwe and Ethiopia still demonstrate an almost total control of the media by the state. Recently, Kenya witnessed a setback in its campaign for media freedom when President Kibaki amended the Kenya Communication Bill of 1998 to allow the state to both confiscate broadcasting material and mandate the withholding of information that may affect the image of a politician. In other words, this bill permits the censoring of news and information. Within such a context, and in the face of continued state control of broadcasting, it is interesting to analyse how radio products such as radio drama continue to thrive and why they do so.

Endnotes

1   This information is based on the production of the programme up to 2006. There have been several changes in KBC since, including the appointment of a new producer, Alex Mbathi, who may have introduced changes that I may not have taken into consideration. I have, however, remained in contact with the former producer, Nzau Kalulu, producer of *Radio Theatre* from early 1995 to 2006.

2   Interview with N. Kalulu, Nairobi, 19 December 2006.

3   Ibid.

4   Radio drama was used outside of VOK premises by the Ministry of Education for educational purposes from 1965, in which case it was not being produced by the state broadcaster. However, the Ministry of Education worked in collaboration with the Ministry of Information, and broadcasting for educational purposes was considered better handled in the former ministry. As such, the Ministry of Education, through the Educational Media Service at the Kenya Institute of Education, produced these programmes.

5   These radio stations were introduced in different periods: KenyaRadio in 1928; AIS in 1949; KBS in 1959.

6   The term *nyayo* means footsteps. This was a show by the president that he was following in the footsteps of Kenyatta.

7   'Paramoia' is a word that Kariuki (1996) uses to summarise Moi's paranoid state during his period of rule, especially from 1982 after a major attempted coup that made him realise that his leadership was under threat. Moi's 'reaction' to threats included the removal of Charles Njonjo, an MP in the Moi government, from active politics after he was accused of engineering the 1982 coup; the assassination of Robert Ouko, who at the time of his death in 1990 was Kenya's foreign minister; and so on. Kariuki outlines several reasons for this paranoia, including the fact that Moi found an enemy in the Kikuyu, who wanted to take over power from Kenyatta after his death through what was called the 'Change-the-Constitution Group' of 1967.

8   The Kenyan Air Force had attempted to overthrow his government in August 1982. The first institution that the Air Force took over was the radio station, VOK. With the help of

the Kenya Armed Forces, however, the coup was put down. Moi's wrath was such that almost 80 of the coup plotters were hanged for their crime and over 200 given long jail sentences.

9   Interview with N. Kalulu, Nairobi, 10 January 2005.

10   Ibid.

10

IsiZulu Radio Drama and the Modern Subject
Restless Identities in South Africa in the 1970s[1]

Liz Gunner

Introduction

The genre of radio drama, often serial radio drama, in isiZulu had by the 1970s established a large and loyal audience both in Natal (now KwaZulu-Natal) and on the Rand, the populous industrial and gold-mining centre of South Africa, with Johannesburg at its heart. The drama of the airwaves, which became one of the new forms of culture produced regularly for isiZulu-language listeners in South Africa from the late 1950s onwards, grew out of cultural and political duress, and thrived (Gunner, 2000a). The serial dramas in isiZulu soon acquired their own unique voice and style. They drew on the appetite of their listeners for voice, for aurality and for narrative, and capitalised on the strengths of radio as a technology of communication and modernity. By the 1970s the plays were being aired daily in short segments spliced with bridging music, running for an average of 30 episodes. The sites of the plays moved between the urban and the rural and the in-between, producing a socioscape (Anderson, 1991) with a thick sense of variety and a palimpsest of places. Their storylines were often finely detailed and intricately involved. Most involved the unit of the family. This socioscape of the airwaves meant that disenfranchised black listeners to radio were often constructing new social identities for themselves and new subjectivities as they listened to football commentaries, music programmes and the radio dramas, known widely as *imidlalo yomoya* (literally 'plays of the air'). I argue here that the element of control and social engineering of which the South African Broadcasting Corporation (SABC) and

Radio Bantu were capable had its limits. Beyond the ruthless manipulation of the music industry and music for black listeners that certainly existed (Coplan, 1979; Hamm, 1995), there was a space of discursive freedom, a place for reinvention in which new identities could be explored and old truths re-evaluated. Radio drama in isiZulu at times became such a space.[2]

My focus in this chapter is on three isiZulu radio plays from the decade of the 1970s when African-language radio in South Africa was firmly in the hands of the SABC, dominated then by apartheid ideologues (Tomaselli, Tomaselli & Muller, 1989; Nixon, 1994). I explore how the serial plays show different faces of an emergent genre and how the deep tensions and resistant creativities of the era manifested themselves in the voices of the dramas. I argue that the writers, actors and producers of radio plays were working with different emphases and playing with different strands of the social and national imaginaries to which radio and radio drama gave access. Radio for African listeners, in the form of the station Radio Bantu, was envisaged by the apartheid government as a means of controlling a restive, modernising black populace. Yet, as a technology of modernity, it helped create modern subjects and subjectivities. The South African state had itself embarked on a modernist and modernising project through its haphazardly thought-through apartheid policies (Hyslop, 1993; Posel, 1993). Jonathan Hyslop (1993:397) shows how the National Party's policy of Bantu Education (begun in the early 1950s) was a massive operation in social control, particularly of urban youth. More than that, through this 'ruthless' project of Bantu Education 'the Nationalist government was able to create a "stable" apartheid system from the early 1960s until the end of the 1970s' (Hyslop, 1993:406). This was a project of policing biopolitics (Foucault, 1978) and enforced 'modernisation' for its African population within the often reactive and self-contradictory race policies of the era. The modernity that radio drama helped create was of a different make. Radio drama in isiZulu proved a perversely resistant medium and genre. The resilience and restlessness of the language itself, the addressivity of its genres, and the creativity of producers and consumers alike made it impossible to control or even monitor with more than minimal success.

In drama in particular, the intimacy of the medium allowed a dwelling on emotion and interior life that was crucial in the creation of modern subjectivities. More than this, the dramas, in their new configuration of emotions, could cut across entrenched cultural expectations and present differently engendered 'emotion discourses' (Lutz & Abu-Lughod, 1990; Abu-Lughod, 2000). The focus in many dramas on the family and ordinary life was another part of the construction of the modern. The dramas in their frequent focus on the family and the self produced a discourse of the modern related to social life. This produced its own alternative versions of power, which quietly coexisted with the wider public production of apartheid-driven discourse.

Both the writers of the scripts, who were often also producers and actors, and the broadcasters were able to set out what Charles Taylor (1989:14) in his *Sources of the Self: The Making of Modern Identity* has called a 'sense of the importance of the everyday in human life'. Taylor (1989:14, 23) regards this affirmation of the production and reproduction of everyday life as 'one of the most powerful ideas in modern civilization'.

Space, voice and radio

Part of the intimate inwardness of radio was its ability to enable the inner eye to move over scapes of the urban and rural at a time of legal spatial restrictions for black listeners. Like the medium of print, radio could provide a means of travel. For radio, it was primarily the voice that allowed multiple journeys and passages, and enabled the medium to act as an entry into new modes of being and of becoming modern. It allowed a play of the inner eye and ear over 'tradition' and the modern, which meant that the contestations over culture and national identities present in the decade of the 1970s in South Africa played themselves out through radio in opaque ways. 'Tradition' in the form of the varied genres of the cultural archives could be present within a drama and yet be accessed differently, as these genres nested within a longer narrative form where they became not discrete moments of experience, but elements in a longer dramatic conversation. In such a frame, as for instance in the first play I discuss, *Ubongilinda Mzikayifani* ('You Must Wait for Me, Mzikayifani!'), listeners could chew over segments of praise poetry (*izibongo*) and assess them as part of the expressive whole offered by the characters within the unfolding drama. The classic expressive genres such as praise poetry thus became part of the interpersonal and family tussle in which listeners were involved over many weeks. The older genres related back to a free-standing, ongoing performative rendition. Yet they also became an element in the new medium, held in a web of associations that linked to character, narrative development, resolution and thoughts on a moral order relating to 'the production and reproduction of everyday life', as Taylor puts it.

Voice, in the material form of the radio, also created socioscapes, or what Appadurai (1991) has termed 'ethnoscapes'. These, through their access to new images of social life, spread by the media and 'complex transnational flows' (Appadurai, 1991:209), undercut the restrictions on black movement that were a cornerstone of segregationist laws. Radio in practice, as David Hendy (2000) mentions, has often been a multiskilled and multitasked operation. Yet the slender resources allocated to the African-languages service of Radio Bantu intensified this multiskilling, sometimes with unexpected results. The limitations in terms of budget and staffing on black radio meant that voice created a complex set of memories, loyalties and imaginings, as broadcasters constantly doubled up, playing different roles and taking listeners to different social sites. Koos Hadebe, who joined the Johannesburg SABC in its downtown Commissioner Street offices in 1974, was one of four full-time staff members for the Radio Zulu service. Together with Thetha Masombuka, he was football commentator, covered music programmes and acted in serial dramas. Voice was a crucial element of the circulatory power of the new medium and of drama within it. Broadly, it allowed the oral and the aural to be enfolded within the new medium. On a micro level, it created strong and complex loyalties as listeners began to identify with a particular personality through his or her voice. The layers of archives that built up from the multiple personae of a particular person as a character in a drama, as a news or sports presenter, or even as a producer, were part of these loyalties and became a way of shaping radio culture in ways not expected by the initiators of Radio Bantu. They became a means of rooting lives in a modernity constructed against the grain of the ideologues. Listeners could travel with the same voice. It could take them to known physical locations such as the football stadiums at sites around the Rand in Daveyton, Benoni, Witbank, Attridgeville and Mamelodi where teams such as Witbank Aces, Moroka Swallows, Orlando Pirates and Kaiser Chiefs battled for supremacy.[3] It could also transport them to sites of the imagination through drama that listeners inhabited and took over as their own. Thus, voice – that fluid phenomenon – allowed listeners to build up a web of associations across programmes and over time and place. It produced different discourses of the social, of interpersonal relations, of the family and home, even of the nation, and thus it produced its own social power.

For some listeners, time and place knotted together as key radio moments often relating to football, radio drama or both, and they arranged their lives around radio coverage of these events. In the South Africa of the 1970s, radio and the intimacy of urban or peri-urban domestic life were often linked with a certain key material item – the Welcome Dover stove. Take, for instance, moments from the boyhood of Tinyiko Maluleke, now a senior academic, whose voice is often heard in his role as a political commentator on SABC radio stations. Let us move to Soweto in the early 1970s – to Meadowlands. It is 14:00 on a Saturday afternoon in winter; two small boys are hard at work cleaning out the stove in the main family room in the standard matchbox house beloved of apartheid township planners. The stove is the famous Welcome Dover – its long chimney going outside, its four top plates, two side doors, one for the wood and coal to heat it, the other for cooking, and its armoury of cleaning implements in a shelf beneath the cooking/baking compartment. Why are they there and not playing outside? It is so that their task of cleaning and preparing the Welcome Dover for lighting, and then lighting it to warm the house in the cold Highveld winter, can be over by 15:00. Why 15:00? Because that is when the football commentary would start and the voice of the famed Thetha Masombuka – on Radio Zulu – would transport young and old all over the country to the grounds of contest where teams such as Moroka Swallows and Kaiser Chiefs would battle it out for primacy.[4] One did not need a pass, or money for travel through apartheid-mapped cities, to move in the mind to that pitch, spurred on by the fevered eloquence and soaring tones of Thetha Masombuka as he created verbal pictures of skill, daring, energy, spectacular goals, near misses, penalties, fouls, off-sides – and in the process built up images of future culture heroes and lauded the prowess of beloved teams.[5] These were images of what could easily become a proto-national pitch, a binding together of listeners into an imagined community. Masombuka's football commentary may not have created a nationalist discourse, but it made a free space, cherished in a time of heavy censorship and restrictions on the movement of black people.[6] Among the commentators themselves, there was a sense of a constituency and of 'serving the nation', partly because of the range of listeners drawn from the different language groups, and also through a sense of the sheer number of people who depended on them.[7]

Running alongside the multilingual, multi-ethnic shadow nation that football commentary on the Rand called into being was the intense focus on the domestic that came from the serial dramas. The listeners to these were both urban and rural. They communicated with producers by mail at the end of each drama and their views, even when seemingly perverse, were treasured by the producers, dramatists and actors as intimate ties with an unseen, yet present community of listeners.[8] It was within the site of these dramas, I argue, that a new kind of modernity shaped itself.

Voice, space and the domestic

The radio serial *Ubongilinda Mzikayifani* played for 20 episodes on Radio Zulu in 1974. It was produced in the cramped Radio Zulu studios at Number 1 Commissioner Street, then the hub of downtown Johannesburg, with a number of well-known names among the cast. Produced and written by Bhekisisa Kunene, who was also a frequent newscaster,[9] it included Wiseman Mkhize as the unsuccessful suitor, Sokalezwe. Minor roles were played by Alexius Buthelezi, by then a household name in the black world of choral music and radio, and three other well-known actors, Johnny Magagula, Sagius Thwala and Sophie Mgcina. Elijah (Thetha) Masombuka played the part of Mzikayifani, the lyrical yet sensible wooer of the resourceful young woman, Nomgcagco, played by Idah Nkosi, whose words are the play's title: 'You Must Wait for Me, Mzikayifani!'

The play used the stereotypical traditional setting of a courtship tussle where two youths vie for the affections of an attractive young woman, with much of the action taking place at the river where girls would go to draw water for their families' needs. The drama, though, worked with a play of emotion, more widely and with more interiority and narrative length than would be expected in the classic oral genres on which it drew. It thus set the cultural archives upon which it partially depended within a different configuration. Lila Abu-Lughod (2000:96, 99) has pointed out the striking differences between the emotional styles and imaginaries created by 'traditional' Egyptian and Arab forms of cultural expression and narrative and poetic traditions, and those of TV melodrama. The epic poem about Abu Zayd al-Hilali, when transposed to television, becomes, she tells us, a melodrama

> ... about interpersonal relationships and individual longings and passions set in the domestic sphere ... Instead of formulaic phrases about tears and their plenitude, what could be thought of as the phenomenology of emotion, TV drama tries to produce their inner beings ... through close-ups of facial expressions and melodramatic acting.

Something similar happens in *Ubongilinda Mzikayifani*. The older genres are put to work in new ways and move in a different pattern of emotionality. This is particularly true of the women's 'traditional' genres in which confessional emotion has always had a place. The classic women's genres of Zulu poetry include the intimate, emotional ballad style of the famous poem of lost love, *Nomagundane* ('Miss Rats'), recorded in the 1960s by Princess Magogo of the royal house when she sang it for David Rycroft (Rycroft, 1975; 1975/6). This style allowed for interiority and the holding of individual emotion and dramatic development, and can be seen as a very modern genre, a forerunner of the focus on emotion and interior life developed by radio dramas. Other women's classic genres include the shorter personal, yet formulaic love songs of young girls (Joseph, 1983; 1987) and the autobiographical, confessional mode of praise poetry for children (*izangelo*) and women's praise poetry (Gunner, 1979). These beautifully allow space for individual emotion and very condensed, often highly allusive narrative. However, with the exception of the remarkable *Nomagundane*, the shorter poetic styles allow little room for any narrative development or any extended setting such as that allowed in a serial drama. Yet *Nomagundane* has the seeds of a modern radio drama: a young woman who has been jilted by her lover, perhaps under pressure from his mother, describes to her sister, Nomagundane, in slowly unfolding details how this happened. She relives scraps of dialogue and sketches actions between the principal players, which gradually become significant as events unfold to their final denouement of rejection. In the ballad, there is no reassertion of a moral order (which almost invariably marks the radio dramas), yet the similarities are striking. The dwelling on emotion and interior life and the sketching of an intense, individual subjectivity form a central dynamic of the ballad. This is what the serial allows, in fact forces into being, when it makes use of oral genres. It does not cut across the known forms, but expands them, makes them elastic and at the same time introduces a much wider frame of interpersonal relationships, family relationships and intrigues.

In *Ubongilinda Mzikayifani*, domestic and interpersonal relationships come under the finest scrutiny. The older genres that the drama brings into play are those of men's poetry, not women's, although the latter can be understood as silently present. The two young men who are in competition display different kinds of masculinity. One, Sokalezwe, is boastful and fluent in his self-praises (*izibongo*). He is, as his name proclaims, the 'Nation's Best Bachelor'. His rival, the winner in the love triangle, is Mzikayifani ('Households Are Not All the Same') who, the serial makes quite clear, will make a far better husband and lover. The chief claim of the drama to show the move to inner life, interiority and hence the modern subject comes through its dwelling on the trials of young love, set within the home and family. A related modern focus is on marriage, love, constancy and equality. Also present are the voices of a strong mother and a determined daughter. They find a way through misfortune and turn dire events in their favour by dint of the energy of speech and, in Nomgcagco's case, through an intense hold on her sense of what is right.

Thus in the same year – 1974 – that Thetha Masombuka was holding his listeners' rapt attention with his football commentary, he took the leading role in what was to become one of radio drama's small classics, which was aired again in 2000, six years into the post-apartheid period. In this 20-episode play, short in comparison to most, Masombuka played the role of Mzikayifani, the lovesick young man whose sweetheart inexplicably turns him down, enigmatically saying: 'You have to wait for me, Mzikayifani!' On one level, *Ubongilinda Mzikayifani* could not be further from the hectic world of football. Its setting is deeply rural. It exploits the old cultural tropes of courtship at the river or stream, with the young girls continually going to draw water and being waylaid by their admirers. Yet, within this almost formulaic narrative, there are finely drawn variations. Mzikayifani shows the emotions of equality, not conquest. A blueprint for the sharing of sorrows and burdens is set out in his address to her. When Nomgcagco (in episode 2) shares with him her anxiety over her father's illness, he answers:

No, Nomgcagco! Indeed, we would face anything terrible together, whatever happens – we would bear the sorrow of [his] illness together. It's always like that. The sorrows of the world bring people closer. You would never expect, surely, to be made to carry the grief of your house alone? We are here, with our love. Nomgcagco, surely you see that your sorrow is my sorrow too? That's why I say, Nomgcagco, give me your word that we will indeed be one. May nothing of this world part us![10]

Yet Nomgcagco, as a woman of action, contained emotion and few words, has little time for Mzikayifani's eloquence. His finely turned phrases and her forceful brevity bump against each other: 'My! Are you a child! Haven't you taken in what I've just said to you?' she replies. As the complicated plot unwinds, we see Nomgcagco forced to pretend to give her love and promise of marriage to Sokalezwe. It is he who has stolen the medicine bag of her father's doctor (*inyanga*), making it impossible for him to cure her father. If Nomgcagco agrees to marry Sokalezwe, he promises that he will return the bag to its rightful owner, her father's doctor. Meanwhile, Mzikayifani's language increases in intensity and lyricism as he presses his case, always at the river. In episode 7 he draws on the beauty of the natural world and, with a lyricism reminiscent of Elizabethan sonnets, he paints a pastoral picture for the context of their love. This time his words work strongly on Nomgcagco's emotions:

> *Mzikayifani:* Come ... let's go and sit under a willow and listen to the rustling of the leaves, singing a song for us, Nomgcagco, that we'll never part. We'll hear the birds above; we'll see the white egrets flapping their wings in their flight to tell us that the birds of the air approve of our everlasting love. Then, Nomgcagco, we'll feast our eyes on the little 'water boatmen' skimming and dipping ecstatically in the water. And the water itself will be babbling on, singing a song of mourning as it leaves the pool and tumbles down a deep hollow. Come closer Nomgcagco, Nomgcagco!

> *Nomgcagco:* I do feel your words, Mzikayifani.

As the two strands of the drama move forward, the sick father see-saws between near death and a return to health, and his herbalist doctor (*inyanga*) frets and fumes at the loss of his potent medicine bag. Mzikayifani pursues his courtship of Nomgcagco – always at the same high level of eloquence and intensity; she listens, her emotions held in check. She schemes how to retrieve the precious medicine bag from the devious and persistent Sokalezwe.

By episode 17, Nomgcagco, to the dismay of her mother and the girls of her age group, has agreed to marry Sokalezwe, accepting him by ambiguously saying: 'I have felt your sting, child of a great man. Words fail me.' The drama moves swiftly to its climax and denouement in the final two episodes. Nomgcagco's father's health improves and his doctor is able to use his powers again. He sends a terrible storm to destroy the home of whoever stole his medicine pouch. News of the demise of Sokalezwe's father comes, as his home has been struck by lightning and burnt to ashes. So it is Sokalezwe, boastful, unreliable and unscrupulous, who is punished for his selfishness and greed. Episode 20 can be seen as the moral heart of the play. Nomgcagco questions the thief Sokalezwe: 'Was it you or your father who stole the medicine bag?' She does not give up until she knows it was the son whose 'love' she dismisses as he returns the stolen bag to her. Nomgcagco is rewarded for her courage, loyalty to her father and her general virtue. Mzikayifani is rewarded as well – for his steadfastness in his pursuit of Nomgcagco and, it would seem, for his amazing way with words, for his command of language and perhaps for the equality of intimacy that his words seem to promise.

This drama shows the scope of the rich and lyrical language of courtship and exploits to the full an ornate vocabulary steeped in images of a bountiful, harmonious nature. It constructs an enclosed world, yet one with its own interior dissonances and moral threats. It holds in its setting no whisper of a modernising, restless social order and yet, in its dwelling on the emotions and the interiorities of its two chief characters, the youth Mzikayifani and the resilient, compassionate Nomgcagco, it is intensely modern. Thetha Masombuka's voice, which shifted between the passionate eloquence of the character Mzikayifani in an unnamed rural place and his own rich depictions of action, style, physique and player biographies in the stadiums of the Rand, was itself a medium for the multiple worlds in which people lived and within which they negotiated their identities.

There is another way in which *Ubongilinda* may have held a deep fascination for its listeners. Although intensely modern in its emotional framing, while drawing on the classic genres, it made use of indigenous cultural archives in its depictions of sickness and health. The herbalist doctor's power to heal Nomgcagco's father and to play a part in re-establishing a moral order that had been displaced showed a different biopolitics being brought into play. The healing of Nomgcagco's father and the retribution for the theft of his doctor's medical knowledge was not brought about through Western medicine. It was knowledge and power that drew unambiguously on 'tradition'. This can be seen as part of a kind of cultural translation as the modern, and a particular kind of modernity, is given shape in the drama and shared with its 'world' of listeners, flowing in their lives between urban and rural spaces, and new ethnoscapes. As Timothy Mitchell remarks in relation to an essay by Dipesh Chakrabarty (2000) on shifts in Bengali culture in response to a Western, colonising modernity: 'The modern subject emerges not through the simple adoption of European categories of thought but through a continuous process of cultural translation' (Mitchell, 2000:xvii). The drama, seemingly so caught in timeless 'tradition', was nevertheless a space for the staging of a modernity that spoke directly to the dilemmas of love and interpersonal relationships, and the values of older moral orders with which listeners constantly engaged even as they negotiated something new. Most importantly, the female characters, and in particular the central figure of Nomgcagco, moved boldly and surely among moral difficulties, emotions and men. At the drama's heart was the family.

Women without a home: *Abangane Ababi*

Although working within certain prescribed frames, one of which was an almost invariably linear narrative line, many of the scripts of the 1970s were relentless in their exploration and, in a perverse way, celebration of the life and language of the times. *Abangane Ababi* ('Bad Friends'), which ran from early May 1979, is on one level a moral fable of a young girl who narrowly escapes corruption and disgrace. Only at the very end of its 36 episodes is a kind of moral and social equilibrium restored. The play, by Abigail Zondi and again from the Johannesburg studios, is a discussion of the options for young women in a hybrid and modernising world, and the risks of these options. The segments, with interlocking bridging music, knit together border territories of place and morality. The play is set in the south of Natal, near the tiny hamlet of uMkomazi and the coastal town of uMzinto. An anonymous and unidyllic rural space features as the place the young woman, Nomathemba, tries to move away from. There is also a location (a black township) and a shebeen run by a free woman of uncertain reputation called Aunty Sarah. There is a group of 'mothers', eloquent, assertive and constantly anxious about the behaviour of Nomathemba. Finally there is Nomathemba's mild, good-natured and dull fiancé who is mostly kept off the air by the author until the plot needs him, when vice fails and virtue is restored. Shadowing the naive Nomathemba is the worldly-wise Danisile (whose name means 'disappointed') who has recently returned home after a failed marriage. When she urges Nomathemba to go to the 'bioscope' (cinema) with her at nearby uMkomazi, saying that after marriage she can be sure that her husband will leave her at home and take other women to the cinema, Nomathemba is intrigued and interested. The drama thus explores the difficulties of marriage in either a 'traditional' or a more modern setting. Abigail Zondi was one of the few women writers for radio of the era and present as a subtext is the knowledge that under customary law, which was operational at the time, a woman was a minor all her life. The politics of gender plays itself out in the play's language. It is full of racy, domestic humour that echoes the feisty banter of women's praise poetry and the energy of daily domestic dialogue: 'Am I the only one to be defeated by marriage? I'm going! Don't chase me out like a dog that's been eating eggs!' Danisile defiantly says to the 'mothers' as they hustle her from the house when she is visiting Nomathemba. Danisile, although treated sympathetically, is not held up as a role model. Unlike Danisile, Nomathemba has a strong and close relationship with her mother, but she frets that her mother continues to treat her as a child. She explores the border spaces beyond the rural home and begins to work for the shebeen queen, Aunty Sarah, finally living with a shady character, a man of the streets with little money and little work, called Mjika Jo – a name still favoured by taxi owners and painted, slogan-like, on their vehicles.

Emotion in *Abangane Ababi* is vested not in a love relationship, but in the encounters between the generations of women and between a young woman and the brawling border world of bars, and the hybrid modernising and in-between spaces of the 1970s. It becomes a discourse of the social (Lutz & Abu-Lughod, 1990). What the drama gives voice to is the range of registers in modern isiZulu and the hybrid nature of the modern African culture in which it is embedded. On the bus and, at another point, in a taxi, an Indian character speaks Fanagalo (a basic, mixed-up isiZulu used on the mines); Mjika Jo speaks an isiZulu city argot, throwing in phrases such as *'Ek sê!'* (Afrikaans 'I say!'). Finally, Mjika Jo and Nomathemba fight over their gender roles as they sell beer in their shack: 'You get up and pour for them!' says Nomathemba. 'No!' replies the conservative but not 'traditional' Mjika Jo, 'I'm a man!' In this drama, the denouement, forgiveness and restoration of order take place in hospital, in Ward A, where the badly beaten up Nomathemba is recovering, with her anxious fiancé Magwaza and the 'mothers' at her bedside. The end is one option of a moral order, yet it is set unforgettably within a tough modernising, subaltern world familiar to many listeners as the space that needs inclusion. *Abangane Ababi* thus takes its listeners into the unmapped spaces beyond set cultural norms and shows young women treading the tricky spaces of choice in interpersonal relationships and freedom from a stifling, if secure site of 'tradition'. The family becomes the point of both departure and uncertain inclusion as Nomathemba moves into an emotional and moral terrain about which the archives of culture have little to tell her. Interestingly, though, the 'mothers' in the form of her own loving mother and her friends play a prominent part in binding her to them in love as the play ends with Nomathemba, battered by experience, in her hospital bed. Here, the company of women and the voices of women dominate and new subjectivities emerge.

Control at all costs: *uBhekifa*

Not all the Zulu Radio dramas of the 1970s sidestepped the preferences of the apartheid mandarins of the SABC and Radio Bantu. Listeners and writers/producers also had to contend with apartheid ideologues and uneasiness about incursions from the north and the broadcasts of Radio Freedom, which was at that time operating from Dar es Salaam (see the chapter by Steve Davis in this volume). *uBhekifa* ('Watch Your Inheritance') is on one level nothing less than dramatised propaganda. It mines cultural archives in order to set them in a narrative that passes on a message of fear of outsiders. It reproduces a static picture of 'native culture' at risk from dangerous outsiders. It constructs a narrow ethnicity entirely in keeping with the apartheid blueprint that inspired the setting up of the African-language radio stations of Radio Bantu. Yet it too may have been so polysemic that its driving message of fear of the outside world was submerged in a wider fascination for place as a metonymic ideal of nation. This serial drama shows that the crude propaganda so blatant in the isiZulu-language news items (Scott, 1999) could also be presented as drama through metaphor, narrative and recourse to the aural resources of the new genre. Even here, however, language and the palimpsest of voice itself proved a resistant medium that could prompt multiple responses rather than a single predictable one.

uBhekifa, the name of one of the central characters, a policeman from the quiet town of Pietermaritzburg, north-west of the city of Durban, was on the air for 40 episodes, or approximately eight weeks, from mid-March 1970. This drama must have been intended to scare black youth in particular away from embracing the radical oppositional positions that were growing in strength throughout the country at the time. It would also be a warning to others of the 'dangers' lurking to the north of South Africa's borders. There was much for the South African state to be anxious about, particularly as regards the youth:

> Coming of age politically in the 1960s, SASO's [South African Students Organisation] founders had watched most of Africa pass rapidly through the transition to independence, including the neighbouring territories of Botswana, Lesotho and Swaziland. By 1970, the Portuguese were fighting unwinnable colonial wars in Angola and Mozambique, and Ian Smith's rebel government in Rhodesia was under pressure from world sanctions …
> In South Africa the literature of African anti-colonialism was supplemented by collections of the post-independence speeches of Julius Nyerere of Tanzania on the theme of *ujamaa* and African socialism … Also influential were the writings of the Martinique-born psychiatrist, Frantz Fanon …

Fanon ridiculed colonialism's self-serving definitions of right and wrong …
Feelings of anger and hatred in the oppressed, he said, were not symptoms
of moral weakness but healthy responses to the indignity of being treated
as subhuman (Karis & Gerhart, 1997:104).

The year 1970 was when a large (exiled) African National Congress delegation
visited the Soviet Union and held lengthy talks on 'irregular warfare', and it was the
year before 'Operation J' attempted – unsuccessfully – to land 50 armed guerrillas
on the Transkeian coast (Karis & Gerhart, 1997:51). The fears of a black uprising and
of infiltrators corrupting a supposedly docile and innocent indigenous populace on
one level dominate the drama *uBhekifa*.

In addition to the subaltern modernising of isiZulu that marked the 1970s, it was
also a period when new isiZulu words denigrating radicals began to be frequently
used in SABC news broadcasts in isiZulu (Nene, in Scott, 1999). One such term that
features frequently in *uBhekifa* is *amaphekulazikhuni* (literally: what blows over
the burning faggots), meaning Bolshevists or militant communists. Throughout the
1970s the onslaught on oppositional forces waged by the apartheid state through the
medium of radio, and in particular the news broadcasts and news commentaries,
was ferocious. The African-language news services may have been particularly
heavily policed (Gqibitole, 2002; Lekgoathi, this volume). In an interview with the
journalist Sally Scott in the Durban-based *Daily News* on 23 August 1999, the veteran
newscaster Thokozani Nene spoke of the difficulties of those years of censorship
and control. He would, he said, read the carefully prepared and heavily censored
news always prefacing them with the disclaimer that he was reading not what he
believed, but what had been prepared. This became standard practice among the
isiZulu-speaking newscasters during those years. Nene also tried another route – he
would end his readings with short snatches from the praise poem (*izibongo*) of one
or other of the Zulu kings – Shaka, Cetshwayo, Mpande, Dingane; he would vary
his choice of royal personage and he would address them *to* his listeners: 'You,
offspring of Zulu son of Malandela …' In the interview with Sally Scott he recalls
that it was not long before the white authorities announced that they felt Nene's
unusual way of rounding off the news was a form of incitement.

uBhekifa, like the two dramas discussed above, was produced in the SABC
Johannesburg studios. It was scripted by P. V. Dlamini, produced by the illustrious
Alexius Buthelezi and the voice of the narrator was the star football commentator
Soks Kubheka, who also played the role of the policeman, uBhekifa. Other radio
personalites, including the football commentator Thetha Masombuka, had minor
parts. Place in *uBhekifa* is neither idyllic and alive, nor filled with the turbulent
energy of borderlands. The narrator moves listeners to the north of present-day

KwaZulu-Natal, to the uBombo mountains, near the border with Swaziland and Mozambique. The outside world, in the form of either Johannesburg with its criminals, sleazy shebeens and communists, or the dangerous 'north', contrasts with a carefully evoked, overdetermined rural space. The opening lines, spoken as a man returning home after years in Johannesburg gazes around him, paint a scene of extreme natural beauty and tranquillity: the trees are etched as if on a background of gold. It is a peopled landscape. The man sees cattle and herdboys in the distance; he sees the homestead of the chief of the district. His eyes follow the course of the stream called Inguya, which passes below the homestead; he makes a mental note of where it flows into the larger stream of Zanezigodo and follows it in his mind's eye through the mountain gorges until it reaches the dark forest of Dukithole (lost calf). He gazes at the waterfall on its edge until evening falls, when he realises he must continue his journey home. The overwhelming sense is of the artificiality of the scene, its constructedness. It is a painted, static scene, as if seen and manipulated prosthetically from a great distance.

The careful marking of the landscape, its great natural beauty and its over-precise mapping of social order is set against a symbolic tale of ogres and hyenas that emerge at night from the forest of Dukithole to eat innocent children. This is a tale to which the returning traveller listens as he sits waiting for the chief. He listens, a stranger on the edge of events, as the children cluster around the grandmother narrator, who is a consummate storyteller. This again is a set scene, what 'native life' is about. Clearly, the ogres and the hyenas that hunt in packs and eat children represent the intruders, the *amaphekulazikhuni* who, we are soon told, have asked the chief for refuge from the police and are living in the dark forest of Dukithole.

The plot, running over 40 episodes, twists and turns, but maintains suspense and intrigue. The strangers, who are ruthless once it is clear that the chief will not assist them, attempt to set his people against him and threaten to destroy him and his community. In another piece of ethnic programming through narrative, the strangers are not mother-tongue isiZulu speakers. When the young boy, Masilo, who has listened fearfully to his grandmother's story of the ogres and hyenas in the forest, encounters the three strange men as he struggles to free a trapped calf from a hole, they speak to him as brutal outsiders. The leader speaks to him in isiXhosa. Simple isiXhosa phrases, roughly spoken, are thrown in as markers of difference: '*Heyi kwedini, wenzantoni apho? Thetha! Thetha masinyane!*' ('Hey young boy, what are you doing there? Speak! Speak quickly!') The two other men with the isiXhosa speaker are even more alien and come from 'a country to the north'. The outsiders, like the ogres of folk tales, live in the forest and the caves within the forest and are again marked as 'Other'. As the serial unfolds, the strangers are progressively 'Othered'. They are from Zambia, by episode 10 they are called '*amaphekulazikhuni zamakhomanisi*' (terrorist lackeys of the communists), and the stage is set for a battle between the forces of stability – those of the *inkosi* (chief) Bhekumuzi Zondi – and the *amaphekulazikhuni*, the terrorists. There is a great deal of suspense, a turncoat villain and a beautiful girl whose loyalty is in question for a long time. Has she defected to the *amaphekulazikhuni* or not? As one would expect, the terrorists are defeated, the girl is proved loyal and order is restored. The model of a dominant Afrikaner nationalism, holding the smaller ethnic consciousness in check and defeating the invading strangers, is reasserted and the ideology of a broader unity of Zulu and Xhosa that unites into a larger African nationalist identity is crushed. There is very little family interaction; a bleak emotional world of fear dominates; there are only lightly sketched, largely instrumental relationships; and there are no intimate family scenes of the everyday apart from the tale of ogres told by a grandmother.

Even in this most ideologically rampant of dramas, however, there is a certain Bakhtinian dialogism. The scene of natural beauty so carefully etched at the drama's opening has affinities with fictional descriptions of the land drawn to evoke feelings of belonging and patriotism. Edouard Glissant's seminal novel *The Ripening* (1986), to take a single example, uses views of the land to evoke a deep sense of Martinican and Caribbean identity and the need for revolutionary change. The early descriptions, although on one level set and static, have the capacity to represent a freed country rather than one under threat from vicious outsiders. Here too, in this seemingly most controlled of dramas, there is the interpretive capacity to move between the narrowly ethnic and a broader transethnic identity. There are no archival records of the millions of postcards and letters (and phone calls) that poured in to Radio Zulu from involved listeners (Switzer, 1985; Gunner, 2000a) as the radio dramas unrolled.[11] Thus the written listener responses to *uBhekifa* are unknown. It may have elicited a mixture of responses – suspense, fear, delight in the play of natural imagery, nostalgia, even the delight of recognition for the set 'home' it created. Yet the memory of one urban and 'conscientised' youth of the era, the writer Mandla Langa, was of its manifest hostility to an imagined world beyond ethnic divisions and a static 'Africa'.[12]

Present incursions

UKhozi FM (as Radio Zulu is now called) has a listenership conservatively estimated at five million and it is the only one of the country's nine publicly owned African-language stations that pays its way. The *imidlalo yomoya* (plays of the air), as the radio dramas are called, continue to be played daily on weekdays. Although they have lost a Friday slot, Monday to Thursday 19:40 to 20:00 is protected with an almost religious zeal. It is reluctantly moved only for the most important Premier League football games or for a national emergency. Its huge listenership covers urban and rural areas mainly in KwaZulu-Natal and Gauteng. Its interactive audience makes itself known in programmes such as *Vuka Mzansi!* ('Wake up the South!') from 06:30 to 09:00, which has phone-ins on a range of topical subjects from the role of modern husbands to the place of black culture in the modern nation. It has a daily women's programme with phone-ins from listeners in quite isolated rural communities, and a great deal of sport, music and religious programmes. None of this thick presence of voice could have been easily imaginable to broadcasters such as Thokozani Nene as they struggled under the constraints of restrictive and misinforming news items ordained by their superiors. Yet the drama in the hands of its determined writers with their loyal, ever-loving listeners built something unimagined by the controllers. Language, voice and an own 'knowledgeable community' built their own rules. The stories of the everyday grew quietly, daily. They provided a means of constructing a version of the modern that sustained and provoked listeners and helped them navigate the journey to the present. This twist of the modern may be one reason why *Ubongilinda Mzikayifani,* the jewel from the 1970s, played again on the airwaves in 2000, as the post-apartheid era contemplated a new set of demands and imaginaries, and recognised the need for an inclusivity of imagination, even a kind of nostalgia and a 'continuous process of cultural translation' such as that presented in *Ubongilinda Mzikayifani.*

Endnotes

1   This chapter draws in part on my article 'Resistant medium: The voices of Zulu radio drama in the 1970s' (Gunner, 2002). I am grateful to Wiseman Masango for his utterly unstinting help with transcribing the dramas and for his energy as my research assistant while I was working on them. All the translations were done by myself from Wiseman Masango's transcriptions. My deep thanks also to SABC, Old Fort Road, Durban for allowing me access to the Drama Tape Archives and for its staff's generous cooperation. Thanks to my colleagues Dina Ligaga, Dumisani Moyo and Pamila Gupta for comments on versions of the article.

2   See Lekgoathi (2009) on Radio Bantu in Sepedi and Gqibitole (2002) on Radio Bantu and drama in isiXhosa-language programmes.

3   Interview with K. Hadebe, SABC, Auckland Park, Johannesburg, 29 November 2000.

4   Interview with T. Maluleke, Pietermaritzburg, 5 April.

5   I am grateful to Tinyiko Maluleke for sharing these reminiscences of his boyhood days with me.

6   On sport and nationalism in South Africa, see Nixon (1994), chap. 5, 'Apartheid on the run: The sports boycott'. See also Couzens (1983).

7   Interview with Hadebe.

8   Telephonic interview with W. Mahlangu, Johannesburg-Durban, 6 August 2006.

9   Interview with W. Masango, Pietermaritzburg, 20 April 2000.

10   *Ubongilinda Mzikayifani*, transcribed by Wiseman Masango and translated by Liz Gunner.

11   Interview with V. V. O. Mkhize, Johannesburg, 17 June 2009.

12   Interview with M. Langa, Pietermaritzburg, 22 March 2001.

3

Radio and Community
Voices of Change

11

Radio Okapi – 100 per cent Congolese

Stephanie Wolters[1]

On Monday, 25 February 2002 I walked down the main street in Goma, the capital of North Kivu Province in eastern Democratic Republic of Congo (DRC). In my hand was a radio tuned to 105.2 FM. Just six weeks earlier, the eruption of the nearby Nyiragongo volcano had sent tens of thousands of people fleeing across the border into neighbouring Rwanda. Many parts of the town now lay under a blanket of hardened lava, while thousands of people had lost their homes and remained displaced. In spite of this, there was cause to celebrate this day ...

> *'Karibuni na MaBibi na MaBwana. Mimi ni Martin Sebujangwe ...'* At precisely 08:00 Goma time, Radio Okapi's first broadcast – the news in Kiswahili read by Martin Sebujangwe – rang out over the airwaves on 105.2 FM in Goma, 94.8 FM in Kisangani and 103.5 FM in Kinshasa. For listeners in rebel-held Kisangani and Goma, this was the first time they had been able to hear a broadcast from Kinshasa since the war divided the country into government- and rebel-held zones in 1998. In Goma, I did not have to turn my radio on to follow the broadcast. The air around me was filled with the sounds from dozens of radio. The effect was magical – instantly the country was reunited through the airwaves, bridging the divide created by the front line and re-establishing the sense that the DRC was one country. It was an emotional moment and the start of a new era in Congolese broadcasting.

Some 2 000 kilometres to the south, that same morning, another crucial event was taking place. At Sun City in South Africa, the long-awaited and oft-delayed Intercongolese Dialogue – peace negotiations among all the Congolese belligerents, the unarmed opposition and civil society – was being launched. The timing was not a coincidence; the founders of Radio Okapi had been able to convince the mediators of the peace talks that everyone would benefit if the two events coincided

– and so they did. Back in the DRC, thanks to Radio Okapi's team of journalists at Sun City, listeners were able from the start to follow closely the evolution of the talks in South Africa, while the various political and rebel factions quickly realised that if they wanted to reach the Congolese population, speaking to Radio Okapi was the best way to do so. This auspicious start was to pave the way for the success of Radio Okapi, which quickly became a shining example of the positive impact that quality journalism can have on peace and nation building.

Political context

On 17 January 2001 Congolese President Laurent Kabila was assassinated by one of his bodyguards in his office in Kinshasa. Within 48 hours, his son Joseph Kabila, a relative unknown who had until then been the head of the army, was appointed as his successor. These events were to lead rapidly to a wholesale shift in the Congolese government's attitude towards the outside world. The government of Joseph Kabila quickly broke with the isolationist policies of the Laurent Kabila era to re-engage with key regional and international actors and international organisations such as the United Nations (UN). Within the year, this re-engagement had paved the way for the full deployment throughout the country of a UN peacekeeping force – the United Nations Organisation Mission in the Democratic Republic of the Congo (MONUC) – and for the tenuous start of peace talks between the various national actors involved in the Congolese war. It was at this crucial stage in the country's history that Radio Okapi was born.

Laurent Kabila had come to power in 1997 as part of an alliance of Congolese politico-military movements backed heavily by Rwanda and Uganda and a loose-knit alliance of other international actors. Rwandan and Ugandan soldiers did the bulk of the fighting in the military campaign that led to Kabila's overthrow of veteran dictator Mobutu Sese Seko in May 1997. At the heart of their involvement were their own national and regional security agendas. Both countries expected Kabila to subsequently allow them to pursue these aims without interference. Rwanda in particular initially played a significant role in the Congolese military and security apparatus following Kabila's ascent to power, occupying many of the most senior positions and significantly influencing security policy. Gradually, however, Kabila began to distance himself from his former allies and assert more influence over domestic matters. When Kabila announced in late July 1998 that all foreign troops would have to leave DRC soil by 1 August, the stage was set for a new confrontation.

At the same time that Kabila was distancing himself from his backers, the volatile security situation in the east, where a variety of armed groups were still engaged in ongoing fighting and where relations between various ethnic groups were tense, continued to deteriorate. Coupled with Kabila's break with his regional allies, this led to the outbreak of full-scale war in August 1998. Within days, Rwandan troops and a small number of Congolese troops had flown to western DRC and were making their way towards Kinshasa, capturing the Inga power dam and cutting off electricity to the capital for three weeks. The intervention of Zimbabwean, Namibian and Angolan troops on Kabila's behalf prevented what was to be a lightning-strike second coup and set the stage for a prolonged war.

Although on the ground it was clear from the start that the real military force in this war was coming from Rwanda and Uganda, a domestic proxy emerged within days of the start of the violence. The Congolese Rally for Democracy was launched in August and would remain the primary vehicle for Rwandan involvement in the DRC throughout the war. In October that year another rebel group was to emerge: the Movement for the Liberation of the Congo (MLC), led by Congolese businessman Jean-Pierre Bemba and backed by Uganda. Within months of the start of the war, these two movements would control close to half of the country, cutting all contact between rebel- and government-held areas. More rebel groups would emerge in the months and year that followed, but the country would remain divided by a front line for the next four years.

Background to Radio Okapi

Most UN peacekeeping missions include a radio component, but from the start, Radio Okapi was different. The key difference lay in the partnership that Radio Okapi's founders forged between the UN Department of Peacekeeping Operations and the Swiss media non-governmental organisation Fondation Hirondelle. The primary aim of this partnership was to safeguard Radio Okapi's editorial independence from UN interference and to create credible objective content for a Congolese target audience, to expedite the procurement and hiring process, and to prepare for the long-term sustainability of the radio station following the inevitable withdrawal down the line of the UN force. Never before in the history of UN peacekeeping radio had there been a partnership with an outside agency.

Editorial independence

Maintaining editorial independence free from UN and other interference, and creating credible, objective content of interest to a Congolese audience have been the cornerstone of Radio Okapi's success. Even today, however, it remains a constant battleground. From the start, various departments within MONUC and at UN headquarters balked at the idea of an independent radio station geared towards a Congolese audience. Many had a more traditional view of UN radio – that it was there to inform UN staff and troops as much as the population of the host nation, and that it should serve as the mouthpiece for the UN system, not as an independent, credible radio service that might even be critical of UN actions and policies.

The directors and staff of Radio Okapi made no concessions to these views. The founders, David Smith[2] of the UN Department of Peacekeeping Operations and Philippe Dahinden of Fondation Hirondelle, both knew that the only way to establish Radio Okapi's credibility among the Congolese population and to actively support the peace process was to provide credible and objective programming on all matters related to the Congolese political and military situation. This was especially so because the Congolese population harboured great distrust of the UN and the international community, a legacy born of the events surrounding the UN peacekeeping force deployed to a secessionist Katanga Province immediately after independence, Patrice Lumumba's death in 1961 and the close relationship between Mobutu and the international community. There was a lot of baggage on this issue and it would take a lot to overcome this initial hurdle. This situation is not unique to the DRC – in many countries the UN has a poor reputation, deservedly or not, and many UN peacekeeping radio stations have stuck to the institutional line and have consequently failed to achieve credibility and therefore have had little impact. Radio Okapi is not only the UN's biggest ever radio station, but also arguably its most successful. I firmly believe that this is owing to one thing only: the editorial independence of the radio station and its willingness to give voice to criticism of the institution that houses it. Without this, Radio Okapi would have been just another expensive peacekeeping radio that the population would have written off as a UN propaganda machine. Instead, it has become a cornerstone of the Congo's transition to a peaceful and democratic nation.

Logistics

From a purely organisational point of view, convincing MONUC that the establishment of Radio Okapi was a priority, not a luxury that could wait until later, was a difficult task. The deployment of a UN peacekeeping mission throughout a country as vast as the DRC and with as little road infrastructure as the DRC – there are only 1 200 kilometres of tarred roads in a country the size of Western Europe – is a bit like attempting to build Rome in one day. Every location to which UN military and civilian staff members were deployed had to essentially be rebuilt, and everything from earth-moving equipment to paint had to be flown in. The logistical effort was massive. In this context, building radio studios was not high on the UN's to-do list! However, by the time of its launch five months after the start of work, Radio Okapi had fully functional studios and FM transmitter sites in three cities: Kinshasa, the network capital, and Kisangani and Goma, both of which were in rebel-held territory.

In the months that followed, the network would be completed with the construction of FM transmitters and studios in Kananga, Mbandaka, Kindu, Gbadolite, Bukavu and Kalemie. In subsequent years, the political situation led to the establishment of studios and transmitters in Bunia, Lubumbashi and Matadi, as well as a number of FM relays throughout the country, sometimes piggybacked on existing community radio stations. The establishment within less than a year of a national radio network comprising nine FM stations would not have been possible without MONUC's enormous logistical capacity. However, an equally important component was the determination of Radio Okapi's international staff to give the radio as broad a reach as possible, as quickly as possible. In the DRC media context, Radio Okapi's reach was nothing short of revolutionary.

The DRC media scene

Broadcast media

The broadcast media in the DRC have been dominated since independence by the state-run Office Zairois de Radio-diffusion et de Television (ORTZ), now known as Radio Television National Congolaise (RTNC). For several decades, ORTZ maintained a national network of television and radio stations that ran both national and local content and programming. However, ORTZ/RTNC has always been a state broadcaster dominated by propaganda favourable to the Mouvement Populaire de la Revolution, the ruling party during the Mobutu era, and to the various Kabila governments. It has never been a credible public-service broadcaster that broadcasts objective information. Even during the 2006 national elections, which were organised by MONUC and heavily observed by the international community, RTNC did not play a neutral role.

Like most government institutions, ORTZ/RTNC's infrastructure deteriorated as a result of years of neglect and lack of investment, and the quality of its content declined considerably. This did not change with the arrival in power of Laurent or Joseph Kabila, and to this day RTNC remains in need of significant restructuring and a significant injection of capital to rebuild its dilapidated infrastructure.

Prior to the overthrow of Mobutu, several other broadcasters had a reach beyond Kinshasa, notably Raga and Tele Kin Malebo. However, they had only a restricted national footprint, being limited to relays in only a small number of major cities and also lacking a short-wave capacity for radio broadcasts. All broadcasters, from RTNC to Raga, were split during the 1998–2002 war, with those stations in government-held areas operating as their own network and those in rebel-held areas operating as another separate network. There was, therefore, no national news service at all for that period.

Aside from the broadcasters with a national reach, countless local radio and TV stations have come and gone over the years. Although none of these stations' political content approached the level of propaganda of ORTZ/RTNC, they were rarely critical of the government and hardly provided an alternative venue for opposition views. This was clearly the case, because their ability to operate depended on the government's approval and, especially during the Mobutu years, political dissent was not tolerated. Media freedom has also been limited under both Laurent and Joseph Kabila, and there have been countless examples of radio and television stations being shut down because they have aired views that were unpalatable to the government. In 2006–07, both during and after the national election campaign, the government several times shut down the radio station belonging to Kabila's main political rival, Jean-Pierre Bemba, because it had criticised the government. Other stations have suffered the same fate. Often these closures are hidden behind alleged violations of the rules and regulations governing media operations. In addition, journalists throughout the country and across all media are frequent targets of harassment, intimidation and arrest. This practice has continued despite the establishment of the High Media Authority, an independent media watchdog, in 2003.

Print media
Congolese print media are essentially limited to Kinshasa, with only a few publications existing in other cities. In Kinshasa, dozens of daily and weekly newspapers are available, but only a handful are published regularly and can be considered to reach a minimum standard of quality. Among these are *Le Potential*, *Le Phare*, *La Reference Plus*, *L'Avenir* and *Le Palmares*, all of which are dailies. *Le Potential* and *Le Phare* are generally considered to be the best and the most neutral, although this too is a question of degree. The print run for these papers, which cost one US dollar, hovers between 2 000 and 3 000, and distribution is limited to Kinshasa. Print journalists are subject to the same type of harassment as are the editors and owners of the newspapers.

Quality of journalism
The quality of the content in Congolese media outlets remains extremely low. Although there are a number of good journalism schools and a large number of talented journalists, the standard of journalism is undermined by the prevalent culture of corruption within the Congolese media. Congolese media owners pay

extremely low salaries, forcing journalists to supplement their income by writing 'sponsored' stories paid for by one or other individual, usually politicians or businessmen. Editors allow these stories to be run regardless of whether they are biased or even remotely based on facts. Another prevailing practice is that of paying *'coupage'* – essentially a fee to journalists who attend a press conference or cover an event. Even if the event is newsworthy and should be covered as a matter of course, a journalist will expect to be paid. These practices have not only undermined the quality of the journalistic output and sullied the profession, but have also made journalists more vulnerable to government crackdowns. The government frequently uses the lack of journalistic ethics and the high levels of corruption within the profession as a front to arrest or harass journalists who have reported credibly and objectively, but critically on a government-related matter.

A related problem is the prevalence of radio and TV stations that are established for the sole purpose of spreading propaganda about the owner, usually an important and wealthy businessman with political aspirations or a political agenda, or an established politician. Here too, content has little to do with facts and more with providing the perspective of the media owner and showing him in a positive light. Even President Joseph Kabila has a number of private radio stations throughout the country dedicated to making him sound and look good. The governor of Katanga Province, Moise Katumbi, who is a wealthy businessman, not only has his own radio station, but also pays the journalists and editors from other broadcast media in the province to cover positively any events in which he is involved.

Today the bottom line in Congolese media remains money. Whoever has it can buy journalists and good coverage, buy off criticism, or go so far as to establish his/her own media outlet as a vehicle for his/her ambitions and views, all depending on the extent of his/her means. This presents the most serious challenge to the establishment of any credible Congolese media outlets.

Radio Okapi: Nuts and bolts

It is into this jaded media context and unstable political environment that Radio Okapi was born. Both of these matters would be a boost to the station's initial popularity and to its long-term success. Provided it produced high-quality content, the poor media environment would boost Radio Okapi's profile, because it did not face a domestic competitor with the objective of producing quality journalism and could therefore quickly rise to the top as the best. And the unstable political environment and peace talks provided the station with a story of overwhelming national interest in a country in which the tradition of listening to the radio is extremely strong.

But these achievements were not de facto. The real success of Radio Okapi was born of the ability of its founders to use the massive resources of a UN peacekeeping mission to support the establishment of a credible, independent Congolese radio station with a national reach. This involved careful planning and staff selection, extensive training, and very hard work. An equally important objective for Smith and Dahinden was the desire to see the Congolese situation improve and to prove that Congolese journalists could produce quality content.

Radio Okapi journalists

News that the UN peacekeeping mission was to establish a radio service spread quickly. In Kinshasa, the production hub of the radio network and where the largest numbers of staff members are concentrated, hundreds of applications were gathered. The most promising were identified and they participated in a comprehensive six-week training course during which the best were selected for hire. Hiring followed a similar pattern in other parts of the country.

Radio Okapi was able to pay significantly better salaries than any domestic media outlet and was therefore able to take its pick from the best and the brightest of the Congolese media scene. Nonetheless, over the eight years since the station was launched, the staff has received significant training in a range of subjects, from IT to editing technology, as well as basic storytelling and production skills. In addition, the ability to pay good salaries also meant that Radio Okapi staff members did not have to supplement their incomes by running sponsored stories or collecting a 'coupage' fee when covering a press conference or an event. From the start, the station has had a very strict anti-corruption policy that has been strictly enforced. Nonetheless, as is bound to happen in a country with an entrenched corruption problem, there have been some incidents.

The question of salaries is an important one, as few local media outlets are able to pay similar high salaries. It is likely that salaries at Radio Okapi will also have to go down once the UN withdraws. It will be a very real challenge for a new structure to maintain quality in spite of an inevitable drop in the salaries paid to its staff.

Security of Radio Okapi staff

Just as crucial to the ability of Radio Okapi journalists to do their jobs in a professional manner is the level of security that is provided by the fact that one is working under the umbrella of the UN. This cannot be underestimated, as it has generally allowed Radio Okapi journalists to report on matters in a critical manner without being exposed to the dangers of retribution.

Because they are local staff, Radio Okapi journalists do not have the same status of immunity as the international UN staff. However, because they are employed by the UN, they do enjoy a level of protection that other Congolese journalists do not, and this is the key reason why they have been able to report freely on a broad range of controversial issues. But in the case of Radio Okapi, MONUC was frequently very slow to respond to threats to Congolese journalists. In the most egregious case, Franklin Moliba-Sese, a young journalist based in Gbadolite, the capital of the territory controlled by Bemba's MLC, was arrested and jailed by the MLC after reporting a story related to child soldiers in the rebel movement. At the time, the international staff member normally in charge in Gbadolite was on vacation, as were Bemba and his number two, Olivier Kamitatu. This meant that attempts to free Moliba-Sese were being conducted between Kinshasa and Gbadolite by phone, and not at the highest level of either organisation. Consequently, they were fruitless, and Moliba-Sese remained in prison for several more days before a Radio Okapi staff member flew to Gbadolite in an attempt to negotiate with the MLC leadership. Discussions with the military leadership of the movement did not succeed, nor did an unexpected encounter with Bemba, who had just returned to Gbadolite from an extended stay in Libya and who responded to the request to free Moliba-Sese with threats to jail other Radio Okapi personnel. Once all efforts to negotiate with the MLC had failed, Radio Okapi's directors decided to expose the matter to the international media. Within 24 hours of the BBC, Radio France International, and various other international media outlets running the story prominently and repeatedly, Moliba-Sese was released.

MONUC's response to this matter was extremely disappointing. It took the most senior leadership of the organisation several days to take any real notice of the matter, and even then they were slow to react. One response from a member of the senior management team was that as Bemba was out of the country, MONUC did not know how to reach him and could not assist in resolving the problem.

By far the most serious incidents took place in Bukavu in July 2007 and November 2008. Serge Maheshe, the station chief in Bukavu, was shot and killed in front of his house by unidentified armed men in July 2007. His two friends who were with him at the time of his murder were later arrested and accused of planning his murder, but were later acquitted. The investigation into Maheshe's murder and the subsequent legal proceedings have been described as botched by MONUC and international organisations, and to this day it remains unclear who killed him and for what reason. However, it cannot be ruled out that his murder was linked to his role at Radio Okapi.

In November 2008 Didace Namujimbo, another journalist at Radio Okapi Bukavu, was assassinated in circumstances similar to those of Maheshe's murder. Here too the investigation fell short of being satisfactory.

In the case of Maheshe, threats had been made prior to his murder and MONUC has been accused of not taking these threats seriously enough. Subsequently threats have been made against other journalists in Bukavu and other parts of eastern DRC, and the UN has responded more rapidly by redeploying Radio Okapi staff to other stations. In the deaths of both Maheshe and Namujimbo, the possession of a UN ID and local immunity did not deter the assassins, and in neither case have the perpetrators been found or arrested. Even with the protection of the UN, little can be done to render the Congolese justice system more functional and more accountable to the victims of violent crime.

The question of safety will always be a preoccupation, but it does seem that the UN umbrella can and has acted as a deterrent in the case of Radio Okapi staff. This, along with the question of salaries, will be the most crucial issue in Radio Okapi's transition to an independent entity following MONUC's withdrawal.

Languages

The DRC is a vast and a diverse country, with over 200 languages and dialects. However, five languages are prevalent and were therefore chosen to be the official languages of the radio station: Lingala, which originates in western DRC, but which is the closest the Congo comes to having a local lingua franca; Kikongo, used in the west and centre; Tshiluba, used in the centre; Kiswahili, predominant in the east; and French, which is used across the country. News bulletins are produced in all five languages, while other programming is generally produced only in French.

The multiple languages presented a particular production challenge, as all FM stations contributing to the national hub could not initially file their stories in all five languages. For example, Goma might file a story in Lingala, Kiswahili and French, but not in Kikongo and Tshiluba, as fewer people speak those languages in eastern DRC. This problem was eventually tackled by hiring translators at all the stations, but it highlights one of the many challenges of working in a country of this size and diversity.

In some UN missions, programmes are also broadcast in languages understood by the civilian and military UN staff. However, the founders and directors of Radio Okapi stated from the start that Radio Okapi would be '100% Congolais – 100% Congolese'. This meant not only that all languages used on the radio were in use in the Congo, but also that all presenters, without exception, were Congolese and not international staff.

International staff

Nonetheless, Radio Okapi has always had a certain number of international staff members. However, the objective of the station's founders was to keep this number to a minimum, in part because international staff is more costly, but primarily because the long-term goal has always been to make Radio Okapi a functional, Congolese-run radio station. In the start-up days, and for several years thereafter, at least one international staff member was working at every station in the network. The primary role of the international staff member was to ensure the timely delivery of stories and programming components to the network hub in Kinshasa; to ensure that content was accurate, well researched and well sourced; and to manage and sometimes provide on-the-job training to Congolese Radio Okapi staff. The quality of journalism varied greatly across the country. In some areas such as Goma, where there had been many significant news events over the years and where journalists have had exposure to reporting big news stories, the journalists hired by Radio Okapi already had significant experience and were of a very high calibre. In other more isolated parts of the country, this was less the case. It was particularly in these latter areas that international staff played a key role.

In Kinshasa, all the senior positions at Radio Okapi – such as radio director, news editor, programme manager and technical director – were initially occupied by international staff. However, from the start the objective was to gradually transfer skills to Congolese staff. Today all the senior editorial positions at the radio are occupied by Congolese staff members and the total number of international staff has been significantly reduced. At this stage, there is no doubt that the editorial side of the radio station is ready to be entirely run by the Congolese staff, as it must be if the station is to become a sustainable Congolese media entity.

Funding, resources and sustainability

This brings us to the question of Radio Okapi's long-term sustainability. From the start, Radio Okapi has been supported by a combination of international donor agencies, whose funding has been channelled primarily through Fondation Hirondelle, and by MONUC, which has provided significant infrastructure and in-kind support without which the station could not function. International donors include the British, Canadians, Swedes, French, Germans and Americans, all of whom have contributed significant funds to support the operations of Radio Okapi, notably the acquisition of equipment and the payment of salaries to international and Congolese Fondation Hirondelle staff, and various other expenses.[3] The UN has contributed to Radio Okapi through the payment of Okapi's UN staff, but more significantly by providing the infrastructure that forms the backbone of the Radio Okapi network, i.e. offices, satellite communications networks and the use of the UN's massive air transport network in the country. Although these networks were established for the benefit of MONUC as a whole, without them it would have been much more difficult to establish and run Radio Okapi. When the UN Organisation Support Mission in the DRC (MONUSCO – the mission's name was changed when it was a given a new mandate in June 2010) leaves, it will take this infrastructure with it, which means that it will have to be replaced by something else, which will also require additional funding.

MONUSCO, Fondation Hirondelle and various donors are currently planning for the departure of the UN mission and for the future of Radio Okapi post-MONUSCO. A number of scenarios have been proposed, all of which are based on the assumption of a continued inflow of donor funds to support the operation in the future. Although it is probably safe to assume that donors will remain committed to the project in the short to medium term, Radio Okapi's long-term sustainability cannot be built on the assumption that donor funds will continue to flow indefinitely. Planning for the post-donor future of Radio Okapi must start now, because it can remain alive only if it becomes self-funded, either as a commercial network of stations or as a series of independent stations.

Whatever the scenario, the transition to a more independent status will come with a host of issues. Security of journalists will be at the top of the list, although as long as the international donor community plays a role, Radio Okapi journalists are likely to enjoy greater safety than their colleagues in the private sector. Resources, although likely to continue to come from donors, will no doubt be reduced, and this will inevitably mean a downsizing of the staff, a decrease in salaries and a general scaling down of the operation. At present, Radio Okapi employs over 200 journalists in 13 cities across the country. Although the staff contingent will inevitably have to be reduced, it is highly desirable that, as much as possible, the geographic spread of the network be maintained.

Radio Okapi's legacy

Eight years into its existence, Radio Okapi is still going strong. Programming is now at 24 hours a day, a total of ten stations are functional, and local and international polls regularly rank it as one of the most-listened-to radio networks in the country. More important than its popularity perhaps is the fact that it is considered to be a credible and objective source of information on the latest political, economic, humanitarian, social and other developments in the country. It is regularly used as a source of information by local and international media outlets. Radio Okapi's editorial excellence and independence are recognised across the board, even by those who have been criticised by it. In September 2010 the International Press Institute awarded Radio Okapi its annual Media Pioneer Award.

One of Radio Okapi's other key achievements is the opening up of the country. In February 2002 the radio station reunited the country across the four-year-old front line. In the months and years that followed Radio Okapi journalists travelled to and reported from towns and areas that had not been covered by any media in decades. Through Radio Okapi, the Congolese population learned how its fellow countrymen had fared during the war, and of the many common realities and differences in their experience. Radio Okapi journalists covered conflicts, massacres, human rights violations and positive moments such as the 2006 elections on a national scale. Never before has the Congolese population had regular access to this much information about its own country. There is little doubt that this has fostered a greater understanding throughout the country and contributed significantly to the process of reunification and reconciliation. It has also made it harder – and cellphones have played a key role here – to hide things such as human rights violations and corruption.

Radio Okapi's flagship political debate programme, launched initially during the Intercongolese Dialogue as a 45-minute round-table discussion of the ongoing negotiations and later continued as *Dialogue entre Congolais* ('Dialogue between Congolese'), eight years later remains the DRC's most significant and hard-hitting discussion programme. From day one, the programme has attracted leaders from all areas to participate in discussions on issues ranging from party politics to the mining industry to sexual violence. The programme has undoubtedly set new standards for free speech and debate in the DRC.

Radio Okapi's election coverage during the 2006 election campaign was comprehensive and all-inclusive, allowing listeners access to the views of the country's many political actors on a wide range of key issues.

The standard of journalism practised at Radio Okapi has raised the bar for journalists throughout the country, as well as in Africa as a whole. Radio Okapi's journalists have demonstrated to their own professional community, as well as to their general audience, that excellent journalism can be produced by Congolese journalists and that quality journalism can make a difference. There are many examples of stories that have been covered by Radio Okapi journalists – especially in regional programming[4] – that have led to the issue being addressed and resolved. Radio Okapi's programming has also demonstrated how important it is for people to have access to quality information about issues that directly affect their lives, especially in a post-conflict country in transition like the DRC.

Even on an internal level within the UN, Radio Okapi has made a positive impact, demonstrating how useful a credible and independent radio station housed within a peacekeeping mission can be for the mission's own image. While MONUC/MONUSCO's image among the Congolese has often been rather poor, Radio Okapi has enjoyed steady support from the Congolese population, many of whom feel that Radio Okapi is the mission's most important achievement. This would never have been the case had the radio station taken a more traditional path and acted simply as the mouthpiece of the UN system. There is no question that the success of an independent and free Radio Okapi has had a positive spillover effect on the image of MONUC/MONUSCO.

What next?

Radio Okapi is the product of tremendous hard work and dedication to the principles of excellent journalism, independent and credible media, and the importance of information in the processes of nation and peace building. The DRC has been lucky to have Radio Okapi in its midst these momentous last eight years during which the country was divided by a front line, moved on to a peace process, saw the formation of a transitional government and a new constitution, and finally held national elections for the first time in decades in 2006. Radio Okapi has been there to inform the Congolese population about all of these events and developments, from all angles and from the perspectives of all the actors involved.

But in spite of these considerable achievements, the consolidation of democracy is far from having been achieved. In fact, there are worrisome signs that the political space is narrowing, that political dissent and media freedom are increasingly less tolerated, and that the national elections planned for 2011 could prove to be less transparent and representative than the 2006 elections. The DRC thus needs the independent and credible voice of Radio Okapi more than ever, and will do so for decades to come.

Endnotes

1   Stephanie Wolters was Radio Okapi's first news editor.
2   Stephanie Wolters and David Smith are co-directors of Okapi Consulting, a company that specialises in media development in conflict zones and in research and political analysis in Africa.
3   Almost half of Radio Okapi's Congolese staff were hired and paid by Fondation Hirondelle. This was part of the agreement between Hirondelle and the UN, and allowed for a more rapid and flexible hiring process.
4   Twice a day, in the morning and in the evening, the regional stations split off from the national network for half an hour and broadcast a local and regional news and information programme that is produced by the local team on the ground.

12

Talk Radio, Democracy and the Public Sphere
567MW in Cape Town

Tanja Bosch

Introduction

Talk radio in South Africa is not a new phenomenon, although its prevalence has increased in the post-apartheid era. While there is a range of talk shows on the broad-spectrum programming of the public broadcaster, on commercial music radio and on community radio, there are only two commercial talk stations, both owned by media company Primedia. Radio 702, based in Johannesburg, was formed in 1980 and moved to a talk format in 1988; sister station 567MW Cape Talk was formed in 1997. While there are many hybrid talk-radio formats, including those mentioned above, this chapter defines talk radio as a format 'characterised by conversation that is initiated by a programme host and usually involving listeners who telephone to participate in the discussion about topics such as politics, sports, or current events' (Rubin & Step, 2000:636). The focus is thus on the format that is exclusively talk, as opposed to other formats where talk exists peripherally or in addition to other material such as music.

This chapter explores commercial talk radio, with 567MW as a case study. In particular, the chapter explores how the radio station positions itself via its talk in relation to how the audience is constituted; and how this process creates a democratic public sphere. More specifically, the broadcast content of 567MW is explored as a potential space for the formation of public opinion, as private individuals use the medium to organise themselves as a public body and participate in critical discussion about matters of general interest (Habermas, 1989).

The South African democracy is still fairly new, with increased citizen participation in the political sphere since 1994; but democratisation does not necessarily lead to a politicised society (Lee, 2002). This makes the media, and by implication talk radio, important in offering a space for political discussions and channelling public opinion.

While the construct of the Habermasian public sphere has been widely critiqued, most notably for its exclusion of women and the poor (see, for example, Felski, 1989 and Fraser, 1992), it remains a useful theoretical frame through which to explore talk radio, as it centres on the premise of citizens being able to enter into public discussion on an equal basis. In later writings, Habermas recognises the existence of alternative public spheres and their capacity for challenging dominant ideology (Downey & Fenton, 2003), which is perhaps more relevant for considering the talk-radio model.

This chapter argues that the station creates a space for the development of a public sphere within the context of a deliberative democracy. Given the theoretical limitations of the public-sphere model, the chapter further acknowledges the existence of multiple public spheres (and their creation via the radio), while arguing that the public sphere of talk radio in South Africa, although sometimes elitist, commodified and otherwise flawed, nonetheless creates the space for mediated discussion and negotiated citizen roles, despite the interpellation of the audience as consumers.

Talk radio in South Africa

First, let us briefly explore the background to talk radio in South Africa. With the exception of Radio 702, the closest South Africa came to talk radio was the full-spectrum programming of the South African Broadcasting Corporation's Springbok Radio, which aired a range of non-music programming, including talk shows and radio dramas. Radio 702 was established in 1980 as a youth music station, but was repositioned as a talk radio station in 1986, at a time when all forms of debate were heavily censored (De Beer, 1998). According to De Beer (1998), this switch was because of the station's inability to compete with the music-driven Radio 5, broadcasting on FM, largely because of the poor quality of its AM signal. During apartheid, Radio 702 was the only independent source of broadcast news. The station was originally located in the former independent homeland of Bophuthatswana, allowing for the broadcast of politically divergent content. Today, Radio 702 is the only talk-radio station broadcasting to the larger Gauteng Province, with 567MW catering to the Western Cape. There are frequent programming overlaps, with some daytime and late night programmes simulcast on both stations, while others (including the news) are more localised.

567MW was first conceptualised in 1997 as a news format station for the city of Cape Town and went on air on 14 October that year with SAfm-style features and lengthy interviews. 'At that time we worked hard to gain an academic, thinking audience. We wanted to reach the thinkers, the policy makers', said Colin Cullis, operations manager.[1] Cullis explained that this style of broadcasting lasted through to 2000, with a static audience of between 65 000 and 100 000 by 2002. 'And around two years ago we started realising that being successful is not telling people this is what you think.' As programme manager Africa Melane said: 'You don't need a PhD to listen to 567MW. Not anymore.'[2]

Overview of the literature

While no literature on talk radio in South Africa was found, there is a fair amount of international research, particularly in the form of audience studies, that deals with talk radio in the United States specifically. Many of these studies deal primarily with talk-radio discourse, the characteristics of callers and non-callers, and the interpersonal nature of talk radio. Armstrong and Rubin (1989), for example, find that talk radio provides callers with an accessible and non-threatening alternative to interpersonal communication. Similarly, Hollander (1996) finds that talk-radio listeners (as compared to non-listeners) have greater feelings of political self-efficacy, are more politically active and are more likely to read newspapers. These authors also find that talk radio is usually associated with negative political factors such as cynicism about government and lower perceptions of government's responsiveness to citizens' needs.

Hofstetter and Gianos (1997) examine differences among groups of listeners to political talk radio using data from a survey of adults in San Diego and find that among more active audience members, limited motivational data suggests that political talk radio serves a mix of needs, including seeking political information, interpreting reality or seeking companionship. Rubin and Step (2000) examine the impact of motivation, interpersonal attraction and parasocial interaction on listening behaviour, information acquisition, attitudinal effects and behavioural effects.

On the other hand, Hofstetter et al. (1994) find little evidence for the hypothesis that political talk radio leads to alienation, social and political isolation, cynicism, and political withdrawal. Respondents reported widespread exposure to talk radio, although they often did not discriminate accurately among political, non-political and other programming. Exposure was associated with traditional forms of political participation, beliefs in self-efficacy linked to specific political behaviours and psychological involvement in politics. Increased penetration of the public may have altered the nature of the political talk-radio audience so that exposure to talk radio is more closely associated with customary forms of political involvement than with social and political alienation.

In the United States, the prevalent assumption informing existing research seems to be that talk radio via 'talk-show democracy' has altered how people obtain political information and as such is politically powerful; and that regular listeners are usually also more politically active (Cappella, Turow & Jamieson, 1996). Lee (2002) acknowledges that much talk-radio research characterises talk shows as forums for public deliberation and further argues that while talk radio provides political information to listeners and serves as a forum for the public to criticise the government, it also sometimes serves as a form of infotainment that displaces serious political journalism.

The present study builds on this research, exploring the notion of 'talk-show democracy' in the South African context. However, the study departs methodologically from previous work, as the focus is primarily on broadcast content (including listener contributions) as the primary unit of analysis, together with a survey administered to a snowball sample of 50 listeners.

Talk radio and the public sphere

The contested concept of the public sphere, originally articulated by Habermas (1989), is used as the theoretical frame for the discussion of 567MW. In some ways, the exclusivity of the bourgeois public sphere Habermas proposes is an appropriate summary of the arguments presented here about the role talk radio plays. The central argument is that the public sphere developed by 567MW may be a bourgeois public sphere in terms of both class and race, but that it still remains a powerful public sphere.

Historically, the political public sphere represented a critical voice that analysed and opposed government action, whereas it has been conceptualised very differently in modern society as the use of public relations to create or manipulate a false public. To some extent, as argued below in the discussion on the audience, it is a false public insofar as it claims membership of an 'imagined' community (see Anderson, 1983), but at the same time Cape Talk 567MW also plays a role in promoting rational-critical debate, which is the lifeblood of the public sphere. The call-in shows that form the frame of this debate, which constitute the backbone of the programme schedule, provide an unstructured outlet for public discourse (Herbst, 1995).

One of Habermas's critiques of the modern state is the decline of rational, meaningful argument; and the Cape Talk station revives this function through its interaction between hosts and listeners on the air, demonstrating how the public sphere exists as part of a private world that then moves into the public domain. Habermas (1989:136) conceptualised the public sphere as 'a sphere which mediates between society and state, in which the public organises itself as the bearer of public opinion'. More than the mere expression of opinions, public opinion and a public sphere are formed only when listeners become political actors. The creation of the public sphere is thus not the moment at which listeners express opinions or frustrations on the air, but rather the moment at which real debate occurs, mediated by the programme host.

Broadcasting can often create the illusion of a public sphere via political talk shows, but the authentic creation of the public sphere demands the listener as engaged participant versus as mere spectator (Price, 1996). All the respondents in the survey indicated that they had voted in the last national elections, with most of them further indicating that they had also voted in local municipal elections. When asked about their attitudes towards politics, none of the respondents chose the option 'I have no interest in politics'. Here we see confirmation of previous research findings that talk-radio listeners tend to take an interest in political matters and that they are generally politically active. Moreover, this is further indication of the talk-radio listener as political actor versus mere spectator in the performance of talk radio.

In terms of political discussion, 567MW broadcasts are often very moderate in terms of political affiliation, and this may be seen as a possible strength. Unlike US talk radio, the political affiliations of the presenters are often unknown and in the highly politicised terrain of South Africa, this might be quite appealing to listeners and an opportunity for programme hosts to more effectively mediate political discussions. Initially, 567MW was perceived by listeners to be hostile towards the new African National Congress (ANC) government, as opposed to embracing 'sunshine' journalism, and the programming still gives space to callers who are critical of the majority party. Lee (2002) has argued that in some ways this is the role of talk radio – that it serves as a platform for people to voice discontent towards government, that it is an arena for expressing anguish resulting from social and political problems, and that the discussions do not necessarily articulate any responses. The purpose of democratic talk is to create citizens who think as a public and make reasoned political judgements (Barber, 1984:197). With the help of programme hosts, discussions on 567MW are more than just a series of calls expressing listener opinions. Rather, over the period of a programme or even the broadcast day, opinions are aggregated, analysed and often coalesced into cogency.

As the public broadcaster is increasingly perceived by listeners to broadcast a pro-government agenda, talk radio also emerges as a critical and alternative space for more conservative listeners (Orgeret, 2008). 567MW then also becomes a quasi-hegemonic force that sets agendas and controls the nature of discourse in the public sphere. Certainly, an agenda-setting function is executed in the selection of news items and discussion topics – but by listeners and callers themselves, who use the 'open line' function of the call-in shows to set the topics and tone of the debate.

In this way, 567MW illuminates public discourse and debates about the nature of the public sphere (Herbst, 1995) and contributes to a democratic public sphere. But in this serendipitous selection of certain discussion topics (and the exclusion of others), power is created and transferred through an economy of discourse or conversation. In this way, power is transferred along conduits of dialogue according to the knowledge one has (Foucault, 1980). This is seen in the process of callers setting the agenda for public debate, raising issues and concerns that might be considered middle class, and resulting in the exclusion of the concerns of poorer neighbourhoods on the periphery of the city, both literally and figuratively.

However, there is no indication that members of these poorer communities do not listen to the station and they do occasionally call in and deliberately attempt to shift the focus. But this middle-class content, the discussion of issues prevalent in middle-class contexts and the coverage of middle-class suburbs are dominant, despite the station's deliberate attempt to diversify its audience. Examples of 'middle-class content' include coverage of issues pertinent to the more affluent Southern Suburbs neighbourhoods in Cape Town, as well as issues such as rates and property values, financial matters (e.g. retirement annuities), etc. One way in which it has attempted to diversify the audience is via the introduction of black presenters such as Aden Thomas and, during 2008, Soli Philander (who replaced Lisa Chait). Thomas explained how the idea behind his appointment to the show was that 'ordinary' people would start to call in and that they would talk about 'ordinary' things. Here the assumption is that the subject matter would not be overtly political, but would deal with light-hearted humorous matters, perhaps almost keeping in line with Thomas's former role as a DJ on a jazz-format, commercial radio station. He highlighted one instance as being a typical example of this:

> I asked people to call in and tell me what their one secret ingredient for a great curry would be. And someone called in saying condensed milk! And that's the power of talk radio, that people would talk about this among themselves later that morning and say, did you hear that crazy person who wanted to put condensed milk in a curry![3]

For those who listen, 567MW plays a role in terms of social cohesion, drawing listeners together through their sharing of similar cultural experiences and reproducing ritualised experiences that affirm common identities, values and memories (Curran,

2002). One example of these kinds of ritualised experiences is national sporting events, which are high on the 567MW news agenda. The majority of survey respondents indicated that they perceived themselves to be very similar to other listeners and that listening made them 'feel more part of the Cape Town community'. Radio station broadcasts, and audience engagement with these broadcasts, result in the constitution of the audience as a singular 'imagined' community.

The recognition afforded the station by political leaders is further evidence of the potential of talk radio to promote public-sphere debates. For example, the former mayor of Cape Town, Helen Zille, as well as the former Western Cape premier, Ibrahim Rasool, regularly agreed to interviews and sessions during which they took often-hostile questions from listeners and answered them directly on the air. Similarly, a number of press conferences around important news events have been broadcast live on the station. For example, former ANC chairperson Mosiuoa Lekota held a press conference live on 8 October 2008 to discuss the formation of a breakaway political party. Similarly, shortly before the 2009 national elections, the president of the ANC Youth League, Julius Malema, agreed to an interview with Redi Direko to explain why he refused to participate in a panel debate with other political leaders, even though he had not been interviewed by any other news media. Here we see that political leaders recognise the space offered by talk radio to reach audiences and generate political discussion. Political leaders and other members of civil society recognise the power inherent in talk radio and seek it out as the platform on which to raise their issues and generate public discussion on matters of general social and political interest.

Audience contributions to public-sphere debates

The audience (represented by callers) is a central component of this notion of the station's role in developing a democratic public sphere. According to the Radio Audience Measurement Survey conducted by the South African Advertising Research Foundation (SAARF, 2009), 567MW had 152 000 listeners in 2009, a fairly small audience by commercial-radio standards. This chapter makes some general observations about listeners based on survey responses and caller-generated on-air content. The audience is of primary importance to talk radio, which is largely sustained by audience-generated talk. With most shows on 567MW built on contributions from callers, they also define, to a large extent, the character of the station.

The callers to the programmes are what define the character of the station, and from the moment that they call in and 'this partial manifestation of opinion is reflected and broadcast to a virtually undefined larger public ... it participates in the construction of the public sphere' (Ferry, 1992:19, cited in Winocur, 2003). Engagement with programme hosts about individual contributions on aspects of daily life solidifies this experience for listeners. The 567MW shows thus move from personal identification to larger group identification, as the show presenter generalises specific experiences into a larger social frame for the interest of the general audience (Wilcox, 1995). The calls to the station are thus a critical component of delineating the boundaries of the public sphere generated by the radio station.

Barber (1984) has argued that even if citizens' contributions are not well thought out or knowledgeable, they are crucial for maintaining a sense of collective civic identity and for generating collective views. As such, these contributions form a deliberative democracy, which has been defined as 'a process whereby citizens voluntarily and freely participate in discussions on public issues. It is a discursive system where citizens share information on public issues, talk politics, form opinions, and participate in political processes' (Kim, Wyatt & Katz, 1999:361).

While some (e.g. Schudson, 1997) argue that everyday talk is not political, this chapter argues that it is 'via meandering and in part never fully predictable talk that the political can be generated, that the links between the personal and the political can be established' (Dahlgren, 2002:12). In other words, the talk that is being considered here is not always overtly political, does not always deal with political topics and can often take the form of seemingly informal everyday conversation.

The characteristics of the 567MW callers are also of importance, as they determine the nature of the contributions. In general, listeners to talk shows in the United States have been described as being 'better educated, more affluent, slightly older, and more involved in the political process than others' (Wilcox, 1995:3). This appears to be the same for 567MW, and in the South African context, race is an additional confounding variable. Many of the callers are white, and black callers often call in only when the programme host is also black. Presumably a perception of homogeneity results in an imagined cultural affinity.

Other research (e.g. Pan & Kosicki, 1997) argues that talk radio attracts like-minded audiences. On 567MW there is little engagement between listeners, with most of the interaction between presenter and caller, with the former mediating debate, but also often playing the role of 'devil's advocate', because there is little major direct disagreement between callers. Hutchby (1996) has demonstrated the power inequality between hosts and callers on British talk radio, and to some extent this is the same on 567MW, merely by extension of the nature of the medium. The host has (and frequently exercises) the power to give callers more time to make their arguments or merely to cut them off; and this power is exercised insofar as the hosts exert their own standards for the level of debate. Callers thus have the illusion that they are communicating with one another, although their contributions are mediated by the programme host, who also guides and directs the discussion. While it is callers who set the agenda, the host frequently suggests conversation topics, and even when it is a designated 'open line', which one may call with any topic of discussion, the host may disregard some topics or encourage further contributions towards others. The formation of public opinion thus occurs in a manner slightly different to the original 'coffee shop' conceptualisation of Habermas's public sphere.

Talk-radio research (e.g. Winocur, 2003) shows that calling the radio is not an activity exclusive to one social sector, but that at middle to high socio-cultural and intellectual levels, participation mainly acquires the form of criticism or opinion. These kinds of calls occur within the framework of a discourse in which the individual 'feels entitled to rights, and participating is perceived as an act of public intervention to denounce social and political injustice ... on issues of collective interest in which the interlocutor is not only the host of the programme but the whole audience' (Winocur, 2003:33). This is certainly a current perception of 567MW callers, most of whom do not appear to be working class.

Here one also finds cultivation theory at work, with callers' complaints often clustered around certain issues, although ironically, for instance with regard to issues such as crime, these callers are often less likely to have been directly affected. Despite international literature that offers support for perceptions of the increased political awareness and involvement of talk-radio listeners, another level of listener complaints on 567MW often seems related to poor understandings of political processes, despite the fact that listeners are often more politically active. For example, when the mayor of Cape Town was on air, she often received complaints that should have been addressed directly to local councillors. On several occasions she pointed this out to callers and reversed the role play by asking them whether they had voted in local municipal elections and pointing out the problems associated with their lack of involvement in local political processes. Here one sees the clear divide emerging between talk-radio listeners and those who call in to participate in on-air discussions. In addition, the station increasingly seems to be actively cultivating a role as a 'go-between', i.e. the first place to go when one has a problem. For example, the station urges callers to phone in with traffic and other similar problems that they want the authorities or public officials to address.

Interestingly, the station's audience is not uniform, even though its members perceive themselves to be similar and even though callers appear to be generally similar. The survey component of this project revealed that some listeners do not fit the assumed demographics in terms of race and class, and that the 567MW audience might quite feasibly be further grouped into two distinct categories: callers and non-callers. There is an implicit assumption that callers are 'somehow representative of the public out of which they emerge' (Coleman, 1998:8), but programme manager Africa Melane estimates that only about 10 per cent of listeners actually call in to the station[4] and that of these, a fair proportion call in on a regular basis, although, according to operations manager Colin Cullis, 'sometimes people call in once a year because they have a story to tell'.[5] Every call that is made to the station is logged and if a caller has rung previously, the computer system immediately alerts the station to this. 'We are getting people and opinions from a variety of backgrounds', said Melane, but added that callers are often selected deliberately to reflect the diversity of the city.

Even though the audience is located at a spatial and sometimes temporal distance (in the case of pre-recorded segments), programming still reflects a clear assumption that the audience is uniform. In many ways, the ideological self-constitution of the audience is such that it is part of the imagined community of 567MW, just by virtue of tuning in. Advertising is a key part of this type of programming and there is a high incidence of advertisements that clearly target an economically viable middle-class market. But even though the audience is targeted primarily as consumers, the nature of debate indicates that despite its aims, the audience of 567MW does not constitute a market, but a public, with the importance of broadcasts being their capacity as vehicles to transfer meaningful messages instead of merely to deliver audiences to advertisers (Price, 1996).

Not all public spheres are democratic (Winocur, 2003), and 567MW is no different. Not everyone participates – the debate may not be closed to those who are not sufficiently imbued with the requisite level of English-language competence or cultural capital, but nonetheless, they do not feel driven enough to participate actively. When we occasionally hear these voices, it is usually because they are solicited via interviews linked to specific, sometimes-sensational events. Participatory democratic talk values the open-ended exploration of common thoughts and experiences (Barber, 1984), as well as the subjective viewpoints of individuals, although in the case of marginal voices, the approach is almost tabloid in the selection of cases that are centred on controversial events. For example, another exclusive 567MW interview was with a local woman who killed her drug-addict son. This open-ended and emotive monologue demonstrates how the purpose of talk in a democracy is to transform private values into public ones 'through the process of identifying and empathising with the values of others' (Barber, 1984:137).

Conclusions

Habermas (1989:438) emphasises the 'pluralistic, internally much differentiated mass public', exploring the possibility that autonomous public spheres can bring conflicts from the periphery to the centre of public life via the mass media in order to generate critical debate among a wider public (Downey & Fenton, 2003). This discussion of 567MW certainly provides some evidence for the existence of these kinds of autonomous public spheres, and through their provision of a platform for discussion, they constitute participatory space for citizens to understand democracy and widen social access to political knowledge.

In South Africa, the talk-radio format is still competing for audiences and advertisers, and despite its perceived popularity, audience numbers cannot compete with those of national commercial music-format stations. According to the former programme manager: 'Talk radio is not a hugely appealing format, yet the medium acts as a catalyst, and it operates within a culture of accountability. Talk radio is not as captivating as you might think.'[6]

However, the present study has demonstrated that 567MW certainly plays a role in the development of a public sphere in Cape Town, despite the potential limitation of the medium and the relatively small audience size. Despite the heterogeneous nature of the audience, the talk component brings its members together through the radio and allows them each in his/her different way to imagine his/her active participation and thus to contribute towards the public sphere of South Africa's emergent democracy. 567MW is an autonomous public sphere, simply independent from the dominant public sphere, which mainstream commercial media and the public broadcaster represent (as opposed to being a counter-public sphere that would also challenge the dominant public sphere). It offers a space in which members of different, more-limited publics talk across lines of cultural diversity (Fraser, 1992:117).

Talk shows have a potential democratising aspect, not because they offer opportunities for discussion, but because they juxtapose people who normally live separate lives and present them with the opportunity to express their opinions (Lunt & Stenner, 2005). 567MW is a powerful medium in its ability to privilege certain forms of talk and play an agenda-setting role in the city, particularly as it provides the opportunity and space for important forms of political speech to flourish.

Endnotes

1   Interview with Colin Cullis, July 2006.
2   Interview with Africa Melane, 31 October 2007.
3   Informal interview with Aden Thomas, April 2008.
4   Interview with Melane.
5   Interview with Cullis.
6   Interview with Tony Fahey, 12 July 2006.

13

Radio and Religion
A Case of Difference and Diversity

Maria Frahm-Arp

Introduction

In late 2006 I was invited to be a guest on *Believe It or Not*, a programme that is aired on Sunday nights on Talk Radio 702, a talk-radio station that broadcasts to Gauteng Province and shares programmes with its sister station 567MW in Cape Town. *Believe It or Not* is a radio show that discusses topics such as religion, mysticism, the occult and the transcendental. A few things struck me as I participated in the show: firstly, it offered a relatively unique space for religious debate in South Africa. Secondly, the manner in which Kate Turkington, the programme host, ran the show clearly positioned her as a leader of a new 'religious community'. Lastly, the fact that *Believe It or Not* was the longest-running talk show on Radio 702 seemed to suggest something about listeners' abiding, or perhaps newfound, interest in religion.

I began to wonder what this might be saying about religion and radio in South Africa in the 21st century and what one might find by comparing this programme with radio stations that specifically support one religious viewpoint or denomination. I had in mind the Catholic station Radio Veritas and the Islamic station Radio Islam, both community radio stations and thus very different in key ways from the commercially based Radio 702, the home of *Believe It or Not*. This chapter, then, is the result of a comparison of three very different religious radio spaces.[1] It argues that the medium of radio affects the nature of religious expression in different ways, making it difficult for us to generalise about how radio impacts on religion. Three particular trends are examined: the chapter explores the notion that radio builds religious communities; it questions whether radio can transform how religion is experienced; and it comments on the authority of the new religious 'leaders' who are emerging due to radio.

Post-apartheid South Africa has moved, albeit with jerky steps, into a modern democratic state, yet as people have become more educated and economically empowered, there has not been a demise of religion, as Weber (1976) predicted. In the period 1982–2002 religious participation grew;[2] simultaneously, South Africa became a secular state. This co-existence of a secular state and a growth in religious practice highlights what many scholars recognise more generally – that the notion of secularisation is not a given in the modern context, nor is it a sound theoretical starting point for any discussion on religion (Asad, 2003; Casanova, 1994). If the census statistics and the participation of South Africans in churches, mosques and temples are to be believed, religion is an important component in the lives of most South Africans and needs to be understood more comprehensively. Religious radio too needs to be analysed as a part of this wider canvas.

With the advent of democracy in South Africa came the beginning of a new openness to and respect for the religions of the world. A variety of faith-based community radio stations in English and other South African languages began to emerge. An exception to the single-faith religious radio position is *Believe It or Not*, which explores religious expressions from paganism to Islam not from one faith-based perspective, but from the perspective of interest in all religions. This reflects the larger societal trend in which people tend to participate in the religions dominant in their communities,[3] but among some people there is a growing appreciation for different religions. Collectively, this means that a study of radio and religion needs to compare and contrast various types of religious programming both from a faith-based perspective and a multifaith viewpoint.

South Africa has undergone rapid social change in the last 20 years and one of the key discussions that has emerged has been about a 'crisis of identity' where, as in much of the globalised world, old stabilities have become increasingly splintered and the locus of individual identities has shifted from one core to another (Hall, 1996:595–96). Castells (1997) argues that, in a context of instability and change, identity has become increasingly powerful, because it offers individuals a source of meaning. Yet all our human 'identities are in some sense ... social identities' (Jenkins, 1996:4). Therefore, Jenkins (1996) maintains that where radical social change has taken place in a society, it follows that there will also be shifts and that people may look to new sources for the basis of their individual identities.

Consumption can be seen as a key new way of shaping identity and radio can be part of this process. In order to live according to the constructs of their identities, people will consume goods, move in particular public spaces, eat various foods and interact with certain groups of people, all of which are aligned to their values or their identities (Campbell, 1987). For example, Muslims will consume halal food, Pentecostal Charismatic Christians will buy designer clothes as a way to signal their wealth when they go to church on Sundays (Frahm-Arp, 2010), teenagers hang out in certain shopping malls (Hetherington, 1998) and the young black upwardly mobile class in South Africa buy labels like Stoned Cherrie and shop in the Zone at Rosebank in Johannesburg to signal their identification with a particular idea of black urban upward mobility (Nuttall, 2004). Identity therefore goes beyond the social roles people play (Castells, 1997:6–7) and embraces the things they consume, which includes the types of radio they listen to. Put another way, and in relation to radio and religion, by tuning in to different radio stations and programmes, people are living out particular religious identities either as members of a specific faith or as those who are willing to question world religions. As theorists such as Hetherington (1998), Nuttall (2004) and Campbell (1987) argue, the very act of consumption is an act of identification with what is consumed. It is consumed because the individuals want to identify with the particular commodity.

Religion, however, is more than just something that is consumed in order for people to shape a sense of identity. Yet what is meant by religion when everything from witchcraft, 'muthi healings', on-line Evangelical youth dating sites, religious tourism and forms of Muslim political protests are all thrown together under the same label? By religion, I follow Birgit Meyer's (2006:6) definition that 'broadly speaking, religion refers to the ways in which people link up with, or even feel touched by, a meta-empirical sphere that may be glossed as supernatural, sacred, divine, or transcendental'.

This chapter examines the relationship between radio and religion in South Africa by comparing Radio Islam, Radio Veritas and *Believe It or Not* on Radio 702. Each station does not use radio in isolation, but engages various forms of media such as the Internet, Twitter and Facebook, but radio currently remains the central operating space. In their edited collection *Religion, Media and the Public Sphere*, Birgit Meyer and Annelies Moors (2006:19) argue that:

> ... religions have come to play an increasingly public role in offering alternative imaginations of communities. At the same time, in the process of going public – by becoming enmeshed with identity politics, by being drawn close to forces of commercialization, and by adopting new media technologies – religions have been transformed.

At first glance, as will be discussed below, it seems that radio is changing the shape of religion: on conservative Islamic and Catholic radio stations, women are presenters, and these presenters appear to form a new type of religious leadership. Not only does it appear as if a new religious leadership is emerging, but new religious communities are formed through radio and these link local communities into global networks.

This chapter looks at the multiple layers of meaning held within the experience of broadcasting religion on air and argues that while different religions use the same multimedia approach, their aims and the effect of radio on religion are quite different. Radio Islam creates a whole imagined world that engages in all the elements of the listener's daily life. In her work on media, Meyer has argued that some religious media create a *habitus* for the listener. In the context of Radio Islam there is not a complete *habitus*, but if engaged with on an ongoing basis, this station, by virtue of the all-encompassing nature of its programmes, offers a specific way of being in the world. Radio Veritas strengthens local communities and links these into the larger global Catholic Church, and both these stations use up-to-date multimedia resources to promote a conservative religious message. This conservative message in turn raises questions about the actual power of the new female and lay male presenters on these stations. *Believe It or Not* creates a very different liberal community and experience of a religious forum in which all forms of transcendental experience are discussed and no religious system is specifically supported.

Stations and programmes: Religious communities?

The variety of languages spoken in South Africa is in a small way reflected in the programmes on which I focus, although English dominates the usage. *Believe It or Not*, on Radio 702, airs all its content in English; Radio Islam and Radio Veritas broadcast the majority of their programmes in English, although Radio Islam also has some Arabic and isiZulu programmes; while Radio Veritas has isiZulu, Sesotho, Portuguese and Afrikaans shows, thus drawing in language-specific Catholic communities in South Africa.

Radio Veritas

Radio Veritas, started by Fr Emil Blaser, a Dominican monk, is a non-profit, self-supporting Catholic radio station based in Eldorado Park in Johannesburg. The station broadcasts 24 hours a day over the Internet or on DSTV channel 170. The programmes are all local, but after 21:00 the station broadcasts programmes from the EWTN Global Catholic Network. In addition to the English programmes, there is a daily Sesotho programme between 15:00 and 16:00, a two-hour isiZulu programme on Thursdays between 19:00 and 21:00, an Afrikaans broadcast on Wednesdays between 18:00 and 19:00, and three Portuguese programmes between 19:00 and 20:00 thrice weekly. While it is true that the varied language programmes cater to

South Africa's cross-language Catholic communities, class and income still exclude many. The accessibility of the station's programmes is limited to people who have DSTV (a subscription cable network) or who have computers where they can access the station online. Only on Sunday mornings is the English programme streamed on Radio 2000 for a mere two hours. Thus, despite its aim to be inclusive, Radio Veritas remains a station for people who have access to more expensive forms of media.

The aim of the station is to give hope, encouragement, education and entertainment to Catholic Christians trying to live out their Catholic faith.[4] It has an easy-to-use website that is updated every day, which gives information about personalities, programmes and community news. Presenters are both male and female, and the religious experts who are brought in include women who may be nuns, spiritual directors, workers in faith-based organisations or theologians. The station gives no general or secular news, but does give news of the events and happenings within the Catholic world and reports on issues directly affecting this community. From the website, there are links to a few other religious sites, but there is no active engagement with blogs and Twitter.

Radio Islam

Radio Islam bills itself as 'Your Learning Station'.[5] This is a fast-moving, informative station that aims to keep listeners in touch with the worldwide Muslim community. The station was started in 1993 and on 10 April 1997 made its first signal broadcast. By far the dominant language used on the station is English, with 96 per cent of programmes in English, 2 per cent in Arabic and 2 per cent in isiZulu. The station is based in Lenasia, Gauteng and offers an almost round-the-clock service. Claiming to have over 100 000 listeners, its aim (in 2007) was to broadcast via signal throughout southern Africa.[6]

With nine news bulletins per day as well as daily prayers, Radio Islam claims to be the only radio station a Muslim needs to tune into to stay up to date with current affairs, international news, health, cooking, gardening, child care, religion, the community and finances. In all these programmes, the focus is not on offering Cape Malay recipes or the latest fashion trends in South Africa, but on teaching women and men how to live according to the laws of Islam. There is a move away from cultural traditions to offering a code of living such that in all things believers are assured that they are observing *sha'ria* law. Its four primary objects are promoting Islam to all via the airwaves, uplifting humankind, striving to be an authentic Islamic voice, and providing alternative news and current events programmes.[7] From the website there are links to other sites, blogs and Twitter addresses, making this a multimedia space.

Believe It or Not

Believe It or Not currently broadcasts on Sunday evenings between 20:00 and 23:00 on Radio 702, and offers a very different engagement with religion. While the other two stations are community stations, are funded by their religious constituents and appeal specifically to people interested in either Catholicism or Islam, *Believe It or Not* is a radio show that views religion from a very different angle, questioning all religions, but not specifically encouraging listeners to join any religion. The programme is part of Radio 702, which is a talk-radio station primarily concerned with running a profitable business. On any given Sunday the programme covers a diverse range of issues. On Sunday, 7 October 2007, for instance, an hour was dedicated to discussions with Buddhist monks regarding the revolt in Burma. This was followed by an hour given to issues of healing with a phone-in session to herbalist Margaret Roberts, followed by a discussion about healing with dolphins. Finally there was an hour-long phone-in with a well-known psychic.

Radio as a form of community building

It has been argued that radio, especially talk radio, which all three of these stations employ in some ways, leads to the formation of a sense of belonging and imagined communities (Nyamnjoh, 2005, and Bosch in this volume). What is of most interest here, however, is not whether radio helps to form religious communities, but the nature of these communities and their local or global connections. Radio Veritas strengthens the ties of the immediate cultural-religious communities of different local Catholic groups and then links them into the imagined global Catholic world. Radio Islam, however, forms more than a community, offering a way of being in the world that is not quite a *habitus* in the Bordieuian sense, but the station provides listeners with cultural capital in the form of programmes about language – particularly Arabic – etiquette, gender roles, life expectations and the teachings of Islam. *Believe It or Not* does not try to create any form of community, but in effect does so through the very nature of phone-in talk-show radio (see Bosch in this volume), which creates a sense of community and is further strengthened by the longevity of the show itself.

Radio Veritas uses a multimedia approach to create both local and global communities. The pope is the head of the Catholic Church, but has remained an elusive figure in the lives of ordinary believers for much of the history of the church. By broadcasting the pope's weekly address, together with his travel plans and latest proclamations, this station brings him into the living rooms and lives of ordinary believers. As Meyer's (2006) work on the sensory importance of religion and media shows, through radio these listeners are able to engage with the very voice of their leader, and his presence is felt and made real – the listener is drawn right into the pope's community and space. The medium of radio has therefore changed the Catholic community's understanding of themselves as a body led by the pope – he is now a real, heard and experienced figure. In the process, a greater uniformity and coherence are created, as everyone, all over the world, can listen to the same message at the same time and thereby also be governed by the same regulatory practices promoted by the pope. What is argued here is that, through radio, the discourse of unity has been altered, because it has moved from speaking about what the pope might have said to a select group in the Vatican to actually hearing the pope speak. By listening to a station like Radio Veritas, people identify with and embrace the creation of a unified Catholic world that identifies with the pope in a far more immediate way then it did a generation or two ago. Through this, a conservative consumption of Catholicism is maintained and promoted.

At the same time, Radio Veritas is also creating local *conservative* religious communities. This is done not just through the radio programmes, particularly those in the four dominant languages within the South African Catholic community, but also through the on-line media of the website, where notice is given of different local events, together with local news about people and clergy within the community. Prayer requests for those who have got married, have recently died or are ill are powerful ways of linking people into a community, because they are given knowledge about one another's lives.

On Radio Islam, the list of people who send in their announcements about weddings, funerals and community events that are aired is similarly impressive. People seem to engage with the station and their letters/emails show that this is a forum and community that they want to communicate with. These announcements create a strong sense of community and belonging – of knowing what is happening in the lives of others. On 15 August 2007 the website reportedly had over 90 000 visitors, showing how active a site it is and the numerical strength of this community.[8]

Where Muslims are a minority, religion is de facto confined to the private sphere and believers come together to create a community 'that is no more than a congregation of believers who follow their own rules of conduct' (Roy, 2005:148). At the same time, there is also a pull to be part of a larger transnational Islam, one where once again culture is stripped away and the rules of Islam regulate all aspects of the life of the believer.

In South Africa, Islam is very much in the minority and the Islamic community is divided into three different cultural groups, as Vahed and Jeppie (2005:252) show: the Malay or Cape Muslims, who were classed as 'coloured' under apartheid; the Indian Muslim group; and the black Muslim group, which is currently the fastest-growing group and is largely made up of immigrants from other parts of Africa.

Within this divergent community, the majority look to conservative Middle Eastern forms of Islam and support the idea of a universal ummah, while a smaller minority are more liberal and seek to disconnect themselves from the Middle Eastern voice of Islam. Radio Islam falls within conservative Salafi Islam and looks to create Muslim unity by placing more focus on how to live out sha'ria law rather then on keeping cultural practices alive. Roy (2005:149) has argued that in conservative diaspora Muslim contexts there has been a push towards divesting the different groups of their cultures and offering them a deculturation process that provides a religion that focuses on norms and rules (Salafism) rather than on values (liberal or ethical Islam). This conservative Muslim radio station does not reject culture as such, but it downplays the variety of cultural forces that influence believers, encouraging them rather to be influenced by the more global conservative religious *Weltanschuung* that it offers.

The plethora of programmes on cooking, housekeeping, gardening, dress codes and family relationships on Radio Islam are an attempt at focusing away from different cultural norms of behaviour, for example Cape Malay culture, and refocusing on correct religious practices in all circumstances of ordinary life. This is a religion that individuals self-consciously take on and in which they become the regulators of their own behaviour according to the norms and rules of their religion rather than the culture they find themselves in. Through this process, these religious rules and regulations for daily living become, as Meyer (2006) has argued, a new *habitus* of Islam, and this *habitus* is mediated not through the family, but via the media. In the case of Radio Islam, its website and the various Twitter sites and blogs associated with it offer believers everything they need to know about the world, from the rand–dollar exchange rate to the weddings taking place in the community in the following week. It would be too strong to suggest that Radio Islam offers a *habitus*, but it does offer listeners cultural and religious capital through its teaching, and this in turn offers them the basis on which their identities can be shaped and anchored. In this it is different from the community created by Radio Veritas, which promotes the multiple social and linguistic cultures that make up the South African Catholic Church. Radio Islam tries to draw listeners out of cultural and community networks and into a religious community network in which its (Radio Islam's) particular type of conservative Islam shapes the self-understanding and behaviour of believers. To strengthen further the idea that while radio might help create imagined religious communities, these communities differ significantly, we turn our attention now to *Believe It or Not*.

Believe It or Not has its sense of community built up through phone-in conversations, emails and texts messages sent to Kate Turkington – it is thus a community built around a personality. Turkington regularly has guests on the show who host events that people might find interesting, but unlike the other two stations, the programme does not use these as vehicles for community building. The sense of community is built, at least according to Turkington, by the people who phone in: 'they make the show and the *Believe It or Not* community.'[9] The technology of radio therefore opens up a loosely imagined community of people who come together and exchange ideas and debate points of view through the radio with the aid of the telephone and email. For these listeners, engagement with this community and the consumption of this form of radio identifies them with a new religious discourse – one in which membership of a religion is not important, but openness to learning about all religions is valued.

Radio as transformer of religion

Radio has not only made various imagined communities possible, although these may be very different in nature and constitution, but, I argue, it is has also transformed the religions that are aired (cf. Meyer, 2006). Yet it may do so in different ways. Below are three very different examples that highlight this point. The first is the Catholic Mass that is aired every Sunday on Radio Veritas, which speaks to the mediated nature of the transcendental, which is made possible through radio. The second is the politics of radio in South Africa, which has directly changed the presentation of Islam, as Radio Islam has to have female presenters in order to keep its licence. The third is the economics of radio, which shape the nature and content of programmes, e.g. *Believe It or Not*: 'Not only do modern media such as print, photography, TV, film, or internet shape sensational forms, the latter themselves are media that mediate, and thus produce, the transcendental and make it sense-able', argues Meyer (2006:14).

Each Sunday morning between 12:00 and 13:00 Radio Veritas airs a live performance of Mass from the studio. Listeners are invited to phone in their intentions and prayer requests. The Mass follows the Catholic Missal and includes the relevant prayers, set readings, canticles, hymns and homilies. This is the central and most important programme on the station. Participating in Mass is the aspect that fundamentally divides Catholics from Protestant, Orthodox or Independent Christians. Only Catholic Christians can take part in a Catholic Mass and so this ritual draws the boundary between those who are truly a part of the community and those who may stand at the margins and listen in. This mediated Mass is one of the greatest technological innovations of radio, because it mediates the transcendental into the very homes of the listeners. Until the advent of radio, Mass could only be heard in a church; now the church has come into the home or workplace. For Catholic laity, there is a centuries-old history that began in the Middle Ages and regards hearing Mass as more important than receiving the actual elements of the Mass.[10] This means that the transforming moment in the Mass for the laity is hearing the words of the Mass rather than actually eating the bread and drinking the wine. Through radio, therefore, it can be said that God becomes present in the lives and sensations of Catholic believers. The ancient religious necessity of being *physically* present at Mass is now transformed and kept up to date through the new media of radio and the Internet. Priests in the Johannesburg diocese support this new mediation of God. As an example of this, Jesuit priest Anthony Egan argued that the church needs to use media to remain relevant and engage with people.[11] This engagement with God in the Mass does not happen in a vacuum, but in the broader context of the social and cultural processes that the physical Catholic churches have built up and which the other programmes on the station deepen.

In a very different way, Radio Islam offers an example of religious transformation through the politics of radio. Although this station initially presented a conservative form of Islam, it had to comply with Independent Communications Authority of South Africa (ICASA) regulations and therefore has employed female presenters. More liberal Islamic radio stations such as Radio Cape have had female presenters since their inception and the communities that listen to the station support gender equality among the staff. In conservative Islam, women are not allowed to engage in any way with the public or be visible in public spaces. Yet because of ICASA regulations that stipulated that Radio Islam would only get its licence if it employed female presenters, this conservative religious principle had to be dropped and now women present programmes and engage in the public space. The presenters, both male and female, speak with knowledge and authority, and they form a new type of religious leadership that seems to directly shape the discourse about their faith, which is presented to the people who listen in. The female presenters on this station are thus among the first generation of female organic 'religious leaders' of conservative Islam in South Africa.

This is a powerful example of how external forces can shape religious practice, but in 2010–11, when I carried out further research on Islamic women in Johannesburg, I began to explore the question of whether the advent of female presenters actually changed the institutional shape of religion. In her chapter in this volume, Schulz examines the dynamics behind female presenters on Malian Muslim stations and argues that they are hampered and at times discredited by male religious leaders. On Radio Islam, the female presenters specifically address women and present shows that focus on teaching women how to live out a Salafi form of Islam in which the conservative moral practices and regulations of the religion are adhered to, which state that female believers will be assured of their salvation through the proper and pious observance of Islamic rules. But the presenters of these shows have not become imams in conservative religious mosques and they are not encouraging women to move out of a conservative religious understanding of Islam. The transformation of the religion that has taken place through the politics of radio that calls for gender equality, in the view of this writer, merely masks the conservative message of Islam that is presented and has not significantly altered the formal power dynamics of women in the mosque and the community at large.

Unlike the programmes on Radio Islam and Radio Veritas, *Believe It or Not* has no particular religious agenda around faith or the transcendental. According to the management of Radio 702, every show is responsible for boosting its own ratings, i.e. getting people to listen. Ratings are all important, because it is through them that advertisers are brought into the station. What improves the ratings, according to Turkington, is lively debate or particularly intriguing topics. The type of religious discourse presented on the show is therefore influenced by an economic agenda, and at times there is mediated confrontational dialogue between religious believers and non-believers who are both encouraged to call in and make their point heard. Religious practices of a more unusual kind take up significant amounts of air time, as they lead to debate that brings in callers and therefore improves ratings. This radio programme does not effect changes in a religion in any significant way; what it does is open up a valuable new platform for debate about and education on different religious viewpoints, thus demonstrating how the broader economic politics of radio technology influences how religion is discussed and presented. Closely linked to this discussion of the transformation of religion by radio is the debate on the voice of authority held by different presenters on these stations.

Gender and shaping the 'voice of authority'

In spite of the presence of women in the programmes of Radio Veritas and Radio Islam, one can ask whether any real shift in gender dynamics has come about. Does this signal a change in leadership within these religious groups? Both Radio Veritas and Radio Islam in South Africa have been on the air for more than ten years, yet in neither religious community is there any current move to recognise women as institutional religious leaders. Once again, *Believe It or Not* offers us a different picture – here a woman is the self-styled leader of a loose organic community of religiously liberal and interested followers. What is at issue here is that radio itself does not create new religious leaders; rather, the relevant social contexts and religious ideologies must also be aligned to give these presenters support, otherwise they do not de facto become recognised leaders.

At Radio Veritas, Fr Emil Blaser, who started the station, personifies the station, but it is his strong presence as a Catholic priest that makes him revered as the community's 'father' and leader, and that separates him from the listeners and other presenters who are laity. He leads a daily morning devotion, which sets the tone for the day. The other presenters are lay people, and while they take up more time on air than priests, they actively try to resist being seen as leaders of the community by continually reminding listeners that priests and the Vatican are the true leaders of the faith and that they themselves are just lay people supporting their clergy. Listeners have the most 'contact' with these lay presenters and announcers. In interviews with clergy, the lay interviewers positioned themselves as 'one of the group' or part of the listening community of lay people and ask questions on behalf of the community in interviews and give advice over the air. For example, on Sunday mornings the presenters often introduce the priest saying Mass as follows: 'Morning Father Michael. You are from St Margaret's parish in Johannesburg. *I speak for myself and other listeners* when I say that we don't know anything about you. Could you introduce yourself to us? (15 September 2007; emphasis added).

Radio Islam also has a large proportion of lay presenters and covers every aspect of a person's life, broadcasting religious programmes that provide translations of the Qur'an, Islamic history, an imam's correction of misconceptions or misunderstood beliefs, guidance for Muslim women and prayers/devotions. But even more time is spent on how to live an holistic Muslim life, including advice on remedies for illnesses, child care and marriage problems. The presenters of these programmes offer insight and advice, and are not imams, but while they are 'organic' and 'informal' leaders on air and in the discussions that promote the living of a pious conservative Muslim life, they have not become formal religious leaders in the communities of faith they serve. As with Radio Veritas and the Catholic Church, which do not accept the institutionalised religious authority of anyone except the church's ordained male clergy, so in conservative Islam, institutionalised religious authority is not given to anyone outside the closely regulated male group of imams. This is not to be confused with the role women can play as theologians and religious experts outside of the institutional space of the religion, or with more liberal forms of Islam where women can become institutionalised religious leaders, or with other forms of Christianity where women can become priests.

Kate Turkington on *Believe It or Not* offers us a different picture. She not only directs much of the content and structure of her show, but is also the central figure in this show and the person the listeners want to hear. Every week there are positive comments from listeners, like this one from Sheila on 11 August 2007: 'I love your show and I listen every week. You are just so interesting to listen to.' Kate is a charismatic person in the Weberian sense and has styled herself as something of an alternative religious leader – someone who does not practise, believe or adhere to any religion in particular, but who is interested in transcendental questions and believes in spiritual powers. Like the lay Muslim or Catholic presenters on the other two stations discussed in this chapter, she is the 'organic' leader of this community, but while she will never be a leader whose position is institutionalised by any organisation, she is seen in the broader community as an expert on religion and leader of this alternative discourse on religion. This point was highlighted when she appeared on the TV show *Talk at Three* on 13 May 2011 as an expert on religions. The cultural context of contemporary South Africa, which is far more open to different expression of religion and the nature of talk-show hosts, has allowed Turkington to move into a space as a self-styled religious leader with a following that gives her authority.

Conclusion

On the basis of the discussion above, we can conclude that the different stations and programmes described all have the potential to play a role in shaping listeners' identities. They provide listeners with advice and teaching about their faith, i.e. by providing a meaningful construct and regulatory practices that tell them how they should live out their faith, what it means to them and how they should mould themselves in accordance with their faith. Each of the three case studies echoes Meyer and Moors' (2006) finding that religions themselves can be developed and influenced by outside forces such as radio, but the present research also stresses that radio does not influence religions in the same way. Radio has the potential to transform the religious experience, as in the case of the virtual Mass that is said on Radio Veritas, and it is possible that through radio, completely new religious communities can come into existence, as in the case of the people who tune in to *Believe It or Not*. This chapter has shown how the dynamics between media and religion are not clear cut and that radio can effect change in one religion, but may not effect the same change in another.

Radio Veritas aims to create a sense of Catholic unity and identity among believers by offering them teaching about their faith, giving them information about events and so strengthening their sense of belonging to an imagined community – the Catholic Church. It gives lay people a space and religious voice, but these leaders do not supersede the ordained clergy, who are held, through the very medium of radio, to be the true leaders of the faith. On Radio Islam, all aspects of life are linked to Islam, and religious regulations, not cultural norms are promoted as being that which governs decision making in every aspect of the believer's life. Radio Islam has also given rise to new organic and informal female leaders in the form of presenters and guests featured on the station, but as yet these women are not changing the message of conservative Islam; rather, they are supporting it.

In all three cases, the management boards and outside state regulator, ICASA, have impacted the shape of the radio stations and the types of programmes they present. For Radio Islam, the management board has continually demanded that the programmes present a conservative Muslim perspective. The programming and content of Radio Veritas have from its inception been strongly influenced by the Dominican religious order that manages the station and therefore is the most prominent voice. *Believe It or Not* is controlled by a secular, commercial management board that requires high ratings and stipulates that no preference be given to any particular religious group. This more than anything else has shaped the tone, content and parameters of *Believe It or Not*.

Radio, we have seen, is mediating new forms of religious experience, learning, community and leadership, but none of these is the same across different religions. What is the same is that radio and the closely linked Internet sites, blogs, Twitter and mobile phone engagement that go with it express the continued importance of religion in the lives of South Africans and are opening up swiftly changing new expressions of religion in a variety of differently mediated spaces.

Endnotes

1   The research for this chapter was done from 2007 until 2011 with regular week-long intervals of listening to the different radio stations over this period.

2   According to the 2001 national census, Christians accounted for 79.7 per cent of the population, Muslims made up 1.5 per cent, Hindus approximately 1.3 per cent and Jews 0.2 per cent. A total of 15.1 per cent said they had no religious affiliation, while 2.3 per cent were classified as 'other' and 1.4 per cent were unspecified.

3   I use the term 'communities' because as people migrate from one community to another they often change their religion. In South Africa, this change is largely from an African religion to Christianity or Islam as people move from rural areas to urban areas. In contemporary schools, children are increasingly exposed to the main world religions and the impact of this on their choices of religion has yet to receive detailed analysis.

4   This sentence is a paraphrase of the station's home page at < http://www.radioveritas. co.za > .

5   < http://www.radioislam.co.za/homepage > , accessed 26 June 2007.

6   < http://www.radioislam.co.za/homepage > , accessed 20 May 2011.

7 Ibid.

8 < http://www.radioislam.co.za > .

9 Interview with Kate Turkington, 1 May 2011.

10 This has its origins in the pre-Vatican II church, where at various times in the history of the Catholic Church laity could not receive the body and/or blood of Christ.

11 Interview with Anthony Egan S.J., 25 March 2010.

14

Voices from Without
The African National Congress, Its Radio, Its Allies and Exile, 1960–84[1]

Stephen R. Davis

Introduction

Beginning with the Rivonia arrests in July 1963 and ending with the unbanning of illegal organisations in February 1990, the African National Congress (ANC) and South African Communist Party (SACP) spent nearly 30 years attempting to direct the liberation struggle from exile. The purpose of this chapter is to examine one aspect of this activity – radio broadcasting – as a window into problems faced by this precarious alliance. I argue that leaders within the ANC and SACP generally agreed that radio was an essential component of armed struggle, even if they disagreed about how to put this potential to good use. Parsing out how each constituency approached radio could allow for a better understanding of how these organisations thought about their stalled revolution, internal power struggles and international supporters.

Above all else, anti-apartheid broadcasts must be understood within the wider radioscapes that effloresced in the ether over southern Africa during the latter half of the 20th century. As other scholars have explained (Gunner, 2000a; Tomaselli, Muller & Tomaselli, 2001), the apartheid state foregrounded radio as the primary means for explaining apartheid to internal and external audiences. The significance of radio can be seen in the sheer scale of apartheid radio services. Behind the Voice of America and Radio Moscow, the external service of Radio South Africa was the third-most-powerful short-wave broadcaster in the world, while the inception of the Radio Bantu services initiated a massive investment in the creation of ethnically delimited black radio audiences. Because apartheid officials believed that radio held so much explanatory power, it follows that anti-apartheid groups saw radio as a pivotal terrain of struggle against the South African state. Simply put, radio emerged as both the point and counterpoint of the construction of apartheid and of the anti-apartheid struggle.

It comes as no surprise, then, that the ANC broadcast regularly throughout the exile years, beginning with sporadic transmissions as early as 1968 and eventually operating a service known as Radio Freedom from five African capitals for several hours a day, several days a week, until the early 1990s. Given this significance, from a conceptual standpoint, radio provides a useful, if often overlooked, way of understanding media during the exile period. During this time, anti-apartheid elites used radio to construct images of themselves for foreign and home audiences, articulated a shared movement into a singular image, and narrated a version of South Africa that ran counter to official government explanations.

The focus of this chapter is not so much on the content of Radio Freedom broadcasts as on how radio broadcasting opens a particularly revealing window into the internal politics of the ANC and SACP in exile. Although the relationship between these two organisations is portrayed in many histories as opaque, paying close attention to radio is one method of analysing the obscured struggles that occurred between constituencies within the fragile alliance. Writing at the height of the township rebellion in 1986, Stephen Davis (1987:x) lamented that

> ... the African National Congress's exiled leadership, distrustful of Western media, more comfortable in secrecy than public relations, and sometimes isolated from its own underground inside the country, has earned a reputation as a reluctant and irksome source of information.

The extent of this secrecy, perhaps exaggerated for dramatic effect in a book pledging to take readers 'inside South Africa's hidden war', is nevertheless not an altogether accurate portrayal of an organisation that produced a voluminous amount of printed material, conducted hours of interviews with journalists and broadcast hours of radio programmes.

In this chapter, I ask when radio became a strategic priority for exiles, who controlled and operated the radio units in exile, and why radio broadcasting assumed such an importance in factional struggles between different constituencies within the external mission of the Congress Alliance.[2] The point of this exercise is not to view radio only as a strategy, but to read strategy as evidence that can illuminate how various parties within this alliance perceived the challenges they faced. Broadly speaking, I periodise these broadcasting efforts into three phases: firstly, the broadcasts of Radio Freedom conducted by underground activists within South Africa in the early 1960s; secondly, the *Voice of Freedom* broadcasts conducted by exiled activists from Dar es Salaam in the late 1960s and early 1970s; and, thirdly, the role of Radio Freedom after the emergence of more robust propaganda campaigns following the Soweto uprising.

Radio Freedom

The story of Radio Freedom begins with the turn to the armed struggle undertaken by the Congress Alliance in 1961. A detour into the politics of this era provides a useful introduction to the fractious political dynamic that became ever more exaggerated once these banned political parties reconstituted themselves as an 'External Mission' outside South Africa.

With the adoption of the Programme of Action in 1949, a young and fervent cohort of black leaders exerted ever more influence over the direction of the ANC. In their view, previous ANC leaders were wedded to an older politics of incremental reform and compromise. Because of this, the ANC was ill adapted to meet the new challenges posed by the ascendant National Party government (Mandela, 1994:104, 113–15). By the end of the 1950s the strategy of non-violent passive resistance had largely failed to prevent the implementation of the first wave of apartheid legislation. Further mass protest seemed to march lockstep with increased government repression. A strident chorus of discordant voices emanating from the ANC and from allies within the SACP took stock of this situation and critiqued the efficacy of peaceful mass protest as a means to bring about political change. A heated debate between these constituent bodies of the Congress Alliance ensued. As members from various perspectives discussed the relationship between non-violent strategy and their waning popularity, competitors such as the Pan African Congress (PAC) and the African Resistance Movement positioned themselves at the helm of a new, uncompromisingly assertive politics that embraced armed action as the necessary means to a just end.

These ongoing debates among members of the ANC and the underground SACP drew to a close after the Sharpeville massacre. The violent repression of a peaceful mass protest tipped the scales of the argument towards advocates of armed struggle and away from those advocating an exclusively non-violent struggle (Mandela, 1994). In the summer of 1961 the turn towards armed struggle received the tacit approval of the ANC leadership, while communist leaders began recruiting their members for military training abroad. Prominent figures from the ANC joined with select members of the SACP to form a jointly constituted, but nominally independent armed wing, Umkhonto we Sizwe (MK) (Lodge, 1983:233; Mandela, 1994:272–73). After a few short months of preparation, this ad-hoc army conducted its first armed actions on 16 December 1961, the holiday celebrating the defeat by the Voortrekkers (ancestors of the main constituency of the National Party) of the Zulu chief Dingane.

Over the next two years MK conducted over 200 bombings and acts of sabotage in all major cities in South Africa (Lodge, 1983:233). Despite the impressive number of attacks, the ultimate objective of this campaign often remained unclear, even to those working within MK. Drawing from a crash course in the revolutionary literature of the day, MK strategists generally agreed that the objective of the campaign was to destabilise the economy in the hope that a popular insurrection might ensue (Kasrils, 1998:44; Bernstein, 1999:226–52). This chain of events never occurred. Although MK succeeded in a few spectacular bombings, it failed to provoke a widespread popular insurrection: spectacular as these bombings may have seemed to some, these actions did not inspire the vast majority of South Africans to revolt. Although opinions differed, some felt that the movement neglected to create the political means with which to capitalise on the armed struggle (Lodge, 1983:239; Barrell, 1993:18). It was in this context that the ANC made its first foray into radio broadcasting.

In April 1963 Walter Sisulu disobeyed a banning order confining him to house arrest in Johannesburg and joined the remaining MK high command at the Lillieslief Farm in Rivonia (Bernstein, 1999:252–53). Once at Rivonia, several high-ranking members of the ANC and SACP gathered to produce a recorded statement for broadcast. Like many other actions taken during this hectic period, the details of the discussions around broadcasting remain obscure (Bernstein, 1999:229–31). The decision to take to the airwaves was probably not the culmination of a carefully planned strategy, but rather a hasty act signalling the increasing desperation felt by the MK leadership.

Regardless of the convoluted origins of this broadcast, sometime in early June 1963 Denis Goldberg recorded Sisulu and Ahmed Kathrada as they read two statements, each totalling less than 15 minutes. Then, on the night of 26 June 1963, Goldberg, Ivan Schermbrucker and Cyril Jones travelled to the Johannesburg suburb of Parktown. At the home of Archie Levetan, Goldberg assembled a custom-built aluminium aerial, spray-painted black to avoid detection by police searchlights. Jones left a rented car nearby for Goldberg, while Schermbrucker stood watch and signalled to Goldberg by torchlight and hand-held radio. Goldberg connected the jury-rigged transmitter to a tape recorder, pressed play and broadcast 'Radio Freedom' to an uncertain number of listeners (Mayibuye Centre Archives, n.d.). Less than two weeks after the broadcast, police raided the Lillieslief Farm and arrested seven leaders, including Sisulu, Kathrada and Goldberg.

In the Rivonia trial, prosecutors foregrounded recordings of 'Radio Freedom' in their presentation of evidence – recordings now submitted under the more provocative title of 'Eye for an Eye' broadcasts (Mayibuye Centre Archives, n.d.a; Bernstein, 1999:311). The trial came to a conclusion in June 1964, when Judge Quartus de Wet sentenced the seven Rivonia defendants to life in prison (Mandela, 1994:350–78). Remaining ANC and SACP members either faced arrest and harassment by continuing their activities, dropped out of the movement altogether, or fled the country to join the fledgling External Mission hastily organised by Oliver Tambo, Moses Kotane and Tennyson Makiwane (Callinicos, 2004:253–302).

Voice of Freedom

For all their paranoia about radio and insurrection, whether real or imagined, the South African government had little to fear from either the ANC or SACP during the years after Rivonia. As members from both groups filtered out of the country and settled into an uncertain existence, establishing a radio station was not their foremost concern. In fact, many believed that exile would be a temporary condition – a kind of strategic withdrawal that did not warrant establishing their presence outside the country.

The ANC did not return to the airwaves for another five years. By April 1969 the organisation had received a 15-minute slot on *Voice of Freedom*, a programme broadcast to southern Africa three times a week from the facilities of Radio Tanzania Dar es Salaam (Head, 1974:223; Kushner, 1974:154; Hale, 1975:98; Mosia, Riddle & Zaffiro, 1994:7).[3] *Voice of Freedom* primarily featured news briefs, speeches by officials and documentary features. Alongside ANC representatives, *Voice of Freedom* also featured spokesmen from the Frente de Libertação de Moçambique (FRELIMO), the South West African People's Organisation, the Zimbabwe African National Union and the National Liberation Movement of Comoro Islands, all eagerly seeking to reach home audiences with their own 15-minute segments.

Voice of Freedom differed from the pre-exile Radio Freedom broadcast in that it was not clandestine – the location of the transmission was readily apparent to listeners tuned in to Radio Tanzania and individuals appearing on the air identified themselves as representatives of their respective organisations. In this way, the appearance of the ANC on *Voice of Freedom* was an important 'public' acknowledgement that the External Mission survived in exile and that it was the sole functioning branch of the ANC. This was no small achievement, because the exiles had always maintained that they were merely the external extension of an underground that continued to survive within South Africa. In effect, these broadcasts signalled a shift in the centre of gravity of opposition to apartheid away from an internal movement effectively crushed by government repression and towards a far-flung assemblage of anti-apartheid groupings.

Radio Freedom after the Soweto uprising

Despite this renewed presence on the airwaves, attempts to 'broadcast the battle' to home audiences suffered from a conspicuous absence of any battle to broadcast. As Vladimir Shubin, a Soviet handler for the ANC, observed, after nearly ten years in exile these self-proclaimed liberators 'failed to fire a single shot on South African soil'. Although ANC representatives continued to project an image of incremental success to international donors, internally this stagnation was obvious and took a serious toll on the organisation. Shubin (1999:124) writes that by 1973/74 'the number of people in ANC care was much smaller', dropping as low as 250 cadres in the camps in Tanzania, 130 in Zambia, and about 100 in Botswana, Lesotho and Swaziland.

This nadir of activity was quickly followed by a series of events that rapidly changed the fortunes of the External Mission. In April 1974 a group of army officers overthrew the regime of Portuguese dictator Marcello Caetano. Although Portugal had spent nearly ten years fighting various guerrilla groups in its 'overseas provinces' of Angola, Mozambique and Guinea-Bissau, the toppling of the Caetano regime signalled the end of the Portuguese colonial empire in Africa. In short order, the Movimento Popular da Libertação de Angola and FRELIMO outpaced rival nationalist groups, eventually replacing the outgoing colonial administrations in Angola and Mozambique, respectively (Ellis & Sechaba, 1992:80–85; Hirson, 1995:34). Drawing on their alliances with Marxist liberation movements in exile, the ANC persuaded the new governments in Angola and Mozambique to either allow the organisation to establish guerrilla camps or at least permit the transit of ANC operatives through their territories.[4] For the first time after nearly a decade in exile, the ANC could finally operate in territories adjacent to South Africa and its dependencies. Unfortunately for those who waited for this moment, just when the geopolitical situation finally permitted the resumption of armed struggle in South Africa, the External Mission lacked the strength to immediately exploit this new opportunity. By 1975 the ANC was anaemic; what remained of its guerrilla army was increasingly aged and disillusioned, made even weaker by a dearth of new recruits after Rivonia.

Placing added stress on exiles, these geopolitical changes were followed soon after by the Soweto uprising. This uprising marked a critical time for the entire exile community, because for the first time in 15 years mass protest almost spontaneously re-emerged in South Africa. As rival groups watched events unfold from afar, they implicitly understood that the ongoing uprising inside South Africa suddenly raised the stakes of the struggle for those outside the country. Radio seemed an obvious choice for projecting the legitimacy of contending exile groups over the emergent protest movement in the townships.

At this pivotal moment, the ANC was not the unquestioned standard bearer of protests against apartheid within South Africa. Since the government had declared the ANC an unlawful organisation, an entire generation of South African youths came of age without much knowledge of the organisation's politics. Complicating matters further, black consciousness constituted the political understanding of most students. This affirmation of a specifically black culture and expansive definitions of blackness could be interpreted as a challenge to the inclusive values enshrined by the ANC in the Freedom Charter. At the same time, black consciousness could be understood as an intermediate stage of a new assertive politics that might find final completion in the non-racial vision of the ANC. As exiles pondered how best to meet the challenge of this new protest culture, it became clear that radio would be the primary tool by which movement ideologists might bracket an emergent blackness within a broader philosophy of non-racialism. The animating principle of this ideological sleight of hand was that black consciousness was a preparatory stage that primed activists for participation in a new non-racial front.

Seizing the moment, exiles appealed to international donors for increased funds for propaganda efforts. In the months that followed, Western donors responded to these requests by supporting serious exile radio efforts. Western assistance coalesced around radio, primarily because donors remained constrained by Cold War-era political sensitivities within their respective nations. No matter how abhorrent the apartheid regime appeared to European and North American audiences, the remarkably 'hot' war being fought by Cold War proxies in southern Africa limited the types of support Western donors could offer an ostensibly Marxist liberation movement. In lieu of direct military aid, the Swedish and Dutch development agencies, and later the Dutch anti-apartheid group Omroep voor Radio Freedom, all devised creative strategies for aiding what was, in their view, a just struggle that right-wing critics unfairly tarred as a communist cabal (Mayibuye Centre Archives, n.d.b; Sellstrom, 2002:23–39, 592–608). Radio became the junction where political constraints faced by Western donors intersected with the changing needs of the resurgent ANC. In this scheme, Radio Freedom assumed a dual meaning: it could be portrayed to critics as providing an essentially non-violent 'counterbalance' to a censored society, yet it permitted donors to think of themselves as indirectly supporting the military objectives of the ANC.

Perhaps more importantly, the very idea of Radio Freedom – an exile radio service broadcasting from afar to a captive population – held a particular resonance with a certain European imaginary of the power of electronic mass media as drawn from the Nazi occupation in Western Europe and the Soviet invasions of Hungary and Czechoslovakia (Mayibuye Centre Archives, n.d.b). All three episodes had a familiar arc: 'free radios' beamed defiant broadcasts across closed borders or within closed borders to national resistance groups waging their own guerrilla wars against a domineering foe. Within recent memory, many European donors could recall moments when radio was perceived as having real power, and these individuals certainly saw parallels between their own experience and that of southern Africa (Mayibuye Centre Archives, n.d.b).

A series of promotional cartoons published by Omroep voor Radio Freedom provides a number of suggestive clues as to how Dutch activists represented the role of radio to Western donors. Two promotional cards picture black broadcasters broadcasting literally from underground – one broadcaster speaking into a microphone in a subterranean chamber, another broadcaster in the guise of a guerrilla broadcasting from under the table of his white oppressor. Other cards depict white listeners caught unawares by the intrusion of guerrilla broadcasts on their radios, while black audiences are mobilised by the Pied Pipers of liberation who call the marching tune. The intended effect of these images is to close the gap between emergent protest cultures and exiled political parties by suggesting that donor funding would support daring and illegal broadcasts within South Africa. In this, exiles and the resurgent protest culture within South Africa are seen as one and the same thing. This unproblematic rendering oversimplifies the distance between exiles and internal activists by invoking narratives of broadcasting heroism that have more to do with resonating with Dutch donors than accurately depicting the actual position of Radio Freedom in emergent protest cultures.

Western donor aid enlarged the ANC's Department of Information and Publicity (DIP) into a relatively well-funded fief set amidst the constellation of quasi-autonomous offices and departments that constituted the growing exile bureaucracy. From an existing nucleus of just a few sleepy offices, the DIP grew into a sizable propaganda outfit splayed across several continents. The Swedish International Development Cooperation Agency and Omroep voor Radio Freedom equipped the studio with expensive electronics such as tape recorders, mixing boards and microphones, while Swedish Telecommunications Consulting and National Broadcasting Company (Radio Netherlands) flew a few fortunate radio staff members to their facilities for advanced training (Omroep voor Radio Freedom, 1988). By 1980 the ANC had built similar 'portable studios' in five additional countries – Zambia, Tanzania, Ethiopia, Angola and Madagascar – with each state broadcaster granting an hour a day to Radio Freedom programmes.

All this expansion occurred as a new generation left South Africa for an uncertain future in exile. As thousands of school-age refugees poured across the border, the ANC faced a serious problem integrating these potential recruits into the existing structures of the External Mission. Aside from the sheer size of this exodus, a troubling generational gap existed between the first wave who left in the early 1960s and the 'children of Soweto'. This new generation of exiles carried their own language of protest and left a country that was markedly different from the one many older exiles remembered (Kasrils, 1998:125).

How did demographic shifts and generational gaps within the External Mission impact on Radio Freedom? Depending on educational background, demonstrable ability, familial connections or political allegiance, one recruit could be directed to dig trenches in a training camp in Angola while another could be sent to study at a prestigious Western university. Those sent to work for Radio Freedom, then, could consider themselves relatively fortunate, given their access to educational opportunities abroad (Mayibuye Centre Archives, n.d.b). Within the DIP itself, Radio Freedom staff members also occupied a relatively privileged position in the bureaucratic hierarchy in their immediate location, remaining connected to a wider world of events and privy to advanced knowledge of internal debates and decisions, while a select few actively shaped outside perceptions of the movement. Above all else, radio work demanded that cadres have an understanding of politics, an aptitude for communication, and the ability to interpret and synthesise information. Although incoming recruits did not always meet these expectations, the leadership made every effort to draw radio personnel from among the most educated, articulate or at least well connected of the 'Soweto generation' (Motsuenyane, Burnham & Zamchiya, 1993:70).[5]

Above the level of general staff, the DIP, and Radio Freedom in particular, served as an important 'proving ground' for a new generation of Western-educated intellectuals. From the early 1970s until his death in 1978, Duma Nokwe, an elder ANC exile, assumed most responsibilities for Radio Freedom in Zambia, appeared regularly on the air and helped 'to produce ANC radio announcers and radio journalists' (Sechaba, 1978:12, 31–41). A change of the guard occurred after Nokwe's death when Oliver Tambo placed Thabo Mbeki at the helm of the DIP, making him the de facto head of Radio Freedom as well (Gevisser, 1999b).[6] Articulate, Western educated and with the cachet afforded by a 'royal' movement pedigree, Mbeki – along with Pallo Jordan, his counterpart in the Research Division of the DIP – increasingly served as the new face of a movement in exile eager to place itself at the head of a youthful internal protest movement (Gevisser, 1999a).

The 'armed propaganda' campaign was the first significant test of these reinvigorated structures. Beginning with the bomb attack on oil storage tanks at the Sasolburg refinery complex on 1 June 1980, MK guerrillas attacked a number of military and economic installations in rapid succession, marking their first successful sabotage campaign within South Africa in nearly 20 years. And while the press made ample mention of these large-scale attacks, Radio Freedom reported less-conspicuous operations in an effort to give the overall impression of a nearly continuous assault (US government, 1982; 1983).

While the ANC attempted to escalate guerrilla activity within South Africa, at the same time the exile organisation strained to cope with a series of counter-attacks by the South African government. In early 1981 the chance discovery of a spy ring in Lusaka uncovered the identity of several government agents secretly working in the Angolan guerrilla camps (Ellis & Sechaba, 1992:116–21). Adding to an already tense situation, South African agents succeeded in assassinating several leading figures in the ANC and SACP, including Joe Gqabi, a veteran organiser and ANC representative to Zimbabwe, and Ruth First, SACP member, researcher at Eduardo Mondlane University and wife of MK commander Joe Slovo. Finally, in December 1982 the Botswana police, acting on a tip from an informant, arrested MK commander Joe Modise and head of ordinance Cassius Make as they waited for a rendezvous with internal organisers (Ellis & Sechaba, 1992:119). Police found several handguns, R60 000 in cash and plans for a massive upcoming military operation; later both men were sentenced to brief prison terms on weapons charges. The combined effect of infiltration, assassination and capture effectively precluded the large-scale infiltration then dubbed the 'People's War', which military planners had tentatively scheduled for mid-1983. As Radio Freedom continued to proclaim bombing after bombing and called on listeners to 'join the revolutionary stream led by the ANC that will sweep away fascism and aggression from southern Africa', the rank and file stationed in the Angolan camps began to clamour for a mass deployment that never seemed to arrive (BBC, 1983).

Amid this atmosphere of heightened suspicion between elites and growing impatience among the rank and file, the ANC granted an unusual degree of latitude to National Intelligence and Security, an internal security department known more commonly by the name Mbokodo.[7] Although Mbokodo operated throughout exile structures in African host states, it enjoyed a particularly free hand in Angola, where the leadership felt that infiltration was most damaging and the potential for unrest most acute. One camp cadre suggested Mbokodo could single out almost any individual it deemed suspicious; interrogating some, torturing others and imprisoning several at a secret prison camp known as Quatro, a name derived from 'The Fort', a prison in Johannesburg also known colloquially as 'Number Four' (Trewhela & Hirson, 1990). While the threat from infiltrators was real, the arbitrary nature of some arrests suggests that at least a few Mbokodo agents also manipulated this situation to settle scores, fabricated accusations for personal advancement, or simply attempted to suppress dissenting voices.

The DIP – operating a prominent Radio Freedom unit in Luanda – was not immune from Mbokodo. As Mbokodo 'comrades' surveyed the structures in Angola for infiltrators, they cast a particularly wary eye on the DIP led by a conspicuous coterie of Western-educated 'aristocrats' who cultivated exclusive ties with Western European aid agencies and support groups. In the context of ongoing internal struggles occurring among exiles, this financially independent and ideologically heterodox group posed a serious threat to SACP cadres attempting to monopolise their control over the movement. Singling out the DIP for scrutiny served two purposes. Firstly, Mbokodo could ensure that the external image of the movement did not stray too far from SACP policies and objectives by intimidating or arresting DIP staff. Secondly, by cowing a well-heeled and up-and-coming leadership, Mbokodo could boost its own prestige and power by demonstrating that no one remained beyond its reach.

The arrest of Pallo Jordan – then-head of a research unit supporting propaganda efforts in Luanda – is one episode that casts these internal struggles into high relief. In June 1983 Peter Boroko, the deputy head of Mbokodo in Angola, ordered his men to arrest Jordan and hold him for questioning at Quatro (Ellis, 1994). In a statement made to a later commission of inquiry into human rights abuses, an anonymous member of this security detail gave a particularly candid account of the reasons behind Jordan's arrest. This source revealed that Mbokodo specifically targeted Jordan because he warned DIP staff to avoid a Mbokodo informant within the department, while openly ridiculing security staff as 'amapolisa' (Marais, 1992:18–20). For his impolitic remarks, Mbokodo then imprisoned Jordan without any formal charge, forced him to write and then rewrite his autobiography, and subjected him to a series of humiliating interrogations. During one particularly tense interrogation session, a source recalled that another unnamed agent remarked ''eli intellectual laseMerika liijwayela kabi', meaning 'this American-trained intellectual is uppity' – and thus in need of straightening out (Jobodwana Report, cited in Ellis, 1994).

This unnamed officer interpreted this threat as indicative of the wider ideological rift that divided Western-educated intellectual elites from the East German-trained security chiefs, with junior Mbokodo staff merely parroting the anti-Western gestures of their superiors (Trewhela & Hirson, 1990).[8] Although ideology certainly was the language these 'comrades' used to express their displeasure with Jordan and others like him, this episode also shows how ANC elites were perceived by less-advantaged cadres – all eager to demonstrate the extent of their new-found authority by transgressing the bounds of rank and privilege. Although it is possible that the 'comrades' harboured some special dislike for Jordan in particular, it is more likely that his inopportune comments merely served as a good excuse to send a message to anyone who might contemplate crossing the security service or its allies. After six weeks in captivity, Mbokodo released Jordan without any formal charge.

By early 1983 the ongoing 'armed propaganda' campaign raised the expectations of MK cadres, while increased government surveillance simultaneously inhibited the ANC's ability to infiltrate guerrillas into South Africa (Barrell, 1993:54–55). Furthermore, the arrest of Joe Modise and Cassius Make in Botswana threw plans for the 'People's War' into jeopardy, making the possibility of a mass deployment of MK guerrillas into South Africa ever more remote. Echoing the situation preceding the Wankie Campaign, military leaders decided to preoccupy the increasingly restless rank and file by organising a joint operation with their Angolan hosts (Ellis & Sechaba, 1992:127–28; Barrell, 1993:49; Twala & Benard, 1994:57).[9] Beginning in mid-1983, MK detachments joined Angola army units in the 'Luta Contra Banditos', a counter-insurgency operation designed to push rebels from Malanje Province back to their strongholds in southern Angola (Twala & Benard, 1994:57).

By most accounts, MK guerrillas fought well, but soon lacked supplies in the field, faced deadly ambushes as they pressed into rebel-held territory and were increasingly abandoned by deserting Angolan soldiers. These complications devastated morale. By January 1984 detachments occupying the towns of Kangandala and Caculama mutinied after the military leadership – then meeting in Luanda – refused to travel to the 'Eastern Front' to hear rank-and-file grievances (Stuart, 1984).[10] Undaunted by this refusal, MK units then commandeered trucks and attempted to travel to Luanda to confront the leadership directly. Mbokodo and Angolan army units intercepted the mutineers en route and redirected them to Viana, a transit camp outside Luanda. Over the next few weeks a stalemate settled over Viana, as mutineers formulated their demands and adopted a plan of action, while exile leaders attempted to defuse a mutiny that eventually included nearly 90% of MK personnel in Angola.[11]

The mutiny, later known as the 'Mkatashinga', the Kimbundu word for 'burden', provides a number of suggestive hints about perceptions of radio among the rank and file in MK. At the behest of MK commissar Chris Hani, mutineers elected a 'Committee of Ten' to relay their demands to the leadership. Interestingly, of the ten elected, three – Zaba Maledza, Kate Mhlongo and Grace Motaung – worked for the eight-person Radio Freedom unit operating in Luanda (Twala & Benard, 1994:62). Maledza was the chief propaganda officer in Angola, while Mhlongo and Motaung enjoyed minor celebrity among camp cadres who listened to their segments on Radio Freedom, relayed to the camps via Radio Luanda (Trewhela & Hirson, 1990).[12] After caucusing with mutineers, Maledza, as the leader of the Committee of Ten, then submitted three demands to the ANC leadership: firstly, the dissolution of the security department; secondly, the institution of an inquiry into the stalled armed struggle; and thirdly, the holding of a conference where a new leadership could be democratically elected. The Committee of Ten also invited the remainder of the Radio Freedom staff to meet with mutineers.

The ANC leadership did not meet any of these demands. Instead, in the early morning hours of 7 February 1984, MK commander Joe Modise attempted to take Viana with the help of an armoured column of the Angolan Presidential Guard (Stuart, 1984; Twala & Benard, 1994:64–65). At the same time, a squad of security staff attempted to 'disarm' the Radio Freedom staff at their flat in Luanda. In Viana, mutineers repelled Modise, killing several Angolan soldiers, while at the flat in Luanda, Mbokodo agents failed to peacefully disarm the Radio Freedom staff and instead killed all three occupants in the ensuing melee (Stuart, 1984). After the failed raid at Viana, Chris Hani addressed the entire camp and convinced the mutineers to surrender their arms without further bloodshed (Marais, 1992). After the surrender, Mbokodo took the Committee of Ten into custody, transferring a few to Angolan prisons in Luanda, while holding others in its own detention camps. In March 1984 Maledza died in detention, allegedly hanging himself in his cell, while Mhlongo and Motaung were later seen at a prison hospital receiving treatment for injuries suffered during interrogation (Trewhela & Hirson, 1990; Ellis & Sechaba, 1992:132–34; Twala and Benard, 1994:73). In the wake of the 'Mkatashinga', six of the eight staff members of Radio Freedom were directly implicated in the mutiny, with four of the six now dead, and the remaining two imprisoned by Mbokodo.

A few weeks after the events at Viana, ANC investigators conducted interviews with detainees and compiled these findings into a detailed report on the causes of the uprising. This committee concluded that radio indeed figured prominently in the causes of the uprising, but instead of directing their attention to perceptions of Radio Freedom, they pointed to Radio South Africa and 'radio potato' as sources of corrupting misinformation (Stuart, 1984). Describing the 'political consciousness' of the cadres as 'low' and suggesting that mutineers were easily 'influenced and manipulated' by enemy broadcasts and rumour campaigns, the authors portrayed rank-and-file mutineers as naive dupes, sweeping aside their legitimate grievances and strategies. If anything, the demands made by mutineers – the reform of security structures, a return to democratic leadership and a refocus on the armed struggle – all suggest that 'political consciousness' within the camps was particularly high, but it was the kind of idealism that established authorities found too inconvenient or too threatening.

Although the history of Radio Freedom does not end with the 'Mkatashinga', the direction of the struggle changed dramatically after 1984. In November 1984 rent increases sparked an unprecedented mass uprising in the townships situated in the Vaal Triangle and beyond. After months of unabated unrest the government declared a state of emergency, while presidential advisers privately conceded that a 'civil war had already begun in South Africa, and that the task now was "to contain it"' (Shubin, 1999:269). At the same time, the Nkomati Accord, a non-aggression pact signed between South Africa and Mozambique, deprived the ANC of one of its most valuable transit routes into the Republic, casting doubts on the continued viability of the military campaign and once again raising the spectre of an internal liberation movement wholly independent from its exiled leadership. As township violence continued to spiral out of control, both the government and the ANC increasingly realised that a political settlement was not only possible, but was preferable. Within the ANC, this shift towards 'talks about talks' meant that military objectives, while never completely abandoned, were increasingly subordinated to a new political dynamic that valued a 'seat at the table' over seizure of power (Shubin, 1999:264–72).

Conclusion

Radio can best be thought of as a kind of political theatre. Across the three phases of radio broadcasting, from the underground broadcasts within South Africa at the beginning of the armed struggle to the *Voice of Freedom* broadcasts from Dar es Salaam, and concluding with the Radio Freedom broadcasts from Angola, the ANC and SACP used radio to project a certain image of themselves to audiences at home, in exile and abroad. Exiles were the actors who performed their dramatic narrative of liberation on the stages of other countries. This drama was addressed to three audiences: one at home in South Africa, one abroad comprising foreign patrons and one in exile among those in the training camps. What foreign patrons and home audiences could not see, but which was eminently apparent to those behind the scenes, were the frustrations of exile and the stalled momentum of the armed struggle. The 'Mkatashinga' was a moment when frustration gave birth to revolt and mutineers threatened to seize control of the centre stage.

Endnotes

1 A longer version of the present chapter appeared in June 2009 in the *Journal of Southern African Studies*, 35(2):349–73.

2 The Congress Alliance included the ANC, the South African Indian Congress, the Coloured People's Congress and the Congress of Democrats, a predominantly white organisation consisting of many members of the underground Communist Party of South Africa. This alliance was formed during the Congress of the People in 1955. The term continued to be used during the first decade of exile, but tended to describe only the ANC and SACP.

3   Although it is unclear which organisation took to the airwaves first, the ANC was periodically accompanied by its rival, the PAC, which also received a similar slot on *Voice of Freedom*.

4   While the ANC presence in Mozambique was always somewhat subdued, in Angola the External Mission was granted a significant visible presence. The ANC occupied the South African Embassy in Luanda, broadcast over Radio Luanda, and occupied several guerrilla camps in Luanda, Malanje and Fazenda Provinces.

5   Evidence suggests that promotions within the radio staff were often guided by connections rather than ability. Dumisani Charlton Oupa Khosa, a 'Soweto generation' Radio Freedom staff member and speechwriter for Oliver Tambo, revealed in a statement to the Motsuenyane Commission investigating human rights abuses in the Angolan camps that there 'was a need for better training programmes' and that 'nepotism was becoming a demoralising factor in the organisation'. Khosa mentioned all three problems at an ANC meeting in March 1981 and later found himself under suspicion, eventually spending four years in detention at Quatro, a secret ANC prison camp.

6   According to Mark Gevisser (1999b), Thabo Mbeki also served as an assistant to Nokwe at some point in the 1960s.

7   isiXhosa for 'grindstone'.

8   This description of the demographics of Mbokodo is also supported by other statements made by Quatro detainees.

9   Barrell (1993) and Ellis and Sechaba (1992) note that the National Executive Committee (NEC) reorganised the Revolutionary Council into the Politico-Military Council as a token gesture towards reform in January 1983. This reorganisation opened a few more seats on the highest military council, but included many of the same members of its predecessor body.

10 The most pressing grievance was that many units had not received food in several days. The *Stuart Commission Report* (Stuart, 1984) also suggests that a few cadres preyed on the local population, intimidating them by firing their weapons into the air. Allegedly, three locals were killed by stray bullets in Kangandala.

11 Oliver Tambo revealed this statistic at a 1990 NEC meeting.

12 Trewhela and Hirson's account states that Maledza was 'one of the foremost propagandists in the ANC radio programmes alongside Duma Nokhwe [sic]'. After a brief imprisonment in Quatro in 1980–81, Maledza returned to his post at Radio Freedom, 'where his unwavering opposition to men like Piliso and Modise, and clarity of mind earned him the respect of both friends and foes within the ANC'.

15

Airing the Politics of Nation
Radio in Angola, Past and Present[1]

Marissa J. Moorman

On Sunday, 5 September 2010 in Viana, a satellite city outside Angola's capital, Luanda, the radio journalist Alberto Graves Chakussanga was shot dead with one bullet to his back. At the time of his death, he was a popular radio announcer on an Umbundu-language news programme and the director of national language programming at Radio Despertar (Radio Awakening). Radio Despertar is a private radio station opened in late 2006 by the group Socitel, composed mainly of União Naçional para a Independência Total de Angola (UNITA) members. This new private radio station emerged in the wake of the 1994 Lusaka Peace Accord between the ruling Movimento Popular da Libertação de Angola (MPLA) and the rebel group UNITA that, among other things, spelled the end of UNITA's Radio Vorgan, the Voice of the Black Cockerel, a rebel radio station of the civil-war era that closed in 1998 (Windrich, 2000).

Chakussanga's death was noiseless. Neither neighbours nor family members heard a scuffle, leading some to conclude that he was shot by a gun equipped with a silencer and that the tank of cooking gas missing from his home was meant to make the murder look like the unintended by-product of robbery. Some have suggested he was not a direct target, but a lesson for others.

It is unclear whether Chakussanga's murder was, in fact, politically motivated. But it occurred in a two-week period characterised by political tensions and incendiary discourse that had been absent from the Angolan political scene since the election in 2008. Two days prior to the murder, the Political Bureau of the MPLA issued a statement accusing some, unnamed, Angolans of being 'spearheads' for foreign interests.[2] Just two days after the murder, the MPLA's secretary of information, Rui Falcão Pinto de Andrade, directly accused UNITA leaders (namely its president, Isaias Samakuva) and Radio Despertar of inciting the Angolan population to civil disobedience, thus giving greater specificity to the Political Bureau's earlier memo.

'We cannot', he went on in language reminiscent of the civil-war years, 'give in to poorly thought out and unreflective attitudes expressed by people who did nothing for this country, who destroyed it, and who continue, by any means possible, to want to attain power' (Bessa, 2010).[3]

Some local journalists considered this to be the salutary return of constructive political debate (Kaliengue, 2010; Malavoloneke, n.d.). One described it as the dancing around the ring that good boxers do (Malavoloneke, n.d.), but it is more like a fight between a heavyweight and a featherweight in a stadium owned by the heavyweight's manager. State media dominate. More specifically, the ruling party has privileged access to, and therefore dominates, state media.

Falcão made his announcement at a press conference where journalists asked no questions and which was broadcast immediately on the state-owned and state-operated radio and television stations (Angolan National Radio (RNA) and Angolan Popular Television (TPA)) and published on the front page of the state daily, *Jornal de Angola*, the following day. A day after Falcão's announcement, the minister of social communication, Carolina Cerqueira, repudiated Radio Despertar and called for an investigation by the National Council for Social Communication, suggesting that legal action might be warranted (*Jornal de Angola*, 2010a). Thus, the death of a young and promising radio journalist receded in the thunder of political drama. Radio Despertar teeters on the brink of extinction: ten employees recently reported that they will leave the station for posts at RNA and TPA because of late payment of salaries and a 'lack of consideration' from the management (see Africa Monitor Intelligence, 2010). In the international arena, the non-governmental organisation Committee to Protect Journalists, following Chakussanga's murder and attacks on an independent TV journalist and on the activist and journalist Rafael Marques, condemned the attacks (see CPJ, 2010). Journalists Without Borders showed Angola as the lusophone country with the lowest press-freedom ranking (although still higher than a number of other countries).[4]

Radio broadcasting in Angola has often had a close relationship with politics, nation and state power. This chapter juxtaposes this vignette of radio/media power in the present with a more panoramic view of the history of radio in Angola. I self-consciously use a visual image to fix an aural phenomenon and to bring attention, as almost all scholars of radio do, to radio's ephemeral and contingent nature. In the present, ephemeral messages encouraging the population to civil disobedience are condemned (but also fixed, repeated and spread) in the state media. Radio's capacity to broadcast messages with the power to mobilise is summoned up in the very attempt to control it, particularly so as the ruling party looks ahead to elections in 2012.[5] But propagandists often confuse content with results, and well-intentioned international organisations ignore the nuances of history. In fact, what listeners of radio do with what they hear and how journalists negotiate power are less clear. A look at the past facilitates some tentative proposals about audiences and journalists in the present.[6]

A brief overview of radio in Angola, 1930–1975

Radio broadcasting in Angola began as the work of hobbyists and amateurs in the 1930s. The first radio transmission occurred in 1933 in Benguela from the private transmitter of a Portuguese man who later established the country's first radio station (Lopes, 2000:3). A series of radio clubs followed: in 1938 in Lobito, then in Luanda and Benguela. By the late 1940s all the major cities had radio clubs and a wave of professionalisation began. The Emissora Oficial de Angola (EOA, Official Broadcasting Company of Angola) began broadcasting daily only in the mid-1950s.

The imprint of the colonial imagination was not, however, completely absent from broadcasting. The Huambo Radio Club, the first professional station, took as its slogan 'a Portuguese voice in Africa' (Coelho, 1999:124). But this radio club and others like it had a distinctly local character and focus. While some Portuguese radio hobbyists, and eventually the state when it got involved, intended to strengthen the ties between the metropole and this bit of 'overseas territory' under the wing of the Portuguese nation, results often differed from intentions. The radio clubs' primary activities included news and entertainment, often broadcast live from their studios, and had a markedly local character. Since radio broadcasting was done on short wave, a radio club, no matter where it was located, could broadcast throughout the country. To a certain degree, programmes and personnel also circulated among various cities and stations. For many of those moving from city to city or to other towns, this generated a stronger sense of *angolanidade* (Angolanness) as they came to know different parts of the country and brought their knowledge, experiences and practices from their hometowns with them.[7]

In the 1960s and 1970s radio played a crucial part in the dissemination of a new form of urban Angolan music, created in Luanda's *musseques* (shanty towns), but popular throughout the territory. Even as the armed struggle for liberation from Portuguese colonialism was being fought along the country's borders by three movements (the Frente Nacional para a Libertação de Angola (FNLA), the MPLA and UNITA), life inside the country continued. With the beginning of the anti-colonial war in 1961, the Portuguese colonial state adopted a two-pronged approach to governance that used repression and reform: it squelched all potentially political activity, but also introduced a series of economic, social and cultural changes (encouraging foreign investment, abolishing the legal distinctions that separated 'assimilated' from 'indigenous' and promoting Angolan folklore). Occupying a position in both the repression and the reform, and in the Portuguese military's programme of 'psycho-social action' (a counter-subversion plan adopted in 1967), radio had a variety of effects on daily life.

Radio propaganda during the war was a key component of military strategy. The Portuguese military often put soldiers captured from the anti-colonial movements in front of radio microphones to tell of the horrors of life in liberation movement camps and controlled areas. Liberation movement radio programmes – the FNLA's *Angola Livre* and, most consistently, the MPLA's *Angola Combatente* – broadcast news of military victories, policy positions and messages of encouragement for nationalist sympathisers.

In the meantime, radio clubs and stations flourished throughout the territory – a relationship between radio, news, music, and nation that broadcasters and listeners created and sometimes flew in the face of the colonial state and the Portuguese military. Before going into more detail about the kinds of shows that official and non-official, state and rebel radio broadcast and that Angolans sought out, some theoretical explorations regarding the complexities of radio audition underscore the need to consider both listening and content.

Radio as a cultural technology: Sounding out the nation

Central to Benedict Anderson's analysis of the nation as an imagined community is the concept of print capitalism. In his book *Imagined Communities* (1983), he links cultural processes with technological innovation and economic dynamics. In Anderson's account, print capitalism does not create the nation, but, rather, fuels it with mass-produced novels and newspapers. The new urban music produced in Luanda in the 1960s and 1970s was the key cultural practice through which Angolans imagined the nation. But the music of Luanda's clubs in and of itself would have only a limited impact were it not for the technologies that record and reproduce sound and for the radios and record turntables that transmit it in specific contexts. I propose the concept of 'sonorous capitalism' to shift attention from the novels, newspapers and printing presses Anderson highlights to vinyl records and radio.[8] These latter cultural technologies massified music and thereby helped to make it the most salient cultural practice in the period 1961–74 both in and outside Luanda.

Anderson argues that novels offered Latin American Creoles a way to imagine a community beyond the local by signalling homogeneous empty time (linking events occurring simultaneously, but happening in different places) encapsulated in the word 'meanwhile'. Radio broadcasting performed this same function in late colonial Angola, opening up a variety of 'meanwhiles': different Angolan anti-colonial movements, recreational clubs in Luanda where new bands played nightly, other cities and towns, and the international arena. I use the plural 'meanwhiles' in place of Anderson's singular to signal the complex context and outcome of Angola's nationalisms and anti-colonial nationalisms in general. This underscores how simultaneity is structured as much from spaces outside as inside. Some of these spaces later came to form an independent Angola (guerrillas and political movements that returned, even if not as victors). Others did not and could not (solidarity groups and other nations with or without interests in Angola, but whose broadcasts Angolans tuned in to: the BBC, Radio Netherlands, Radio Brazzaville and radio from Zaire). All of these spaces offered exterior coordinates (other than Portuguese ones) with which Angolans imagined their nation.

Listeners tuned in to foreign and local stations for music and news via the MPLA's programme *Angola Combatente* broadcast from Congo-Brazzaville, Tanzania and Egypt (Lopes, 2000);[9] the FNLA's *Angola Livre*[10] broadcast from Kinshasa; and other foreign news services such as Voice of America and Radio Moscow. Radio connected those within the country to those fighting from outside the country and to those in solidarity with the anti-colonial struggle. Radio clubs and stations existed throughout the colonial territory (linking various localities), while access to international radio framed the territory from without, placing it within the international sphere (of relations between nations), which the Portuguese colonial regime doggedly denied.

Radio, like books or film, is a cultural technology with a specific mode of communication that gives it a particular relation to the production of nation. Joy Hayes (2000:23) argues that the development of the radio medium has two important social implications: 'the creation of a new mode of mass-mediated intimacy and the formation of a new kind of collective space.' Intimacy and collectivity are elemental to nation. Radio produces a sense of intimacy as the voice of the broadcaster enters the ear and home or space of the listener. Like the newspaper and novel, radio also creates intimacy through temporal levelling – one has access to other 'meanwhiles'. Radio, in this sense, may in fact trump novels, and perhaps even newspapers, in terms of giving us a sense of being able to participate, even if only as aural witness to a spatially different 'now'.

At the same time, one tunes in with the knowledge that others in a vast space can do the same. In her study of radio in Zambia in the colonial period, Debra Spitulnik (1998:68) notes that 'with radio, places were experienced as closer together and places that were minimally connected before became strongly linked … while the horizons of people's worlds expanded … it also appears that distances overall became shorter and even more tangible'. Radio pulls people and places closer together while also pushing out the limits of their worlds. Radio listening can unite people in a collective experience: people gather to listen. In this way, radio can produce a sense of collectivity that is at once local – those of us here around the radio – and more dispersed – a larger listening 'we' or, in Hayes's words, a 'virtual commons' where an intimate anonymity reigns.

Tuning in in late colonial Angola

Albina Assis remembered that as a school-age girl (in the mid-to-late 1950s), she and her friends listened to foreign radio stations (Radio Moscow and Danish radio) in order to hear news about Portugal that government censors prohibited on local radio.[11] Once the war had started in 1961, Luandans began to tune in to radio broadcasts from other African countries. Listeners tuned in to news programmes in Portuguese and local languages prepared by the MPLA and FNLA in particular and broadcast from Congo-Brazzaville, Egypt, Tanzania, Zaire, Zambia and Ghana.[12] PIDE (International Police for the Defence of the State – Portuguese secret police) documents note that agents followed Radio Cairo broadcasts in Portuguese (1964) and Radio Tanzania broadcasts of 20-minute duration that encouraged support for independence movements in Namibia (South West Africa), Angola and Mozambique (1965).[13]

People also tuned in to foreign stations to listen to music. Brazzaville's transmitter was strong enough for Angolans throughout the territory to pick it up.[14] The independent sound of Congolese music issued in part from its being broadcast by newly independent African nations, a fact to which Angolan listeners were keenly attuned. Knowledge of independent neighbouring states and Angolans' desire for their own political sovereignty were never far from the sound of the music itself.

The availability of programming offers only part of the picture. In order to have a presence and an audience, people had to own radios or have access to them. How present were radios in the *musseques* of Luanda and throughout Angola? According to a study conducted in the late 1950s, of 344 families surveyed, only four owned radios (Nunes, 1961:22). Here, as in other parts of the continent, radios, like gramophones and later record turntables, were a symbol of, if not elite status, at the very least a desire for 'upward mobility and urbanity' (Waterman, 1990:93).[15] Thus it is no surprise that the economic changes of the late 1960s found Angolans investing in such technology. By the early 1970s radio ownership had increased significantly: a study of the *musseques* found that 42.6 per cent of heads of households reported listening to radio at home, meaning that they owned radio sets. Transistors were even more popular: the study's author claimed that individuals would often forgo other necessities to purchase a transistor (Monteiro, 1973:368–71). The desire to tune in, or at least an indication of the value of the radio, also registered in an increase in radio thefts – the number of such thefts doubled between 1968 and 1970 (Monteiro, 1973:379–80).

Radio listening was not a pastime limited to Luanda or even to urban areas. The same study notes that in some rural areas, more than 10 per cent of families owned radios and that they were a mark of prestige (Monteiro, 1973:371). Reporting from the town of Pereira d'Eça (today Ondjiva) in the southernmost region of the country, a PIDE agent worried about broadcasts from Radio Tanzania heard locally and remarked that 'there are numerous radios in existence among the locals'.[16] Reporting on Malanje Province, another agent recommended that 'due to the elevated number of radios owned by natives of this area, it would be wise to efficaciously interfere with the above-mentioned broadcasts', in this case from Radio Brazzaville.[17]

In Luanda, the association between *musseques*, music and radio was particularly strong.[18] By mid-1968, according to one letter to the editor in the local popular press, foreign broadcasts formed part of Luanda's urban soundscape. Much to the chagrin of the letter's author, these programmes were more popular among the urban 'masses' than were the many shows broadcast by the 20 local stations available at the time – shows closely controlled by colonial government censors:

> It is of this mass, connected to other traditions, educated in other environments that I am going to speak. Now, it doesn't go unnoticed by anyone when we are walking in the street, or on the beaches or when we enter into bars and cross paths with individuals carrying transistor radios, their gullets open, with their *banga* [vanity], showing that that is what is good. Ninety per cent, approximately, of these individuals have their radios tuned in to broadcasts from Brazzaville, the Republic of the Congo and Zambia. This is not news to anyone and I even like to hear those rhythms. What I don't like is the news that they broadcast in Portuguese and in almost all the languages of Angola. We all know the politics that these countries practise against us … Out of curiosity, I asked some individuals why they listened to those stations and undervalued ours and the responses were variable and I note them here: 'because it is hot music', 'it is our music and our friends', 'they also speak our language', 'they play music that the people like'. Mr Director, why don't we combat this Congomania because this is not the Congo it is Angola, for all of us. Why not create a program that broadcasts consecutively music in the same melodic line. Our folklore, which all of us like to hear and that unfortunately we have few opportunities to applaud, would then have greater projection (Da Silva, 1968).

The author describes the swagger and pride of young urban males who use transistor radios as political fashion accessories. Local music, the author suggests, is the remedy for subversive Congolese news and music. Popular practices, in his view, could be coopted and rechannelled to support Portugal's pluri-continental nationalist project. Local music, in this reading, was prophylactic: it offered protection against the insidious effects of 'Congomania' and the craze of anti-colonial nationalism.[19]

From the perspective of Angolan musicians, Congolese music seemed less like an infectious disease and more like a spark of inspiration that returned them to their roots, linked them to other cosmopolitan musical practitioners and reminded them of the armed struggle being waged for Angolan independence. The musician and composer Xabanu recalled that 'those of us here, Angolans in the *musseques*, tuned in to Congolese radio – from the Congo – which played lots of Latin American and Congolese music'.[20] Angolans clamoured for Franco, Dr Nico and Wendo, in part because they sang in Lingala and created an urban African sound: a sound that ethnomusicologist Jorge Macedo also described as 'ours'; a sound that he said 'inflamed our nationalist spirit'.[21]

When Angolans claimed that the Congolese musicians played 'our' music and 'spoke our language' (in the metaphoric sense, since most Angolans did not speak Lingala), they made a rhetorical move identifying with an independent African nation instead of with Portugal. Asserting a pan-Africanist 'we', these Angolans claimed a cosmopolitan nationalism that did not have Portugal, or even Europe, as its template.[22] If the Huambo Radio Club presented itself as 'a Portuguese voice in Africa', then Congolese radio projected an African voice in Africa. Finally, the fact that Congolese radio (from Brazzaville and Kinshasa) intercalated news broadcasts with music – whether the MPLA's *Angola Combatente*, the FNLA's *Angola Livre* or local Congolese news – implicated Congolese music with the nationalist struggle by simple association.

Angola Combatente

Angola Combatente aired at 19:00, a detail that consistently marks the memories of Angolans when they discuss this programme. Owing to the highly politicised nature of the broadcasts, it was dangerous to be seen or heard listening to them. People would gather with select, trustworthy friends and family to hear the broadcasts. Others tuned in alone. Those without radios or the possibility of hearing *Angola Combatente* received the news second hand. Many Luanda residents recounted listening to broadcasts with their heads under pillows or under the bed. Some went further. Manuel Faria sought the cover of night and a remote listening spot: 'I would put my car in the soccer field, because I lived just near there and, you know, there in the soccer field it is dark and what not and I could listen to that little bit of radio at 19:00.'[23] Outside Luanda, people took similar precautions before tuning in: former mine workers at Diamang in eastern Angola recounted memories of hidden audition.[24] Both inside and outside the capital, the spectre of the PIDE (notorious as they were for terrorising *musseque* residents) induced fear and inspired creative listening strategies.

Despite the fear of violence associated with being caught, people listened to *Angola Combatente*. They listened to hear what was going on with the guerrilla struggle on its own terms and to hear words of encouragement. The EOA, on its programme the *Voz de Angola* (Voice of Angola), played good music, but it presented nothing but propaganda and highly censored reports of local and international events on its news broadcasts (Reuver-Cohen & Jerman, 1974:95–96, 99). *Angola Combatente* was therefore an alternative news source on international events in general and items that related to the Angolan liberation struggle in particular.[25] Foreign stations and *Angola Combatente* reported on United Nations resolutions and debates that related to the anti-colonial wars in Angola and other Portuguese colonies, but that never made the local news.

Although only 15 minutes in duration,[26] the programme also communicated, in code, news of those who had fled to join the fight. One PIDE report recorded such transmissions on 16 May 1970: 'Attention papa! Mama had twins!' followed by 'Attention Muigi in Matadi! Your messages have been received with regularity.'[27] For those involved in the clandestine political struggle in Luanda after the war broke out in 1961, *Angola Combatente* gave them a way to stay in touch with what was happening in the guerrilla fronts in the north and east of the country and with exiled political leaders in Brazzaville and Dar es Salaam. News about who had arrived, like the message about the twins (likely announcing the arrival of two new nationalists), and the silence about those who had not provided information that Luanda's politically active anxiously awaited.

Albina Assis recounted how she and others involved in clandestine political groups used the radio and employed their own codes to talk about what they were doing:

> By the time the MPLA started broadcasting ... we would say we're going to '*bençon*'. What is '*bençon*'? A '*bençon*' was a kind of Mass that was held during the month of May for the whole month, which is the month in the Catholic Church – the month of Maria – in which the people would go to the church at 19:00 and stay there for about an hour ... We all had an obligation to hear *Angola Combatente* so that the next day we could report on what was happening and how the war was developing, who had left for

there and who had arrived. We were young girls but we already knew all those codes of the messages.[28]

Assis and her colleagues used the trappings of piety to cover up clandestine political work. Who would dare question young people going off to church in the evening? Indeed, it must have seemed like a real blessing that *Angola Combatente* broadcast at the same hour as mass. The use of this particular code of religious practice underscored the sense of devotion to and sanctity of the cause.[29]

Others listened to *Angola Combatente* with members of their political cells. Xabanu participated in a political cell formed in 1962–63 with other students from the Rangel neighbourhood.[30] He recalled that each person had his/her own friend or small cell with whom he/she would listen to *Angola Combatente* and groups grew as large as ten people. *Angola Combatente* often broadcast instructions on how to organise political cells, hide arms and make bombs.[31] Although he had to leave the group to do military service in the Portuguese army, Xabanu said 'we never stopped listening to our *Angola Combatente* even as the soldiers that we were. We always had the nucleus of a group that would say – *epa*, it is 19:00, let's go listen to *Angola Combatente*! And we would listen ... but if they caught you, look out!' The risks were substantial. As soldiers in the Portuguese army they were listening to the 'enemy', betraying the flag they bore on their uniforms for 'our' *Angola Combatente*.[32] One PIDE agent caught a small group of *cipaios* (African policeman) in the town of Chiumbo in central Angola listening to *Angola Combatente*. The *cipaios* claimed they tuned in for the music, not the talk.[33]

In the early 1970s companies in Angola produced records of local music that often found their way across the border and into the hands of *Angola Combatente* broadcasters. Innovative radio operators took advantage of this to hoodwink authorities and transmit *Angola Combatente* semi-surreptitiously. Roldão Ferreira, whose Kimbundu-language radio show *Kussunguila* played popular urban Angolan music, remembered listening to *Angola Combatente* in public:

At the National African League [the Liga] ... every Thursday we already had the programme schedule for *Angola Combatente*. And I managed to play the music almost simultaneously. The songs were placed, via the guide of *Angola Combatente* in Brazzaville, and we would put them on here as well on the programme *Kussunguila*. [*João Chagas: This didn't cause problems?*] No, no, it didn't. Because we, I and some others, were normally in the São João bar with a number of whites on the other side, listening, attentive, wanting to hear either *Kussunguila* or *Angola Combatente* to know what it was they were saying. And there was such a complication of music that those who were nearby couldn't tell if it was *Angola Combatente* or *Kussunguila* ... because the songs coincided ... We listened to *Angola Combatente* even with the enemies right next to us![34]

Ferreira spoke with pleasure at slipping one by the Portuguese who were curious to know what *Angola Combatente* broadcast. In playing the music from *Angola Combatente* simultaneously with his own *Kussunguila* show (whose name refers to the nightly gathering of elders and youth where stories and fables are told), Ferreira amplified the music's subversive potential. The same music that would have aired on *Voz de Angola* and been considered anodyne by the authorities acquired a direct nationalist resonance when played on local radio synchronised with *Angola Combatente*. The desire of populations throughout the Angolan territory to listen to *Angola Combatente* and their ingenuity in finding ways to do so demonstrate a widespread interest in the activities of the nationalists.[35]

Radio and counter-insurgency

The nationalist guerrillas had set the communications agenda. In the late 1960s the colonial state found itself forced to respond to rebel broadcasts that were accessible to anyone with a short-wave radio.[36] The most direct and obvious state response was to jam the foreign-based transmissions (Coelho, 1999:137),[37] but perhaps the more effective response was to develop a radio network throughout Angola. On 27 March 1961, on the heels of the uprisings in February and March of that year, the overseas minister created the Coordinating Commission for a Radio Broadcasting Plan for the Province of Angola.[38] This plan provided for an increase in broadcasting and for a newly coordinated broadcasting system throughout the province that linked local clubs and commercial stations to the EOA. Only in 1967, after many years of liberation movement broadcasting, did the Angolan Centre for Information and Tourism convene the first Colloquium on Radio Broadcasting to evaluate the success of the prior plan and to discuss radio in frankly political and propagandistic terms (Lopes, 2000:9). This colloquium was part of a larger effort by the colonial government to win the war of ideas. In the same year, 1967, the Portuguese government established the General Council for Counter-subversion (Reuver-Cohen & Jerman, 1974:10). From November 1968 to March 1969 it held a Symposium on Counter-subversion where participants discussed the problem of 'enemy' (i.e. nationalist movements) radio and the usefulness of radio to their own campaign, already under way on *Voz de Angola* (Reuver-Cohen & Jerman, 1974:11).

Documents from the symposium state that *Voz de Angola* was already an effective means of 'electronic warfare'. They report that the radio programme was widely heard both throughout Angola and outside of it. Counter-subversion experts attributed much of the programme's success to its use of 'native tongues' (Reuver-Cohen & Jerman, 1974:99). *Voz de Angola* employed Angolans who spoke local languages in order to broadcast news and information that would reach the widest possible audience. Local-language news broadcasts commonly included interviews with real and imagined deserters from the guerrilla troops, speeches that praised public institutions that provided social assistance to the population, and conversations with 'African heroes', i.e. those loyal to the Portuguese (Reuver-Cohen & Jerman, 1974:95–96).[39] Most Angolans had no trouble seeing this for the propaganda that it was, but they tuned in just the same in order to hear the local music that accompanied the news.

Radio after independence

Given the importance of radio in the late colonial period and its diverse uses in the war and in particular in the hands of the MPLA, whose *Angola Combatente* was the most consistent and insistent anti-colonial radio voice, it is no surprise that radio became an important force of news, information and propaganda after independence. Since civil war and independence were the twin spawn of decolonisation in Angola, war propaganda was particularly prominent, but so were a number of programmes that promoted nation building. RNA came under the wing of the Ministry of Information, which reported directly to and was vetted by the secretary for the ideological sphere of the ruling MPLA. From the point of view of the ruling MPLA, radio was important not only as a weapon against the civil-war enemy UNITA, but also in terms of sorting out disputes internal to the MPLA, in particular what became known as the Nito Alves faction, the attempted coup, and the subsequent repression in which control of the radio and other organs of social communication were key to consolidating the state's position. *Angola Combatente* became a programme that was broadcast to the armed forces engaged in the fight against UNITA and that carried forward the idea that the civil war was Angola's second war of liberation. At the same time, radio came to mark the rhythms of daily life: RNA's children's programme '*pio-pio*' at 10:00 and the news report at 13:00 structured the daily soundscape. In Angolan writer Ondjaki's debut novel about life in 1980s Luanda, *Bom dia camaradas!*, the 13:00 newscast is a constant part of the lunchtime ritual of the protagonist's family. Music programmes promoted new styles of music from different provinces that were meant to create greater representation of different musical genres, from Cabinda to Cunene, as the taint of factionalism made some of the hugely popular music from the 1960s and 1970s unwelcome on the state's broadcasting service (see Moorman, 2008).

During the Angolan civil war, UNITA also actively broadcast propaganda (about military advances, anti-communist policy and hagiographic treatments of the party's leader at the time, Jonas Savimbi). Vorgan, the Voice of the Black Cockerel (UNITA's symbol), broadcast a 'fantasy' world from its 'laboratory of hate', according to Elaine Windrich (2000:215). Yet, people of all political stripes tuned in to Vorgan to hear news different from that broadcast on RNA, even if they did not agree with the ideological line. As Paulo de Carvalho's (2002:103) study of audiences in Luanda shows, the bulk of listeners following shows on what were considered opposition radio, such as Radio Ecclesia, also identified with the MPLA. Political affiliation does not define listenership and is in itself far too complex and historically complicated to be transparent to any particular kind of behaviour, whether radio audition or voting.

Radio in the present

Precisely one month after Chakussanga's death, RNA celebrated its 35th anniversary (precisely 37 days before the Republic of Angola celebrated its 35th year of existence). An editorial in the state daily celebrated the 'glorious' history of radio in the country (*Jornal de Angola*, 2010b). But the history it celebrated was a history prior to those 35 years being celebrated, prior to independence. In other words, the editor of the paper lauded the history of radio in the late colonial period and completely forgot, as one well-known journalist lamented, the radio journalists and history of radio since independence, not to mention the significant contributions of the ruling party's rebel radio programme, *Angola Combatente*.[40] At one level, this stemmed from the arrogance of print media reflecting on radio. The editor, in fact, welcomed the announcement by the minister of social communication of the shift to digital technologies and the expansion of radio operations while, with a paternalistic tone, cautioning that training was necessary, again erasing the many years of radio broadcasting and experience since 1975 (*Jornal de Angola*, 2010b). At another level, it is an example of a strange sort of colonial nostalgia by the very generation that fought for independence. It points to the necessity for a much more complete and nuanced history of radio since independence, particularly one focused on the 1980s and early 1990s.

As to radio listening in the present, a few features stand out. The changes introduced by the 1992 elections, which included agreements to move toward media liberalisation, mean that there are a number of different commercial stations – some specialising in sport, others in music, most with a diversity of programming (e.g. the Catholic station Radio Ecclesia and the first commercial station, Luanda Antenna Comercial). But the state still dominates the airwaves, and current laws, soon to

Radio in Africa

be revised in light of the new constitution adopted in February 2010, restrict radio transmission to FM broadcasters (a high-cost endeavour thanks to the very high cost of constructing infrastructure required to reach a large area). Not even the RNA has full national coverage, as a recent article notes (ANGOP, 2010).

Today in Luanda at least the soundscape is diverse: not only radio news and music, but the sounds of car horns (as drivers try to find a path through record-breaking traffic), the cries of fish vendors, the well-rehearsed chants of political rallies, the songs of sports fans and the groans of cranes fundamental to the frenetic construction work that characterises the capital. This should remind us that a more ample aural canvas than this chapter has represented existed in years gone by as well and that radio listeners hear radio in between and next to other sounds.[41] They also continue to listen together, as a walk down any section of a Luanda street full of security guards evidences. By far the most consistent reason for tuning in, at least on the street, by this all-male group is sports. Radios of all sizes, almost always with improvised antennae, emerge when there is a football match. But music and news programmes also have a broad and consistent audience (many listeners actively engage by calling in and the top hits music show – o Top dos Mais Queridos, based on phone voting – is now in its 20th year).

One Saturday morning I happened on five or six security guards standing around a mid-sized radio with a wire running from the box to the gate in front of which they stood. When I asked what they were listening to, they responded 'o programa do Jójó' (Jójó's programme). This is a popular programme on Radio Despertar in which the radio journalist Manuel António 'Jójó' da Silva satirises the news and takes comic jabs at official announcements and state initiatives. I read this as an auspicious sign of the times: a frank, sometimes critical, and tongue-in-cheek radio programme on the UNITA-associated radio station could be casually listened to, collectively no less, on the street. And then, as I was trying to finish this piece, I heard the news that Jójó had been stabbed by someone posing as a fan when he left Radio Despertar's installations late at night on 21 October 2010. In fact, he says he was leaving a friend's sports bar/house of games when the attack occurred and not the radio station (Miranda, 2010). As in Chakussanga's case, it is impossible to say whether someone in the ruling party ordered this attack, although it is unlikely. The effects of state power are often crude, but its operations are typically subtle and indirect. More likely someone, party nomenklatura or rank-and-file militant, thought that Jójó needed a more explicit lesson.[42]

Broadcasters might be temporarily silenced and more self-censoring, but not in the long term. Angolans today find ways to voice criticisms, just as Angolans during the anti-colonial war found ways to tune in to clandestine radio, even when conditions are not the most propitious and even if circumstances have changed.

Professionalism, not polemics, is the discourse to which broadcasters and radio journalists take recourse today, but it is a tactic they learned in the school of the 1980s.

If UNITA's Vorgan was, in Windrich's phrase, a 'laboratory of hate', it was also a place where some people learned the love of the trade of journalism.[43] And RNA, despite the fact that it still functions more as an official organ of state than as a public service, also was and is a 'laboratory of professionalism'. Many of the journalists who work and worked there are more interested in being skilled professionals than in being ideologues, although some make more political compromises than others. For his part, Jójó says he is ready for new challenges and, who knows, maybe he will soon have a programme on RNA, since criticism from within is more welcome than criticism from without. None of this is likely to cow listeners or make them turn away. They are still more keen to tune in than to tune out.

Endnotes

1   Roughly two-thirds of this article comes from chapter 5 of my book *Intonations: A Social History of Music and Nation, Luanda, Angola, 1945 to Recent Times* (Moorman, 2008). It is reproduced here with permission from Ohio University Press (< http://www.ohioswallow. com >). Note: all translations of documents from Portuguese to English are by the present author.

2   Among others, this referred to the journalist Rafael Marques, whose report on corruption by particular government officials has raised much dust of late. See Marques's website: < http://makaangola.com/ > .

3   When Marques's report came out, Falcão publicly said that it was not the place of the MPLA to respond. He has obviously changed his mind and one prominent blogger, 'Wilson Dada', suggested that Falcão's recent remarks were meant as a recovery for his earlier failure to properly defend the MPLA. See Dada's blog, 'O MPLA, a Oposição, os confrontos de Maputo e a destruição do Roque Santeiro', < http://www.morrodemaianga. com > , accessed 9 September 2010.

4   See   < http://en.rsf.org/spip.php?page = classement&id_rubrique = 1001 > ,   accessed 10 November 2010.

5   Africa Monitor Intelligence (2010) suggests that Radio Ecclesia, the Catholic radio station, has traded greater national broadcast coverage in exchange for depoliticising the tone of some of its news.

6   The last such study was done in Luanda in 2002 (De Carvalho, 2002).

7   Carlos Alberto Pimentel, for example, was offered a job in the early 1970s at the Benguela Radio Club because local listeners were fans of his radio programmes broadcast from the Kwanza Sul Radio Club. Although from Huambo, S. Coelho was hired in 1951 as chief of

production services and principal announcer for the Moçamedes Radio Club, making him the first white Angolan to hold such a position. He also established a studio in Luanda after being released from prison for activities in Huambo and prohibited from living there (see Coelho, 1999). Shows produced at the studio Voz de Luanda (Voice of Luanda) were broadcast throughout the country via the Commercial Radio of Lubango (interview with M. L. Fançony, Luanda, 16 October 2001).

8   Marcus Power (2000:605) argues that in Mozambique 'broadcasting became central to the capitalist development of the colony'. Writing on the history of radio in Angola, Júlio Mendes Lopes (2000:5) states: 'two aspects would mark the origin of radio-broadcasting in Angola: in the first place, the improvement in the colony's economic situation with positive entries in its balance of payments situation which was reflected in commercial activities and, in the second instance, the influx of Portuguese. This allowed for the consolidation of the economic, political, military and administrative structures existing in the territory.' As I mention, state use of the radio followed local entrepreneurial initiatives, and Diamang, the diamond concession, had its own radio transmitter and station. Certainly, the development of radio was linked to capitalist development in the late colonial period, but how, to what extent and what the effects were remain to be investigated.

9   According to Jean Michel Mabeko Tali, the broadcasts from Brazzaville and Dar es Salaam were the most consistent and enduring (personal communication, 25 December 2002).

10 Interview with D. Rocha, Luanda, 12 June 1998.

11 Interview with A. Assis, Luanda, 17 January 2002. Jorge Macedo (interview, Luanda, 11 May 2001) also mentions the importance of Radio Moscow as an alternative news source.

12 Interview with C. V. Dias, Luanda, 18 March 2002.

13 PIDE/DGS, Del. De Angola, Divisão de Informação – 1ª Secção, Processo de Informação: 14.26.A: Postos Emissores Clandestinos: f91 and f12, respectively.

14 Phyllis Martin (1995:148) notes that this transmitter was the most powerful on the continent and was established by General de Gaulle during the Second World War. Christopher Waterman (1990:93) notes the popularity of Congolese music played on the radio in urban Nigeria: 'By the late 1950s, Congolese guitar-band music, strongly influenced by the Cuban rumba and mambo, had become the craze in Lagos, its popularity sustained in part by the clear broadcasts from Brazzaville.'

15 See also Spitulnik (2002:339) and interviews with A. M. Faria, Luanda, 19 March 2002; 'Santocas', Luanda, 22 November 2001; and Xabanu, Ljuanda, 21 November 2001.

16 PIDE/DGS, Del. De Angola, Divisão de Informação – 1ª Secção, Processo de Informação: 14.26.A: Postos Emissores Clandestinos: f12.

17 Ibid.: f22.

18 For another example, see Eduarda (1973:18): 'in the musseques life is lived on the basis of happiness. Radios are turned on from 6 in the morning until midnight! And on the weekends the music never stops.'

19 This sentiment was echoed in a PIDE note that likewise referred to 'Congomania' but noted its decline in the wake of successful programming by the Voz de Angola. See PIDE/DGS, Del. de Angola, Divisão de Informação – 1ª Secção, Processo de Informação: 15.33. A1: Emissora Oficial de Angola, f465.

20 Interview with Xabanu.

21 Interview with Macedo.

22 Bob White (2002) argues similarly for Congo-Leopoldville relative to Afro-Cuban music: 'it provided urban Congolese with an alternative to a particular form of cosmopolitanism – Belgian colonialism – that was strict and stoic if not cruel and in many ways anti-cosmopolitan.' Meredith Terretta (2006) points to the ways in which nationalism and pan-Africanism are not mutually exclusive but, rather, mutually reinforcing.

23 Interview with Faria.

24 Many thanks to Todd Cleveland for sharing his interview material and an article from Diamang's former employees' magazine with me. His interviews were conducted with former mine workers in late 2004 and 2005 in Dundo, Lunda Norte.

25 Transcriptions of broadcasts on Radio Tanzania criticised US and South African involvement with the Portuguese, talked about liberated zones administered by the MPLA, and encouraged Portuguese soldiers to desert and fight fascism (Torre do Tombo, PIDE/DGS/Del. Angola, 'Radio Tanzania', Proc. 15.29/B, ff10–11, 28–30, 34–36, 38–41. Torre do Tombo is the national archive in Lisbon where, among many other things, the documents of the PIDE/DGS – the fascist secret police – are housed; see < http://antt.dgarq.gov.pt/ >).

26 Marga Holness, who has a small collection of transcribed radio programmes broadcast from Tanzania between 1968 and 1970, said that the programmes were generally only 15 minutes long (personal e-mail communication from Marga Holness, 23 October 2003).

27 Torre do Tombo, SCCIA, PdI #190, U.I. cx. 260, f62.

28 Interview with Assis.

29 In chapter 2, 'This is the Voice of Algeria', of A Dying Colonialism, Frantz Fanon (1965) discusses the radical role of radio in the Algerian anti-colonial struggle. As in Angola, it was not just the news being broadcast by the nationalist movements that was interesting, but the ways in which people listened and how they used radio.

30 Interview with Xanabu.

31 Torre do Tombo, PIDE/DGS/Del. Angola, Proc. 14.19.A1, NT 2045, f55. Bittencourt (2008:299) argues that instructions on how to construct bombs and conduct insurrection had little effect.

32 Interview with Xanabu. For another example of soldiers listening to MPLA broadcasts, see Torre do Tombo, PIDE/DGS/Del. Angola, Proc. 14.19.A1: Emissoras Estrangeiras, nt 2045, f3.

33 Torre do Tombo, SCCIA, PdI #190, U.I. cx. 260, f30.

34 RNA, *Angolan Music on the Radio*, hosted by João Chagas, 28 February 2002, Luanda.

35 A local administrator in Mungo town in Huambo province reported a similar incident in 1967. He happened upon a group of 10–15 African men listening to *Angola Combatente* in a bar. They used the telephone as a radio receptor and switched back and forth between stations (Torre do Tombo, SCCIA, PdI #190, U.I. cx. 260, f8).

36 The colonial government, as part of its counter-subversion programme, encouraged the sale of radios and was developing television communications: 'The sale of radios should not be restricted; that should be a solution only in extreme necessity. But only radios which can receive exclusively middle-wave should be sold' (Reuver-Cohen & Jerman, 1974:95).

37 PIDE/DGS, Del. de Angola, Dinf., Processo no. 14.19.A1: Emissoras Estrangeiras, nt 2045, f3, 4, 6–8, 47, 48, 61.

38 *Boletim Oficial de Angola*, vol. 1, no. 15, 12 April 1961, p. 535, cited in Lopes (2000:9).

39 This sort of propaganda was also prevalent in the local press. The popular magazine *Notícia* contained a series of articles over several years covering the war that was entitled 'on the front, with our troops'. Many articles focused on Angolans who were fighting with the Portuguese troops and interviews with those who had abandoned the 'enemy' to come and fight with the Portuguese. See, for example, *Notícia*, 16 November 1968, pp. 21–29.

40 See < morrodemaianga.com > , 8 October 2010 entry, accessed 10 October 2010.

41 Television is also a much greater force these days. TV via TPA broadcasting began in 1975, the year of independence. Currently, the state-run station, TPA, has two channels and there is one independent station, TVZimbo – in many middle-class homes the TV station that is constantly on.

42 In his interview with *Vida*, Jójó said the attack is under investigation by the police and that he knows that his show creates both friends and enemies. Crime in Viana, where the radio is located and where he lives, is high and there are on average 60 such acts each day, he underscored. Jójó then averred that his 'heart belongs to the M[PLA]'.

43 Bela Malaquias and Guida Paulo are two former Vorgan journalists who now work at RNA. Malaquias (interview, Luanda, 6 June 2008) emphasised her commitment to journalism as a profession and her sense of vocation over politics.

16

Radio in Zones of Conflict
Abnormal Measures for Abnormal Circumstances

David Smith

Case study – Somalia

A radio station for Somalis, by Somalis and about Somalis went on the air on 1 March 2010. Radio Bar-Kulan ('meeting place' in Somali) uses FM, short wave, satellite and the Internet to ensure that access is available to all who want it. The history of this station has its roots in peacekeeping. The success of another radio service,[1] described elsewhere in this book, helped convince the people with money that perhaps Somalia needed similar treatment.

Bar-Kulan is still very much a work in progress. It was born out of need and developed through compromise. I am a director of the implementing agency for Bar-Kulan and I cannot overemphasise the importance of radio in a society that is in conflict and is overwhelmingly oral. I also recognise that there is an argument against creating such a service and will try to present a faithful synopsis of that case.

First, however, a brief look at the playing field.

Background

Somalia is a failed state. 'Failed state' is a term thrown around quite often in Africa – sometimes it is used to describe the Democratic Republic of Congo (DRC), the Central African Republic (CAR), Chad and even Nigeria. 'Failed state' is a bit like 'genocide' – it is hard to agree on when the term should be used; 'genocide' fits what happened in Rwanda in 1994, but not what is happening in Darfur today. I would also argue that there are no other clear-cut examples of failed states in Africa apart from Somalia. The DRC, CAR, Nigeria and Chad certainly have their problems, but they also have territorial integrity and a central government that, despite well-documented weaknesses, are in power following national elections. Assessing the extent of the free and transparent nature of these elections is beyond the scope of this chapter.

Somalia has a Transitional Federal Government (TFG). Members of the TFG were appointed and given support by a variety of outside interests, including the United States, Ethiopia, the United Nations (UN) and the African Union (AU). The current president, Sheikh Sharif, was elected by his colleagues at a meeting in neighbouring Djibouti. Officially, the TFG is working towards national elections in 2011.

In order for national elections to take place, something not far from a miracle is needed. The TFG may have good intentions, but it has little else. Ensconced in Mogadishu in a laager-like compound originally built by the Italians as their colonial headquarters, the 550 members of the 'national' assembly do little more than survive. With the military support of a beleaguered AU peacekeeping mission (the AU Mission in Somalia, or AMISOM) down the road, the TFG is able to govern an area smaller than an East Rand mining community in South Africa. The TFG's own armed forces are receiving training from the Americans and others and, at the time of writing, the AU is calling upon member states to boost the numbers of the 6 000-strong Ugandan and Burundian force that keeps the airport and seaport open in Mogadishu. A handful of countries are expected to answer the call, but it is not likely that anywhere near the number of soldiers needed to wrest the country from the hands of the anti-government forces will be provided.

And this brings us to the rest of the country. Pre-referendum Sudan is more united than Somalia. Somalia has been split up into at least four separate entities. Somaliland, in the north, is a breakaway republic not recognised internationally, but operating in all ways bar a seat at the UN as an independent country. Puntland in the Horn of Africa part of the country – the place where the Indian Ocean meets the Gulf of Aden – is officially part of the Somalia recognised by the AU. Unofficially, like Somaliland, it operates de facto as another country, with its president and his administration sitting in the local capital city, Garowe. Then there is south-central Somalia – the large swathe of territory running from the border with Puntland in the north all the way down to the border with the ethnic-Somali region of Kenya. Depending on where you place your finger on the map of this part of the country, the area probably falls under the dominance of either Al-Shabaab or Hizbul Islam, two of the largest anti-government groups; a local semi-autonomous administration such as that of the President of Galmudug in Galkacyo; or the fourth of the broadly defined entities – the liberated zones of Mogadishu held by the TFG and AMISOM.

Although the TFG officially speaks for the entire country at the UN, few Somalis will stand up and say that the TFG speaks for them.

Greater Somali and the diaspora

The ethnic Somali homeland extends well beyond the borders of Somalia. Djibouti, the former French Somaliland, is dominated by ethnic Somalis; the same is true of Ethiopia's southern Ogaden region. Meanwhile, Kenya rarely advertises the fact that a large number of north-eastern Kenyans are ethnic Somalis and, in addition to those born in Kenya, form one of the world's largest refugee populations – Somalis fleeing violence in Somalia have been crossing the border for decades. Nobody knows how many Somalis live in the greater Horn of Africa region – estimates centre on the six-million mark.

Then there are the large diaspora centres far from home – Egypt and South Africa host significant Somali communities, as does Yemen across the Sea of Aden. Further afield, Canada, the United States and several northern European countries are home to Somali communities often numbering in the hundreds of thousands. As is often the case with diaspora communities that originate in countries wracked by internal violence, Somalis overseas are often part of the problem. Money for arms, and even bodies for cannon fodder, including recruits for suicide bombings, come from as far afield as Minnesota in the Midwestern United States (one of the largest Somali diaspora communities).

All of the above communities form target markets for Bar-Kulan. All of them have played a role in making the country ungovernable, and all of them need to be part of the solution if the goals of peace and stability are to be achieved and maintained.

Shortly after Radio Okapi went on the air with studios in three cities in the DRC – Kinshasa, Kisangani and Goma – the head of the UN peacekeeping mission in the country, Amos Namanga Ngongi, announced to the world that the station had electronically removed the front line in a war that, at the time, was being called 'Africa's World War'. Eight years prior to this, radio was being used to call upon Rwandans to slaughter their neighbours. There should be no doubt how powerful radio is on this continent.

The Somali media scene

Understanding that Somalia needs radio to help in the peace process does not require a great intellectual leap. Determining how to effectively deploy such a plan is the hard part.

Radio certainly existed in Somali prior to Bar-Kulan. Dozens of radio stations regularly came and went there. The grandfather stations were established during the colonial period – one in Hargeysa, in what was then the capital of British

Somaliland, and one in Mogadishu, in what was then the capital of Italian Somalia. After independence, the two Somalias merged to form one country, with Mogadishu as the capital of the united state; Mogadishu also became the headquarters for state radio.[2] This remained the case until after the ousting of the former president, Siad Barre, in 1991. Today, state radio in Mogadishu and Hargeysa are, respectively, the mouthpieces for the TFG and the Somaliland administration. Government authorities in Puntland get their message across through their own radio service in Garowe.

South-central Somalia has traditionally been home to the bulk of the population – it is the part of the country most suited to agriculture. The two largest rivers in Somalia, the Shabelle and the Jubba, water this region, and rainfall, although not abundant, is higher than in the north. It is here that most of the radio stations are located.

Operating a radio station in south-central Somalia requires making compromises that go dramatically beyond any normal principle of free speech. Station managers must at the very least take into account the demands of the dominant clan in the area and, increasingly, practise strict censorship in line with the heavy-handed norms of groups such as Al-Shabaab and Hizbul Islam; between them, these groups ban music, sports, female announcers and anything else they consider to be un-Islamic from being broadcast.

In all cases, the footprint of the broadcast area is small. Radio Mogadishu, controlled by the TFG and run from its compound at Villa Somalia, covers little more than the city, simply because it has no recognised authority beyond Mogadishu that would allow it to erect FM relays. Independent radio stations – the term 'independent' is used very loosely here – generally have neither the funding nor the resources or influence to extend their reach beyond a single FM transmitter housed at their studios.

The only radio stations managing to cover the entire Horn of Africa are those broadcasting from outside Somalia. Prior to Bar-Kulan taking to the airwaves, there were two of note – the BBC Somali Service, broadcasting from the United Kingdom, and the Voice of America Somali Service, broadcasting from the United States. To call either of these services independent and credible Somali radio stations would require quite a stretch of the imagination. In the case of the BBC, credible as its English-language World Service is, the Somali service struggles with a perception that it favours coverage of a subclan of the Hawiye and also focuses on international Western media material translated into Somali. The Voice of America is perceived as closely tied to the US government: daily transmissions of US government editorials as part of its output do not improve its credibility.

Outside of Somalia, the diaspora turns to the Internet for information. There are more Somali-language websites than radio stations. The most popular is Shabelle.net, to which Somalis turn in large numbers for a simple reason – it is fast. If something is happening in Somalia or of interest to Somalis, the chances are that Shabelle.net will have it first. Being fast, however, comes at a price – and that price is factual accuracy. Shabelle.net journalists are notoriously poorly paid and poorly trained, making news coverage erratic and an editorial line virtually non-existent. Left unchecked, rumours become de facto fact.

Shabelle.net is not alone when it comes to broadcasting or posting fiction. Virtually all Somali media outlets have an agenda. In some cases, it is a moveable agenda set by money. Universal TV, an overseas-based commercial channel, is the largest Somali television service. Universal actively sells decoders to Somalis throughout the diaspora, with agents as far afield as Washington, DC, Toronto and London. While no one can fault its distribution plan, there are weaknesses in its content control. At the very least, the station operates an advertorial policy where content producers can sponsor air time; editorial checks are waived, meaning that money will ensure that any content goes on air.

There is little to say about print media simply because the print run of the largest newspaper is small. There are numerous titles in Somalia, but for a variety of reasons, including high illiteracy rates, low disposable income and distribution difficulties, print runs rarely exceed a few hundred copies.

This is the media space Bar-Kulan has moved into.

Getting started

Okapi Consulting believed that Somalia, Somalis and the diaspora needed a place where they could meet easily to come up with a plan for peace, stability and prosperity in their homeland. The plan does not involve rocket science. It involves using appropriate technology to take advantage of and facilitate something Somalis have always been quite good at – talking. The problem up to now has been finding a place where they could talk in relative security and include the largest possible number of participants. This is where *by whatever means necessary* comes into play. Somalia is at war. The country is in an emergency situation – it is an abnormal situation that requires abnormal measures. The resources one uses in such situations are not necessarily the ones one uses in stable societies during times of peace and prosperity. An explanation is necessary.

There is what appears to be a never-ending argument over whether the UN should be involved in radio. The argument against goes something like this. The UN does not understand local conditions on the ground. The UN steals local talent, pays unsustainable salaries and upsets the local economic balance. The UN does not obey local rules and regulations. The UN broadcasts propaganda. There is an element of truth in all these statements, just as there is an element of truth in most clichés and stereotypes. I argue that the situation on the ground in countries such as Somalia, the DRC, Sudan and the CAR requires urgent action. Discussions on long-term agreements and strategy can follow later. UN peacekeeping missions provide a useful emergency tool to cut through diplomacy/bureaucracy/red tape or whatever else one wants to call it and get down to work saving lives. Once again, an explanation is necessary.

Radio Okapi is the second-largest radio network in Africa after the South African Broadcasting Corporation. It has played an enormous role in helping to bring peace to the DRC. It would not have existed if the UN had not decided that it would exist. Without Radio Okapi, Africa's third-largest country would have been left with a state broadcaster without means or credibility; commercial radio stations that see no role for themselves other than one that makes money (nothing wrong with that, but it does not rebuild broken countries); and community stations that serve communities, not countries. Provided the UN manages to find a way to turn Radio Okapi over to the Congolese people once the peacekeeping mission ends, the DRC and its people will be dramatically better off – they will have a trusted information and entertainment source that would not otherwise have been there.

That brings us back to Somalia. Bar-Kulan exists because the UN and the AU say it should. Bar-Kulan was conceived at a workshop in October 2008 at the AU headquarters in Addis Ababa. Okapi Consulting was invited, among others, to address the AU's public information specialists in its Peacekeeping Division. Peacekeeping within the AU is new when compared to its big brother, the UN. Unlike the UN, there is no tradition of setting up radio stations as part of AU peacekeeping missions. Operations in Burundi, Sudan and Somalia were not established with radio as part of the mix. The Burundi mission has come and gone; Sudan has been transformed into a hybrid mission that includes the UN's Department of Peacekeeping Operations (DPKO);[3] and AMISOM, the Somalia operation, is struggling to survive.

At the Addis Ababa workshop, Okapi Consulting presented the case for using radio as a tool for peace in zones of conflict. The presentation was, by all accounts, well received and a request was made for a follow-up document on how a radio project could be developed for application to the Somalia situation. In our Johannesburg offices, a plan was developed for the AU for what at the time was no more than a generic peacekeeping-type radio operation that would, if implemented, work in concert with the mission in Somalia. It was a simple plan that called for little more than a basic studio operation in Mogadishu allowing for interaction between Somalis and AMISOM. With hindsight, it was not a good plan.

The fatal flaw in the plan was that it called for the creation of a radio service that would belong to the peacekeeping mission. AMISOM's intentions are good, but there is no peace to keep in Mogadishu. The mission is to a large extent on the defensive and doing, with only limited success, damage control. A fairly large number of Somalis do not like AMISOM and would prefer that the Ugandans and Burundians pack their bags and go home. To be fair, many Somalis feel this way about any foreign intervention in their country – recent invasions by Ethiopia have left a sour taste in their mouths.

There may come a day – and that day may not be far off – when AMISOM receives the human, material, and financial resources it needs to enforce and keep the peace, and do this in an area that is considerably larger than a few neighbourhoods of Mogadishu. Until this happens, however, the unfortunate status quo is unlikely to change. The status quo goes something like this: Somali insurgents fire at AMISOM installations, sometimes injuring or killing peacekeepers. AMISOM fires back, using, among other things, mortar fire and tank shells. More often than not, civilians are hit. One of the most-often-hit areas is the main market in the city, Bakara Market. In what has so far been a public relations disaster for AMISOM, any responsibility on its part for civilian deaths is generally denied.

Linking a radio service to AMISOM at the moment would be suicide for credibility. But that said, AMISOM must work; it has to be fixed. The AU is aware of this and so is the international donor community. The UN has hired two public relations firms to help AMISOM get on the right track in its relationship with Somalis (more on that later).

Meanwhile, back in Addis Ababa, the AU liked the radio plan. Few organisations would not like the idea of a radio station that offered support to their efforts. The plan found its way to the UN headquarters in New York, from where DPKO decided something needed to be done. A call for tenders went out to parties interested in providing the following: a radio station for AMISOM as well as public-information support and capacity building for the mission. The proposed operation was to be financed by the UN Support Office for Somalia through the AMISOM trust fund. The UN also offered to throw a certain amount of logistical support into the deal.

The UN invited Okapi Consulting to bid for the project. The directors of Okapi have considerable experience within UN peacekeeping operations in the domain of public information and, more precisely, in the field of radio for peacekeeping missions. The possibility of actually putting in place a radio service for Somalia, with the support of the UN, sounded extremely attractive and an opportunity not to be missed. Providing public-information support to AMISOM sounded less interesting. This is where one must remind oneself of the maxim *by whatever means necessary.*

The UN's Procurement Division has come under the spotlight in recent years for less-than-honourable reasons; accusations of corruption are not new to the organisation. In an effort to appear transparent and fair, the UN spread its net far and wide to solicit tender bids. Some of the world's biggest public relations firms threw their hats into the ring. One of the conditions attached to the bid required the eventual winner to put up a large amount of cash as surety. In order to meet all the requirements of the bid, Okapi Consulting went into partnership with two other organisations and formed a consortium – Okapi brought to the table its radio experience in zones of conflict, while the other partners brought experience in public-information capacity building and the necessary cash – not an ideal situation but, under the circumstances, one that works. And this is the point: an ideal situation in Somalia is not likely, at least not in the short to medium term.

Foot in the door

Okapi Consulting, together with its consortium partners Albany Associates and Bell Pottinger, won the bid. Albany and Bell Pottinger have written vast amounts of material on the support they provide to AMISOM, Radio Mogadishu and the TFG. This chapter is concerned only with the need for radio for peace in Somalia, and this is where Okapi Consulting fits in.

The UN has never outsourced an entire public-information service. In the DRC, a partnership with a Swiss non-governmental organisation that led to the creation of Radio Okapi was the start of precedent-setting activity. The UN is not usually very keen on handing over the reigns of information production to non-UN entities. There is no across-the-board agreement in New York that partnerships and outsourcing are a good idea – many at UN headquarters believe all such projects should be handled in-house. I do not necessarily disagree. However, in an emergency situation, one uses the tools at hand, and at hand in this situation was a contract to produce what was at the time an ill-defined idea for a radio service for Somalia.

There are no secrets in Somalia. Once word got out that a South African-based outfit was getting UN money to set up some sort of Somali radio station, an out-of-tune orchestra of newly assembled opponents of the project appeared almost instantly (read: people and organisations that felt the UN money should have gone to them). The list included out-of-work journalists, existing partisan radio stations in Somalia, Radio Mogadishu, the TFG, AMISOM, other UN agencies and certain members of the diplomatic community. An argument can be made in favour of most or all of the above. The point is, a decision had to be made and the longer it takes to make a decision in a country that is at war, the more damage will be done to life and limb.

Once the contract was awarded, the goal was to get on the air as soon as possible and become a vital source of information from the start. It is usually more difficult to stop such a project once it is operational than it is to get permission to launch, therefore the best approach is to start before somebody decides to stop you!

What kind of radio does Somalia *really* need?

Somalia needs a radio service that people believe and trust. It needs a radio service that *involves* the stakeholders – Somali youth, Somalis in the diaspora, Somalis who want their homeland to be stable and prosperous. Somalia needs a radio service that will last and be able to stand on its own feet. This was not, however, the type of radio service set out in the contract Okapi Consulting was asked to fulfil – the international community, especially when organisations such as the UN or AU are involved, has a tendency to dilute terms of reference for fear of upsetting any concerned parties. The Somalia contract called for the establishment of production facilities in Nairobi, with a satellite link to Mogadishu, for broadcasting programming from an FM transmitter based at AMISOM, as well as ensuring that two hours of short-wave programming per day covers the entire Somali territory and a website provides information to the diaspora. This was not a bad plan, it was just not enough.

Rumours were rife in late 2009 that the UN was setting up AMISOM radio. Certain quarters – within AMISOM and within the UN itself – believed that this was the case. It was incredibly obvious that any radio station set up with the AMISOM name attached to it would not enjoy the support or trust of the Somali people. I would, to some extent, like to be wrong about this – AMISOM is made up of brave individuals who work under horrendous conditions in Mogadishu. They do not want to be there; they would like to be at home with their families. They do not need a radio station; they need a stronger mandate and more – many more – resources. They also need to prove to Somalis that they are on the same side.

Establishing Bar-Kulan began by establishing what it was not. Meetings with journalists, diplomats, humanitarian workers and any others with an interest in Somali affairs inevitably began with the disclaimer that the new radio service being set up was *not* AMISOM radio and *not* UN radio, but *was* to become an all-Somali service for Somalis everywhere. The name Bar-Kulan came after canvassing Somalis worldwide – it had to be found quickly so we could move beyond calling it *the radio that is not AMISOM.*

The project officially got off the ground in November 2009. The UN provided a building in Nairobi from where all consortium partners could direct their operations. Bar-Kulan occupies the ground floor of the building. Between November and March

2010, journalists were recruited throughout Somalia, paying special attention to ensure that all of the major clans were represented on the staff. Many members of the crack start-up team used to launch Radio Okapi were brought in to put Bar-Kulan together, including the website designer and the musical genius who designed the jingles, music beds and theme songs. The website < http://www.bar-kulan.com > was launched in February 2010. The first broadcasts went on air on 1 March from short-wave transmitters in the United Arab Emirates and South Africa.

The ability to produce content moved faster than the ability to send a live signal to the transmitters, forcing Bar-Kulan to relay recorded programming through the Internet to the transmitter site. This meant no live news, but it did create an opportunity to test the signal while providing on-the-job training to the new team. The initial content consisted of station identification, Somali music, short features of a cultural nature and anchor programming of a religious nature focusing on passages from the Qur'an that teach tolerance, peace and peaceful coexistence. Under strict supervision, Bar-Kulan's religious affairs editor meets regularly with Somali Islamic scholars to choose the Qur'anic content and suitable Hadiths that conform to the aim of the station – i.e. to promote the creation of a constructive environment for Somalis at home and abroad to work together to lift their country out of chaos.

This programming remains central to everything Bar-Kulan puts on the air. Two weeks after the first recorded programmes were broadcast, live programming was introduced with the commissioning of an FM transmitter in Mogadishu. The transmitter, protected by AMISOM, heralded several important firsts for Bar-Kulan:

- the first broadcast of signal from Somali territory;
- the first live broadcast;
- the first news content; and
- the first regularly scheduled use of Bar-Kulan's new Somali-wide network of regional correspondents.

FM, launched on 14 March 2010, increased the programming day to nine hours. Exactly two months later, on 14 May, the length of the broadcast day jumped to 16 hours and live streaming was added to the website.

Keeping in mind that youths are the main target of Bar-Kulan and remembering that most Somalis are less than 20 years old, the production of content aims to keep young Somalis close to their radios. Web-based surveys indicate that most Somalis, regardless of their age, want to hear religious programming. This is followed by news, sport and music. If future surveys indicate a change in interests, the Bar-Kulan schedule will change. As this is a Somali station and the hope is that it will one day become a permanent fixture in the Somali broadcasting landscape, listeners will to a large extent help determine what goes on the air (provided it is in line with the aim of Bar-Kulan to promote a peaceful, stable and prosperous Somalia).

The Soccer World Cup in South Africa could not have come at a better time for Bar-Kulan. On its staff is the only FIFA-accredited, Somali-speaking sports journalist in the world. It should not surprise anybody to hear that there are large numbers of sports-mad Somalis who, like the rest of the world, wanted to follow the World Cup. Bar-Kulan broadcast every game in its entirety with live, in-studio commentary in Somali and studio guests, including the former national coach of the Somali team. Anecdotal evidence[4] indicates that a large and loyal listenership was established during the World Cup. Without any external marketing campaign, the number of listeners to live streaming during the World Cup averaged about 2,500 per day, a figure that has been maintained post-World Cup.

Music is a more sensitive issue in Somalia than in most other parts of the world. Extremist groups in Somalia have banned music on stations in parts of the country – the argument being that it is un-Islamic. Although most Islamic scholars do not agree with this, the reality on the ground is that to play music in certain areas, notably south and central Somalia, can be a life-threatening activity. Bar-Kulan is able to cover Somalia with content from its music library of over 6,000 Somali titles because its studios are not within the zones controlled by the extremists. This does not mean, however, that the choice of music played is not heavily scrutinised. The playlist, as is the case with all content, does not include any titles that promote violence or intolerance. What it does include is a rotation ensuring that there is the widest possible selection of Somali music genres throughout every broadcast day – modern, vocal, oldies, instrumental and traditional all have their slots on the playlist, and there is absolutely no random jukebox mode.

Thematic programming focusing on women, youth, health, business and technology, and culture has regularly scheduled slots. Producers are assigned programmes in order to ensure continuity and develop an expertise in the subject.

Okapi Consulting's policy of gender equity is a greater challenge in Somalia than in many other places. Traditionally, Somali women face a steep uphill battle when trying to enter the professional world. Apart from few jobs being available and the education system being in ruins, the few places that are available for formal education do not usually go to women. It is an aim of the project to ensure that women are well represented not only as journalists and producers, but also as technicians and members of management. This subject leads to the question of what still needs to be done.

Finding Somali journalists to work on the project is easy; finding female Somali journalists is not. Finding female Somali technicians is extremely difficult, as is finding Somalis of any gender with media management skills. Training will be a big part of the development of Bar-Kulan during the second year. Funding to make this training as well as other aspects of the project's growth possible is and likely will remain a challenge. That said, *the show must go on!*

There are two other important challenges to address in year two: (1) extending FM signal coverage on the ground and (2) making programming more interactive. Regarding FM relays, negotiations with local authorities throughout the Horn of Africa have thus far yielded various levels of success, from 'Yes, please put up as many FM transmitters in our area as you possibly can' to 'No, we don't want Bar-Kulan here because we believe you will be biased against our clan'. Where negotiations are successful, challenges still remain. It cannot be taken for granted that transmitter technicians are lining up to install equipment in Somalia. They do exist, but they are not always easy to find. Once they are found and once the necessary bureaucratic paperwork (visas, entry permits, re-entry permits) is out of the way, secure sites with reliable power sources must be found. These sites do exist; it just takes time to identify and then secure them.

One of Bar-Kulan's primary goals is to ensure that Somalis everywhere have easy access at any time of day or night to the service. This means creating partnerships with Somali-language radio stations throughout the world and expanding what is on offer on the website – both in print and audio format (eventually adding video as well); and this leads to the second big challenge – interactivity.

Cellphones have done more to make radio interactive than any other electronic device. Not so long ago, just about the only way to have live, personal contact with a radio station was by walking directly into the studio. This, of course, was not an option for most people. Indirectly, there was always the post office. However, postal service is less than reliable, if available at all, to the majority of people living on the African continent. Cellphones, especially the SMS function, put the power of *instant content and reaction* into the hands of the listener. In other words, the listener is more than a listener, becoming a person empowered to generate content.

The first year of the project is drawing to a close. But before that happens, it is likely that Bar-Kulan will have the capability to interact directly with Somalis through SMS, phone calls and text content on the Internet at an extremely low cost to the listener. This interaction will spawn new programming, including debates and round tables involving, hopefully, not only Somali youth and other interested parties, but some of the belligerents as well.

North America, Western Europe and Kenya – three regions with large Somali diaspora populations – dominate visits to the Bar-Kulan website. As content in general and the amount of English-language content[5] in particular increase, including audio and eventually video, the number of visits is also likely to rise. The Bar-Kulan website is not separate from the radio service; they are integrated as one media access operation. The days of websites being simply an add-on to radio, newspaper and television operations are long over; to ignore this fact is professional folly.

So what have we learned?

There are no hard and fast rules when operating within a zone of conflict. Somalia is in a state of emergency and as such requires emergency measures. *By whatever means necessary* seems to be the order of the day. As the implementer of Bar-Kulan, I believe that difficult decisions must be made and difficult compromise agreements must be entered into when the stakes are as high as they are in Somalia. *Somalia has known neither peace nor stability for more than two decades. The status quo is not the answer. Somalia is an oral society – to reach people one must talk to them. Radio is the way to do this in Somalia, while the Internet is a reasonable alternative for Somalis elsewhere.*

Is it going to work? There is a war in Somalia – we do not know when it will end or who will win. However, as lottery-ticket buyers say, 'You can't win if you don't have a ticket'. We will never know how significant a role dialogue through radio can play in bringing peace to Somalia unless we try to get such a dialogue going. There are some excellent precedents out there to remind us of the pivotal role, both positive and negative, radio has already played in conflicts on our continent.

Bar-Kulan is on the air. The biggest step has already been taken. Continued and expanded political and financial support will increase the odds of its survival. A Bar-Kulan foundation is being established as a conduit for funding for the project. UN financial support lasts two years, one of which is almost over. Support for year two does not cover a fraction of the proposed expansion outlined here.

Motivation is a big part of the mix when working towards project success. Finding motivated Somalis is easy. They, just like almost every other person on this planet, want their home to be a safe and secure place. A healthy and credible Bar-Kulan today provides a good foundation for strong, independent media in a future stable and prosperous Somalia, and such a day will come.

Endnotes

1   Radio Okapi, the peacekeeping radio network covering the Democratic Republic of Congo and housed within the United Nations peacekeeping mission based in that country; see chapter 11 in this volume.

2   Adam (1997) provides a comprehensive look at state radio in the pre- and early post-independence periods.

3   The AU/UN Hybrid Operation in Darfur.
4   The security situation in much of Somalia makes public-opinion polling extremely hazardous.
5   The number of Somalis living in the diaspora who do not read Somali is on the increase – a trend that is likely to continue.

17

Multiple Publics, Multiple Languages
Radio and the Contestations of Broadcasting Language Policy in Uganda

Monica B. Chibita

Introduction

Radio in sub-Saharan Africa has over the last two decades been dubbed *the people's medium* (Bourgault, 1995; Daloz & Verrier-Frechette, 2000; Van der Veur, 2002; Mwesige, 2009). Literacy rates in most sub-Saharan countries remain below average. In any case, the print media are still mostly published in the colonial languages, so they tend to serve only a small elite. Television has to a large extent served as an entertainment medium, out of the reach of many rural populations because of its cost and its reliance on electricity. Radio, on the other hand, is relatively affordable and transcends literacy and language barriers. It has been ideal for enabling the majority of rural populations of this region to participate in public debates on important issues affecting their everyday lives, particularly in languages they are comfortable with. The deployment of the different languages on radio, however, has been a subject of debate. Often, the perceptions of policymakers have been at variance with those of ordinary citizens. Policymakers have tended to see radio's role more as a conduit of pre-packaged information than as an arena for the contestation of ideas, representations and identities.

Language, complexities and citizens

Sub-Saharan Africa's linguistic heterogeneity poses a challenge to radio in optimising its role. The question of achieving the optimum language regime for radio remains a vexing one. As Fardon and Furniss (2000:3–4) observe:

To broadcast in one language is to fail to broadcast in another, and that is always taken as a message. Because the message of language choice may be divisive, a particular array of languages used on air may function as a symbolic mark of inclusion into a state, region or nation.

In linguistically heterogeneous societies, arriving at the optimum language policy to maximise citizens' democratic potential is no simple proposition. In this chapter, I discuss the potential of Uganda's indigenous-language radio in this regard, placing it in historical context and highlighting the resultant language dynamics. I propose a broadcasting language policy that would allow for a more pluralistic deployment of Uganda's different languages in the public domain with a view to increasing the opportunities of Ugandans to participate in public debate via radio. The chapter draws on 26 interviews with academics, local leaders, media managers and owners, and language policy advocates in Uganda and nine focus group discussions with radio listeners from different regions of Uganda. The interviews were conducted between 2005 and 2010.[1]

Language, radio and leaders

Political leaders have to contend with the tensions among radio's role in binding individual ethnic communities together, breaking barriers across such communities and bringing them into the global community. Part of the legacy of colonialism has been that by virtue of their social positioning and educational placement, a small elite exists whose members have the flexibility to maximise the opportunities that media such as radio have to offer at these different levels. As a result, as Mazrui (1996:113) argues, leaders in these countries have fallen prey to viewing the elite as the citizens they must address in the first instance. Mazrui contends that except at election times, political leaders pay scant attention to the communication needs of the majorities, who, for historical reasons, are able to interact with the outside world only in their mother tongue or a related language. Rather, politicians focus their attention on the elite. In this context, a discussion of the impact of language policy on the uses of radio in enhancing public participation in a multilingual setting becomes relevant.

The medium of radio has contributed greatly to the growth of a public space for debate on common issues in different African countries. How to best deploy language in this medium, though, remains a major preoccupation on the continent. According to Ricento (2000:10), the earliest works on language policy and planning were influenced by the discourse of decolonisation and state formation. As such, some scholars in discussing language policy for the media in post-colonial sub-Saharan African countries have favoured an approach that involves promoting a privileged public language or group of languages. By implication, this has meant limiting or denying recognition to other languages (Patten, 2001).

Scholars such as Mazrui (1996), Pawlikova-Vilhanova (1996) and Mohochi (2003) still see language as important in constituting such a space in a post-colonial African context. This is particularly so because the majority of sub-Saharan countries inherited linguistically heterogeneous entities and centrally controlled media systems. As a result, their language policies prioritised national consolidation. Thus, Mazrui (1996) contends that language policy for the broadcast media in this context is important for the involvement of citizens in public affairs and policymaking at various levels. In aid of achieving a 'national public sphere', Mazrui advocates downplaying both the colonial language and the majority of the indigenous languages. Instead, he argues for the use of one indigenous language in public communication. In East Africa, this model to a large extent underlies broadcasting language policy in Tanzania, which dictates that English and Kiswahili shall be the languages of broadcasting (United Republic of Tanzania, 2005).

The above position has some merit, to the extent that political leaders need an efficient way to address their citizens and citizens need a language to communicate across ethnic groups. However, it overemphasises a single, unified 'public sphere' as the sole focus of language policy. Radio in this perspective easily becomes a noticeboard for one-way communication. Furthermore, such a view does not pay sufficient attention to the fact that the language of radio must make both intellectual and emotional sense for ordinary citizens to be able to optimally utilise radio. The availability of radio in languages other than the colonial ones enables audiences to express themselves on issues such as agriculture, health, land, the budget, the environment, taxes and trade relations with neighbours. However, optimising radio in this way may be hampered by a policy that favours the use of one language for radio with the aim of creating a unified 'public sphere'.

Some critics of Habermas's (1989:27) notion of the public sphere, 'where private people come together as public and discuss matters of common concern', have advocated multiple 'sphericules' (Ekeh, 1975; cf. Gitlin, 1998) as more viable democratising sites in the African context (cf. Willems, 2007). These arguments are grounded in the understanding that colonialism created a situation in Africa where, even though the post-colonial state would like to assume one unitary public called 'the nation', there are in fact multiple publics. Language and ethnicity have been central to the consolidation of these publics and a lot of the politics of everyday life takes place in these 'sphericules' rather than in an imagined 'national public sphere'. Ugandan radio offers a good example of this phenomenon. A popular format on the commercial (and community) stations is the *ekimeeza* (meaning round table). These are open-air talk shows that sometimes take place in English, but mostly in the indigenous languages.[2] Since their inception in the late 1990s they have been immensely popular and have also attracted the government's attention. They were banned for the second time in September 2009 because of their perceived role in influencing public opinion.[3] These forums' utilisation of indigenous languages constitutes a powerful boost to the creation of smaller spheres of public opinion formation that could feed into the broader (national) public sphere. Language policy appears to be central in making this happen.

The current media landscape

Broadcasting in Uganda was a state monopoly until the early 1990s. In 1993 the National Resistance Movement (NRM) government liberalised the broadcasting sector, allowing for numerous privately owned stations to be licensed. The former Radio Uganda and Uganda Television were converted into the Uganda Broadcasting Corporation (UBC) by an Act of Parliament in 1995. The UBC now broadcasts in 24 languages, including English, Kiswahili and Luganda. Although the Act declares the UBC a public broadcaster, it is fully owned and controlled by the government and continues to operate as a state broadcaster (Mwesige & Ouma, 2008).

According to the Uganda Communications Commission,[4] as of February 2009 there were 181 registered radio stations in the country, nearly 123 of which are on air. Forty-six of these are based in the capital city and the rest in a few of the other metropolitan centres throughout the country. Most of the privately owned FM stations broadcast either in English and/or Luganda, or one of the major, commercially viable languages from the region that they serve. The latter include Lwo for the northern region; Luganda for the central and eastern regions; and the mutually intelligible Runyoro, Rutooro, Runyankore and Rukiga, also known as 'the 4Rs', for the western region. With this arrangement, many of Uganda's languages are typically heard on the state broadcaster only for a few minutes every week and some not at all on any of the commercial media. There is a sprinkling of financially constrained community radio stations whose potential is curtailed by the pressure to survive. To fully understand the dynamics of the operation of indigenous-language radio in Uganda and its implications for the political uses to which Ugandans put radio, however, it is important to appreciate the history of participation in the country.

A short history of Ugandan participation[5]

Uganda was a British colony between 1894 and 1962. During this period, two forces were of specific relevance to the evolution of language policy. One was the Baganda ethnic group, which served as the closest ally of the colonial government. The Baganda were used as agents of the indirect rule project (Karugire, 1980:109–16; Kabwegyere, 1995:61–67; cf. Mamdani, 1997:109–37 for a comprehensive treatment of the establishment of indirect rule in Uganda). The other was the Christian missionaries, who had a vested interest in which languages played a central role in Uganda's affairs, as this had a bearing on their evangelisation mission (Kabwegyere, 1995:188–97).

After attaining independence in 1962, the country experimented with a multiparty democratic system that lasted until 1967, when the then-prime minister, Dr Apollo Milton Obote, abrogated the constitution, abolished the traditional kingdoms, made himself president and declared a state of emergency (Karugire, 1988:58; Kabwegyere, 1995:210–14). This allowed him to rule by decree until he was overthrown by Idi Amin Dada in a *coup d'état* in 1971. By this time, not only were basic freedoms eroded, but the country was greatly polarised along ethnic and religious lines.

Amin's era was followed by a period of political instability characterised by *coups d'état* and gross human rights abuses (Karugire, 1988:86–95). Between 1979 and 1985 there was a 'musical chairs' situation involving different ethnic groups who variously felt marginalised or excluded. The current NRM government came to power in 1986 after a five-year guerrilla war against Gen. Tito Okello Lutwa's military junta, which had overthrown Obote's second government.[6]

Among the reforms introduced by the NRM government was the promulgation of a new democratic constitution in 1995 that was the culmination of a broad consultative process. The constitution guaranteed freedom of the press and of association. The NRM government also introduced a system of participatory politics at the grass roots consisting of five tiers (RC1 to RC5[7]) (Mamdani, 1997:215–17; cf. Golooba-Mutebi, 2004). A combination of these reforms seems to have sown the seeds for a new and pluralistic radio culture.

The language mix

Uganda is made up of four broad linguistic groups, the Bantu, Eastern Nilotic, Western Nilotic and Sudanic. There is limited mutual intelligibility within languages in each group, and none across the four groups. According to the Summer Institute of Linguistics,[8] at least 36 different languages are spoken in Uganda. English is the official language and Kiswahili the second official language. Luganda is the language spoken by the largest number of Ugandans (17.3 per cent),[9] but is largely unintelligible to the non-Bantu populations of northern and eastern Uganda. Although the Constitution of the Republic of Uganda (Uganda, 1995) recognises the existence of the different indigenous languages, it does not name a *national* language, and politically explosive discussion has surrounded debates on this topic. The debate has mostly centred on the roles of two key languages in the public domain, Luganda and Kiswahili.

The British maintained the dominant local languages as the languages of official business only at the local level. This was in order to combat any efforts by the different ethnic groups to cooperate with one another in the independence struggle. The colonial language policy thus served to maintain separate development in the different regions (Kabwegyere, 1995:144–45). English, which was the official language of business and debate, turned out to be a privilege of the colonial masters and those Ugandans with a Western education. The average Ugandan at the district level was limited by language to discussing the local politics of his/her district or ethnic group. Such policies over the years have widened the gap between the elite and the rest of the Ugandan population, and confounded any attempt to imagine a 'Ugandan public sphere'. As Kabwegyere (1995:190–97) observes, public debate in Uganda has typically been conducted at two separate levels, one dominated by the elite and often conducted in English, and another dominated by the remainder of Uganda's population and conducted in indigenous languages.

It is important to note, however, that public debate on language in Uganda has seldom dwelt on the role of the different languages in enabling all Ugandans to optimise radio for political participation. This could be because the majority of Ugandans have never seen a need to rally together as a nation, since the British policy of indirect rule had encouraged a more insular approach to politics. It could also be that the current two-tier language policy, where the members of a small elite are proficient in English while the majority operate mainly in their indigenous languages, suits the political leadership. Uganda's situation in this respect is different from Tanzania's where, using Kiswahili as a vehicle, the political leadership has succeeded in rallying together a sense of 'nation'. This sense appears to transcend ethnic and class barriers (Vavrus, 2002:375–76). Asked whether most Tanzanians have accepted this state of affairs willingly, Abdallah Katunzi, for instance, said:

The majority of Tanzanians living in rural areas have no problem with the policy – the use of Kiswahili. For most of them, Kiswahili was their second language and hence the straightforward choice for a national language. As of now, Kiswahili is widely spoken as the first language to most young people.[10]

For Ayub Rioba, the question of willingly accepting the policy or not does not even arise. The fact is that Tanzanians are using Kiswahili and it has, in his words, 'united elite and common man'.[11]

In complex linguistic contexts like Uganda's, however, it would seem that for the majority to optimise the opportunities that radio offers, there is justification for a multi-tier language regime that caters for communication within ethnic groups, across ethnic groups and across the country's borders. Such a regime would be driven by both state policy and the agency of media proprietors and ordinary citizens. In this way, ordinary Ugandans could enjoy the closeness and spontaneity of their ethnic communities through, for instance, community radio and indigenous-language programming on local and national radio. They could at the same time have a sense of 'Ugandan-ness' and remain abreast of government policy and activity through state radio. They could also, through the available international channels, continue to feel regionally and globally relevant. All this would require a careful deployment of the indigenous languages, Kiswahili and English. However, Uganda's post-independence governments have been reluctant to address the complexities of the language situation decisively. Official documents stop short of assigning any language except English and Kiswahili a role in the public domain (see, for instance, Policy Review Commission, 1992).

Re-examining language policy for radio

Ugandan political leaders in the past have not seen indigenous-language radio as a key component of a broader diversity that relates to enhanced public presence and political participation for all citizens. Rather, they have looked at indigenous-language radio stations as conduits of government policies and programmes to a largely illiterate public. Beyond this, government has chosen to let the agency of media owners and audiences dictate the use of the indigenous languages on radio, as long as vital public information is available in English on all channels. This policy is problematic for a number of reasons.

Since less than a quarter of Ugandans understand or speak English, there is an increased need to provide information and facilitate debate on issues that concern ordinary Ugandans in as many of the indigenous languages as possible. This would enable the majority to participate in policy formulation and hold government accountable. In the absence of this, a gap is created (or exacerbated) between the members of a small elite who have facility with English and the majority who can only participate meaningfully in radio using an indigenous language. Besides, there is no one indigenous language that all non-English-speaking Ugandans can benefit from at the moment. The likely consequence of this scenario is that the governors become insensitive to the real needs of the majority because the latter have no avenue for expressing themselves adequately.

The current broadcasting language policy also promotes a high level of ethnic insularity that makes it difficult to have any semblance of a simultaneous national debate on any issue. In a recent debate about land rights and tenure in Uganda, for instance, radio stations serving different ethnic groups discussed their specific land concerns mostly shaped by their particular colonial experiences. However, no consensus seemed to be emerging on the national land question, i.e. on what kind of land policy would be in the best interest of all Ugandans. As a result, although the Land Bill was passed, sections of the Buganda subregion continue to express dissatisfaction with it. Similarly, Uganda has been involved in a process of regional integration with Kenya, Tanzania, and lately Burundi and Rwanda. However, it has been difficult for Ugandans to discuss the pros and cons of this move as a nation on radio, as radio stations have tended to examine issues from an insular regional or ethnic perspective. Such situations would appear to justify the need for a common language (or languages) for public communication to help build a national consensus around issues of public concern.

Others in this debate, however, have argued that the whole fuss about a 'unifying' language is uncalled for, as one language does not necessarily make for unity. Proponents of this position cite countries such as Burundi, Rwanda and Somalia that have been bedevilled by civil strife for decades in spite of having a common ethnic language.

Still, from the government's perspective, it could be argued that the universal use of a language like Luganda or Kiswahili could help consolidate some form of a unified 'public sphere' and could contribute to 'national consolidation'. For historical reasons, most Ugandan governments have preferred Kiswahili to any indigenous language for this purpose. Idi Amin declared Kiswahili the national language in 1972, although he did nothing to actualise this. The NRM government has sought to promote Kiswahili to the level of a national language because of its perceived neutrality and its potential to catalyse the development of a political and economic bloc in the fast-unifying East Africa region. Furthermore, government statements have referred to the maintenance of a multilingual language policy with all the indigenous languages playing an equal role as 'backward and divisive' (see, for instance, Policy Review Commission, 1992). The NRM's pro-Kiswahili policy has met with resistance, particularly from the Baganda ethnic group. For the purposes of maintaining peace, therefore, the NRM government has had to continue offering lip service to the indigenous languages in the short term. The result, at least for radio, has been a fuzzy non-policy on language.

From the horse's mouth: Interviews and insights[12]

In this section I discuss insights from interviews I conducted with local leaders, media owners and managers, and ordinary radio listeners in central, eastern, northern and western Uganda. The broad areas of inquiry included the significance of the indigenous languages for participation in and through the broadcast media (and particularly radio). The inquiry also covered attitudes towards the use of Uganda's different languages in the broadcast media, the perceived efficacy of indigenous-language radio and suggestions for the ideal policy for regulating linguistic diversity in Uganda's broadcast media. I will relate some of the findings from the interviews to the arguments on language and political participation raised hitherto.

There was unanimity among all media owners and managers interviewed that indigenous-language broadcasting plays a vital role in enhancing ordinary people's participation in the democratic process. Key informants, including local leaders and district information officers, said indigenous-language radio enables the majority of Ugandans to access accurate information in languages they understand. It enables them to participate through the media in issues that concern them. It also gives them a sense of relevance and belonging.

Interviewees further argued that the importance of indigenous-language radio in the democratic process is demonstrated by the significance that local and national politicians attach to local stations: 'Every standing politician has to come to radio. And now they are all setting up their own radio stations.'[13]

The following comment from a district information officer summarises what many perceive as the unique significance of indigenous-language radio:

> When the programme is in Lumasaba (the majority local language in Mbale), you get very good points that come from people who have not even gone to school. The audience of radio is in the rural areas. Here real people talk to their leaders ... The media has [sic] a very big role, especially in our area here. Print circulates only among the elite, and the majority of ordinary Ugandans are illiterate. Radio broadcasts in languages they understand so they pay more attention.[14]

However, there appeared to be no consensus among ordinary Ugandan radio listeners on whether or not it would be appropriate to have a single official language for broadcasting in Uganda. The position of English was seen as non-problematic by most interviewees at the grass-roots level, but none of the other indigenous languages (apart from Luganda) was considered a serious contender for the position of official language of broadcasting. The discussion at this level therefore once again boiled down to the possible role of Kiswahili and Luganda in the broadcast media. There was, surprisingly, no discernible consensus in favour of Luganda, even though it is spoken by the largest percentage of Ugandans, has the most developed orthography, and is the de facto lingua franca of the central, eastern and parts of the western regions.[15]

The majority of those interviewed did not think it was viable to have an indigenous language as the official language of broadcasting because of historical ethnic tensions, as well as the fear of losing individual ethnic identities. The following response from a middle-aged focus group participant in Sironko, eastern Uganda, to the suggestion that Luganda be considered as the official language of broadcasting captures the level of emotion that often typifies this aspect of the debate:

Ekyo kifu![16] (That is [a] dead [suggestion].) It cannot work. It would cause inferiority complex [sic] in other ethnic groups. For example, if it is Luganda for the eastern and central regions, this makes Baganda feel superior over other tribes. Our people high there in the mountains [the area surrounding Sironko is mountainous] don't understand Luganda and are not even interested in listening to it.

In all but the central region (the home of the Baganda ethnic group), many saw Kiswahili as the lesser of two evils if they had to choose a 'unifying language' for radio. Many, even in the central region, admitted that Kiswahili could unite Ugandans since it is widely spoken in the neighbouring East African countries and some areas in Uganda, and that it is a 'neutral' language that would eliminate discrimination among Ugandans.

The strongest arguments in favour of Luganda as the official language of broadcasting, on the other hand, were based on underlying fears expressed in statements such as 'our local languages should not merely be erased by Kiswahili' and the fact that it is indigenous to Uganda, unlike Kiswahili. The proponents of Luganda also argued that Luganda is easier for Ugandans to learn than either English or Kiswahili. They added that it is accepted in most of Uganda and cuts across socio-economic barriers. Interviewees also repeatedly raised the issue of Kiswahili's reputation as a language of violence and barbarism.[17] For some interviewees (especially in the central region), the choice of any language besides Luganda was unimaginable, because of the historical position of power of the Baganda ethnic group. One interviewee put it simply: 'I have travelled widely in this country, and when someone speaks Luganda, everyone listens. But Swahili [Kiswahili]? They feel alienated.'[18]

What emerges from the interviews is that many ordinary Ugandans are torn between the need to communicate and actualise themselves in an ethnically comfortable context and the need to be relevant beyond their ethnic environs. They would like to find a solution that enables them to be part of their ethnic 'sphericules' without being left out of debate at the national, regional and global levels. It also appears that political debate is not necessarily their greatest motivation for listening to or participating in radio. Plain self-expression and strengthening social networks rank at least as high as politics.

The interviews with media owners yielded predictably pragmatic positions. For them, a language was only as good as the audience and revenues it garnered, and all language decisions are primarily based on this consideration. A former minister of information offers this analysis:

> [Y]ou see, the stations we have are commercially driven. They are not motivated to have variety for its own sake. They prefer to deal with large language blocks. If people were economically strong, then stations would attempt to reach out to them. But most groups are poor .... This [of course] is a threat to democracy.[19]

Listeners were also asked to evaluate the efficacy of their participation in indigenous-language radio programmes. Some said listeners' contributions are indeed taken seriously and responded to. Others, however, were modest about the effect of their contributions, saying it depends on a number of factors, such as the issue in question and whether the radio guest has the power to do anything about it. Indeed, the majority opinion across the regions I visited was that government officials in particular responded only to inconsequential listeners' suggestions and that listener contributions on interactive local-language programmes had little effect on governance beyond the cosmetic. A 32-year-old taxi driver and participant in a focus group discussion with Open Gate FM listeners in Mbale captured the latter, more pessimistic view:

> There isn't much our calling [in to radio] can do once government has decided on something. Our calling only affects local issues like garbage

collection in town here. However, there are some instances when ordinary people have been listened to. For example, the Domestic Relations Bill ... was shelved when people (especially Muslims) complained and women demonstrated against it. But it seems our participation does not change political issues because what most people tell the MPs is not what they [MPs] deliberate [sic] and pass as Laws.[20]

Most listeners interviewed also indicated that they preferred to listen to and participate in political satires and dramas rather than straight political debate. They said the participation of ordinary people in programmes of a specifically political nature is limited to periods of high political activity like elections, by-elections or referendums. This suggests that conclusions about the significance of indigenous-language radio for Ugandans' participation in the democratic process need to be tempered with caution. One would need to go deeper and inquire into what kind of programming the stations are broadcasting in the indigenous languages, who is able to participate meaningfully in these programmes and with what motive.

Furthermore, there seemed to be a strong feeling among those interviewed that government does not take radio as seriously as it does the print media. One interviewee attributed this to the fact that the print media are read by members of the elite and government 'fears' members of the elite more than it 'fears' the ordinary people because the former are more likely to sustain a challenge to government programmes through debate.

Listeners interviewed suggested that any programme in a familiar indigenous language (with the exception of music and international sport) tends to be more popular than a similar programme in, say, English or Kiswahili, or a language not well understood in a given region. This implies that, in the Ugandan context, to achieve maximum impact and participation from radio, indigenous-language broadcasting would need to be set free rather than proscribed in the way that it has been, say, in neighbouring Tanzania. Official attempts at making radio more inclusive have emphasised the use of regional languages (hence Luganda for the central and eastern regions, Lwo for the northern region, Ateso/Ngakarimojong for the north-east and the 4Rs for the west). These, however, have ignored the fact that Uganda's ethnic groups are not always neatly distributed in specific sections of the country (for instance, there are Lwo in northern as well as eastern Uganda, and there are migrant labourers, particularly from south-western and northern Uganda, in other parts of Uganda; Runyankore-speaking pastoralists have also settled in parts of the central and north-eastern regions).

A different proposal emerging from the interviews in this regard was that since some ethnic groups are not necessarily located in one region, radio stations could adopt Luganda to address Bantu speakers, Lwo to address the Nilotes and Ateso to address Nilo-Hamites (mostly the Ateso and Ngakarimojong) and broadcast in all three languages. This proposal, informed by the logic of language rationalisation, has been borne out by the operation of many state radio stations in Africa. This solution, however, would leave out Kiswahili, which is becoming an increasingly important language regionally. It would also fall short on the imperative of making Ugandans globally relevant. Furthermore, it would be unsatisfactory for many who derive a sense of satisfaction from identifying with their own ethnic group through a specific language. Finally, it would not address the need for a 'unifying' language, which seems to be a high priority at least for political leaders.

Conclusions

There seems to be a degree of consensus among Ugandans from different regions and stations in life that indigenous-language radio is key to their participation in the broadcast media. Evidently, overtly political programmes (such as political talk shows) are not necessarily the most popular programmes among the ordinary Ugandans interviewed. This suggests that conclusions about causal links between participatory political programmes and political participation may be premature. It also points to a need to reassess the political contribution of popular programming in African contexts.

The interviews reveal a level of caution about the efficacy of the simple act of, say, calling in to indigenous-language radio. It appears that here too some opinions are 'more equal than others' and that call-in radio shows can be a mere charade when politicians often come to them with predetermined action plans. This finding agrees with Mwesige's (2004) findings on political talk shows in Uganda.

The interviews also support the disparities in emphasis between the public sphere and public 'sphericules' orientations discussed earlier. There appears to be a gap between the agenda of political leaders and that of ordinary Ugandans with regard to the role of indigenous-language radio. Government agents interviewed were focused on identifying or legislating a politically neutral language of cross-ethnic communication for the media in order to ease administration and facilitate regional economic and political integration. The majority of ordinary citizens interviewed, however, saw the role of indigenous-language radio more in terms of identification, cultural expression and cultural preservation. For media owners and managers, language policy was a practical matter and the majority favoured leaving market forces to shape language policy for radio. Their major question was: In the

Ugandan context, what language recipe maximises audience size and advertising revenue?

Given Uganda's political history and ethnic mix, could it be that the apparent paralysis over broadcasting language policy has been related to the fact that governments' real interest is in those languages that in some way help them maintain their position of power? If this were so, it would seem unlikely that political leaders would agitate for a language regime merely for the purposes of enhancing cultural expression or strengthening political diversity.

There is no inclination towards altering the position that English occupies in relation to Kiswahili or any of the indigenous languages. This perhaps attests a growing recognition among different sectors of the population of the need for relevance beyond national borders. For many interviewed, it would not be problematic to maintain the status quo, with English as the language of wider communication, backed up by Kiswahili, and the indigenous languages continuing to serve specific ethnic communities.

However, Fardon and Furniss (2000), in discussing the Nigerian language situation, identify two possible models for a context such as Uganda's. One is the multilingual model, where stations broadcast short slots of a wide range of languages every day. The other is the separate language service model, where radio is set up to broadcast one major language for each region on different channels *simultaneously*. The multilingual model is underpinned by the recognition of the major political forces that make up the state. This model is unpopular with commercial broadcasters, which see it as inefficient, while its inherent tendency to be repetitive can bore sections of the audience.

Fardon and Furniss (2000:3–4) see more potential for success with the separate language service model, citing the BBC, Deutsche Welle, the Voice of America and Radio Moscow, which have succeeded in 'building a separate regular audience' for the different languages. While the above models would serve the major languages, community radio would perhaps be best placed to fill in the gaps for the other languages to ensure that they too have forums for public expression and representation.

From the Ugandan situation, it could be argued that linguistically heterogeneous countries perhaps need to debate language in a broader context and think of solutions that bear in mind new political, economic and cultural imperatives. Radio has the flexibility to permit the nurturing of an environment where all citizens feel free to express themselves in languages that make sense to them, but also where they are able to participate in debates that address broader issues beyond their ethnic or national environs. It is important to remember, however, that language practice on radio is not always or *only* dictated by state policy, but is also influenced by market forces, as well as the agency of audiences, and media owners and managers.

Endnotes

1 In 2001 Uganda's National Resistance Movement government put in place a Constitutional Review Commission, chaired by Prof. Frederick Ssempebwa, to review the 1995 Constitution of the Republic of Uganda. This commission had, among other things, the mandate of identifying a possible national language 'to unify Ugandans'. As in previous instances, Kiswahili and Luganda emerged as the two languages in contention. The debate in the local papers in the early 2000s was polarised along support for or opposition to Kiswahili and Luganda. The language debate came to a climax in 2005 when the report was debated in parliament. Most of the key informant and respondent interviews, as well as the focus group discussions, were conducted in 2005. A few follow-up interviews were conducted in 2009 and 2010 to enable comparison.

2 Usually one of the commercially viable languages.

3 See Mwesige (2004; 2009) for a comprehensive treatment of the role of political radio talk shows in Uganda's politics; see also < http://www.bbc.co.uk/worldservice/trust/whatwedo/where/africa/uganda/2009/09/090930_uganda_ekimeeza_interview.shtml >, accessed 23 April 2010.

4 < http://www.ucc.co.ug >.

5 See Chibita (2009) for a more detailed discussion.

6 Having been ousted by Idi Amin in 1971, Obote had managed to stage a comeback in 1980.

7 RC was short for Resistance Council, conforming with the name of the ruling National Resistance Movement.

8 < http://www.ethnologue.com/show-country.aspn?name = UG >.

9 It has been argued, however, that some mutually intelligible language blocks like the 4Rs may compare favourably with Luganda in terms of numbers of speakers.

10 Interview with Abdallah Katunzi, assistant lecturer, University of Dar es Salaam, 2010.

11 Interview with Ayub Rioba, lecturer at the University of Dar es Salaam, media expert and chairperson of the Media Institutions of Southern Africa – Tanzania Chapter, 2010.

12 The bulk of these interviews were part of a doctoral research project at UNISA and later post-doctoral work under the Sida-Makerere research collaboration.

13 Interview with radio manager, Mbarara, 2005. A large proportion of FM stations in Uganda are owned by politicians at different levels of government.

14 Interview with a district information officer, Mbale, 2005.

15 < http://www.ethnologue.com/show-country.aspn?name = UG >, accessed 2 March 2010.

16 Note that the comment is made by a non-Muganda in Luganda!

17 Kiswahili has been the language of the military since colonial times and was associated with atrocities committed against civilians during the Idi Amin era.

18 Focus group participant, central region, 2006.

19 Interview with a former minister of information, Nsaba Butuuro, 2005.

20 Interview with taxi driver and participant in a focus group discussion with Open Gate FM listeners, Mbale, 2006.

References

Abu-Lughod, L. (1998) Feminist longings and postcolonial conditions. In Abu-Lughod, L. (ed.), *Remaking Women: Feminism and Modernity in the Middle East*, pp. 3–31. Princeton: Princeton University Press.

— (2000) Modern subjects: Egyptian melodrama and postcolonial difference. In Mitchell, T. (ed.), *Questions of Modernity*, pp. 87–114. Minneapolis: University of Minnesota Press.

— (2002) Egyptian melodrama: Technology of the modern subject. In Ginsburg, F., Abu-Lughod, L. & Larkin, B. (eds), *Media Worlds: Anthropology on the New Terrain*, pp. 112–33. Berkeley: University of California Press.

Adam, Suleiman M. (1997) *Gather Round the Speakers: A History of the First Quarter Century of Somali Broadcasting*. London: Haan.

Adorno, T. (1973) *Dialectic of Enlightenment*. London: Lane.

Africa Monitor Intelligence (2010). No. 506, 7 October 2010. < http://www.africamonitor.info > , accessed 14 October 2010.

Alidou, O. (2005) *Engaging Modernity: Muslim Women and the Politics of Agency in Postcolonial Niger*. Madison: University of Wisconsin Press.

Anderson, B. (1983) *Imagined Communities*. London: Verso.

— (1991) *Imagined Communities: Reflections on the Origin and Spread of Nationalism*. London: Verso.

ANGOP (2010) RNA aposta na modernização dos meios técnicos. 4 October. < http://www.angonoticias.com > , accessed 6 October 2010.

Appadurai, A. (1990) Disjuncture and difference in the global culture economy. *Theory, Culture and Society*, 7:295–310.

— (1991) Global ethnoscapes: Notes and queries for a transnational anthropology. In Fox, R. (ed.), *Recapturing Anthropology: Working in the Present*, pp. 191–210. Santa Fe: School of American Research Press.

— (1993) Patriotism and its futures. *Public Culture*, 5(3):411–30.

Armour, C. (1984) The BBC and the development of broadcasting in British colonial Africa 1946–1956. *African Affairs*, 83(332):359–402.

Armstrong, C. B. & Rubin, A. M. (1989) Talk radio as interpersonal communication. *Journal of Communication*, 39:84–94.

Article 19 (1996) *Broadcasting Genocide: Censorship, Propaganda, and State-Sponsored Violence in Rwanda 1990–1994*. London: Article 19.

Asad, T. (1986) The idea of an anthropology of Islam. Center for Contemporary Arab Studies Occasional Papers Series, Georgetown University.

— (2003) *Formations of the Secular: Christianity, Islam, Modernity*. Stanford: Stanford University Press.

Asma'u, N. (1997) *Collected Works of Nana Asma'u, Daughter of Usman dan Fodio*, ed. J. Boyd & B. Mack. East Lansing: Michigan State University Press.

Atton, C. (2002) *Alternative Media*. London: Sage.

Augis, E. (2002) Dakar's Sunnite Women: The Politics of Person. PhD thesis, University of Chicago.

Avleh, B. (2010) My interview with World Bank country director. < http://www.citifmonline.com/site/blogs/blog/35 > , accessed 13 June 2010.

Bakhtin, M. M. (1981) *The Dialogic Imagination: Four Essays*, ed. M. Holquist. Austin: University of Texas Press.

Banda, F. (2003) Community Radio Broadcasting in Zambia: A Policy

Perspective. Doctoral thesis, University of South Africa.

Bantu (1961) Radio Bantoe: 'n Pad oopgekap na nuwe hoogtes van ontwikkeling. April:149-54.

Barber, B. (1984) *Strong Democracy: Participatory Politics for a New Age.* Berkeley: University of California Press.

Barber, K. (2000) *The Generation of Plays: Yorùbá Popular Life in Theatre.* Bloomington: Indiana University Press.

Barnard, S. (2000) *Studying Radio.* London: Arnold.

Barrell, H. (1993) *MK: The ANC's Armed Struggle.* London: Penguin.

BBC (British Broadcasting Corporation) (1983) *BBC Monitoring Reports*, 20 October, ME/7469/B/1.

— (2006) *African Media Development Initiative: Research Summary Report.* London: BBC World Service Trust. < http://downloads.bbc.co.uk/worldservice/trust/pdf/AMDI/AMDI_summary_Report.pdf > , accessed 13 June 2010.

Bennett, S. (2001) Americans' exposure to political talk radio and their knowledge of public affairs. *Journal of Broadcasting and Electronic Media*, March:72-86.

Berger Guy (2009) Introduction: Beyond broadcasting. In Banda, F., Duncan, J., Mukundu, R. & Machado, Z. (eds), *Beyond Broadcasting: The Future of State-owned Broadcasters in Southern Africa*, pp. 5-13. Grahamstown: Highway Africa.

Berkeley, B. (2001) *The Graves Are not yet Full: Race, Tribe, and Power in the Heart of Africa.* New York: Basic Books.

Bernstein, R. (1999) *Memory against Forgetting: Memoirs from a Life in South African Politics.* London: Viking.

Bessa, C. (2010) Maior partido da oposição incita à disobediência civil. *Jornal de Angola*, 8 September.

Biener, H. (2008) Human radio for peace, democracy and rights: Zimbabwe. < http://www.evrel.ewf.uni-erlangen.

de/pesc/peaceradio-ZBW.html > , accessed 4 October 2008.

Bittencourt, M. (2008) *'Estamos juntos': o MPLA e a luta anticolonial, Vol. I.* Luanda: Kilombelombe.

Bjorkman, I. (1989) *Mother, Sing for Me: Peoples Theatre in Kenya.* London: Zed Books.

Boafo, S. T. K. (1991) Communication technology and development in sub-Saharan Africa. In Sussman, G. & Lent, J. A. (eds), *Transnational Communications: Wiring the Third World*, pp. 103-24. London: Sage.

Boal, A. (1979) *Theater of the Oppressed.* London: Pluto Press.

Bosch, T. (2006) Radio as an instrument of protest: The history of Bush Radio. *Journal of Radio Studies*, 13(2):249-65.

Bourgault, L. M. (1995) *Mass Media in Sub-Saharan Africa.* Bloomington: Indiana University Press.

Bowen, J. (1993) *Muslims through Discourse: Religion and Ritual in Gayo Society.* Princeton: Princeton University Press.

Boyd, J. (2001) Distance learning from purdah in nineteenth-century northern Nigeria: The work of Asma'u Fodio. *Journal of African Cultural Studies*, 14(1):7-22.

Brennan, J. R. (2010) Radio Cairo and the decolonization of East Africa, 1953-1964. In Lee, C. J. (ed.), *Making a World after Empire: The Bandung Moment and Its Political Afterlives*, pp. 173-95. Athens: Ohio University Press.

Brenner, L. (1993) Constructing Muslim identities in Mali. In Brenner, L. (ed.), *Muslim Identity and Social Change in Subsaharan Africa*, pp. 59-78. Bloomington: Indiana University Press.

— (2001) *Controlling Knowledge: Religion, Power and Schooling in a West African Muslim Society.* Bloomington & Indianapolis: Indiana University Press.

Brooks, P. (1976) *The Melodramatic Imagination.* New Haven: Yale University Press.

Brown, D. (2007) *Ethnic Minorities, Electronic Media and the Public Sphere: A Comparative Study*. Cresskill: Hampton Press.

Bryant, J. & Thompson, S. (2002) *Fundamentals of Media Effects*. Boston: McGraw-Hill.

Bull-Christiansen, L. (2004) *Tales of the Nation: Feminist History or Patriotic History? Defining National History and Identity in Zimbabwe*. Uppsala: Nordiska Afrikainstitutet.

Callinicos, L. (2004) *Oliver Tambo: Beyond the Engeli Mountains*. Cape Town: David Philip.

Camara, S. (1976) *Gens de la parole: essai sur la condition et le rôle dans la société Malinké*. Paris: La Haye.

Campbell, C. (1987) *The Romantic Ethic and the Spirit of Modern Consumerism*. Oxford: Basil Blackwell.

Cappella, J. N., Turow, J. & Jamieson, K. H. (1996) *Call-in Political Talk Radio: Background, Content, Audiences, Portrayal in Mainstream Media*. Philadelphia: Annenberg Public Policy Center, University of Pennsylvania. < http://www. annenbergpublicpolicycenter.org/ Downloads/Political_Communication/ Political_Talk_Radio/1996_03_political_ talk_radio_rpt.pdf > , accessed 1 June 2009.

Carver, R. (2000) Broadcasting and political transition: Rwanda and beyond. In Fardon, R. & Furniss, G. (eds), *African Broadcast Cultures: Radio in Transition*, pp. 188–97. Oxford: James Currey.

Casanova, J. (1994) *Public Religions in the Modern World*. Chicago: University of Chicago Press.

Castells, M. (1996) *The Power of Identity: The Information Age, Vol. 1: The Rise of the Network Society*. Oxford: Blackwell.

— (1997) *The Power of Identity: The Information Age, Vol. II: Economy, Society and Culture*. Oxford: Blackwell.

Chakrabarty, D. (2000) Witness to suffering: Domestic cruelty and the birth of the modern subject in Bengal. In Mitchell, T. (ed.), *Questions of Modernity*, pp. 49–86. Minneapolis: University of Minnesota Press.

Chalk, F. (1999) Hate radio in Rwanda. In Adelman, H. & Suhrke, A. (eds), *The Path of a Genocide: The Rwanda Crisis from Uganda to Zaire*, pp. 93–107. New Brunswick: Transaction.

— (2007) Intervening to prevent genocidal violence: The role of the media. In Thompson, A. (ed.), *The Media and the Rwandan Genocide*, pp. 375–80. London: Pluto Press.

Chibita, M. B. (2009) The politics of broadcasting, language policy and democracy in Uganda. *Journal of African Media Studies*, 12(2):275–307.

Chiumbu, S. (2004) Redefining the national agenda: Media and identity – challenges of building a new Zimbabwe. In Melber, H. (ed.), *Media, Public Discourse and Political Contestation in Zimbabwe*. Uppsala: Nordiska Afrikainstitutet.

Chrétien, J.-P. (2007) The democratic alibi. In Thompson, A. (ed.), *The Media and the Rwandan Genocide*, pp. 55–61. London: Pluto Press.

Chrétien, J.-P., Dupaquier, J.-F., Kambanda, M. & Ngarambe, J. (1995) *Rwanda: les médias du génocide*. Paris: Karthala.

Citifmonline (2010) Another NPP activist escapes assault in Tamale. 26 May. < http://www.citifmonline.com/site/ politics/news/view/6310/2 > , accessed 13 June 2010.

Coelho, S. (1999) *Angola: história e estórias de informação*. Luanda: Executive Centre.

Cole, C. (2010) *Performing South Africa's Truth Commission: Stages of Transition*. Bloomington: Indiana University Press.

Coleman, S. (1998) BBC Radio Ulster's talkback phone-in: Public feedback in a divided public space. *The Public*, 5(2):7–19.

Connerton, P. (1989) *How Societies Remember*. Cambridge: Cambridge University Press.

Conrad, D. & Frank, B. (eds) (1995) *Status and Identity in West Africa: The Nyamakalaw of Mande*. Bloomington: Indiana University Press.

Coplan, D. (1979) The African musician and the development of the Johannesburg entertainment industry, 1900–1960. *Journal of Southern African Studies*, 5(2):135–64.

— (2007) *In Township Tonight! Three Centuries of South Africa's Black Music and Theatre*. Johannesburg: Jacana.

Coulon, C. (1988) Women, Islam, and Baraka. In Cruise O'Brien, D. & Coulon, C. (eds), *Charisma and Brotherhood in African Islam*, pp. 113–33. Oxford: Clarendon Press.

Coulon, C. & Reveyrand, O. (1990) *L'Islam au féminin: Sokhna Magat Diop Cheikh de la Confrérie Mouride*. Travaux et Documents 25. Senegal: Centre d'Etude d'Afrique Noire.

Couzens, T. (1983) An introduction to the history of football in South Africa. In Bozzoli, B. (ed.), *Town and Countryside in the Transvaal: Capitalist Penetration and Popular Response*, pp. 193–214. Johannesburg: Ravan Press.

CPJ (Committee to Protect Journalists) (2010) Angolan radio presenter gunned down. 8 September 2010. < http://cpj. org/2010/09/angolan-radio-presenter-gunned-down.php#more > , accessed 10 November 2010.

Craib, I. (1992) *Modern Social Theory: From Parsons to Habermas*, 2nd ed. London: Harvester Wheatsheaf.

Curran, J. (2002) *Media and Power*. London: Routledge.

Curran, J. & Park, M. J. (2000) Beyond globalization theory. In Curran, J. & Park, M. J. (eds), *De-Westernizing Media Studies*, pp. 2–15. London: Routledge.

Dagron, A. G. (2001) *Making Waves: Stories of Participatory Communication for Social Change*. New York: Rockefeller Foundation.

Dahlgren, P. (2002) In search of the talkative public: Media, deliberative democracy and civic culture. *Javnost: The Public*, 9(3):5–26.

Dallaire, R. with Beardsley, B. (2004) *Shake Hands with the Devil: The Failure of Humanity in Rwanda*. New York: Random House.

Daloz, J. P. & Verrier-Frechette, K. (2000) Radio pluralism as an instrument of political change: Insights from Zambia. In Fardon, R. & Furniss, G. (eds), *African Broadcast Cultures: Radio in Transition*, pp. 180–87. Oxford: James Currey.

Da Silva, A. J. G. (1968) Finger in the wound. *Notícia*, 22 June.

Davis, S. M. (1987) *Apartheid's Rebels*. New Haven: Yale University Press.

De Beer, A. (1998) *Mass Media towards the Millennium: The South African Handbook of Mass Communication*. Pretoria: Van Schaik.

De Carvalho, P. (2002) *Audiençia de media em Luanda*. Luanda: Editora Nzila.

De Certeau, M. (1984) *The Practise of Everyday Life*. Berkeley: University of California Press.

Des Forges, A. (1999) *Leave None to Tell the Story: Genocide in Rwanda*. New York: Human Rights Watch.

De Vries, H. & Weber, S. (eds) (2001) *Religion and Media*. Stanford: Stanford University Press.

De Witte, M. (2008) Spirit Media: Charismatics, Traditionalists, and Mediation Practices in Ghana. PhD thesis, University of Amsterdam.

Diawara, M. (1997) Mande oral popular culture revisited by the electronic media. In Barber, K. (ed.), *Readings in African Popular Culture*, pp. 40–48. London: International African Institute.

— (2003) *Empire du verbe et l'éloquence du silence: vers une anthropologie du discours dans les groupes dits domines au Sahel*. Cologne: Ruediger Koeppe.

Douglas, M. (1966) *Purity and Danger: An Analysis of the Concept of Pollution and Taboo.* New York: Praeger.

Downey, J. & Fenton, N. (2003) New media, counter publicity and the public sphere. *New Media and Society,* 5:185–202.

Dunbar, R. A. (2000) Muslim women in African history. In Levtzion, N. & Pouwels, R. (eds), *The History of Islam in Africa,* pp. 397–417. Athens: Ohio University Press.

Dutkiewicz, P. & Shenton, R. (1986) 'Etatization' and the logic of diminished reproduction. *African Review of Political Economy,* 13(37):108–15.

Eduarda, M. (1973) O musseque e as suas gentes. *Boletim cultural (repartição de cultura e turismo):*18.

Eickelman, D. (1992) Mass higher education and the religious imagination in contemporary Arab societies. *American Ethnologist,* 19(4):643–55.

Eickelman, D. & Anderson, J. (1999) *New Media in the Muslim World.* Bloomington: Indiana University Press.

Ekeh, P. P. (1975) Colonialism and the two publics in Africa: A theoretical statement. *Comparative Studies in Society and History,* 17(1):91–112.

Ellis, J. (2000) Scheduling: The last creative act in television? *Media, Culture and Society,* 22(1):25–38.

Ellis, S. (1989) Tuning in to pavement radio. *African Affairs,* 88(352):321–30.

— (1993) Rumour and power in Togo. *Africa,* 63(4):462–76.

— (1994) Mbokodo: Security in the ANC camps, 1961–1990. *African Affairs,* 93(371):279–98.

Ellis, S. & Sechaba, T. (1992) *Comrades against Apartheid: The ANC and the South African Communist Party in Exile.* London: James Currey.

Ellis, S. & Ter Haar, G. (2004) *Worlds of Power: Religious Thought and Political Practice in Africa.* Johannesburg: Wits University Press.

Engelbrecht, P. J. (1962) Radio Bantoe brei uit. *Bantu,* August:495–96.

Englund, H. (2011) *Human Rights and African Airwaves: Mediating Equality on the Chichewa Radio.* Bloomington: Indiana University Press.

Evers Rosander, E. (1997) Le dahira de Mam Diarra Bousso de Mbacké. In Evers Rosander, E. (ed.), *Transforming Female Identities: Women's Organizational Forms in West Africa,* pp. 160–74. Uppsala: Nordiska Afrikainstitutet.

Facebook (2010) Radio Gold 90.5: *Alhaji and Alhaji.* < http://www.facebook.com/permalink.php?story_fbid = 11753 0378289031&id = 106457296042136 > , accessed 13 June 2010.

Fanon, F. (1965) *A Dying Colonialism.* New York: Monthly Review Press.

Fardon, R. & Furniss, G. (2000) African broadcast cultures. In Fardon, R. & Furniss, G. (eds), *African Broadcast Cultures: Radio in Transition,* pp. 1–19. Oxford: James Currey.

Felski, R. (1989) *Beyond Feminist Aesthetics: Feminist Literature and Social Change.* Cambridge, Mass.: Harvard University Press.

Ferry, J. (1992) Las transformaciones de la publicidad politica. In Ferry, J. & Wolton, D. (eds), *El nuevo espacio publico.* Barcelona: Gedisa.

Fiske, J. (1992) Popularity and the politics of information. In Dahlgren, P. (ed.), *Journalism and Popular Culture,* pp. 45–63. London: Newbury Park.

Foucault, M. (1973) *The Order of Things: An Archeology of the Human Sciences.* New York: Vintage.

— (1977a) *Discipline and Punish: The Birth of the Prison.* London: Allen Lane/Penguin.

— (1977b) *Madness and Civilization: A History of Insanity in the Age of Reason.* London: Tavistock.

— (1978) *History of Sexuality, Vol. 1: An Introduction.* Trans. by R. Hurley. New York: Random House.

— (1980) *Power/Knowledge: Selected Interviews and Other Writings 1972–1977.* New York: Pantheon.

Fraenkel, P. (1959) *Wayeleshi*. London: Weidenfeld & Nicholson.

Frahm-Arp, M. (2006) Professional Women in South African Pentecostal Charismatic Churches. Doctoral thesis, University of Warwick.

— (2010) *Professional Women in South African Pentecostal Charismatic Churches*. Leiden: Brill.

Fraser, N. (1992) Rethinking the public sphere: A contribution to the critique of actually existing democracy. In Calhoun, C. (ed.), *Habermas and the Public Sphere*, pp. 109–42. Cambridge, Mass.: MIT Press.

Freedom House (2009) Ghana. < http://www.freedomhouse.org/template.cfm?page = 251&country = 7614&year = 2009 > , accessed 13 June 2010.

Freire, P. (1972) *Pedagogy of the Oppressed*. Harmondsworth: Penguin.

Frere, M.-S. (2007) Francophone Africa. In Baratt, E. & Berger, G. (eds), *50 Years of Journalism. African Media since Ghana's Independence*, pp. 33–51. Johannesburg: African Editors Forum.

— (2008) *Le paysage mediatique congolais: etats des lieux, enjeux et defis*. Kinshasa: France Co-operation International.

Fujii, L. A. (2006) Killing Neighbors: Social Dimensions of Genocide in Rwanda. PhD thesis, George Washington University.

Furedi, F. (1990) *The Mau Mau War in Perspective*. Nairobi: Heinemann Kenya.

Gaffney, P. (1994) *The Prophet's Pulpit: Islamic Preaching in Contemporary Egypt*. Berkeley: University of California Press.

Gatwa, T. (1995) Ethnic conflict and the media: The case of Rwanda. *Media Development*, 3:18–20.

Gerstl-Pepin, C. (2007) Introduction to the special issue on the media, democracy, and the politics of education. *Peabody Journal of Education*, 82(1):1–9.

Gevisser, M. (1999a) The bag carrier. *Sunday Times*, 6 June.

— (1999b) The Thabo Mbeki story. *Sunday Times*, 16 May.

Ghanaweb (2007a) Media research slams journalists. 7 May. < http://www.ghanaweb.com/GhanaHomePage/NewsArchive/artikel.php?ID = 123652 > , accessed 13 June 2010.

— (2007b) Stop plagiarizing GNA stories. 30 March. < http://www.ghanaweb.com/GhanaHomePage/NewsArchive/artikel.php?ID = 121708 > , accessed 13 June 2010.

Ginsberg, F. D., Abu-Lughod, L. & Larkin, B. (eds) (2002) *Media Worlds: Anthropology on New Terrain*. Berkeley: University of California Press.

Gitelman, L. (2006) *Always Already New: Media, History, and the Data of Culture*. Cambridge, Mass.: MIT Press.

Gitlin, T. (1998) Public sphere or public sphericules? In Liebes, T. & Curran, J. (eds), *Media, Ritual and Identity*, pp. 175–202. London: Routledge.

Glissant, E. (1986) *The Ripening*. London: Heinemann.

Goffman, E. (1981) *Forms of Talk*. Philadelphia: University of Pennsylvania Press.

Golding, P. & Harris, P. (1997) Introduction. In Golding, P. & Harris, P. (eds), *Beyond Cultural Imperialism: Globalization, Communication and the New International Order*, pp. 1–9. London: Sage.

Golooba-Mutebi, F. (2004) Reassessing popular participation in Uganda. *Public Administration and Development*, 24:289–304. < http://www.interscience.wiley.com > , accessed 25 March 2009.

Gonda, V. (2008) Government looking for land for mass burial, after killing 78 miners. 11 December. < http://www.swradioafrica.com/news111208/massburial111208.htm > , accessed 12 December 2008.

Gqibitole, K. M. (2002) Contestations of tradition in Xhosa radio drama under apartheid. *English Studies in Africa*, 45(2):33–46.

Gunner, L. (1979) Songs of innocence and experience: Zulu women as composers and performers of *izibongo* Zulu praise poetry. *Research in African Literatures*, 10(2):239–67.

— (2000a) Wrestling with the present, beckoning to the past: Contemporary Zulu radio drama. *Journal of Southern African Studies*, 26(2):223–37.

— (2000b) Zulu radio drama. In Nuttall, S. & Michael, C. A. (eds), *Senses of Culture: South African Culture Studies*, pp. 231–55. Oxford: Oxford University Press.

— (2002) Resistant medium: The voices of Zulu radio drama in the 1970s. *Theatre Research International*, 27(3):259–74.

— (2005) Supping with the devil: Zulu radio drama under apartheid – the case of Alexius Buthelezi. *Social Identities*, 11(2):161–69.

— (2006) Zulu choral music: Performing identities in a new state. *Research in African Literatures*, 37(2):83–97.

Habermas, J. (1989) *The Structural Transformation of the Public Sphere: An Inquiry into a Category of Bourgeois Society*. Cambridge, Mass.: MIT Press.

Hale, J. (1975) *Radio Power: Propaganda and International Broadcasting*. Philadelphia: Temple University Press.

Hall, S. (1980) Encoding/decoding. In Hall, S., Hobson, D., Lowe, A. & Willis, P. (eds), *Culture, Media and Language*, pp. 105–14. London: Routledge.

— (1996) The question of cultural identity. In Hall, S., Held, D., Hubert, D. & Thompson, K. (eds), *Modernity: An Introduction to Modern Societies*, pp. 1–17. Cambridge: Polity Press.

— (1997) *Representation: Cultural Representations and Signifying Practices*. California: Sage.

Hall, A. & Cappella, J. N. (2002) The impact of political talk radio exposure on attributions about the outcome of the 1996 US presidential election. *Journal of Communication*, June:332–50.

Hamelink, C. J. (1986) Information technology and the Third World. Paper presented at the 15th Conference of the International Association for Mass Communication Research, New Delhi, 25–30 August.

Hamm, C. (1991) 'The constant companion of man': Separate development, Radio Bantu and music. *Popular Music*, 10(2):147–73.

— (1995) *Putting Popular Music in Its Place*. Cambridge: Cambridge University Press.

Hannerz, U. (1992) *Cultural Complexity: Studies in the Social Organization of Meaning*. New York: Columbia University Press.

Hartley, J. (2000) Radiocracy: Sound and citizenship. *International Journal of Cultural Studies*, 3(2):153–59.

Haugerud, A. (1995) *The Culture of Politics in Modern Kenya*. Cambridge: Cambridge University Press.

Hawkesworth, M. (1997) Confounding gender. *Signs: Journal of Women in Culture and Society*, 22(31):649–85.

Hayes, J. E. (2000) *Radio Nation: Communication, Popular Culture, and Nationalism in Mexico 1920–1950*. Tucson: University of Arizona Press.

Head, S. (1974) *Broadcasting in Africa: A Continental Survey of Radio and Television*. Philadelphia: Temple University Press.

Heath, C. (1986) Broadcasting in Kenya: Policy and Politics, 1928–1984. Doctoral thesis, University of Illinois.

Hendy, D. (2000) *Radio in the Global Age*. Cambridge: Polity Press.

— (2007) *Life on Air: A History of Radio 4*. Oxford: Oxford University Press.

Herbst, S. (1995) On electronic public space: Talk shows in theoretical perspective. *Political Communication*, 12:263–74.

Hetherington, K. (1998) *Expression of Identity: Space, Performance, Politics*. London: Sage.

Higiro, J.-M. V. (2007) Rwandan private print media on the eve of the genocide.

In Thompson, A. (ed.), *The Media and the Rwandan Genocide*, pp. 73–89. London: Pluto Press.

Hills, J. (2002) *The Struggle for Control of Global Communication: The Formative Century*. Urbana: University of Illinois Press.

Hirschkind, C. (2006) *The Ethical Soundscape*. New York: Columbia University Press.

Hirson, B. (1995) *The Revolutions in My Life*. Johannesburg: Wits University Press.

Hoffman, B. (1995) Power, structure, and Mande *jeliw*. In Conrad, D. & Frank, B. (eds), *Status and Identity in West Africa: The Nyamakalaw of Mande*, pp. 36–45. Bloomington: Indiana University Press.

Hofmeyr, I. (1993) *We Spend Our Years as a Tale that Is Told: Oral Historical Narrative in a South African Chiefdom*. Johannesburg: Wits University Press.

Hofstetter, C. & Gianos, C. (1997) Political talk radio: Actions speak louder than words. *Journal of Broadcasting and Electronic Media*, 41(4):501–15.

Hofstetter, C. R. & Barker, D., with Smith, J., Zari, G. & Ingrassia, T. (1999) Information, misinformation, and political talk radio. *Political Research Quarterly*, 52(2):353–69.

Hofstetter, C. R., Donovan, M. C., Klauber, M. R., Cole, A., Huie, C. J. & Yuasa, T. (1994) Political talk radio: A stereotype reconsidered. *Political Research Quarterly*, 47:467–79.

Hollander, B. (1996) Talk radio: Predictors and use and effects on attitudes about government. *Journalism and Mass Communication Quarterly*, 73(1):102–13.

Horwitz, R. B. (2001) 'Negotiated liberalization': Stakeholder politics and communication sector reform in South Africa. In Morris, N. & Waisbord, S. (eds), *Media and Globalization: Why the State Matters*, pp. 37–55. Lanham: Rowman & Littlefield.

Hutchby, I. (1996) *Confrontation Talk*. Hillsdale: Lawrence Erlbaum.

— (2001) 'Witnessing': The use of first-hand knowledge in legitimating lay opinions on talk radio. *Discourse Studies*, 3(4):481–97.

Hutson, A. (1999) The development of women's authority in the Kano Tijaniyya, 1894–1963. *Africa Today*, 46(3/4):48–64.

Hyden, G., Leslie, M. & Ogundimu, F. F. (eds) (2002) *Media and Democracy in Africa*. Uppsala: Nordiska Afrikainstitutet.

Hyslop, J. (1993) 'A destruction coming in': Bantu Education as response to social crisis. In Bonner, P., Delius, P. & Posel, D. (eds), *Apartheid's Genesis 1935–1962*, pp. 393–410. Johannesburg: Ravan Press.

Ibuka (2001) *Dictionnaire nominatif des victims du genocide en prefecture de Kibuye*. Kigali.

Ilboudo, J.-P. (2000) Rural radio in Africa: Strategies to relate audience research to the participatory production of radio programmes. In Fardon, R. & Furniss, G. (eds), *African Broadcast Cultures: Radio in Transition*, pp. 42–71. Oxford: James Currey.

ICTR (International Criminal Tribunal for Rwanda) (2003a) *The Prosecutor v. Ferdinand Nahimana, Jean-Bosco Baraygwiza, and Hassan Ngeze*. ICTR case no. 99-52-T, Judgment and Decision, 3 December.

— (2003b) Three media leaders convicted of genocide. Press release, 3 December. < http://69.94.11.53/ENGLISH/PRESSREL/2003/372.htm >

Ilanga laseNatal (1952) 16 April.

Internews (n.d.) Media in conflict: Case study – Rwanda, 2. < http://www.internews.org/mediainconflict/mic_rwanda.html >

IREX (2008) *Media Sustainability Index 2006/2007: Development of Sustainable Independent Media in Africa*. Washington, DC: IREX.

Jenkins, R. (1996) *Social Identities*. London: Routledge.

Jones, D. (2002) The polarizing effect of new media messages. *International Journal of Public Opinion Research*, 14(2):158–74.

Jornal de Angola (2010a) Crimes na Rádio da Unita. 9 September. < http:// jornaldeangola.sapo.ao/20/0/crimes_na_radio_da_unita > , accessed 9 September 2010.

— (2010b) Editorial 'Percurso glorioso'. 7 October. < http://jornaldeangola.sapo.ao/19/42/percurso_glorioso > , accessed 15 October 2010.

Joseph, R. (1983) Zulu women's music. *African Music*, 6(3):53–89.

— (1987) Zulu women's bow songs: Ruminations on love. *Bulletin of the School of Oriental and African Studies*, 50(1):90–119.

Kabwegyere, T. B. (1995) *The Politics of State Formation and Destruction in Uganda*. Kampala: Fountain.

Kafewo, S. (2006) *African Media Development Initiative: Ghana – Research Findings and Conclusions*. London: BBC World Service Trust. < http://www.radiopeaceafrica.org/assets/texts/pdf/GHA_AMDI_Report_pp4%201.pdf > , accessed 13 June 2010.

Kaliengue, J. (2010) UNITA e MPLA: o regresso da política. *O País Online*, 10 September. < http://www.opais.net/pt/opais/?det = 15656&id = 1929&mid = &u > , accessed 11 September 2010.

Karaan, M. (2003) Islamic identity as perceived by community media: A study of the Voice of the Cape. *Annual Review of Islam in South Africa*, 6:16–19.

Karis, T. G. & Gerhart, G. M. (1997) *From Protest to Challenge: A Documentary History of African Politics in South Africa, 1882–1990, Vol. 5: Nadir and Resurgence, 1964–1979*. Bloomington: Indiana University Press.

Kariuki, J. (1996) Paramoia: Anatomy of a dictatorship in Kenya. *Journal of Contemporary African Studies*, 14(1):69–86.

Karugire, S. R. (1980) *A Political History of Uganda*. Nairobi: Heinemann.

— (1988) *Roots of Instability in Uganda*. Kampala: Fountain.

Kasrils, R. (1998) *Armed and Dangerous: From Undercover Struggle to Freedom*. Bellville: Mayibuye.

Katz, E. & Wedell, G. (1977) *Broadcasting in the Third World: Promise and Performance*. Cambridge, Mass.: Harvard University Press.

— (1978) *Broadcasting in the Third World: Promise and Performance*. London: Macmillan.

Kellow, C. & Steeves, H. L. (1998) The role of radio in the Rwandan genocide. *Journal of Communication*, 48(3):107–28.

Kendall, M. (1982) Getting to know you. In Parkin, D. (ed.), *Semantic Anthropology*, pp. 197–209. London & New York: Academic Press.

Kenyatta, J. (1968) *Suffering without Bitterness: The Founding of the Kenya Nation*. Nairobi: East African Publishing House.

Kim, J., Wyatt, R. & Katz, E. (1999) News, talk, opinion, participation: The part played by conversation in deliberative democracy. *Political Communication*, 16:361–85.

Kimani, M. (2007) RTLM: The medium that became a tool for mass murder. In Thompson, A. (ed.), *The Media and the Rwandan Genocide*, pp. 110–24. London: Pluto Press.

Kirschke, L. (2000) Multiparty transitions, elite manipulation, and the media: Reassessing the Rwandan genocide. *Viertljahresschrift für Sicherheit und Frieden*, 18(3):238–44.

Kitzinger, J. (1999) A sociology of media power: Key issues in audience research. In Philo, G. (ed.), *Message Received*, pp. 3–20. Harlow: Longman.

Kivikuru, U. (2006) Top-down or bottom-up? Radio in the service of democracy:

Experiences from South Africa and Namibia. *International Communication Gazette*, 63(1):5–31.

Kleiner-Bosaller, A. & Loimeier, R. (1994) Radical Muslim women and male politics in Nigeria. In Reh, M. & Ludwar-Ene, G. (eds), *Gender and Identity in Africa*, pp. 61–69. Münster & Hamburg: LIT.

Kruger, F. (2007) Is radio in Africa democratic? Unpublished paper presented to the panel discussion at the colloquium on Radio, Publics and Communities in Southern Africa, WISER, University of the Witwatersrand, Johannesburg, 26 October.

Kruger, L. (1999) *The Drama of South Africa*. London: Routledge.

Kuperman, A. (2001) *The Limits of Humanitarian Intervention: Genocide in Rwanda*. Washington, DC: Brookings Institution Press.

Kushner, J. M. (1974) African liberation broadcasting. *Journal of Broadcasting*, 18(3):299–310.

Larkin, B. (2008) *Signal and Noise: Media, Infrastructure and Urban Culture in Nigeria*. Durham: Duke University Press.

Launay, R. (1992) *Beyond the Stream: Islam and Society in a West African Town*. Berkeley: University of California Press.

Lawson, C. & McCann, J. A. (2005) Television news, Mexico's 2000 elections and media effects in emerging democracies. *British Journal of Political Science*, 35:1–30.

LeBlanc, M. N. (1999) The production of Islamic identities through knowledge claims in Bouaké, Côte d'Ivoire. *African Affairs*, 98(393):485–509.

Lee, F. (2002) Radio phone-in talk shows as politically significant infotainment in Hong Kong. *Harvard Journal of Press/Politics*, 7(4):57–79.

— (2007) Talk radio listening, opinion expression and political discussion in a democratic society. *Asian Journal of Communication*, 17(1):78–96.

Lekgoathi, S. P. (1995) Reconstructing the History of Educational Transformation in a Rural Transvaal Chiefdom: The Radicalisation of Teachers in Zebediela from the Early 1950s to the Early 1990s. MA dissertation, University of the Witwatersrand.

— (2009) 'You are listening to Radio Lebowa of the South African Broadcasting Corporation': Vernacular radio, Bantustan identity, and listenership, 1960–1994. *Journal of Southern African Studies*, 35(3):575–94.

Levene, M. (2005) *Genocide in the Age of Nation State, Vol. 1*. London: Tauris.

Li, D. (2002) Echoes of violence. *Dissent*, 49(1):78–85.

— (2004) Echoes of violence: Considerations on radio and genocide in Rwanda. *Journal of Genocide Research*, 6(1):9–28.

Ligaga, D. (2005) Narrativising development in radio drama: Tradition and realism in the Kenyan radio play *Ushikwapo Shikamana*. *Social Identities*, 11(2):131–45.

Lodge, T. (1983) *Black Politics in South Africa since 1945*. New York: Longman.

Lonsdale, J. (2004) Moral and political argument in Kenya. In Berman, B., Eyoh, D. & Kymlicka, W. (eds), *Ethnicity and Democracy in Africa*, pp. 73–95. Oxford: James Currey.

Lopes, J. M. (2000) *Contribuição à história de radiodifusão em Angola*. Luanda: Rádio Nacional de Angola.

Lunt, P. & Stenner, P. (2005) The Jerry Springer Show as an emotional public sphere. *Media, Culture and Society*, 27(1):59–81.

Lutz, C. & Abu-Lughod, L. (1990) Introduction: Emotion, discourse and the politics of everyday life. In Lutz, C. & Abu-Lughod, L. (eds), *Language and the Politics of Emotion*, pp. 1–23. Cambridge: Cambridge University Press.

Lyons, R. & Straus, S. (2006) *Intimate Enemy: Images and Voices of the*

Rwandan Genocide. New York: Zone/ MIT Press.

Macho, T. (2006) Stimmen ohne koerper: Anmerkungen zur technikgeschichte der stimme. In Kolesch, D. & Kraemer, S. (eds), *Stimme: Annaeherungen an ein Phaenomen*, pp. 130–46. Frankfurt/ Main: Suhrkamp.

Mahmood, S. (2001) Feminist theory, embodiment, and the docile agent: Some reflections on the Egyptian Islamic revival. *Cultural Anthropology*, 16(2):202–36.

— (2005) *Politics of Piety: The Islamic Revival and the Feminist Subject.* Princeton: Princeton University Press.

Maja-Pearce, A. (1995) Zimbabwe. In Article 19, *Who Rules the Airwaves? Broadcasting in Africa*, pp. 123–32. London: Article 19.

Mak'Ochieng, M. (1996) The African and Kenyan media as the political public sphere. *Communicatio*, 22(2):23–32.

Malavoloneke, C. (n.d.) A Despertar, a UNITA, o MPLA e o 'Bilo'. *Seminário Angolense.* < http://www.club-k.net/ opiniao/17-opiniao/5960 > , accessed 21 September 2010.

Mamdani, M. (1997) *Citizen and Subject: Decentralized Despotism and the Legacy of Late Colonialism.* Delhi: Oxford University Press.

Mandaville, P. (2007) Globalization and the politics of religious knowledge: Pluralizing authority in the Muslim world. *Theory, Culture and Society*, 24(2):101–15.

Mandela, N. (1994) *Long Walk to Freedom.* Boston: Little, Brown.

Mano, Winston (2004) African National Radio and Everyday Life: A Study of Radio Zimbabwe and Its Listeners. PhD thesis, University of Westminster.

Marais, H. (1992) *Hani Opens Up.* Work in progress, June.

Martin, P. (1995) *Leisure and Society in Colonial Brazzaville.* Cambridge: Cambridge University Press.

Marx, K. (1970) *Critique of Hegel's Philosophy of Right.* Cambridge: Cambridge University Press.

Masuku, J. (2006) Surviving in a risky operating environment. *OpenSpace*, 1(5):67–70.

Matambanadzo, P. (2008) Call to relocate Chiadzwa families. *The Herald*, 12 December. < http:// www1.herald.co.zw/inside. aspx?sectid = 1517&cat = 1 > , accessed 12 December 2008.

Matlwa, K. (2007a) Call me a coconut but African tongues are destined for obscurity. *Sunday Times*, 7 October.

— (2007b) *Coconut: A Novel.* Johannesburg: Jacana.

Matza, T. (2009) Moscow's echo: Technologies of the self, publics, and politics on the Russian talk show. *Cultural Anthropology*, 24(3):489–522.

May, Tim (2003) *Social Research: Issues, Methods and Process*, 4th ed. Buckingham: Open University Press.

Mayibuye Centre Archives (n.d.a) Interview with Denis Goldberg by Wolfie Kodesh. MCA6-279.

— (n.d.b) *Dutch Opposition to Apartheid: Facts and Fallacies.* Karel Roskam Collection, Mayibuye Centre Archives.

Mazrui, A. A. (1996) Language policy and the foundations of democracy. *International Journal of the Sociology of Language*, 118:107–24.

Mbaine, E. A. (2003) Viability and sustainability of public service broadcasting. *Broadcasting Policy and Practice in Africa*, 19:138–61.

Mbeki, T. (1998) *The African Renaissance.* Johannesburg: Konrad Adenauer Stiftung.

McGreal, C. (2002) US funds penetrate Zimbabwe airwaves. *The Guardian*, 24 January.

McGuire, M. (2002) *Religion: The Social Context*, 5th ed. Belmont: Wadsworth.

McMillan, K. (2005) Racial discrimination and political bias on talkback radio in

New Zealand: Assessing the evidence. *Political Science*, 57(2):75–91.

Mda, Z. (1993) *When People Play People: Development Communication through Theatre.* Johannesburg: Wits University Press.

Melvern, L. (2000) *A People Betrayed: The Role of the West in Rwanda's Genocide.* London: Zed Books.

— (2004) *Conspiracy to Murder: The Rwandan Genocide.* London: Verso.

Mendelsohn, M. & Nadeau, R. (1996) The magnification and minimization of social cleavage by the broadcast and narrowcast new media. *International Journal of Public Opinion Research*, 8(4):374–89.

Metzl, J. F. (1997) Rwandan genocide and the international law of radio jamming. *American Journal of International Law*, 91(4):628–51.

Meyer, B. (2004) 'Praise the Lord': Popular cinema and Pentecostalite style in Ghana's new public sphere. *American Ethnologist*, 31(1):92–110.

— (2005) Religious remediations: Pentecostal views in Ghanaian video-movies. *Postscripts*, 2/3, special issue 'Mediating Film and Religion', guest edited by Stephen Hughes and Birgit Meyer.

— (2006) Religious sensations: Why media, aesthetics and power matter in the study of contemporary religion. Public lecture, Vrije Universiteit Amsterdam.

— (2009) *Aesthetic Formations: Media, Religion, and the Senses.* New York: Palgrave Macmillan.

Meyer, B. & Moors, A. (2006) Introduction. In Meyer, B. & Moors, A. (eds), *Religion, Media, and the Public Sphere*, pp. 1–28. Bloomington: Indiana University Press.

Mhlambi, T. N. (2009) The Early Years of Black Radio Broadcasting in South Africa: A Critical Reflection on the Making of Ukhozi FM. Master's mini-dissertation, University of Cape Town.

Mill, J. S. ([1859] 2001) *On Liberty.* Kitchener: Batoche Books.

Miran, M. (1998) Le Wahhabisme à Abidjan: dynamisme urbain d'un islam reformiste en Côte d'Ivoire contemporaine (1960–1996). *Islam et sociétés au sud du Sahara*, 12:5–74.

— (2005) D'Abidjan à Porto Novo: associations islamiques et culture religieuse réformiste sur la Côte de Guinée. In Fourchard, L. A. M. R. O. (ed.), *Entreprises religieuses transnationales en Afrique de l'ouest*, pp. 43–72. Ibadan & Paris: IFRA/ Karthala.

Miranda, J. (2010) António Manuel 'Jójó': de bem com a vida. *A Vida* online, 8 November. < http://www.opais.net/ pt/revista/?det = 17063&id = 1639& mid = &utm_medium = email&utm_ source = Newsletter&utm_ content = 654003458&utm_ campaign = NewsletterOPas08- 11-10OJornaldaNovaAngola- VersionA&utm_term = AntnioManuelJoj- Debemcomavida > , accessed 8 November 2010.

Mironko, C. (2006) Means and motive in the Rwandan genocide. In Cook, S. (ed.), *Genocide in Cambodia and Rwanda: New Perspectives*, pp. 163–89. New Brunswick: Transaction.

— (2007) The effect of RTLM's rhetoric of ethnic hatred in rural Rwanda. In Thompson, A. (ed.), *The Media and the Rwandan Genocide*, pp. 125–35. London: Pluto Press.

Misse, F. & Jaumain, Y. (1994) Death by radio. *Index on Censorship*, 4(5):72–74.

Mitchell, N. (2004) *Agents of Atrocity: Leaders, Followers, and the Violation of Human Rights in Civil War.* New York: Palgrave Macmillan.

Mitchell, T. (2000) Introduction. In Mitchell, T. (ed.), *Questions of Modernity*, pp. xi–xxvii. Minneapolis: University of Minnesota Press.

Mobile Industry Review (2007) SW Radio Africa sidesteps Zimbabwe government's transmission jamming using text updates. 29 March. < http://www.mobileindustryreview.com/2007/03/sw_radio_africa_sidesteps_zimbabwe_governments_transmission_jamming_using_text_updates.html > , accessed 4 December 2008.

Moghalu, K. (2005) *Rwanda's Genocide: The Politics of International Justice*. New York: Palgrave.

Mohochi, E. S. (2003) Language choice for development: The case for Swahili in Kenya. *Journal of African Cultural Studies*, 16(1):85–94. < http://www.jstor.org/stable/3181387 > , accessed 24 March 2009.

Monteiro, R. L. (1973) *A família nos musseques de Luanda*. Luanda: Fundo de Acção Social no Trabalho em Angola.

Moorman, M. J. (2008) *Intonations: A Social History of Music and Nation, Luanda, Angola, 1945 to Recent Times*. Athens: Ohio University Press.

Mosia, L., Riddle, C. & Zaffiro, J. J. (1994) From revolutionary to regime radio: Three decades of nationalist broadcasting in southern Africa. *Africa Media Review*, 8(1):1–24.

Motsuenyane, S. M., Burnham, M. & Zamchiya, D. M. (1993) *Reports of the Commission of Enquiry into Certain Allegations of Cruelty and Human Rights Abuse against ANC Prisoners and Detainees by ANC Members*. Johannesburg: Commission of Enquiry into Certain Allegations of Cruelty and Human Rights Abuse against ANC Prisoners.

Moyo, D. (2006) *Broadcasting Policy Reform and Democratisation in Zambia and Zimbabwe, 1990–2005: Global Pressures, National Responses*. Oslo: Unipub.

Mukundu, R. (2006) *African Media Development Initiative Report: Zimbabwe, Research Findings and Conclusion*. London: BBC World Service Trust. 21 December.

Mutoko, C. (2009) Interview with *Pulse* pull-out magazine. *The Standard*, 16 January.

Mutonya, M. (2005) Mugiithi performance: Popular music, stereotypes and ethnic identity. *Africa Insight*, 35(2):53–60.

Mwesige, P. (2004) *'Can You Hear Me Now?': Radio Talk Shows and Political Participation in Uganda*. Ann Arbor: Proquest.

— (2009) The democratic functions and dysfunctions of political talk radio: The case of Uganda. *Journal of African Media Studies*, 1(2):221–45.

Mwesige, P. & Ouma, B. (2008) *Public Broadcasting: An Assessment of Uganda Broadcasting Corporation*. Kampala: Eastern Africa Media Institute.

Myers, M. (2000) Community radio and development: Issues and examples from francophone West Africa. In Fardon, R. & Furniss, G. (eds), *African Broadcast Cultures: Radio in Transition*, pp. 90–101. Oxford: James Currey.

— (2009) Radio, convergence and development in Africa: Gender as cross-cutting issue. Paper presented to the International Development Research Centre and Carlton University round-table discussion on a research agenda, Butare, Rwanda, 10–13 September (updated November 2009). < http://www.cmts-cmst.org/gender-as-a-cross-cutting-issue.pdf > , accessed 19 May 2010.

Myjoyonline (2007) Myjoyonline live radio streaming is back. 20 July. < http://news.myjoyonline.com/news/200707/6812.asp > , accessed 13 June 2010.

— (2008) NPP to rig elections; anonymous tape claims. 27 December. < http://news.myjoyonline.com/elections/200812/24373.asp > , accessed 13 June 2010.

— (2010a) Audit report queries misapplication of funds at Information Ministry. 24 February. < http://news.

myjoyonline.com/news/201002/42565.
asp >, accessed 13 June 2010.
— (2010b) Ben Ephson should have
been arrested if he were not
NDC – Kwaku Kwarteng. 31 May.
< http://news.myjoyonline.com/
politics/201005/46973.asp >, accessed
13 June 2010.
— (2010c) Egbert faults police but
condemns man who compares Mills
to chimp. 29 May. < http://news.
myjoyonline.com/news/201005/46911.
asp >, accessed 13 June 2010.
— (2010d) Government forms propaganda
unit. 19 March. < http://news.
myjoyonline.com/politics/201003/43616.
asp >, accessed 13 June 2010.
— (2010e) 'I will kill my MCE before he
kills me' – Assin North MP. 1 April.
< http://news.myjoyonline.com/
news/201004/44200.asp >, accessed 13
June 2010.
— (2010f) Ken Agyapong flares up: Take
NPP to Ashanti, I am tired, useless man.
29 April. < http://news.myjoyonline.
com/politics/201004/45414.asp >,
accessed 13 June 2010.
— (2010g) Kwaku Baako, A.B.A. Fuseini
fight over GH¢1.5 million 'chop chop'
allegation. 22 February. < http://news.
myjoyonline.com/news/201002/42479.
asp >, accessed 13 June 2010.
— (2010h) Police arrest two NPP
sympathizers over 'criminal
accusations'. 19 February.
< http://news.myjoyonline.com/
news/201002/42285.asp >, accessed 13
June 2010.
— (2010i) Radio presenter in Kumasi vows
mob attack on Luv FM. 22 March.
< http://news.myjoyonline.com/
news/201003/43724.asp >, accessed 13
June 2010.
— (2010j) Regulate serial calling on radio.
23 March. < http://news.myjoyonline.
com/news/201003/43771.asp >,
accessed 13 June 2010.
— (2010k) The media should unite the
country – Prof. Karikari. 26 April.

< http://news.myjoyonline.com/
news/201004/45263.asp >, accessed 13
June 2010.
Mytton, G. (1983) *Mass Communication in
Africa*. London: Edward Arnold.
— (2000) From saucepan to dish: Radio
and TV in Africa. In Fardon, R. &
Furniss, G. (eds), *African Broadcast
Cultures: Radio in Transition*, pp. 21–41.
Oxford: James Currey.
Nageeb, S. A. (2004) *New Spaces and
Old Frontiers: Women, Social Space,
and Islamization in Sudan*. Lanham:
Lexington.
Nassanga, L. (2008) Journalism ethics and
the emerging new media culture of
radio talk shows and public debates
(*Ekimeeza*) in Uganda. *Journalism*,
9(5):646–63.
New York Times (2003) Fanning Rwanda's
genocide. House editorial, 5 December.
Ngugi wa Thiong'o (1997) Women in
cultural work: The fate of the Kamiriithu
people's theatre in Kenya. In Barber,
K. (ed.), *Readings in African Popular
Culture*, pp. 131–37. Bloomington:
Indiana University Press.
Nicholson, H. (2005) *Applied Drama: The
Gift of Theatre*. Basingstoke: Palgrave
Macmillan.
Nixon, R. (1994) *Homelands, Harlem and
Hollywood: South African Culture and
the World Beyond*. London: Routledge.
Njogu, K. (ed.) (2005) *Culture,
Entertainment and Health Promotion
in Africa*. Nairobi: Twaweza
Communications.
Nombre, U. (2000) The evolution of radio
broadcasting in Burkina Faso: 'From
mother radio to local radios'. In Fardon,
R. & Furniss, G. (eds), *African Broadcast
Cultures: Radio in Transition*, pp. 83–90.
Oxford: James Currey.
Norris, P. (ed.) (2009) *Public Sentinel:
News Media and Governance Reform*.
Washington, DC: World Bank.
Nunes, J. A. P. (1961) Inquéritos socio-
económicos dos muçeques de Luanda:
salários, alimentação, habitação,

mobilário e baixelas. *Mensário administrativo Portugal*:22.

Nuttall, S. (2004) Stylizing the self: Rosebank, Johannesburg. *Public Culture*, 16(3):430–52.

Nyamnjoh, F. B. (1999) African cultural studies, cultural studies in Africa: How to make a useful difference. *Critical Arts: A Journal of Cultural Studies in Africa*, 13(1):15–39.

— (2005) *Africa's Media: Democracy and the Politics of Belonging*. Pretoria: UNISA Press.

O'Doul, R. (n.d.) The people's voice. < http:/www.g21.net/africa7.html >

O'Sullivan, S. (2005) 'The whole nation is listening to you': The presentation of the self on a tabloid talk radio show. *Media, Culture, and Society*, 27(5):719–38.

Ochieng, P. & Kirimi, J. (1980) *The Kenyatta Succession*. Nairobi: Transafrica.

Ogot, B. (1995) The politics of populism. In Ogot, B. & Ochieng, W. (eds), *Decolonization and Independence in Kenya 1940–1993*, pp. 187–213. London: James Currey.

Ogot, B. & Ochieng, W. (eds) (1995) *Decolonization and Independence in Kenya 1940–1993*. London: James Currey.

Ogude, J. (1999) *Ngugi's Novels and African History: Narrating the Nation*. London: Pluto Press.

Omosa, M. & McCormick, D. (2004) *Universal Access to Communication Services in Kenya: A Baseline Survey: Final Report to the Communication Commission of Kenya and International Development Research Centre*. < http:/ www.cck.go.ke/html/baseline_survey_ final_report > , accessed 9 March 2009.

Omroep voor Radio Freedom (1988) *Radio Freedom*. Karel Roskam Collection, Mayibuye Centre Archives.

Orgeret, K. (2008) From his master's voice and back again? Presidential inaugurations and South African television – the post-apartheid experience. *African Affairs*, 107(429):611–29.

Orth, R. (2006) Rwanda's Hutu extremist insurgency: An eyewitness perspective. In Cook, S. (ed.), *Genocide in Cambodia and Rwanda: New Perspectives*, pp. 215–56. New Brunswick: Transaction.

Owen, D. (2000) Popular politics and the Clinton/Lewinsky affair: The implications for leadership. *Political Psychology*, 21(1):161–77.

Pan, Z. & Kosicki, G. (1997) Talk show exposure as an opinion activity. *Political Communication*, 14:371–88.

Patten, A. (2001) Political theory and language policy. *Political Theory*, 29(5):691–715.

Pawlikova-Vilhanova, V. (1996) Swahili and the dilemma of Ugandan language policy. *Asian and African Studies*, 5(2):158–70.

Peacefmonline (2010) Asante chief descends on Kwasi Pratt. 23 March. < http://news.peacefmonline.com/ social/201003/40642.php > , accessed 13 June 2010.

Perse, E. (2001) *Media Effects and Society*. Mahwah: Lawrence Erlbaum.

Peters, J. D. (2004) The voice and modern media. In Kolesch, D. & Schrödl, J. (eds), *Kunst-Stimmen*, pp. 85–100. Berlin: Theater der Zeit Recherchen 21.

Pfau, M., Cho, J. & Cho, K. (2001) Communication forms in US presidential campaigns: Influences on candidate perceptions and the democratic process. *Harvard International Journal of the Press/Politics*, 6(4):88–105.

Phelan, J. M. (1987) *Apartheid Media: Disinformation and Dissent in South Africa*. Westport: Lawrence Hill.

Policy Review Commission (1992) *Education for National Integration and Development: Government White Paper on the Education Report*. Entebbe: Government Printer.

Posel, D. (1993) Influx control and labour markets in the 1950s. In Bonner, P., Delius, P. & Posel, D. (eds), *Apartheid's*

Genesis 1935–1962, pp. 411–430. Johannesburg: Ravan Press.

Power, M. (2000) *Aqui Lourenco Marques!* Radio colonization and cultural identity in colonial Mozambique, 1932–74. *Journal of Historical Geography*, 26(4):605–28.

Power, S. (2001) Bystanders to genocide: Why the United States let the Rwandan genocide happen. *Atlantic Monthly*, 288(2):89.

Price, M. (1996) *Television, the Public Sphere and National Identity*. Oxford & New York: Oxford University Press.

Purpura, A. (1997) Knowledge and Agency: The Social Relations of Islamic Expertise in Zanzibar Town. PhD thesis, City University of New York.

Pype, K. (2009) Media celebrity, charisma and morality in post-Mobutu Kinshasa. *Journal of Southern African Studies*, 35(3):541–55.

Radio Gold (2009) Radio Gold and Oman FM criticised over bad reportage. < http://www.myradiogoldlive.com/ index.php?option = com_content&task = view&id = 946&Itemid = 1 > , accessed 6 June 2010.

Ranger, T. (2004) Nationalist historiography, patriotic history and the history of the nation: The struggle over the past in Zimbabwe. *Journal of Southern African Studies*, 30(2):215–34.

Reeves, G. (1993) *Communications and the Third World*. London: Routledge.

République du Rwanda (1994) *Recensement général de la population et de l'habitat au 15 août 1991: analyse des résultats définitifs*. Kigali, April.

Reuver-Cohen, C. & Jerman, W. (eds) (1974) *Secret Government Documents on Counter-subversion*. New York: IDOC.

Reveyrand-Coulon, O. (1993) Les énoncés féminins de l'islam. In Bayart, J.-F. (ed.), *Religion et modernité politique en Afrique noire: Dieu pour tous et chacun pour soi*, pp. 63–100. Paris: Karthala.

Ricento, R. (2000) *Ideology, Politics and Language Policies*. Amsterdam: John Benjamins.

Robinson, F. (1993) Technology and religious change: Islam and the impact of print. *Modern Asian Studies*, 27(1):229–51.

Rosenthal, E. (1974) *'You Have Been Listening …': A History of the Early Days of Radio Transmission in South Africa*. Cape Town: Purnell.

Ross, K. (2004) Political talk radio and democratic participation: Caller perspectives on Election Call. *Media, Culture, and Society*, 26(6):785–801.

Roy, O. (2005) *Globalised Islam: The Search for a New Ummah*. New Delhi: Rupsa.

Rubin, A. & Step, M. (2000) Impact of motivation, attraction, and parasocial interaction on talk radio listening. *Journal of Broadcasting and Electronic Media*, 44(4):635–54.

Rycroft, D. (1975) The Zulu ballad of Nomagundwane. *African Language Studies*, XVI:61–92.

— (1975/6) The Zulu bow songs of Princess Magogo. *African Music*, 5(4):41–97.

SAARF (South African Advertising Research Foundation) (2009) Radio Audience Measurement Survey (RAMS). < http://www.saarf.co.za/ > , accessed 1 June 2009.

SABC (South African Broadcasting Corporation) (1961) *SABC Annual Report*. Johannesburg: SABC.

SABC Sound Archive, Polokwane (1980) *Highlights of 'Hlokwa la Tsela'* – interview with Hezekiel Justice Tshungu, Tape T (NS/69), T (NS/70), nos. 1 & 2.

— (2001) *Madireng a Afrika* – interview with Hezekiel Justice Tshungu, Tape T (NS/2001), no. 10, 5 August.

— (n.d.) File T (NS/89), Tape no. 33.

Schabas, W. (2000) Hate speech in Rwanda: The road to genocide. *McGill Law Journal*, 46:141–71.

Schatzberg, M. & Khadiagala, G. (1987) Introduction. In Schatzberg, M. (ed.), *The Political Economy of Kenya*. New York: Praeger.

Schmidt, L. E. (2000) *Hearing Things: Religion, Illusion and the American Enlightenment*. Cambridge, Mass.: Harvard University Press.

Schudson, M. (1997) Why conversation is not the soul of democracy. *Critical Studies in Mass Communication*, 14(4):297–309.

Schulz, D. (1999a) In pursuit of publicity: Talk radio and the imagination of a moral public in urban Mali. *Africa Spectrum*, 99(2):161–85.

— (1999b) Pricey publicity, refutable reputations: *Jeliw* and the economics of honour in Mali. *Paideuma*, 45:275–92.

— (2001a) Music videos and the effeminate vices of urban culture in Mali. *Africa*, 71(3):325–71.

— (2001b) *Perpetuating the Politics of Praise: Jeli Praise Singers, Radios and Political Mediation in Mali*. Köln: Rüdiger Köppe.

— (2003) 'Charisma and brotherhood' revisited: Mass-mediated forms of spirituality in urban Mali. *Journal of Religion in Africa*, 33(2):146–71.

— (2006a) Morality, community, 'publicness': Shifting terms of debate in the Malian public. In Meyer, B. & Moors, A. (eds), *Religion, Media, and the Public Sphere*, pp. 132–51. Bloomington: Indiana University Press.

— (2006b) Promises of (im)mediate salvation: Islam, broadcast media, and the remaking of religious experience in Mali. *American Ethnologist*, 33(2):210–29.

— (2007) Evoking moral community, fragmenting Muslim discourse: Sermon audio-recordings and the reconfiguration of public debate in Mali. *Journal for Islamic Studies*, 27:39–72.

— (2008) Piety's manifold embodiments: Muslim women's quest for moral renewal in urban Mali. *Journal for*

Islamic Studies, 28:26–93. Special issue: 'Reconfigurations of Gender Relations in Africa', guest editors M. Janson & D. Schulz.

— (2010) 'Channeling' the powers of God's word: Audio-recordings as scriptures in Mali. *Postscripts*, 4(2):135–56.

— (2011) Renewal and enlightenment: Muslim women's biographic narratives of personal reform in Mali. *Journal of Religion in Africa*, 41(1):1–31. Special issue: 'Conversion in Africa'.

— (forthcoming) 'Touched by divine grace': Religious objects and the mediation of spiritual power in urban Mali. In Zillinger, M., Behrend, H. & Dreschke, A. (eds), *Trance Media and New Media*. Frankfurt: Campus.

Scott, J. C. (1985) *Weapons of the Weak: Everyday Forms of Peasant Resistance*. New Haven: Yale University Press.

Scott, S. (1999) A way with words. *Daily News*, 23 August.

Sechaba (1978) Duma Nokwe honourable son of Africa. *Sechaba*, 12(2):12–41.

Sellstrom, T. (2002) *Sweden and National Liberation in Southern Africa*. Uppsala: Nordiska Afrikainstitutet.

Shubin, V. (1999) *ANC: A View from Moscow*. Bellville: Mayibuye.

Silverman, D. (2000) *Doing Qualitative Research: A Practical Handbook*. London: Sage.

Singhal, A. & Rogers, E. (2003) *Combating AIDS: Communication Strategies in Action*. New Delhi: Sage.

Smart, B. (1985) *Michael Foucault*. London: Routledge.

Snyder, J. (2000) *From Voting to Violence: Democratization and Violence*. New York: Norton.

Snyder, J. & Ballentine, K. (1996) Nationalism and the marketplace of ideas. *International Security*, 21(2):5–40.

Soares, B. (2005) *Islam and the Prayer Economy: History and Authority in a Malian Town*. Ann Arbor: University of Michigan Press.

Soley, L. (1995) Heating up clandestine radio after the Cold War. In Pease, E. C. & Everette, E. D. (eds), *Radio: The Forgotten Medium*. New Brunswick & London: Transaction.

Soyinka, W. (1967) *Kongi's Harvest*. London: Oxford University Press.

Sparks, C. (1992) Popular journalism: Theories and practice. In Dahlgren, P. (ed.), *Journalism and Popular Culture*, pp. 24–44. London: Newbury Park.

Spitulnik, D. (1998) Mediated modernities: Encounters with the electronic in Zambia. *Visual Anthropology Review*, 14(2):63–84.

— (2000) Documenting radio culture as lived experience: Reception studies and the mobile machine in Zambia. In Fardon, R. & Furniss, G. (eds), *African Broadcast Cultures: Radio in Transition*, pp. 144–63. Oxford: James Currey.

— (2002) Mobile machines and fluid audiences: Rethinking reception through Zambian radio culture. In Ginsburg, F., Abu-Lughod, L. & Larkin, B. (eds), *Media Worlds: Anthropology on New Terrain*, pp. 337–54. Berkeley: University of California Press.

Squires, C. (2000) Black talk radio: Defining community needs and identity. *Harvard International Journal of the Press/Politics*, 5(2):73–95.

Sterne, J. (2003) *The Audible Past*. Durham: Duke University Press.

Stolow, J. (2005) Religion and/as media. *Theory, Culture and Society*, 22(4):119–45.

Straus, S. (2006) *The Order of Genocide: Race, Power, and War in Rwanda*. Ithaca: Cornell University Press.

Stuart, J. (a.k.a. H. R. Loots) (1984) *Stuart Commission Report, African National Congress*. < http://www.anc.org.za/ancdocs/misc/stuartreport.html >

Switzer, L. (1985) *Media and Dependency in South Africa: A Case Study of the Press and the Ciskei Homeland*. Athens: University of Ohio Press.

Taylor, C. (1989) *Sources of the Self: The Making of Modern Identity*. Cambridge, Mass.: Harvard University Press.

Temple-Raston, D. (2002) Journalism and genocide. *Columbia Journalism Review*, 41(3):18–19.

— (2005) *Justice on the Grass: Three Rwandan Journalists, Their Trial for War Crimes, and a Nation's Quest for Redemption*. New York: Free Press.

Terretta, M. (2006) Nationalists go global: From Cameroonian (UPC) *vilage maquisards* to pan-African freedom fighters. Paper presented at the Equatorial African Workshop, University of Wisconsin-Madison, 14 October.

Tettey, W. (2001) The media and democratization in Africa: Contributions, constraints and concerns of the private press. *Media, Culture and Society*, 23(1):5–31.

— (2004) The politics of radio and radio politics in Ghana: A critical appraisal of broadcasting reform. In Beck, R.-M. & Wittmann, F. (eds), *African Media Cultures: Transdisciplinary Perspectives*, pp. 215–39. Köln: Rüdiger Köppe.

— (2009a) News media and governance reform: Sub-Saharan Africa. In Norris, P. (ed.), *Public Sentinel: News Media and Governance Reform*, pp. 277–304. Washington, DC: World Bank.

— (2009b) Transnationalism, the African diaspora, and the deterritorialized politics of the Internet. In Mudhai, O. F., Tettey, W. J. & Banda, F. (eds), *African Media and the Digital Public Sphere*, pp. 143–63. New York: Palgrave Macmillan.

— (2010) Sexual citizenship, heteronormativity, and the discourse of homosexual rights in Ghana. In Puplampu, K. P. & Tettey, W. J. (eds), *The Public Sphere and Politics of Survival in Ghana: Voice, Sustainability and Public Policy*, pp. 38–66. Accra: Woeli.

The Herald (2007) Chombo warns NGOs. 5 January.

— (2008) Water situation remains critical in Zimbabwe. 3 December. < http://nzcn.wordpress.com/2008/11/11/water-situation-remains-critical-in-zimbabwe/ >

Theunissen, M., Nikitin, V. & Pillay, M. (1996) *The Voice, the Vision: A 60-year History of the SABC and the Path to the Future*. Johannesburg: Advent Graphics.

Thompson, A. (ed.) (2007) *The Media and the Rwanda Genocide*. London: Pluto Press.

Tomaselli, K., Muller, J. & Tomaselli, R. (2001) *Currents of Power*. New York: Academic Press.

Tomaselli, R., Tomaselli, K. G. & Muller, J. (eds) (1989) *Currents of Power: State Broadcasting in South Africa*. Bellville: Anthropos.

Trevor, J. (1975) Western education and Muslim Fulani/Hausa women in Sokoto, northern Nigeria. In Brown, G. & Hiske, M. (eds), *Conflict and Harmony in Education in Tropical Africa*, pp. 247–70. London: Allen & Unwin.

Trewhela, P. & Hirson, B. (1990) Inside Quadro: The end of an era. *Searchlight South Africa*, 5 July. < http://www.revolutionary-history.co.uk/supplem/Hirson/Quatro.html >

Tudesq, A.-J. (1983) *La radio en Afrique noire*. Paris: Anthropos/INA.

Turner, B. (2007) Religious authority and the new media. *Theory, Culture and Society*, 24(2):117–34.

Twala, M. & Benard, E. (1994) *Mbokodo: Inside MK, a Soldier's Story*. Johannesburg: Jonathan Ball.

Uganda (1995) Constitution of the Republic of Uganda. Entebbe: Government Printer.

Umar, M. S. (2001) Education and Islamic trends in northern Nigeria, 1970s–1990s. *Africa Today*, 48(2):127–50.

UNESCO (UN Educational, Scientific and Cultural Organisation) (1996) *Statistical Yearbook*. Rome: UNESCO.

United Republic of Tanzania (2005) *The Broadcasting Services (Content) Regulations*. Dar es Salaam.

US Government (1982) *Foreign Broadcast Information Service (FBIS)*, 10 January, U3.

— (1983) *Foreign Broadcast Information Service (FBIS)*, 16 September, U5.

Vahed, G. & Jeppie, S. (2005) Multiple communities: Muslims in post-apartheid South Africa. In Daniel, J., Southall, R. & Lutchman, J. (eds) *State of the Nation 2005*, pp. 252–86. Cape Town: HSRC Press.

Van der Veur, P. R. (2002) Broadcasting and political reform. In Hyden, G., Leslie, M. & Ogundimu, F. F. (eds), *Media and Democracy in Africa*, pp. 81–106. New Brunswick: Transaction.

Vavrus, F. (2002) Language in development. *TESOL Quarterly*, 36(1):373–97. < http://www.jstor.org/stable/3588418 >, accessed 25 March 2009.

Venter, D. J. & Neuland, E. (2005) *NEPAD and the African Renaissance*. Johannesburg: Richard Havenga.

VOK (Voice of Kenya) (1984) *VOK Brochure*. Nairobi: VOK.

Volpi, F. & Turner, B. (2007) Introduction: Making Islamic authority matter. *Theory, Culture and Society*, 24(2):1–19.

Wachanga, D. N. (2007) Sanctioned and Controlled Message Propagation in a Restrictive Information Environment: The Small World of Clandestine Radio Broadcasting. Doctoral thesis, University of North Texas, < http://digital.library.unt.edu/permalink/meta-dc-5113:1 >, accessed 4 December 2008.

Warner, M. (2002) Publics and counterpublics. *Public Culture*, 14(1):49–90.

Waterman, C. (1990) *Jùjú: A Social History and Ethnography of an African Popular Music*. Chicago: University of Chicago Press.

Weber, M. (1976) *The Protestant Ethic and the Spirit of Capitalism*. London: Allen & Unwin.

Weix, G. G. (1998) Islamic prayer groups in Indonesia: Local forums and gendered responses. *Critique of Anthropology*, 18(4):405–20.

White, B. (2002) Rumba and other cosmopolitanisms. *Cahiers d'etudes Africaines 168*, 42(4):678. Special issue, 'Musique, joie et crise dans le cosmotropole Africain', edited by B. White.

White, S., Oates, S. & McAllister, I. (2005) Media effects and Russian elections, 1999–2000. *British Journal of Political Science*, 35:191–208.

Wilcox, T. (1995) Squawk talk: Call-in talk shows and American culture. < http://web.mit.edu/comm-forum/forums/squawktalk.html >, accessed 1 June 2009.

Willems, W. (2007) Interogating public sphere and popular culture as theoretical concepts: On their value in African studies. Paper presented at the Centre for African Studies, University of Cambridge, 19 November.

Williams, R. (1961) *The Long Revolution*. London: Chatto & Windus.

Windrich, E. (2000) The laboratory of hate: The role of clandestine radio in the Angolan war. *International Journal of Cultural Studies*, 3:206–18.

Winocur, R. (2003) Media and participative strategies: The inclusion of private necessities in the public sphere. *Television and New Media*, 4(25):25–42.

Winston, B. (1995) How are media born? In Downing, J., Mohammadi, A. & Sreberny-Mohammadi, A. (eds), *Questioning the Media: A Critical Introduction*, pp. 54–74. London: Sage.

— (1998) *Media Technology and Society: A History from Telegraph to the Internet*. London: Routledge.

Yanovitzky, I. & Cappella, J. N. (2001) Effects of call-in political talk radio shows on their audiences: Evidence from a multi-wave panel analysis. *International Journal of Public Opinion Research*, 13(4):377–97.

Zaller, J. (1992) *The Nature and Origins of Mass Opinion*. New York: Cambridge University Press.

— (1996) The myth of a massive media impact revived: New support for a discredited idea. In Mutz, D., Sniderman, P. & Brody, R. (eds), *Political Persuasion and Attitude Change*, pp. 17–78. Ann Arbor: University of Michigan Press.

Index

EAO, *see* Emmissora Oficial de Angola
Economist, The, report by Economist
        Intelligence Unit 29
educational programming 137
educational soap opera, Kenya 156
        Tushauriane ('Let Us Consult Each
                Other') 156
        Ushikwapo Shikamana ('If
                Assisted, Assist Yourself')
                156
        Usiniharakishe ('Do Not Rush Me')
                156
Egypt 242, 258
        Radio Cairo 243
        Sauti-al-Arab (Voice of the Arabs),
                Egypt 7
        Sauti ya Cairo (Voice of Cairo) 7
elections 27
        democratic, South Africa 140–1
        general, Kenya 45
electronic media 8–9
        see also technology
Emmissora Oficial de Angola (EAO)
        240
emotional reciprocity 22
emotion discourses 164–5
entertainment (infotainment) sites 37,
        38
        African musicians 129
        music-oriented programmes 39
        songs with covertly political
                messages 129
Ethiopia 230, 258
ethnic communities 38
ethnoscapes 165–6
everyday life
        Kenya 149–50
        moral narratives 150
        moral themes taken from 153–5
        Zimbabwe 105, 108–12
External Mission 228, 231

faith-based community radio stations
        209
First, Ruth 232
Fondation Hirondelle, Swiss media
        NGO 185, 186, 193–4
forum theatre model (Boal) 42–3

francophone countries, media changes
        in 10–11
freedom of expression 19, 31, 32
French Radio Dakar 135
Frente de Libertação de Moçambique
        (FRELIMO) 227, 228
Frente Nacional para a Libertação de
        Angola (FNLA) 240, 243
        Angola Livre broadcast 241, 242,
                245

gay and lesbian rights 9, 23
Ghana 10, 13, 243
        Accra-based Top Radio 29–30
        Asempa FM, *Ekosii Sen* talk
                programme 29
        broadcasting reform 11
        Citi FM's *Citi Breakfast Show* 25
        'hierarchisation of voices' 11
        Hot FM discussion 31
        Joy FM station 2, 24
        Kumasi-based Fox FM 30
        media 20–1
        National Fire Service investigation
                29–30
        NDC and NPP political parties 27
        Oman FM 27
        'pentecostalite style' 13
        political talk radio 21, 27
        Radio Gold, *Alhaji Alhaji* talk
                programme 24
        Radio Gold, Election Forensics
                programme 27
        Radio Gold, Internet online site 25
        social networking 24
        talk radio 2, 9, 22, 27–8
        see also under diaspora
Glissant, Edouard 177
        The Ripening, novel 177
Goldberg, Denis 226
Gqabi, Joe 232
griots (*jeli,* praise singer) and women 5
Guinea 10

Habyarimana, President Juvénal 91, 99
Hani, Chris 234, 235
Hitler's speeches 4–5
Huambo Radio Club, Angola

Portuguese voice in Africa slogan
240

ICTR, *see* International Criminal
Tribunal for Rwanda
identity and consumption 209–10
Independent Broadcasting Authority
142
Independent Communications
Authority of South
Africa (ICASA) 142, 221
regulations and female presenters
217
Indian people 140
Zimbabwians 110
indigenous transformation 108
information and communication
technologies 24–6
international communication,
complexities of 105
International Criminal Tribunal for
Rwanda (ICTR), UN 84
International Police for the Defence of
the State (PIDE) 243, 246
Islamic faith 13
Cape Malay culture 215
cultural groups 214
Middle Eastern forms 215

Johannesburg
community station 13
religious radio 2
Yfm 141
see also Radio 702
Jordan, Pallo 231, 233–4
journalism
ethics 189
politicised 28
popular music serving as 107
'sunshine' 201
journalists 32
'*coupage*' fee 190
salaries 189, 190
stringers (informal) 58
threats to Congolese 191
training 190
Journalists Without Borders 239
judicial system 32

Kabila, President Joseph 184–5, 188,
189
Kabila, President Laurent 184, 188
Kamiriithu Community Education and
Cultural Centre, Kenya 153
KANU, *see* Kenya African National
Union
Katatura Community Radio, Namibia
144
Kathrada, Ahmed 226
Kenya 13, 118, 149, 258, 267, 277
applied theatre 46
campaign for media freedom 161
Citizen Radio FM: *Jambo Kenya*
37, 44–6
civic education of voters 45–6
Communication Bill 161
Constitution 36
context of FM radio 38–9
dialogic and democratic cultures
39–45, 47
Easy FM breakfast show 37, 43–4
FM radio broadcasting 9, 36
interactive talk show, *The Big Issue
of the Day* 42
Kiss 100 FM breakfast show 37,
41–3
Mau Mau and independence
struggles 159–60
Metro FM 38
multiparty political system 36
participatory democracy 41
people's parliament 9, 45–6
Radio Mang'elete 106–7
talk radio shows 9
urban youth lingi (*sheng*) 39
see also Radio Theatre
Kenya African National Union (KANU)
36, 38, 45–6, 159
Kenyan Broadcasting Corporation
(KBC) 3, 15, 37–8, 154–5
state-controlled broadcaster 40
see also Voice of Kenya (VOK)
Kenya Broadcasting Services (KBS)
152
KenyaRadio, colonially controlled
station 152
Kenyatta, Mzee Jomo regime, Kenya
159

Suffering without Bitterness book
159
Kibaki, President Mwai 157, 161
Kiu (Q) FM, Kiswahili radio station 43
  Nation Media, Kenya 43
Kongi's Harvest play (Soyinka) 40
Kotane, Moses 227

languages 110-11, 270-3
  African 2, 118, 135, 139, 141,
    144-5, 148, 166
  Afrikaans 139, 211
  Arabic 211, 212
  Bantu speakers 282
  chiShona 110
  colonial 272
  contested use of 6
  dialects 110
  English 38, 39, 139, 211, 212, 267,
    273, 283
  French 192
  Gikuyu accent, Kenya 43
  indigenous 6, 271, 273, 275, 278,
    283
  isiXhosa 118, 121, 146, 156
  isiZulu 3, 118, 121, 135, 156, 163,
    164, 175, 211, 212
  Kikongo 192
  Kiswahili 38, 39, 44, 192, 275,
    279-80, 283
  Lingala 192
  local 22, 136, 243
  Luganda 273, 275, 279
  Mande-speaking cultural realm,
    Mali 75
  North and South Sotho 118
  Portuguese 211, 243
  region and ethnicity 34-5
  Sesotho 121, 146, 211
  Setswana radio 121
  Tshiluba 192
  Tswana 118
  use in Kenya 38-9
Latin American Creoles, novels 241-2
Lesedi FM 141, 143, 144-5
Lesotho 145-6, 228
Harvest FM 144
listeners 137
  adults 108

black 165
  identities 220
  participation by 103, 197, 280-1
  political awareness 205
  talk-radio 199
listenership increased 136-7
literacy rates 270
live call-in programme 23
local discussion and news programmes
  6
Lumumba, Patrice 186
'Luta Contra Banditos' counter-
    insurgency operation 234
Lutwa, Gen. Tito Okello 274

Madagascar 230
mainstream or non-mainstream
    categorisation 39
Make, Cassius 234
Makiwane, Tennyson 227
Malawi Broadcasting Corporation 12
  Nkhani za m'maboma (News from
    the Districts) 12
  political bias 12
  Radio 1 and Radio 2 FM 12
Mali 5, 10, 20
  Arab Muslim world 68
  audo recordings, local radio
    broadcasts 65
  democratisation of media 13
  endogamous artisanal specialists
    (*nyamakalaw*) 73
  ethics of cassette listening 71
  families of free or aristocratic
    descent (*horon*) 75
  gender-specific ideals of moral
    conduct 69
  gender-specific norms of religious
    preaching 75
  Islamic moral revival 63, 64, 65, 77
  jeli speaker-as-ventriloquator 75-6
  listeners' aural perceptual
    predisposition 71
  male preachers 64, 75
  mass-mediated religious
    sermonising 77
  moral lessons (*ladili*) 65
  musical change and performance
    styles 5

death notices (*Zviziviso Zverufu/ Izaziso Zemfa*) 12, 103, 108, 111–16
news (*Nhau/Izindaba*) 108
weather reports 108
write-in greetings and music dedication (*Kwaziso/Ukubingelelana*) 108, 113–15
Radio Zulu, later Ukhozi FM 141, 166, 167
Rawlings, President 30, 31, 33
rediffused high frequency modulation (FM) system 121, 122
religion and radio 208–11
  churches 11
  debates 208
  gender and 'voice of authority' 218–20
  transformation 216–18
  Turkington, Kate 208, 219–20
  women as presenters 210–11
religious communities 211–13
research methodology 108–12
  face-to-face interviews 109
  interviews 109–11
  questionnaires 111
Rivonia, Lillieslief Farm 226
  defendants 227
RNA, *see* Angolan National Radio
Rwanda 4, 184, 258, 277
  alternative model of media effects in genocide 98–100
  Congolese Rally for Democracy 185
  conventional wisdom, problems with 88–9
  direct incitement 87
  ethnic categorisation 99
  foreign stations 85
  genocide 5, 83
  hate radio 83–4, 89, 100
  high- and low-genocide periods 92
  Hutu ethnic group 85–6, 92, 99–100
  inflammatory broadcasts 93
  media liberalisation 83
  non-systematic content analysis 89
  propaganda campaign against Tutsi 87

radio broadcasts and genocidal violence 86–7
Radio Machete 86, 100
radio media effects in genocide 84–7
Radio Muhabura 85, 94
Radio Rwanda 85
Tutsi ethnic group 83, 85–7, 92, 99–100
Rwanda and hypothesis testing 89
  broadcast range and regional patterns of violence 90–1
  broadcasts and violence 91, 98–100
  content analysis 93–4
  exposure 90
  face-to-face mobilisation 95–7
  ICTR Media Trial decision 91–2
  qualitative analysis of perpetrator interviews 95–8
  quantitative analysis of perpetrator interviews 94–5

SABC, *see* South African Broadcasting Corporation
SACP, *see* South African Communist Party
Salafi–Sunni reformist trends, Egypt, Saudi Arabia 64
Samakuva, President Isias 238–9
Savimbi, Jonas 250
semi-private FM stations 10
Senegal 10, 64, 102
serial callers 27–8
Sharif, President Sheikh 257
Sharpeville massacre 225
Short Wave Radio Africa (SWRA), London 51, 52, 56, 57, 108
  Callback programme 53–4
  free short message service 54
  mass radio 59–60
  radio broadcasts into Zimbabwe 53–4
  stringers (informal journalists) 58
sidewalk radio (*radio trottoir*) 138, 147–8
Sierra Leone 4
Sisulu, Walter 226
social and economic factors 103–4

Swedish International Development
        Cooperation Agency 230
Swedish Telecommunications
        Consulting 230
Swiss non-governmental organisation
        263
talk radio 9, 22, 140, 198–9
    and democratic citizenship 21–6
    international research 199–200
    interviews 199
    open-air shows 273
    partisan politicisation of 34–5
    political audience 199–200
    political awareness and
            involvement 205
    propaganda tool 27–8
    and public sphere 200–3
    shows 6, 9, 20, 198
Tambo, Oliver 227, 231
Tanzania 102, 228, 230, 242, 277
    Radio Tanzania 227, 243, 244
Taylor, Charles 165
    *Sources of the Self: The Making of
            Modern Identity* 165
technology
    audio 134
    blogs 221
    cellphones 23–4, 39, 102, 134, 267
    digital age and radio 102, 103
    email 102
    Facebook 24, 210
    hyper-portable video 134
    Internet 2, 102, 134, 210, 221, 260
    live online streaming 2
    mediating religion 67
    mobile communications 102
    mobile phones 2, 221
    new media 66
    podcasting 2
    storing and broadcasting sound and
            voice 73–4
    text messaging 22, 25
    Twitter 210, 221
    websites 260, 267
telephones, access to 23–4
television 85, 106, 270
    access 134
    drama 6

TFG (Transitional Federal Government),
        see under Somalia
Thiong'o, Ngugi wa 149, 153
    Maitu Njugira ('Mother, Sing for
            Me') 153
    Ngahika Ndeeda ('I Will Marry
            when I Want')
Thobela FM 121–2, 126, 145, 146
    public affairs in siSwati 145
    Tshivenda women's programme
            145
Tracey, Hugh 135
training of staff members 143–4
transistor radios 85
Traoré, President 64, 70
Truth and Reconciliation Commission
        6
Tsvangirai, Morgan 49, 115
Tutu, J. P. 135
    musical variety troupe Gay Gaieties
            135

Uganda 102, 184, 185
    Baganda ethnic group 274
    broadcasting languages 14, 273
    Christian missionaries 274
    Constitution of the Republic of
            Uganda 275
    current media landscape 273
    democratic constitution 274
    ethnic groups 281
    interviews and insights 278–82
    Kigadi-kibaale Community Radio
            107
    Land Bill 277
    language policy 271–2, 276–8
    linguistic groups 274–6
    multiple public spheres or
            'sphericules' 9
    National Resistance Movement
            (NRM) 273, 274
    participation 274, 278
    privately owned FM stations 273
    radio and languages 272–3
    state monopoly 273
Uganda Broadcasting Corporation
        (UBC) 273
    state broadcaster 273

Printed and bound by CPI Group (UK) Ltd, Croydon, CR0 4YY

23/04/2025

14661042-0002